ZAMBIA

AF693220

INVESTMENT AND BUSINESS GUIDE

VOLUME 2

BUSINESS, INVESTMENT OPPORTUNITIES AND INCENTIVES

International Business Publications, USA
Washington DC, USA - Zambia

ZAMBIA

INVESTMENT AND BUSINESS GUIDE

VOLUME 2 BUSINESS, INVESTMENT OPPORTUNITIES AND INCENTIVES

UPDATED ANNUALLY

We express our sincere appreciation to all government agencies and international organizations which provided information and other materials for this guide

Cover Design: **International Business Publications, USA**

International Business Publications, USA. ***has used its best efforts in collecting, analyzing and preparing data, information and materials for this unique guide. Due to the dynamic nature and fast development of the economy and business environment, we cannot warrant that all information herein is complete and accurate. IBP does not assume and hereby disclaim any liability to any person for any loss or damage caused by possible errors or omissions in the guide.***
This guide is for individual use only. Use this guide for any other purpose, included but not limited to reproducing and storing in a retrieval system by any means, electronic, photocopying or using the addresses or other information contained in this guide for any commercial purposes requires a special written permission from the publisher

2016 Edition Updated Reprint International Business Publications, USA
ISBN 1-5775-1907-8

For customer service and information, please contact:

in the USA: **International Business Publications, USA**
P.O.Box 15343, Washington, DC 20003
Phone: (202) 546-2103, Fax: (202) 546-3275.
E-mail: rusric@erols.com

Printed in the USA

ZAMBIA

INVESTMENT AND BUSINESS GUIDE

VOLUME 2

BUSINESS, INVESTMENT OPPORTUNITIES AND INCENTIVES

TABLE OF CONTENTS

STRATEGIC AND BUSINESS PROFILES

Capital and largest city	Lusaka 15°25′S 28°17′E15.417°S 28.283°E
Official languages	English
Recognised regional languages	> 0.5%
Ethnic groups	> 0.5%
Demonym	Zambian
Government	Presidential republic
• President	Edgar Chagwa Lungu
• Vice President	Inonge Mutukwa Wina
Legislature	National Assembly
Independence	
• from the United Kingdom	24 October 1964
• Current constitution	24 August 1991
Area	
• Total	752,618 km^2 (39th) 290,587 sq mi
• Water (%)	1
Population	
• 2015 estimate	16,212,000 (69th)
• 2010 census	13,092,666
• Density	17.2/km^2 (191st) 44.5/sq mi
GDP (PPP)	2014 estimate
• Total	$61.786 billion[5]
• Per capita	$4,113
GDP (nominal)	2014 estimate
• Total	$26.611 billion
• Per capita	$1,810
Gini (2010)	57.5 high
HDI (2014)	▲ 0.586[7] medium · 139th
Currency	Zambian kwacha (ZMW)
Time zone	CAT (UTC+2)
Drives on the	left
Calling code	+260
ISO 3166 code	ZM
Internet TLD	.zm

The **Republic of Zambia** is a landlocked country in Southern Africa, neighboring the Democratic Republic of the Congo to the north, Tanzania to the north-east, Malawi to the east, Mozambique, Zimbabwe, Botswana and Namibia to the south, and Angola to the west. The capital city is Lusaka, in the south-central part of the country. The population is concentrated mainly around Lusaka in the south and the Copperbelt Province to the northwest.

Originally inhabited by Khoisan peoples, the region was colonised during the Bantu expansion of the thirteenth century. After visits by European explorers in the eighteenth century, Zambia became the British protectorate of Northern Rhodesia towards the end of the nineteenth century.

For most of the colonial period, the country was governed by an administration appointed from London with the advice of the British South Africa Company.

On 24 October 1964, the country became independent of the United Kingdom and then-prime minister Kenneth Kaunda became the inaugural president. Kaunda's socialist United National Independence Party (UNIP) maintained power from 1964 until 1991. From 1972 to 1991 Zambia was a single-party state with the UNIP as the sole legal political party under the motto 'One Zambia, One Nation'. Kaunda was succeeded by Frederick Chiluba of the social-democratic Movement for Multi-Party Democracy in 1991, beginning a period of social-economic growth and government decentralisation. Levy Mwanawasa, Chiluba's chosen successor, presided over the country from January 2002 until his death in August 2008, and is credited with campaigns to reduce corruption and increase the standard of living. After Mwanawasa's death, Rupiah Banda presided as Acting President before being elected President in 2008. Holding office for only three years, Banda stepped down after his defeat in the 2011 elections by Patriotic Front party leader Michael Chilufya Sata.

In 2010, the World Bank named Zambia one of the world's fastest economically reformed countries. The Common Market for Eastern and Southern Africa (COMESA) is headquartered in Lusaka.

STRATEGIC PROFILE

Background:	The territory of Northern Rhodesia was administered by the South Africa Company from 1891 until takeover by the UK in 1923. During the 1920s and 1930s, advances in mining spurred development and immigration. The name was changed to Zambia upon independence in 1964. In the 1980s and 1990s, declining copper prices and a prolonged drought hurt the economy. Elections in 1991 brought an end to one-party rule, but the subsequent vote in 1996 saw blatant harassment of opposition parties.

GEOGRAPHY

Location:	Southern Africa, east of Angola
Geographic coordinates:	15 00 S, 30 00 E
Map references:	Africa
Area:	total: 752,614 sq km land: 740,724 sq km water: 11,890 sq km
Area - comparative:	slightly larger than Texas
Land boundaries:	total: 5,664 km border countries: Angola 1,110 km, Democratic Republic of the Congo 1,930 km, Malawi 837 km, Mozambique 419 km, Namibia 233 km, Tanzania 338 km, Zimbabwe 797 km

Coastline:	0 km (landlocked)

For additional analytical, business and investment opportunities information,
please contact Global Investment & Business Center, USA
at (202) 546-2103. Fax: (202) 546-3275. E-mail: rusric@erols.com

Maritime claims:	none (landlocked)
Climate:	tropical; modified by altitude; rainy season (October to April)
Terrain:	mostly high plateau with some hills and mountains
Elevation extremes:	lowest point: Zambezi river 329 m highest point: unnamed location in Mafinga Hills 2,301 m
Natural resources:	copper, cobalt, zinc, lead, coal, emeralds, gold, silver, uranium, hydropower
Land use:	arable land: 7% permanent crops: 0% permanent pastures: 40% forests and woodland: 39% other: 14%

Irrigated land:	460 sq km
Natural hazards:	tropical storms (November to April)

Environment - current issues:	air pollution and resulting acid rain in the mineral extraction and refining region; chemical runoff into watersheds; poaching seriously threatens rhinoceros, elephant, antelope, and large cat populations; deforestation; soil erosion; desertification; lack of adequate water treatment presents human health risks
Environment - international agreements:	party to: Biodiversity, Climate Change, Desertification, Endangered Species, Hazardous Wastes, Law of the Sea, Nuclear Test Ban, Ozone Layer Protection, Wetlands signed, but not ratified: Climate Change-Kyoto Protocol
Geography - note:	landlocked; the Zambezi forms a natural riverine boundary with Zimbabwe

PEOPLE

Population:	9,770,199 note: estimates for this country explicitly take into account the effects of excess mortality due to AIDS; this can result in lower life expectancy, higher infant mortality and death rates, lower population and growth rates, and changes in the distribution of population by age and sex than would otherwise be expected (est.)
Age structure:	0-14 years: 47.36% (male 2,324,128; female 2,303,349) 15-64 years: 50.14% (male 2,433,250; female 2,465,747) 65 years and over: 2.5% (male 105,694; female 138,031)
Population growth rate:	1.93%
Birth rate:	41.46 births/1,000 population
Death rate:	21.97 deaths/1,000 population
Net migration rate:	-0.16 migrant(s)/1,000 population
Sex ratio:	at birth: 1.03 male(s)/female under 15 years: 1.01 male(s)/female 15-64 years: 0.99 male(s)/female 65 years and over: 0.77 male(s)/female total population: 0.99 male(s)/female
Infant mortality rate:	90.89 deaths/1,000 live births
Life expectancy at birth:	total population: 37.29 years

For additional analytical, business and investment opportunities information, please contact Global Investment & Business Center, USA at (202) 546-2103. Fax: (202) 546-3275. E-mail: rusric@erols.com

	male: 37.06 years female: 37.53 years
Total fertility rate:	5.53 children born/woman
HIV/AIDS - adult prevalence rate:	19.95%
HIV/AIDS - people living with HIV/AIDS:	870,000
HIV/AIDS - deaths:	99,000
Nationality:	noun: Zambian(s) adjective: Zambian
Ethnic groups:	African 98.7%, European 1.1%, other 0.2%
Religions:	Christian 50%-75%, Muslim and Hindu 24%-49%, indigenous beliefs 1%
Languages:	English (official), major vernaculars - Bemba, Kaonda, Lozi, Lunda, Luvale, Nyanja, Tonga, and about 70 other indigenous languages
Literacy:	definition: age 15 and over can read and write English total population: 78.2% male: 85.6% female: 71.3% (1995 est.)

GOVERNMENT

Country name:	conventional long form: Republic of Zambia conventional short form: Zambia former: Northern Rhodesia
Government type:	republic
Capital:	Lusaka
Administrative divisions:	9 provinces; Central, Copperbelt, Eastern, Luapula, Lusaka, Northern, North-Western, Southern, Western
Independence:	24 October 1964 (from UK)
National holiday:	Independence Day, 24 October (1964)
Constitution:	2 August 1991
Legal system:	based on English common law and customary law; judicial review of legislative acts in an ad hoc constitutional council; has not accepted compulsory ICJ jurisdiction
Suffrage:	18 years of age; universal
Executive branch:	**chief of state:** President Edgar LUNGU (since 25 January 2015); Vice President Inonge WINA (since 26 January 2015); note - the president is both chief of state and head of government **head of government:** President Edgar LUNGU (since 25 January 2015); Vice President Inonge WINA (since 26 January 2015 **cabinet:** Cabinet appointed by president from among members of the National Assembly **elections/appointments:** president directly elected by simple majority popular vote for a 5-year term (eligible for a second term); special presidential election held on 20 January 2015 to complete President SATA's term in office (next to be held

	in late 2016); SATA died 28 October 2014; vice president appointed by the president **election results:** Edgar LUNGU elected president; percent of vote - Edgar LUNGU (PF) 48.8%, Hakainde HICHILEMA (UPND) 47.2%, other 4%
Legislative branch:	unicameral National Assembly (158 seats; 150 members are elected by popular vote, 8 members appointed by the president, to serve five-year terms) elections: last held on 20 September 2011 (next to be held in 2016) election results: percent of vote by party - NA; seats by party - PF 60, MMD 55, UPND 28, ADD 1, FDD 1, independents 3; seats not determined 2
Judicial branch:	Supreme Court (the final court of appeal; justices are appointed by the president); High Court (has unlimited jurisdiction to hear civil and criminal cases)
Political parties and leaders:	Forum for Democracy and Development or FDD [Edith NAWAKWI]; Heritage Party or HP [Godfrey MIYANDA]; Movement for Multiparty Democracy or MMD [vacant]; Party of Unity for Democracy and Development or PUDD [Dan PULE]; Patriotic Front or PF [Michael SATA]; Reform Party [Nevers MUMBA]; United Democratic Alliance or UDA (a coalition of RP, ZADECO, PUDD, and ZRP); United Liberal Party or ULP [Sakwiba SIKOTA]; United National Independence Party or UNIP [Tilyenji KAUNDA]; United Party for National Development or UPND [Hakainde HICHILEMA]; Zambia Democratic Congress or ZADECO [Langton SICHONE]; Zambian Republican Party or ZRP [Benjamin MWILA]
Political pressure groups and leaders:	NA
International organization participation:	ACP, AfDB, C, CCC, ECA, FAO, G-19, G-77, IAEA, IBRD, ICAO, ICFTU, ICRM, IDA, IFAD, IFC, IFRCS, ILO, IMF, Intelsat, Interpol, IOC, IOM, ITU, MONUC, NAM, OAU, OPCW, PCA, SADC, UN, UNAMSIL, UNCTAD, UNESCO, UNIDO, UNMEE, UNMIK, UNTAET, UPU, WHO, WIPO, WMO, WToO, WTrO
Diplomatic representation in the US:	chief of mission: Ambassador Atan SHANSONGA chancery: 2419 Massachusetts Avenue NW, Washington, DC 20008 telephone: 1 (202) 265-9717 through 9719 FAX: 1 (202) 332-0826
Diplomatic representation from the US:	chief of mission: Ambassador David B. DUNN embassy: corner of Independence and United Nations Avenues mailing address: P. O. Box 31617, Lusaka telephone: 260 (1) 250-955 FAX: 260 (1) 252-225
Flag description:	green with a panel of three vertical bands of red (hoist side), black, and orange below a soaring orange eagle, on the outer edge of the flag

ECONOMY

Zambia's economy has experienced strong growth in recent years, with real GDP growth in 2005-13 more than 6% per year. Privatization of government-owned copper mines in the 1990s relieved the government from covering mammoth losses generated by the industry and greatly increased copper mining output and profitability to spur economic growth. Copper output has increased steadily since 2004, due to higher copper prices and foreign investment. Zambia's dependency on copper makes it vulnerable to depressed commodity prices, but record high copper prices and a bumper maize crop in 2010 helped Zambia rebound quickly from the world economic slowdown that began in 2008. Zambia has made some strides to improve the ease of doing business. Regulatory changes by the current government in 2012-2013 included Statutory Instruments (SI) Number 33 (mandating use of the kwacha for domestic transactions) and SI Number 55 (monitoring foreign exchange transactions). Along with problems of fiscal management and weakening global copper prices, these SI's were perceived as undermining confidence in Zambia's economy and currency, leading to sharp depreciation of the kwacha in March 2014. In response, the Minister of Finance revoked SI 33 and 55 in late March 2014. Despite a strong economy, poverty remains a significant problem in Zambia, made worse by a high birth rate, relatively high HIV/AIDS burden, and by market distorting agricultural policies.

GDP (purchasing power parity):
$25.47 billion (est.)
country comparison to the world: 124
$24.01 billion (2012 est.)
$22.39 billion (2011 est.)
note:data are in 2013 US dollars

GDP (official exchange rate):
$22.24 billion (est.)

GDP - real growth rate:
6% (est.)
country comparison to the world: 37
7.2% (2012 est.)
6.8% (2011 est.)

GDP - per capita (PPP):
$1,800 (est.)
country comparison to the world: 196
$1,700 (2012 est.)
$1,600 (2011 est.)
note:data are in 2013 US dollars

Gross national saving:
14.5% of GDP (est.)
country comparison to the world: 111
19.4% of GDP (2012 est.)
23.7% of GDP (2011 est.)

GDP - composition, by end use:
household consumption:

60%
government consumption:
26.5%
investment in fixed capital:
19.1%
investment in inventories:
1%
exports of goods and services:
36.2%
imports of goods and services:
-42.9%
(est.)

GDP - composition, by sector of origin:
agriculture:
19.8%
industry:
33.8%
services:
46.5% (est.)

Agriculture - products:
corn, sorghum, rice, peanuts, sunflower seeds, vegetables, flowers, tobacco, cotton, sugarcane, cassava (manioc, tapioca), coffee; cattle, goats, pigs, poultry, milk, eggs, hides

Industries:
copper mining and processing, emerald mining, construction, foodstuffs, beverages, chemicals, textiles, fertilizer, horticulture

Industrial production growth rate:
8% (est.)
country comparison to the world: 25

Labor force:
6.275 million (est.)
country comparison to the world: 66

Labor force - by occupation:
agriculture:
85%
industry:
6%
services:
9% (2004)

Unemployment rate:
15% (2008 est.)
country comparison to the world: 140
50% (2000 est.)

Population below poverty line:
60.5%

Household income or consumption by percentage share:
lowest 10%:
1.5%
highest 10%:
47.4%

Distribution of family income - Gini index:
57.5
country comparison to the world: 9
50.8 (2004)

Budget:
revenues:
$4.814 billion
expenditures:
$6.687 billion (est.)

Taxes and other revenues:
21.6% of GDP (est.)
country comparison to the world: 150

Budget surplus (+) or deficit (-):
-8.4% of GDP (est.)
country comparison to the world: 199

Public debt:
31.8% of GDP (est.)
country comparison to the world: 114
29.5% of GDP (2012 est.)

Fiscal year:
calendar year

Inflation rate (consumer prices):
7.1% (est.)
country comparison to the world: 189
6.6% (2012 est.)

Central bank discount rate:
8.39% (31 December 2009)
country comparison to the world: 12
14.49% (31 December 2008)

Commercial bank prime lending rate:
10.4% (31 December 2013 est.)
country comparison to the world: 64
12.15% (31 December 2012 est.)

Stock of narrow money:
$2.299 billion (31 December 2013 est.)
country comparison to the world: 122
$2.185 billion (31 December 2012 est.)

Stock of broad money:
$5.047 billion (31 December 2013 est.)
country comparison to the world: 128
$4.86 billion (31 December 2012 est.)

Stock of domestic credit:
$5.458 billion (31 December 2013 est.)
country comparison to the world: 110
$3.833 billion (31 December 2012 est.)

Market value of publicly traded shares:
$3.004 billion (31 December 2012 est.)
country comparison to the world: 81
$4.009 billion (31 December 2011)
$NA (31 December 2010 est.)

Current account balance:
-$1.25 billion (est.)
country comparison to the world: 123
-$189.9 million (2012 est.)

Exports:
$8.547 billion (est.)
country comparison to the world: 100
$9.414 billion (2012 est.)

Exports - commodities:
copper/cobalt, cobalt, electricity; tobacco, flowers, cotton

Exports - partners:
China 43.4%, South Africa 7.2%, Democratic Republic of the Congo 6.7%, South Korea 5.4%, India 4.7%, UAE 4.3%, Egypt 4.1%

Imports:
$8.216 billion (est.)
country comparison to the world: 109
$7.961 billion (2012 est.)

Imports - commodities:
machinery, transportation equipment, petroleum products, electricity, fertilizer, foodstuffs, clothing

Imports - partners:
South Africa 36.7%, Democratic Republic of the Congo 19.8%, China 10.4%, Kuwait 6%

For additional analytical, business and investment opportunities information, please contact Global Investment & Business Center, USA at (202) 546-2103. Fax: (202) 546-3275. E-mail: rusric@erols.com

Reserves of foreign exchange and gold:
$2.833 billion (31 December 2013 est.)
country comparison to the world: 110
$3.042 billion (31 December 2012 est.)

Debt - external:
$5.985 billion (31 December 2013 est.)
country comparison to the world: 115
$5.618 billion (31 December 2012 est.)

Stock of direct foreign investment - at home:
$NA

Stock of direct foreign investment - abroad:
$NA

Exchange rates:
Zambian kwacha (ZMK) per US dollar -
5.3 (est.)
5.1 (2012 est.)
4,797.1 (2010 est.)
5,046.1
3,512.9 (2008)

ENERGY

ectricity - production:
11.19 billion kWh
country comparison to the world: 93

Electricity - consumption:
7.96 billion kWh
country comparison to the world: 95

Electricity - exports:
578 million kWh
country comparison to the world: 65

Electricity - imports:
23 million kWh
country comparison to the world: 103

Electricity - installed generating capacity:
1.679 million kW
country comparison to the world: 112

Electricity - from fossil fuels:
0.4% of total installed capacity

country comparison to the world: 206

Electricity - from nuclear fuels:
0% of total installed capacity
country comparison to the world: 209

Electricity - from hydroelectric plants:
99.6% of total installed capacity
country comparison to the world: 5

Electricity - from other renewable sources:
0% of total installed capacity
country comparison to the world: 144

Crude oil - production:
174.6 bbl/day
country comparison to the world: 119

Crude oil - exports:
0 bbl/day
country comparison to the world: 209

Crude oil - imports:
12,500 bbl/day
country comparison to the world: 75

Crude oil - proved reserves:
0 bbl
country comparison to the world: 210

Refined petroleum products - production:
12,900 bbl/day
country comparison to the world: 102

Refined petroleum products - consumption:
19,260 bbl/day
country comparison to the world: 130

Refined petroleum products - exports:
254 bbl/day
country comparison to the world: 116

Refined petroleum products - imports:
1,272 bbl/day

country comparison to the world: 189

Natural gas - production:
0 cu m
country comparison to the world: 212

Natural gas - consumption:
0 cu m
country comparison to the world: 212

Natural gas - exports:
0 cu m
country comparison to the world: 211

Natural gas - imports:
0 cu m
country comparison to the world: 83

Natural gas - proved reserves:
0 cu m
country comparison to the world: 210

Carbon dioxide emissions from consumption of energy:
2.434 million Mt

COMMUNICATIONS

Telephones - main lines in use:
90,100
country comparison to the world: 148

Telephones - mobile cellular:
4.947 million
country comparison to the world: 102

Telephone system:
general assessment: among the best in Sub-Saharan Africa
domestic: high-capacity microwave radio relay connects most larger towns and cities; several cellular telephone services in operation and network coverage is improving; domestic satellite system being installed to improve telephone service in rural areas; Internet service is widely available; very small aperture terminal (VSAT) networks are operated by private firms
international: country code - 260; satellite earth stations - 2 Intelsat (1 Indian Ocean and 1 Atlantic Ocean), 3 owned by Zamtel

Broadcast media:
state-owned Zambia National Broadcasting Corporation (ZNBC) operates 1 TV station and is the principal local-content provider; several private TV stations; multi-channel subscription TV services are available; ZNBC operates 3 radio networks; about 2

For additional analytical, business and investment opportunities information, please contact Global Investment & Business Center, USA at (202) 546-2103. Fax: (202) 546-3275. E-mail: rusric@erols.com

dozen private radio stations; relays of at least 2 international broadcasters are accessible in Lusaka and Kitwe

Internet country code:
.zm

Internet hosts:
16,372
country comparison to the world: 123

Internet users:
816,200
country comparison to the world: 105

TRANSPORTATION

Railways:	total: 2,157 km narrow gauge: 2,157 km 1.067-m gauge (13 km double-track) note: the total includes 891 km of the Tanzania-Zambia Railway Authority (TAZARA), which operates 1,860 km of 1.067-m narrow gauge track between Dar es Salaam and Kapiri Mposhi where it connects to the Zambia Railways system; TAZARA is not a part of the Zambia Railways system; Zambia Railways assets are scheduled for concessioning (2001)
Highways:	total: 66,781 km paved: NA km unpaved: NA km
Waterways:	2,250 km note: includes Lake Tanganyika and the Zambezi and Luapula rivers
Pipelines:	crude oil 1,724 km
Ports and harbors:	Mpulungu
Airports:	112
Airports - with paved runways:	total: 13 over 3,047 m: 1 2,438 to 3,047 m: 3 1,524 to 2,437 m: 5 914 to 1,523 m: 3 under 914 m: 1
Airports - with unpaved runways:	total: 99 2,438 to 3,047 m: 1 1,524 to 2,437 m: 2 914 to 1,523 m: 65 under 914 m: 31

MILITARY

Military branches:
Zambian National Defense Force (ZNDF): Zambia Army, Zambia Air Force, National Service (paramilitary youth organization)

Military service age and obligation:
national registration required at age 16; 18-25 years of age for male and female voluntary military service (16 years of age with parental consent); no conscription; Zambian citizenship required; grade 12 certification required; mandatory HIV testing on enlistment; mandatory retirement for officers at age 65 (Army, Air Force)

Manpower available for military service:
males age 16-49: 3,041,069
females age 16-49: 2,948,291

Manpower fit for military service:
males age 16-49: 1,745,656
females age 16-49: 1,688,670

Manpower reaching militarily significant age annually:
male: 158,592
female: 158,805

Military expenditures:
1.55% of GDP
country comparison to the world: 59
1.59% of GDP
1.55% of GDP

TRANSNATIONAL ISSUES

Disputes - international:
in 2004, Zimbabwe dropped objections to plans between Botswana and Zambia to build a bridge over the Zambezi River, thereby de facto recognizing a short, but not clearly delimited, Botswana-Zambia boundary in the river

Refugees and internally displaced persons:
refugees (country of origin): 16,684 (Democratic Republic of the Congo)

Illicit drugs:
transshipment point for moderate amounts of methaqualone, small amounts of heroin, and cocaine bound for southern Africa and possibly Europe; a poorly developed financial infrastructure coupled with a government commitment to combating money laundering make it an unattractive venue for money launderers; major consumer of cannabis

For additional analytical, business and investment opportunities information,
please contact Global Investment & Business Center, USA
at (202) 546-2103. Fax: (202) 546-3275. E-mail: rusric@erols.com

IMPORTANT INFORMATION FOR UNDERSTANDING ZAMBIA

PROFILE

OFFICIAL NAME: Republic of Zambia

Geography

Area: 752,614 sq. km. (290,585 sq. mi.); slightly larger than Texas.
Cities: *Capital*--Lusaka (pop. approx. 1 million).
Other cities: Kitwe, Ndola, Livingstone, Kabwe.
Terrain: Varies; mostly plateau savanna.
Climate: Generally dry and temperate.

People

Nationality: *Noun and adjective*--Zambian(s).
Population: Approx. 11.9 million.
Annual growth rate: 1.6%.
Ethnic groups: More than 70 ethnic groups.
Religions: Christian, indigenous beliefs, Muslim, Hindu.
Languages: English (official), about 70 local languages and dialects, including Bemba, Lozi, Kaonde, Lunda, Luvale, Tonga, and Nyanja.
Education: *No compulsory education; 7 years free education.* Net primary school enrollment: 67%. *Literacy*--women: 60.6%; men: 81.6%.
Health: *Infant mortality rate*--102/1,000. *Life expectancy* (2005)--38.4 years. *HIV prevalence (15-49)*--17%.
Work force: *Agriculture*--75%; *mining and manufacturing*--6%; *services*--19%.

Government

Type: Republic.
Independence: October 24, 1964.
Constitution: 1991 (as amended in 1996).
Branches: *Executive*--president (chief of state and head of government), cabinet. *Legislative*--unicameral National Assembly. Judicial--Supreme Court, high court, magistrate courts, and local courts.
Ruling political party: Movement for Multi-party Democracy (MMD).
Suffrage: Universal adult.
Subdivisions: Nine provinces subdivided into 72 districts.

Economy

Natural resources: Copper, cobalt, zinc, lead, coal, emeralds, gold, silver, uranium, hydroelectric power, fertile land.
Agriculture: *Products*--corn, sorghum, rice, groundnuts, sunflower seeds, vegetables, horticultural products, tobacco, cotton, sugarcane, livestock, coffee, and soybeans.
Industry: *Types*--mining, transport, construction, foodstuffs, beverages, chemicals, and textiles.
Trade (2006): *Exports*--$3.54 billion: copper, cobalt, lead, and zinc, cut vegetables, cotton. *Major markets*--South Africa, United Kingdom, Tanzania, Malawi, Japan. *Imports*--$2.7 billion: crude oil, refined petroleum products, manufactured goods, machinery, transport equipment, foodstuffs. *Major suppliers*--South Africa, China, Tanzania, Zimbabwe.
Major donors: Donors provided $1.1 billion in development assistance to Zambia in 2005/6. The World Bank is Zambia's largest multilateral donor. Other key multilateral donors include the International Monetary Fund (IMF), the European Union, UN agencies, and the African Development Bank. Counting direct bilateral assistance and assistance through multilateral agencies, the U.S. is Zambia's largest country donor.

PEOPLE

Zambia's population comprises more than 70 Bantu-speaking ethnic groups. Some ethnic groups are small, and only two have enough people to constitute at least 10% of the population. Most Zambians are subsistence farmers. The predominant religion is a blend of traditional beliefs and Christianity; Christianity is the official national religion. Expatriates, mostly British (about 15,000) or South African, live mainly in Lusaka and in the Copperbelt in northern Zambia, where they are employed in mines and related activities. Zambia also has a small but economically important Asian population, most of whom are Indians. The country is 44% urban. The HIV/AIDS epidemic is ravaging Zambia. Nearly 1 million Zambians are HIV positive or have AIDS. An estimated 100,000 died in 2004. Over 750,000 Zambian children have been orphaned by HIV/AIDS. Life expectancy at birth is 32.7 years.

HISTORY

The indigenous hunter-gatherer occupants of Zambia began to be displaced or absorbed by more advanced migrating tribes about 2,000 years ago. The major waves of Bantu-speaking immigrants began in the 15th century, with the greatest influx between the late 17th and early 19th centuries. They came primarily from the Luba and Lunda tribes of southern Democratic Republic of Congo and northern Angola but were joined in the 19th century by Ngoni peoples from the south. By the latter part of that century, the various peoples of Zambia were largely established in the areas they currently occupy.

Except for an occasional Portuguese explorer, the area lay untouched by Europeans for centuries. After the mid-19th century, it was penetrated by Western explorers, missionaries, and traders. David Livingstone, in 1855, was the first European to see the magnificent waterfalls on the Zambezi River. He named the falls after Queen Victoria, and the Zambian town near the falls is named after him.

In 1888, Cecil Rhodes, spearheading British commercial and political interests in Central Africa, obtained a mineral rights concession from local chiefs. In the same year, Northern and Southern Rhodesia (now Zambia and Zimbabwe, respectively) were proclaimed a British sphere of influence. Southern Rhodesia was annexed formally and granted self-government in 1923, and the administration of Northern Rhodesia was transferred to the British colonial office in 1924 as a protectorate.

In 1953, both Rhodesias were joined with Nyasaland (now Malawi) to form the Federation of Rhodesia and Nyasaland. Northern Rhodesia was the center of much of the turmoil and crisis that characterized the federation in its last years. At the core of the controversy were insistent African demands for greater participation in government and European fears of losing political control.

A two-stage election held in October and December 1962 resulted in an African majority in the legislative council and an uneasy coalition between the two African nationalist parties. The council passed resolutions calling for Northern Rhodesia's secession from the federation and demanding full internal self-government under a new constitution and a new national assembly based on a broader, more democratic franchise. On December 31, 1963, the federation was dissolved, and Northern Rhodesia became the Republic of Zambia on October 24, 1964.

At independence, despite its considerable mineral wealth, Zambia faced major challenges. Domestically, there were few trained and educated Zambians capable of running the government, and the economy was largely dependent on foreign expertise. Abroad, three of its neighbors--Southern Rhodesia and the Portuguese colonies of Mozambique and Angola--remained under white-dominated rule. Rhodesia's white-ruled government unilaterally declared independence in

1965. In addition, Zambia shared a border with South African-controlled South-West Africa (now Namibia). Zambia's sympathies lay with forces opposing colonial or white-dominated rule, particularly in Southern Rhodesia. During the next decade, it actively supported movements such as the Union for the Total Liberation of Angola (UNITA), the Zimbabwe African People's Union (ZAPU), the African National Congress of South Africa (ANC), and the South-West Africa People's Organization (SWAPO).

Conflicts with Rhodesia resulted in the closing of Zambia's borders with that country and severe problems with international transport and power supply. However, the Kariba hydroelectric station on the Zambezi River provided sufficient capacity to satisfy the country's requirements for electricity. A railroad to the Tanzanian port of Dar es Salaam, built with Chinese assistance, reduced Zambian dependence on railroad lines south to South Africa and west through an increasingly troubled Angola.

By the late 1970s, Mozambique and Angola had attained independence from Portugal. Zimbabwe achieved independence in accordance with the 1979 Lancaster House agreement, but Zambia's problems were not solved. Civil war in the former Portuguese colonies generated refugees and caused continuing transportation problems. The Benguela Railroad, which extended west through Angola, was essentially closed to traffic from Zambia by the late 1970s. Zambia's strong support for the ANC, which had its external headquarters in Lusaka, created security problems as South Africa raided ANC targets in Zambia.

In the mid-1970s, the price of copper, Zambia's principal export, suffered a severe decline worldwide. Zambia turned to foreign and international lenders for relief, but as copper prices remained depressed, it became increasingly difficult to service its growing debt. By the mid-1990s, despite limited debt relief, Zambia's per capita foreign debt remained among the highest in the world.

GOVERNMENT

Zambia became a republic immediately upon attaining independence in October 1964. The constitution promulgated on August 25, 1973, abrogated the original 1964 constitution. The new constitution and the national elections that followed in December 1973 were the final steps in achieving what was called a "one-party participatory democracy."

The 1973 constitution provided for a strong president and a unicameral National Assembly. National policy was formulated by the Central Committee of the United National Independence Party (UNIP), the sole legal party in Zambia. The cabinet executed the central committee's policy.

In accordance with the intention to formalize UNIP supremacy in the new system, the constitution stipulated that the sole candidate in elections for the office of president was the person selected to be the president of UNIP by the party's general conference. The second-ranking person in the Zambian hierarchy was UNIP's secretary general.

In December 1990, at the end of a tumultuous year that included riots in the capital and a coup attempt, President Kenneth Kaunda signed legislation ending UNIP's monopoly on power. Zambia enacted a new constitution in August 1991, which enlarged the National Assembly from 136 members to a maximum of 158 members, established an electoral commission, and allowed for more than one presidential candidate who no longer had to be a member of UNIP. The constitution was amended again in 1996 to set new limits on the presidency (including a retroactive two-term limit, and a requirement that both parents of a candidate be Zambian-born). The National Assembly is comprised of 150 directly elected members, up to eight presidentially-appointed members, and a speaker. Zambia is divided into nine provinces, each administered by an appointed deputy minister who essentially performs the duties of a governor.

For additional analytical, business and investment opportunities information, please contact Global Investment & Business Center, USA at (202) 546-2103. Fax: (202) 546-3275. E-mail: rusric@erols.com

The Supreme Court is the highest court and the court of appeal; below it are the high court, magistrate's court, and local courts.

Principal Government Officials

Cabinet of Zambia: February 2015 – present

Portfolio	Incumbent
President Commander-in-chief of the Armed Forces	H.E. Edgar Lungu
Vice President of Zambia	H.E. Inonge Wina
Minister of Agriculture and Livestock	Given Lubinda
Minister of Chiefs and Traditional Affairs	Joseph Katema
Minister of Commerce, Trade and Industry	Margaret Mwanakatwe
Minister of Community Development, Mother and Child Health	Emerine Kabashi
Minister of Defence	Richwell Siamunene[4]
Minister of Education, Science, Vocational Training and Early Education	Michael Kaingu
Minister of Finance	Alexander Chikwanda
Minister of Foreign Affairs	Harry Kalaba
Minister of Gender and Child Development	Nkandu Luo
Minister of Health	Joseph Kasonde
Minister of Home Affairs	Davies Mwila
Minister of Information and Broadcasting Services	Chishimba Kambwili
Minister of Justice	Ngosa Simbyakula
Minister of Labour and Social Security	Fackson Shamenda
Minister of Land, Natural Resources and Environmental Protection	Christbel Ngimbu
Minister of Local Government and Housing	John Phiri
Minister of Mines, Energy and Water Development	Christopher Yaluma
Minister of Tourism and Arts	Jean Kapata
Minister of Transport, Works, Supply and Communications	Yamfwa Mukanga
Minister of Youth and Sports	Vincent Mwale
Attorney General	

Zambia maintains an embassy in the United States at 2419 Massachusetts Avenue, NW, Washington, DC 20008 (tel: 202-265-9717/8/9).

Zambia became a republic immediately upon attaining independence in October 1964. The constitution promulgated on August 25, 1973, abrogated the original 1964 constitution. The new constitution and the national elections that followed in December 1973 were the final steps in achieving what was called a "one-party participatory democracy."

The 1973 constitution provided for a strong president and a unicameral National Assembly. National policy was formulated by the Central Committee of the United National Independence Party (UNIP), the sole legal party in Zambia. The cabinet executed the central committee's policy.

In accordance with the intention to formalize UNIP supremacy in the new system, the constitution stipulated that the sole candidate in elections for the office of president was the person selected to be the president of UNIP by the party's general conference. The second-ranking person in the Zambian hierarchy was UNIP's secretary general.

In December 1990, at the end of a tumultuous year that included riots in the capital and a coup attempt, President Kenneth Kaunda signed legislation ending UNIP's monopoly on power. In response to growing popular demand for multi-party democracy, and after lengthy, difficult negotiations between the Kaunda government and opposition groups, Zambia enacted a new constitution in August 1991. The constitution enlarged the National Assembly from 136 members to a maximum of 158 members, established an electoral commission, and allowed for more than one presidential candidate who no longer had to be a member of UNIP. The constitution was amended again in 1996 to set new limits on the presidency (including a retroactive two-term limit, and a requirement that both parents of a candidate be Zambian-born). The National Assembly is comprised of 150 directly elected members, up to eight presidentially-appointed members, and a speaker. Zambia is divided into nine provinces, each administered by an appointed deputy minister who essentially performs the duties of a governor.

The Supreme Court is the highest court and the court of appeal; below it are the high court, magistrate's court, and local courts.

POLITICAL CONDITIONS

The **politics of Zambia** takes place in a framework of a presidential representative democratic republic, whereby the President of Zambia is head of state, head of government and leader of a multi-party system. Executive power is exercised by the government, while legislative power is vested in both the government and parliament. Formerly Northern Rhodesia, Zambia became a republic immediately upon attaining independence in October 1964.

EDGAR CHAGWA LUNGU 2015 - PRESENT

After being sworn in on the January 25, He has held the office of president after taking over from Guy Scott who was acting president after the passing of 5th republican president Micheal Chiluyfa Sata. So Far His presidency has been criticised with the depreciating kwacha and his drinking problem.[citation needed].However these economic challenges, in particular the depreciating kwacha, have been attributed to the global fall and depressed commodity prices. Zambia derives over 90% of its export earnings to one commodity: COPPER which has lost about 45% of its value on the international commodity market. Numerous individuals and media have repeatedly failed to prove his drinking problem as his health has improved dramatically since his collapse in his early days as president. On 5th January 2016, Edgar Chagwa Lungu became the first president in Zambia's history to successfully conclude the constitutional issue as proposed by the Zambian people when he assented to the 2015 Constitutional Amendment Bill. This Bill is a result of extensive work which started during the Mwanawasa era (The Mwanakatwe Commission) and was later polished by the Michael Chilufya Sata appointed Technical Committee (the Mwanawasa Constitutional Review Commission was rejected by parliament). As Justice Minister, Edgar Chagwa Lungu released the Draft Constitution in a short period of time and was presented to parliament and it was later decided that non-contentious issues will be debated in parliament while the continuous issues will be subjected to a referendum. He has followed this up, as president, by successfully finalising the long standing Constitutional issue.

The major figure in Zambian politics from 1964 to 1991 was Kenneth Kaunda, who led the campaign for independence and successfully bridged the rivalries among the country's various regions and ethnic groups. Kaunda tried to base government on his philosophy of "humanism," which condemned human exploitation and stressed cooperation among people, but not at the expense of the individual.

Kaunda's political party--the United National Independence Party (UNIP)--was founded in 1959 and was in power under Kaunda's leadership from 1964 to 1991. Before 1972, Zambia had three significant political parties--UNIP, the African National Congress (ANC), and the United Progressive Party (UPP). The ANC drew its strength from western and southern provinces, while the UPP found some support among Bemba-speakers in the Copperbelt and northern provinces. Although not strongly supported in all areas of the country, only UNIP had a nationwide following.

In December 1972, Zambian law established a one-party state, and all other political parties were banned; this was later enshrined in the 1973 constitution. Kaunda, the sole candidate, was elected President in the 1973 elections. Elections also were held for the National Assembly. Only UNIP members were permitted to run, but these seats were sharply contested. President Kaunda's mandate was renewed in December 1978, October 1983, and October 1988 in a "yes" or "no" vote on his candidacy.

Growing opposition to UNIP's monopoly on power led to the rise in 1990 of the Movement for Multiparty Democracy (MMD). The MMD assembled an increasingly impressive group of important Zambians, including prominent UNIP defectors and labor leaders. During the year, President Kaunda agreed to a referendum on the one-party state but, in the face of continued opposition, dropped the referendum and signed a constitutional amendment making Zambia a multi-party state. Zambia's first multi-party elections for parliament and the presidency since the 1960s were held on October 31, 1991. MMD candidate Frederick Chiluba resoundingly carried the presidential election over Kenneth Kaunda with 81% of the vote. To add to the MMD landslide, in the parliamentary elections the MMD won 125 of the 150 elected seats and UNIP the remaining 25. However, UNIP swept the Eastern Province, gathering 19 of its seats there.

By the end of Chiluba's first term as President (1996), the MMD's commitment to political reform had faded in the face of re-election demands. A number of prominent supporters founded opposing parties. Relying on the MMD's overwhelming majority in parliament, President Chiluba in May 1996 pushed through constitutional amendments that eliminated former President Kaunda and other prominent opposition leaders from the 1996 presidential elections. In the presidential and parliamentary elections held in November 1996, Chiluba was re-elected, and the MMD won 131 of the 150 seats in the National Assembly. Kaunda's UNIP party boycotted the parliamentary polls to protest the exclusion of its leader from the presidential race, alleging in addition that the outcome of the election had been predetermined due to a faulty voter registration exercise. Despite the UNIP boycott, the elections took place peacefully, and five presidential and more than 600 parliamentary candidates from 11 parties participated. Afterward, however, several opposition parties and non-governmental organizations declared the elections neither free nor fair. As President Chiluba began his second term in 1997, the opposition continued to reject the results of the election amid international efforts to encourage the MMD and the opposition to resolve their differences through dialogue.

Early in 2001, supporters of President Chiluba mounted a campaign to amend the constitution to enable Chiluba to seek a third term of office. Civil society, opposition parties, and many members of the ruling party exerted sufficient pressure on Chiluba to force him to back away from any attempt at a third term.

Presidential, parliamentary, and local government elections were held on December 27, 2001. Eleven parties contested the elections. The elections encountered numerous administrative problems. Opposition parties alleged that serious irregularities occurred. Nevertheless, MMD presidential candidate Levy Mwanawasa, having garnered a plurality of the vote (29%), was declared the victor by a narrow margin, and he was sworn into office on January 2, 2002. Three parties submitted petitions to the Supreme Court, challenging the election results, but the court ruled against the petitioners in February 2005. Opposition parties won a majority of parliamentary seats in the December 2001 election, but subsequent by-elections gave the ruling MMD a majority in parliament.

During his first months in office, President Mwanawasa encouraged the Zambian Anticorruption Commission to aggressively pursue its mandate. In July 2002, in a speech before the Zambian National Assembly, President Mwanawasa provided details on a number of corruption allegations targeting former President Chiluba, and called for parliament to consider lifting Chiluba's immunity from prosecution. Mwanawasa appointed a special Task Force to investigate and prosecute corrupt officials. Zambian courts are now hearing cases involving corruption charges against Chiluba and numerous officials from his regime.

During his first term in office, President Mwanawasa appointed an Electoral Reform Technical Committee (ERTC) and a Constitutional Reform Committee (CRC) to make recommendations for reforms. The ERTC submitted its final report to the President in August 2005. Voter registration began on October 31, 2005 and continued through December 31, 2005. The CRC presented its final report and a draft constitution in December 2005. In February 2006 the government agreed to allow the formation of a Constituent Assembly to consider and adopt the draft constitution, subject to certain conditions. However, to date, a Constituent Assembly has not been formed. The Government of Zambia introduced very limited legislative changes to electoral procedures in mid-2006.

On July 25, 2006, President Mwanawasa dissolved parliament and his cabinet and set September 28, 2006 as the date for presidential, parliamentary, and local government elections. Mwanawasa won the September 2006 election with 1,177,846 votes, while the Patriotic Front's Michael Sata came in second with 804,748 votes. The head of a three-party alliance, Hakainde Hichilema, placed third. In parliamentary elections, the ruling MMD party won a slim majority of seats. International observers commended the overall conduct of the elections, but noted some anomalies.

ECONOMY

Rank	105th
Currency	Zambian kwacha (ZMK)
Fiscal year	calendar year
Trade organisations	WTO, SADC, COMESA
	Statistics
GDP	$24.36 billion
GDP growth	7.3%

GDP per capita	$1700
GDP by sector	agriculture: 20.4%, industry: 32.2%, services: 46.4%
Inflation (CPI)	6.6%
Population below poverty line	60%
Labour force	5.956 million
Labour force by occupation	agriculture: 85%, industry: 6%, services: 9%
Unemployment	14%
Main industries	copper mining and processing, construction, foodstuffs, beverages, chemicals, textiles, fertilizer, horticulture
Ease-of-doing-business rank	84th)
	External
Exports	$8.589 billion f.o.b.
Export goods	copper/cobalt 64%, cobalt, electricity; tobacco, flowers, cotton
Main export partners	China 42.2% South Africa 7.2% DR Congo 7.2% South Korea 5.3% India 4.5% Egypt 4.5% United Arab Emirates 4.4%
Imports	$7.361 billion f.o.b.
Import goods	machinery, transportation equipment, petroleum products, electricity, fertilizer; foodstuffs, clothing
Main import partners	South Africa 36.2% DR Congo 21.3% China 10.1% Kuwait 5.7% (2012 est.)
	Public finances
Public debt	$4.137 billion
Revenues	$4.256 billion
Expenses	$5.256 billion
Economic aid	recipient: $640.6 million
Credit rating	B+ (Domestic) B+ (Foreign) B+ (T&C Assessment) (Standard & Poor's)

Zambia is one of Sub-Saharan Africa's most highly urbanized countries. About one-half of the country's 11.5 million people are concentrated in a few urban zones strung along the major transportation corridors, while rural areas are under-populated. Unemployment and underemployment are serious problems. National GDP has actually doubled since independence, but due in large part to high birth rates and AIDS per capita annual incomes are currently at about two-thirds of their levels at independence. This low GDP per capita, which stands at $1400, places the country among the world's poorest nations. Social indicators continue to decline, particularly in measurements of life expectancy at birth (about 50 years) and maternal and infant mortality (85 per 1,000 live births). The high population growth rate of 2.3% per annum makes it difficult for per capita income to increase. The country's rate of economic growth cannot support rapid population growth or the strain which HIV/AIDS-related issues (i.e., rising medical costs, street children, and decline in worker productivity) places on government resources.

For the first time since 1989 Zambia's economic growth reached the 6%-7% mark(in 2007) needed to reduce poverty significantly. Copper output has increased steadily since 2004, due to higher copper prices and the opening of new mines. The maize harvest was again good in 2005, helping boost GDP and agricultural exports. Cooperation continues with international bodies on programs to reduce poverty, including a new lending arrangement with the IMF in the second quarter of 2004. A tighter monetary policy will help cut inflation, but Zambia still has a serious problem with high public debt.

Zambia was ranked the 127th safest investment destination in the world in the March 2011 Euromoney Country Risk rankings

Over 70% of Zambians live in poverty. Per capita annual incomes are currently at about one-half their levels at independence and, at $627, place the country among the world's poorest nations. Social indicators continue to decline, particularly in measurements of life expectancy at birth (about 38 years) and maternal mortality (729 per 100,000 pregnancies). The country's rate of economic growth cannot support rapid population growth or the strain which HIV/AIDS related issues (i.e., rising medical costs, decline in worker productivity) place on government resources. Zambia is also one of Sub-Saharan Africa's most highly urbanized countries. Almost one-half of the country's 10 million people are concentrated in a few urban zones strung along the major transportation corridors, while rural areas are underpopulated. Unemployment and underemployment are serious problems.

HIV/AIDS is the nation's greatest challenge, with 16% prevalence among the adult population. HIV/AIDS will continue to ravage Zambian economic, political, cultural, and social development for the foreseeable future.

Once a middle-income country, Zambia began to slide into poverty in the 1970s when copper prices declined on world markets. The socialist government made up for falling revenue by increasing borrowing. After democratic multi-party elections, the Chiluba government (1991-2001) came to power in November 1991 committed to an economic reform program. The government was successful in some areas, such as privatization of most of the parastatals, maintenance of positive real interest rates, the elimination of exchange controls, and endorsement of free market principles. Corruption grew dramatically under the Chiluba government. Zambia has yet to address effectively issues such as reducing the size of the public sector and improving Zambia's social sector delivery systems.

Zambia's total foreign debt stood at about $7 billion when Zambia reached the Highly Indebted Poor Countries Initiative (HIPC) completion point in April 2005. In December 2005, the U.S. and Zambian Governments signed an agreement for cancellation of $280 million in bilateral debt. Once debt cancellation under HIPC is completed, almost $6 billion in debt will be eliminated.

The IMF conducts periodic economic reviews under a three-year Poverty Reduction and Growth Facility. In November 2006, the Fund commended Zambia's macroeconomic stability and continued fiscal discipline, but noted lags in the implementation of some reform measures. In 2006, the rate of inflation dropped into single digits for the first time in recent history. The Zambian economy has historically been based on the copper-mining industry. Output of copper had fallen, however, to a low of 228,000 metric tons in 1998, after a 30-year decline in output due to lack of investment, low copper prices, and uncertainty over privatization. Following privatization of the industry, copper production rebounded, reaching almost 400,000 metric tons in 2004 and 440,000 metric tons in 2005. Improvements in the world copper market have magnified the effect of this volume increase on revenues and foreign exchange earnings.

The Zambian Government is pursuing an economic diversification program to reduce the economy's reliance on the copper industry. This initiative seeks to exploit other components of Zambia's rich resource base by promoting agriculture, tourism, gemstone mining, and hydro power.

DEFENSE

The Zambian Defense Force (ZDF) consists of the army, the air force, and Zambian National Service (ZNS). The ZNS, while operating under the Ministry of Defense, is responsible primarily for public works projects. The ZDF is designed primarily for internal defense. The HIV/AIDS epidemic has hit the ZDF especially hard.

The ZDF contributes to African Union and United Nations peacekeeping operations in Africa, and in 2005 became a partner in the African Contingency Operations and Training Assistance (ACOTA) program.

FOREIGN RELATIONS

Zambia is a member of the Non-Aligned Movement (NAM), the African Union, the Southern African Development Community (SADC), and the Common Market for Eastern and Southern Africa (COMESA), which is headquartered in Lusaka.

President Kaunda was a persistent and visible advocate of change in Southern Africa, supporting liberation movements in Angola, Mozambique, Namibia, Southern Rhodesia (Zimbabwe), and South Africa. Many of these organizations were based in Zambia during the 1970s and 1980s.

President Chiluba assumed a somewhat higher profile internationally in the mid- and late 1990s. His government played a constructive regional role sponsoring Angola peace talks that led to the 1994 Lusaka Protocols. Zambia has provided troops to UN peacekeeping initiatives in Mozambique, Rwanda, Angola, and Sierra Leone. Zambia was the first African state to cooperate with the International Tribunal investigation of the 1994 genocide in Rwanda.

In 1998, Zambia took the lead in efforts to establish a cease-fire in the Democratic Republic of Congo. Zambia was active in the Congolese peace effort after the signing of a cease-fire agreement in Lusaka in July and August 1999, although activity diminished considerably after the Joint Military Commission tasked with implementing the ceasefire relocated to Kinshasa in September 2001.

U.S.-ZAMBIAN RELATIONS

The United States and Zambia enjoy warm relations. The United States works closely with the Zambian Government to defeat the HIV/AIDS pandemic that is ravaging Zambia, to promote economic growth and development, and to effect political reform needed to strengthen the nation's emerging democratic institutions. The United States is also supporting the government's efforts to root out corruption. Zambia is a beneficiary of the African Growth and Opportunity Act (AGOA). Total U.S. Government assistance obligated for Zambia in 2006 was approximately $268 million. These funds provided a variety of technical assistance and other support that is managed by the Department of State, U.S. Agency for International Development, Millennium Challenge Account (MCA) Threshold Program, Centers for Disease Control, Department of Treasury, Department of Defense, and Peace Corps. The majority of assistance was provided through the President's Emergency Plan for AIDS Relief (PEPFAR), in support of the fight against HIV/AIDS.

In addition to supporting development projects, the United States has provided considerable emergency food aid during periods of drought through the World Food Program (WFP) and is a major contributor to refugee programs in Zambia through the UN High Commission for Refugees and other agencies.

For additional analytical, business and investment opportunities information, please contact Global Investment & Business Center, USA at (202) 546-2103. Fax: (202) 546-3275. E-mail: rusric@erols.com

U.S. Agency for International Development (USAID)
USAID administered more than $141 million in obligated funding for 2006. This included the management of over $70 million for PEPFAR and $22 million for the MCA assistance to Zambia to fight corruption, reduce administrative barriers, and make customs clearance more efficient, to improve trade. During 2006, USAID focused on the following programs in addition to PEPFAR and MCA:

- Increased private sector competitiveness;
- Improved quality of basic education for more school-aged children;
- Improved health status of Zambians; and
- Reduced impact of HIV/AIDS through a multi-sectoral response.

Peace Corps
A country agreement inviting the Peace Corps to work in Zambia was signed by the United States and Zambia on September 14, 1993. The first group of volunteers was sworn in on April 7, 1994. In 2007, the Peace Corps program in Zambia continues to increase understanding between Zambians and Americans. More than 160 two-year Volunteers and as many as 10 extension and Crisis Corps Volunteers promote sustainable development through their activities in agricultural and natural resource management, health and sanitation, rural education, and humanitarian assistance. Volunteers are working in eight of Zambia's nine provinces building local capacity to manage family fish farms, to promote food security and positive resource management practices near forest reserves, to implement health reforms at the village level, to promote and support rural education, and to extend HIV/AIDS education and prevention efforts through full participation in PEPFAR. Volunteers live primarily in rural villages in remote parts of the country without running water, electricity, or other amenities. New trainees undertake training in local language, culture, and the relevant technical specialty for 9-12 weeks at a center in the Chongwe district of Lusaka province.

Principal U.S. Officials
Ambassador--Carmen Martinez
Deputy Chief of Mission--Michael Koplovsky
Public Affairs Officer--Christopher Wurst
Political/Economic Section Chief--Jill Derderian
Consular Officer--Malia Heroux
Defense Attaché--Lt. Col. David Dougherty
Centers for Disease Control and Prevention--Dr. Marc Bulterys
USAID Mission Director--Melissa Wells
Peace Corps Director--Cynthia Threlkeld
The U.S. Embassy in Zambia is at the corner of Independence and United Nations Avenues (P.O. Box 31617), Lusaka (tel: 260-1- 250955; fax 260-1-252225).

TRAVEL AND BUSINESS INFORMATION

The U.S. Department of State's Consular Information Program advises Americans traveling and residing abroad through Consular Information Sheets, Public Announcements, and Travel Warnings. **Consular Information Sheets** exist for all countries and include information on entry and exit requirements, currency regulations, health conditions, safety and security, crime, political disturbances, and the addresses of the U.S. embassies and consulates abroad. **Public Announcements** are issued to disseminate information quickly about terrorist threats and other relatively short-term conditions overseas that pose significant risks to the security of American travelers. **Travel Warnings** are issued when the State Department recommends that Americans avoid travel to a certain country because the situation is dangerous or unstable.

For the latest security information, Americans living and traveling abroad should regularly monitor the Department's Bureau of Consular Affairs Internet web site at http://www.travel.state.gov, where the current Worldwide Caution, Public Announcements, and Travel Warnings can be found. Consular Affairs Publications, which contain information on obtaining passports and planning a safe trip abroad, are also available at http://www.travel.state.gov. For additional information on international travel, see http://www.usa.gov/Citizen/Topics/Travel/International.shtml.

The Department of State encourages all U.S citizens traveling or residing abroad to register via the State Department's travel registration website or at the nearest U.S. embassy or consulate abroad. Registration will make your presence and whereabouts known in case it is necessary to contact you in an emergency and will enable you to receive up-to-date information on security conditions.

Emergency information concerning Americans traveling abroad may be obtained by calling 1-888-407-4747 toll free in the U.S. and Canada or the regular toll line 1-202-501-4444 for callers outside the U.S. and Canada.

The National Passport Information Center (NPIC) is the U.S. Department of State's single, centralized public contact center for U.S. passport information. Telephone: 1-877-4USA-PPT (1-877-487-2778). Customer service representatives and operators for TDD/TTY are available Monday-Friday, 7:00 a.m. to 12:00 midnight, Eastern Time, excluding federal holidays. Travelers can check the latest health information with the U.S. Centers for Disease Control and Prevention in Atlanta, Georgia. A hotline at 877-FYI-TRIP (877-394-8747) and a web site at http://wwwn.cdc.gov/travel/default.aspx give the most recent health advisories, immunization recommendations or requirements, and advice on food and drinking water safety for regions and countries. A booklet entitled "Health Information for International Travel" (HHS publication number CDC-95-8280) is available from the U.S. Government Printing Office, Washington, DC 20402, tel. (202) 512-1800.

ZAMBIA LEGAL SYSTEM BASICS

The Zambian legal system is based primarily on the English common law tradition. Zambia is overly reliant on the colonial legal system (many of the government's inefficiencies can be traced to its decision to adhere to a system that is ill-fitted for post-colonial rule). For instance, English law is used as a gap filler in all aspects of law from procedure, to contract, to legislative acts. Moreover, the system is structured in the same manner as it was during colonial rule and recognizes traditional customary law only if it is not "repugnant" to "civilized" ideas of justice. Further still, judges and lawyers continue to wear the antiquated dress of judges in the 19th century – especially complicated robes and white-haired wigs – while these customs have been phased out in most of the rest of the world, including England where they originated.

Like the American and South African legal systems (which were heavily influenced by the British tradition), Zambia has a hybrid common law system with a legal authority hierarchy as follows: 1) constitutional law 2) statutory law 3) common law 4) customary law and 5) authoritative texts (which are merely persuasive and not binding).

The Zambian constitution is the highest law of the land and provides for, essentially, the structure of government and the protection of the Zambian people's rights. The constitution is broken into parts and articles. Article five provides for citizenship, while articles 12 through 21 provide for the rights to life, personal liberty, a fair hearing, freedom of conscience and religion, expression, assembly, and protections from slavery, inhuman treatment, deprivation of property, against arbitrary search.

Zambia lies between the Democratic Republic of Congo to the north, Tanzania to the north-east, Malawi to the east, Mozambique, Zimbabwe, Botswana, and Namibia to the south, and Angola to the west. The country measures approximately 752,618 sq km with a population of approximately 11 862 740. The country's leadership is democratic.

Zambia's population comprises more than 70 Bantu-speaking ethnic groups. Some ethnic groups are small, and only two have enough people to constitute at least 10% of the population. Most Zambians are subsistence farmers. The predominant religion is a blend of traditional beliefs and Christianity; Christianity is the official national religion. Expatriates, a majority of whom are British (about 15,000) and South African, live mainly in Lusaka and in the Copper belt in northern Zambia, where they are employed in mines and related activities. Zambia also has a small but economically important Asian population, most of whom are Indians.

The indigenous hunter-gatherer occupants of Zambia began to be displaced or absorbed by more advanced migrating tribes about 2,000 years ago. The major waves of Bantu-speaking immigrants began in the 15th century, with the greatest influx between the late 17th and early 19th centuries. They came primarily from the Luba and Lunda tribes of southern Democratic Republic of Congo and northern Angola but were joined in the 19th century by Ngoni peoples from the south. By the latter part of that century, the various peoples of Zambia were largely established in the areas they currently occupy.

Except for an occasional Portuguese explorer, the area lay untouched by Europeans for centuries. After the mid-19th century, it was penetrated by Western explorers, missionaries, and traders. David Livingstone, in 1855, was the first European to see the magnificent waterfalls on the Zambezi River. He named the falls after Queen Victoria, and the Zambian town near the falls is named after him.

For additional analytical, business and investment opportunities information, please contact Global Investment & Business Center, USA at (202) 546-2103. Fax: (202) 546-3275. E-mail: rusric@erols.com

In 1888, Cecil Rhodes, spearheading British commercial and political interests in Central Africa, obtained mineral rights concession from local chiefs. In the same year, Northern and Southern Rhodesia (now Zambia and Zimbabwe, respectively) were proclaimed a British sphere of influence. Southern Rhodesia was annexed formally and granted self-government in 1923, and the administration of Northern Rhodesia was transferred to the British colonial office in 1924 as a protectorate. In 1953, both Rhodesias were joined with Nyasaland (now Malawi) to form the Federation of Rhodesia and Nyasaland. Northern Rhodesia was the center of much of the turmoil and crisis that characterized the federation in its last years. At the core of the controversy were insistent African demands for greater participation in government and European fears of losing political control.

A two-stage election held in October and December of 1962 resulted in an African majority in the legislative council and an uneasy coalition between the two African nationalist parties. The council passed resolutions calling for Northern Rhodesia's secession from the federation and demanding full internal self-government under a new constitution and a new national assembly based on a broader, more democratic franchise. On December 31, 1963, the federation was dissolved, and Northern Rhodesia became the Republic of Zambia on October 24, 1964.

At independence, despite its considerable mineral wealth, Zambia faced major challenges. Domestically, there were few trained and educated Zambians capable of running the government, and the economy was largely dependent on foreign expertise. Abroad, three of its neighbors--Southern Rhodesia and the Portuguese colonies of Mozambique and Angola--remained under white-dominated rule. Rhodesia's white-ruled government unilaterally declared independence in 1965. In addition, Zambia shared a border with South African-controlled South-West Africa (now Namibia). Zambia's sympathies lay with forces opposing colonial or white-dominated rule, particularly in Southern Rhodesia. During the next decade, it actively supported movements such as the Union for the Total Liberation of Angola (UNITA), the Zimbabwe African People's Union (ZAPU), the African National Congress of South Africa (ANC), and the South-West Africa People's Organization (SWAPO).

Conflicts with Rhodesia resulted in the closing of Zambia's borders with that country and severe problems with international transport and power supply. However, the Kariba hydroelectric station on the Zambezi River provided sufficient capacity to satisfy the country's requirements for electricity. A railroad to the Tanzanian port of Dar es Salaam, built with Chinese assistance, reduced Zambian dependence on railroad lines south to South Africa and west through an increasingly troubled Angola.

By the late 1970s, Mozambique and Angola had attained independence from Portugal. Zimbabwe achieved independence in accordance with the 1979 Lancaster House agreement, but Zambia's problems were not solved. Civil war in the former Portuguese colonies generated refugees and caused continuing transportation problems.

The Benguela Railroad, which extended west through Angola, was essentially closed to traffic from Zambia by the late 1970s. Zambia's strong support for the ANC, which had its external headquarters in Lusaka, created security problems as South Africa raided ANC targets in Zambia. In the mid-1970s, the price of copper, Zambia's principal export, suffered a severe decline worldwide. Zambia turned to foreign and international lenders for relief, but as copper prices remained depressed, it became increasingly difficult to service its growing debt. In response to growing popular demand, and after lengthy, difficult negotiations between the Kaunda government and opposition groups, Zambia enacted a new constitution in 1991 and shortly thereafter became a multi-party democracy. Kaunda's successor, Frederick Chiluba, made efforts to liberalize the economy and privatize industry, but allegations of massive corruption characterized the latter part of his administration. By the mid-1990s, despite limited debt relief, Zambia's per capita foreign debt remained among the highest in the world.

Although poverty continues to be a significant problem in Zambia, its economy has stabilized, attaining single-digit inflation in 2006-2007, real GDP growth, decreasing interest rates, and increasing levels of trade. Much of its growth is due to foreign investment in Zambia's mining sector and higher copper prices on the world market. In 2005, Zambia qualified for debt relief under the Heavily Indebted Poor Countries (HIPC) initiative, consisting of approximately U.S. $6 billion in debt relief.

GOVERNMENT

Zambia became a republic immediately upon attaining independence in October 1964. The constitution promulgated on August 25, 1973, abrogated the original 1964 constitution. The new constitution and the national elections that followed in December 1973 were the final steps in achieving what was called a "one-party participatory democracy." The 1973 constitution provided for a strong president and a unicameral National Assembly. National policy was formulated by the Central Committee of the United National Independence Party (UNIP), the sole legal party in Zambia. The cabinet executed the central committee's policy. In accordance with the intention to formalize UNIP supremacy in the new system, the constitution stipulated that the sole candidate in elections for the office of president was the person selected to be the president of UNIP by the party's general conference. The second-ranking person in the Zambian hierarchy was UNIP's secretary general.

In December 1990, at the end of a tumultuous year that included riots in the capital and a coup attempt, President Kenneth Kaunda signed legislation ending UNIP's monopoly on power. Zambia enacted a new constitution in August 1991, which enlarged the National Assembly from 136 members to a maximum of 158 members, established an electoral commission, and allowed for more than one presidential candidate who no longer had to be a member of UNIP. The first multi-party elections in November 1991 resulted in the victory of the Movement for Multi-Party Democracy (MMD) and the election of President Frederick Chiluba, a former trade Unionist. The present Constitution dates from June 1996. While similar to the 1991 Constitution, it contains amended provisions regarding the qualifications of presidential candidates and grants the President and the National Assembly increased powers in respect of their relationship with the judiciary. The May 1996 amendment set new limits on the presidency (including a retroactive two-term limit, and a requirement that both parents of a candidate be Zambians-by birth or descent). This amendment had the direct effect of excluding former President Kaunda, whose parents were Malawian, from standing in the presidential elections. The UNIP boycotted the November 1996 elections that confirmed the government of MMD and President Chiluba. Executive power is vested in the President, who is elected directly by universal suffrage for a term of five years and may be re-elected only once. The President is the Head of State and the Commander-in-Chief.

On 2 August 1991, the adoption of a new Constitution introduced a multi-party system, thereby ending the monopoly of Kaunda's United National Independence Party (UNIP). The President appoints the Ministers of his Cabinet from among the members of the National Assembly, and they are collectively answerable to the National Assembly. The President has the power to declare a state of emergency and to dissolve the National Assembly. Article 45 of the Constitution provides for the office of the Vice-President, who is appointed from among the members of the National Assembly and performs such functions as are assigned to him by the President of the Republic. Legislative power is vested in the Parliament, which consists of the President and the National Assembly. The National Assembly is composed of 150 members elected by universal, direct suffrage, with not more than eight members nominated by the President, and the Speaker, nominated by the members of the National Assembly. Traditional chiefs are not qualified to be elected as members of the Parliament. Legislation passed by the National Assembly must be assented to by the President in order to become law. Members of the Parliament form parliamentary committees with the mandate to consider specific matters or bills.

The Constitution also provides for a House of Chiefs, an advisory body composed of 27 chiefs from the various provinces. 401 Zambia –*Attacks on Justice, eleventh edition* International Commission of Jurists .The country is divided into nine provinces, including the capital of Lusaka, each of which is administered by a centrally appointed Provincial Secretary and a partially elected Provincial Council. The provinces are subdivided into 55 districts, each administered by a centrally appointed Governor and a partially elected District Council. Presidential and parliamentary elections are to be held on 27 December 2001.

At the beginning of 2001 President Chiluba had seemed eager to amend the Constitution in order to seek a third term, but on 8 May 2001, following pressure from the opposition, international donors and even by members of his own cabinet, Chiluba announced that he would not stand for an unconstitutional third term in office. In the meantime, more than 20 dissident members of the ruling MMD party including the country's Vice-President and eight ministers have been expelled from the Parliament. In May 2001, an impeachment petition was filed against President Chiluba before the House Speaker of the National Assembly. The petitioners, mostly MMD parliamentarians, obtained 65 signatures, enough to compel the Speaker to convene parliament to hear charges of gross misconduct against President Chiluba, who had come under intense criticism for corruption in his government. On 30 May 2001, the Parliament postponed the debate on the impeachment motion.

In December 1990, at the end of a tumultuous year that included riots in the capital and a coup attempt, President Kaunda signed legislation ending UNIP's monopoly on power. In response to growing popular demand for multi-party democracy, and after lengthy, difficult negotiations between the Kaunda government and opposition groups, Zambia enacted a new constitution in August 1991. The constitution enlarged the National Assembly from 136 members to a maximum of 158 members, establishing an electoral commission, and allowed for more than one presidential candidate who no longer had to be members of UNIP. The constitution was amended again in 1996 to set new limits on the presidency (including a retroactive two term limit, and a requirement that both parents of a candidate be Zambian-born.) The National Assembly is comprised of 150 directly elected members, up to 8 presidentially appointed members and a speaker. Zambia is divided into nine provinces, each administered by an appointed governor.

FOREIGN RELATIONS

Zambia is a member of the Non-Aligned Movement (NAM), the African Union, the Southern African Development Community (SADC), and the Common Market for Eastern and Southern Africa (COMESA), which is headquartered in Lusaka. President Kaunda was a persistent and visible advocate of change in southern Africa, supporting liberation movements in Angola, Mozambique, Namibia, Southern Rhodesia (Zimbabwe), and South Africa. Many of these liberation organizations were based in Zambia during the 1970s and 1980s. President Chiluba assumed a visible international role in the mid- and late 1990s. His government sponsored Angola's peace talks that led to the 1994 Lusaka Protocols. Zambia provided troops to UN peacekeeping initiatives in Mozambique, Rwanda, Angola, and Sierra Leone. Zambia was the first African state to cooperate with the International Tribunal investigation of the 1994 genocide in Rwanda.

In 1998, Zambia took the lead in efforts to establish a cease-fire in Democratic Republic of the Congo. After the signing of a cease-fire agreement in Lusaka in July and August 1999, Zambia was active in supporting the Congolese peace effort, although activity diminished considerably after the Joint Military Commission tasked with implementing the ceasefire relocated to Kinshasa in September 2001.

During President Mwanawasa's administration, Zambia contributed troops to support UN peacekeeping operations in southern Sudan. During his tenure as SADC Chair, President Mwanawasa brought the issue of Zimbabwe to the fore in the SADC, taking a lead role in pressuring President Mugabe for reforms in his country. Zambia's history of stability and its commitment to regional peace has made it a haven for large numbers of refugees. Currently, Zambia hosts approximately 87,000 refugees (down from a high of 203,000 in 2002), including roughly 51,000 Congolese, 27,000 Angolans, and 9,000 other nationalities (mainly Rwandans, Burundians, and Somalis). In recent years, Zambia has made serious efforts to repatriate many of these refugees, including organized repatriation for 74,000 Angolan and 17,000 Congolese refugees.

ECONOMY

About two-thirds of Zambians live in poverty. Per capita annual incomes are well below their levels at independence and, at $852, place the country among the world's poorest nations. Life expectancy at birth is about 51 years, and maternal mortality is 649 per 100,000 pregnancies. The country's rate of economic growth cannot support rapid population growth or the strain which HIV & AIDS-related issues (i.e., rising medical costs, decline in worker productivity) place on government resources. Zambia is also one of Sub-Saharan Africa's most highly urbanized countries. Over one-third of the country's 12.9 million people are concentrated in a few urban zones strung along the major transportation corridors, while rural areas are under-populated. Unemployment and underemployment are serious problems. HIV & AIDS is the nation's greatest challenge, with 14.3% prevalence among the adult population.

HIV & AIDS will continue to ravage Zambian economic, political, cultural, and social development for the foreseeable future. Once a middle-income country, Zambia began to slide into poverty in the 1970s when copper prices declined on world markets. The socialist government made up for falling revenue by increasing borrowing. After democratic multi-party elections, the Chiluba government (1991-2001) came to power in November 1991 committed to an economic reform program. The government was successful in some areas, such as privatization of most of the parastatals, maintenance of positive real interest rates, the elimination of exchange controls, and endorsement of free market principles. Corruption grew dramatically under the Chiluba government. Zambia has yet to address effectively issues such as reducing the size of the public sector and improving Zambia's social sector delivery systems.

For 30 years, copper production declined steadily from a 1973 high of 700,000 metric tons to a 2000 low of 226,192 metric tons. The decline was the result of poor management of state-owned mines and lack of investment. With the privatization of the mines in April 2000, the downward trend in production and exports was reversed as a result of investments in plant rehabilitation, expansion, increased exploration, and high copper prices on the international market. Copper production rose to 535,000 metric tons in 2007, but slumping copper prices in late 2008 put significant pressure on the mining companies and government revenue. Zambia experienced positive economic growth for the ninth consecutive year in 2007 with a GDP of U.S. $10.9 billion and a real growth rate of 6% (according to preliminary IMF estimates). The rate of inflation dropped from 30% in 2000 to single-digit inflation of 8.9% by December 2007 due to fiscal and monetary discipline and the growth of the domestic food supply.

Year-on-year inflation grew to double digits in late 2008, due to rising fuel and food prices. In April 2005, the International Monetary Fund (IMF) and the World Bank's International Development Association (IDA) provided Zambia significant debt service relief and debt forgiveness under the Heavily Indebted Poor Countries (HIPC) initiative. Zambia was the 17th country to reach the

For additional analytical, business and investment opportunities information, please contact Global Investment & Business Center, USA at (202) 546-2103. Fax: (202) 546-3275. E-mail: rusric@erols.com

HIPC completion point and has benefited from approximately U.S. $6 billion in debt relief. In July 2005, the G-8 agreed on a proposal to cancel 100% of outstanding debt of eligible HIPC countries to the IMF, African Development Fund, and IDA. Zambia is among the beneficiaries of this additional multilateral debt relief.

Zambia also completed a Poverty Reduction and Growth Facility (PRGF) arrangement with the IMF for the period 2008-2011. The Zambian Government is pursuing an economic diversification program to reduce the economy's reliance on the copper industry. This initiative seeks to exploit other components of Zambia's rich resource base by promoting agriculture, tourism, gemstone mining, and hydropower. The government is also seeking to create an environment that encourages entrepreneurship and private-sector led growth. Zambia's economy has been affected by the global economic crisis and the fall in world copper prices. High inflation, currency volatility, rising unemployment, and restricted access to capital are likely to dampen Zambia's economic performance in 2009.

SOURCES OF LAW

Zambia does not have a single code containing its laws. These are drawn from a variety of sources. The following are sources of law in Zambia:

- Constitution
- Legislation
- Common Law
- Judicial precedent
- Customary Law
- Authoritative texts

Constitution of Zambia

The constitution was adopted in 1991 and was amended in 1996. It abrogates the 1973 constitution, which allowed, as stated above, only one political party. More political parties were allowed to participate as enshrined by the new constitution.

Legislation

Legislation in Zambia is contained in statute books that are available in most libraries. The Ministry of Justice Law library offer legislation. The government website is also helpful in as far as legislation is concerned. Constitutionally, legislation refers to laws that have been passed by parliament and have been assented to by the President. Subsidiary legislation refers to laws passed by other bodies to which parliament have validly delegated such legislative powers. These include government gazettes and municipal bye-laws, *inter alia.*

In Zambia the legislative vests in the National assembly and is assented to by the President. Parliament can confer power on any authority to create binding laws. Currently parliament consists of one House; the National assembly. In terms of the constitution, legislation brought through parliament has to be scrutinized by the National assembly before it goes for assent to the President (article 78(2)). A bill shall not become law unless the President has assented to it and signed it in token of that assent (article 78). By virtue of Article 54(2) (a), the Attorney General is charged with drafting and signing all bills presented before parliament. The Attorney General may delegate functions to the Solicitor General (article 55(5) (b)). Laws made by the National

Assembly and assented to by the president shall be styled "Acts" and the words of enactment shall be "Enacted by the Parliament of Zambia" (article 78(8)).

Precedent

Precedent forms part of the law of Zambia. Decisions of superior courts of record are therefore binding to lower courts. Decisions from South African courts are only persuasive, and courts refer to them in formulating their decisions. Decisions from similar jurisdiction can also be cited for their persuasive value. Magistrates' courts decisions do not become precedent since these are lower courts. They are however bound by decisions of the High Court and the Supreme Court of Appeal. Precedent assists in consistency in legal interpretation and application of the law. It has also been justified for bringing certainty and uniformity to the law. However, precedent has been blamed for causing rigidity of legal systems, preventing development of the law.

Authoritative texts

Written works of eminent authors have persuasive value in the courts of Zambia. These include writings of the old authorities as well as contemporary writers from similar jurisdictions.

INTERNATIONAL LAW

Zambia is signatory to many international instruments. Although the country is quick to ratify, implementation is often slow or never materialises. Zambia belongs to the dualist tradition, thus views international law and domestic law as two separate legal systems. Hence domestication of international law by an Act of Parliament is necessary before international law can be applied. This of course excludes customary international law which is binding on all states. The Attorney General is mandated by article 54(2) (b) to draft and peruse treaties and agreements the government of Zambia is party to.

THE JUSTICE SYSTEM OF ZAMBIA

At the apex of the Zambian justice system is the Supreme Court which is the final court of appeal on all matters. It has a supervisory and review jurisdiction over all courts of Zambia. The Supreme Court has appellate jurisdiction for all legal and constitutional disputes. The High Court, which holds regular sessions in all nine provincial capitals, has authority to hear criminal and civil cases and appeals from lower courts. The Industrial Relations court deals exclusively with industrial and labour matters. There is also a Land Tribunal and Revenues Appeals Tribunal. Magistrate courts have original jurisdiction in some criminal and civil cases; local, or customary, courts handle most civil and petty criminal cases in rural areas.

Local courts employ the principles of customary law, which vary widely throughout the country. Lawyers are barred from participating in proceedings in such courts, and there are few formal rules of procedure. Presiding judges, who usually are prominent local citizens, have substantial power to invoke customary law, render judgments regarding marriages, divorces, inheritances, other civil proceedings, and rule on minor criminal matters. Judgments often are not in accordance with the Penal Code. For example, they tend to discriminate against women in matters of inheritance.

The Constitution and the Judiciary

Judicial power exclusively vests in the judiciary in terms of Article 91(2) of the Constitution. Article 91 (3) of the Constitution further provides that justice shall be administered in accordance with the provisions of an Act of Parliament which shall be independent and subject on. Article 91(1) provides that the judiciary shall consist of the Supreme Court of Judicature comprising:

(a) The Supreme Court, and

(b) The High Court

(c) Such other courts as may be prescribed by an Act of Parliament.

Chapter outline of the constitution

The constitution of Zambia is the supreme law and if any other law inconsistent with the constitution that other law shall, to the extent of its inconsistency, be void (article1(3)). Therefore Zambia has a constitutional supremacy.

The constitution was adopted in 1991 after consultations with the citizens of Zambia. It was amended in 1996. It repealed the constitution of Zambia Act, 1973. It purports to be an autochthonous document. The constitution set out clearly the state structure, bill of rights, the separate arms of government as well as other administrative organs such as the public service commission.

Constitutional clauses analysis:

Fundamental rights and freedoms Article11

Protection of right to life Article 11(a), Article 12

Protection of right to personal liberty Article13

Protection from slavery Article 14

Protection from inhuman or degrading treatment Article 15

Protection from deprivation of property Article16

Right to a fair hearing Article 18(1)

Protection against arbitrary search or entry Article 17(1)

Protection of freedom of conscience and religion Article 19

Protection of freedom of expression Article 20

Protection of freedom of assembly and association Article 21

Rights of child Article 24

Enforcement of protective provisions Article 28

National Sovereignty and the state

Zambia is defined as a unitary sovereign, multiparty and democratic state. (This part sets out that all power resides in the people who shall exercise their sovereignty through the democratic institutions of the state). This part also establishes the Public Seal. The supremacy of the

For additional analytical, business and investment opportunities information,
please contact Global Investment & Business Center, USA
at (202) 546-2103. Fax: (202) 546-3275. E-mail: rusric@erols.com

constitution is set out in this part. The constitution also sets out the anthem and the National Emblem.

Citizenship

Citizenship is the state of belonging. Citizenship guarantees rights of nationality and all other rights from being a national of a particular country. Amongst other inherent rights is the ability to pass on to natural and adopted children since they cannot obtain their independent citizens at that stage. This part talks about acquisition and loss of acquisition. Citizenship in Zambia can be by way of descent, operation of the law or birth, marriage or by registration.

Most notable is the fact that either the mother or the father or both can confer citizenship on children (Article 5). Article 9 provides for the establishment of the Citizenship Board, which deals with any matters pertaining registration as citizens and powers of parliament in making provisions for acquisition of citizenship of Zambia by persons who are not eligible to become citizens of Zambia.

Protection of Fundamental Rights and Freedom of the Individual

Part three is concerned with the promotion and protection of fundamental human rights and freedom of the individual.

Protection of the right to life

Zambia still retains the death penalty, whilst Article 12(1) states that no person shall be deprived of life, it permits the use of death penalty in the execution of the sentence of a curt in respect of criminal offence which that person has been convicted. This is not enough to ensure the full guarantee of the right to life. The right to life, as guaranteed by the second protocol to the International Covenant on Civil and political Rights aiming at the abolition of the death penalty, and the African Charter on Human and Peoples Rights. Imposition of the death penalty itself is not only a violation of the right to life, but also the ultimate form of cruel, inhuman or degrading punishment or treatment.

Protection of the right to personal liberty

The protection guaranteed in the international standards is missing or not fully recognized and entrenched in this constitution. For example International standards of fair trial provide that anyone arrested or detained must be notified at the time of the arrest of the reasons of their arrest or detention and their right, including their right to counsel. This information is essential to allow detained persons to challenge the lawfulness of their arrest or detention and, if they are charged, to start the preparation of their defense. It is essential against arbitrary arrest and detention, to ensure that no detainee is held incommunicado detention, or in a place other than an official detention centre or prison or held in any manner intended to frustrate proper and prompt access to the detainee by legal representatives, doctors or next of kin. Finally, it is not clear why this part on the protection of the right to personal liberty should include exceptions allowing for orders requiring a person to remain within a specific area or prohibiting that person from being within such an area as envisaged by article 16(1)(i).

Protection of Women's rights

The Zambian Constitution is silent on the issue of women's equal participation in electoral politics. Moreover, no provision of the Zambian Constitution ensures substantive equality between women and men, though Article 11 does include a blanket non-discrimination clause that guarantees everyone the enjoyment of fundamental rights and freedoms regardless of "race, place of origin, political opinions, colour, creed, sex or marital status" (emphasis added). Article

For additional analytical, business and investment opportunities information, please contact Global Investment & Business Center, USA at (202) 546-2103. Fax: (202) 546-3275. E-mail: rusric@erols.com

23 of the Constitution further guarantees that, except for certain limitations, "A law shall not make any provision that is discriminatory either of itself or in its effect."

Article 23(4) of the Zambian Constitution allows discrimination in the area of customary Law, family law and other areas such as adoption, marriage, divorce and inheritance. Article 11(1) recognizes and declares every person in Zambia to be entitled to the fundamental rights and freedoms of the individual, whatever "his sex". However, the same article states that the entitlement of these rights and freedoms are subject to limitations contained in this related to Fundamental Rights and Freedoms. Linked to Article 23(4), this means that discrimination against women in areas related to property and inheritance rights is allowed. Article 16 provides for protection against deprivation of property, which may only be carried out under an Act of Parliament providing for payment of adequate compensation.

The right of persons of with disabilities

There is no specific provision in the Zambian constitution that stipulates the rights of persons with disabilities. Article 23 proscribes discrimination in any form against any person and could be used to govern the rights of the disabled. Persons with disabilities should have their rights protected and guaranteed. However, Zambia has a specific legislation on the rights of disabled persons. It is contained in the Handicapped Persons Act of 1968 as amended. The Zambian statute establishes a Council of the disabled, which provides for voluntary registration of disabled persons and of associations that maintain their welfare. A commissioner of the disabled is responsible for the administration of the Act.

The Executive

Article 33(1) states that there shall be a president of the Republic of Zambia who shall be the head of state and of the government and the Commander-in-chief of the defense force. Article 33(2) clearly states that the executive power of the Republic of Zambia shall vest in the president and, subject to the other provisions of this constitution; shall be exercised by him either directly or through officers subordinates to him. In line with the doctrine of separation of powers Article 33(2) emphasizes that exercise of executive power by the president shall be in accordance with the constitution. This serves to curtail any excess on the use of such power. The constitution further provides for the appointment of the Vice-President, ministers and their deputies.

The Attorney general

The attorney General (AG) plays the role of the legal advisor to the government, hence the relationship between the office of the AG and the ministry of justice. The AG is not part of the cabinet per se but works closely with the executive. Article 54(1) of the constitution which is the provision creating this office provides that the AG shall be appointed by the president. It further spells out the qualifications of the persons to be appointed. The AG is the Principal legal advisor to the government and an ex-officio member of cabinet. The AG represents the government in courts or any other legal proceedings to which government is a party.

Government also makes use of the office of the Solicitor General (SL) who shall be appointed by the president as per Article 55(1). The SL may exercise any power or duty imposed on the AG when the AG is unable to act owing to illness or absence and in any case where the AG has authorized the AG.

Apart from the AG's office and the SL's office government also makes use of the office of the Director of Public Prosecutions (DPP), mainly in criminal matters. Article 56(1) set up this office and provides for the appointment of the DPP. The DPP is appointed by the President subject to ratification by the National Assembly, and qualification for appointment to this office is the same as that for a judge of the High Court with experience biased on criminal law, (Article 56(2)).

For additional analytical, business and investment opportunities information, please contact Global Investment & Business Center, USA at (202) 546-2103. Fax: (202) 546-3275. E-mail: rusric@erols.com

Article 56(3) provides that the DPP shall have power in any case which he considers it proper to do so, to;

(a) Institute and undertake criminal proceedings against any person in any court, other than a court martial, in respect of any offence alleged to have been committed by that person;

(b) Take over and continue any such criminal proceedings as have been instituted or undertaken by any other person or authority;

(c) To discontinue, at any stage before judgment is delivered, any such criminal proceedings instituted or undertaken by himself or any other person or authority.

The DPP in person or by delegation to subordinate officers has the power to institute and undertake criminal proceedings against any person before any court. This office can take over and continue or discontinue any criminal proceedings instituted by any person or authority, at any stage before judgment is delivered. Although individuals can prosecute (that is institute criminal proceedings) at the private instance. The drawback of provisions allowing for prosecution at the private instance is that the DPP's office never really gets to totally relinquish its powers to prosecute. Article 56(3) (b) of the constitution acts as a drawback clause that can easily be open to abuse, to frustrate any attempts at private prosecutions. Notwithstanding the issue of a *nolle prosequi*, the DPP's office can still intercept private prosecution proceedings and take over in its capacity as a public prosecutor: thus effectively excluding the person or authority that initiated the proceedings. The DPP's office need not give reasons for such move, save that it is proper to do so.

Further, after rejoining the fray, the DPP's office may then exercise its powers under paragraph (c) to terminate any criminal proceedings, whether started by the office at the public instance or any person at private instance.

It is submitted that this vicious cycle is open to abuse. In effect it means that prosecution can only be undertaken by the DPP and no other individual or authority.

The Legislature

The constitution portrays the government in Zambia as a multi-party and democratic Sovereign State. The constitution further provides that parliament shall consist of the President and the National Assembly. In terms of Article 63(2) membership to the National Assembly is through ordinary elections and being voted into parliament. The elected members shall not exceed one hundred and fifty members (150), not more than eight (8) nominated members and the speaker of the national assembly. Since Zambia is a multi-party democracy members of parliament represent their respective political parties. The constitution is silent on the issue of Women's equal participation in electoral politics.

The Judicature

The constitution provides that the judicature shall be autonomous and shall be administered in accordance with the provisions of an Act of parliament. The judicature shall be independent and subject to only the constitution. The judiciary shall consist of superior court of judicature comprising of;

- Supreme Court
- High Court
- Industrial Court

- Subordinate Courts
- The Local Courts
- Such other courts as may be prescribed by act of parliament.

The judiciary has jurisdiction in all matters civil and criminal, including matters relating to the constitution, and such other jurisdiction as by law conferred on it. The superior courts are courts of record and have power to commit for contempt to themselves and all such powers as were vested in a superior court of record immediately before the commencement of the constitution.

Infringement on judicial independence

The constitution gives very wide powers to the head of state to appoint judicial officers. The president appoints the chief justice and the deputy chief justice. According to article 93(1) the chief justice and deputy chief justice shall subject to ratification by the national assembly, be appointed by the president. Article 93(2) gives the president the power to appoint judges of the Supreme Court. Article 95(1) states that puisne judges shall subject to ratification by national assembly be appointed by the president on the advice of judicial services commission. Furthermore, the president with the advice of the JSC appoints the chairman and deputy chairman of the industrial court. Section 96(1) states that any position appointed under article 93 to act as a judge of the Supreme Court shall continue to act for the period of that person's appointment is marked by the president.

Judges and other judicial officers ought to be hired on full time basis to ensure that they enjoy security of the tenure to enable them to carry out their duties in a competence fashion without fear or favour. Judges on contract are under pressure particularly when their contracts are about to end. This is contrary article 91(2) which promotes judicial independence and frowns upon infringement on this independence by other organs of government. Appointment of judges on acting or contract basis is detrimental to judicial independence since such judges are put in a state of suspense regarding whether they would be confirmed or not. In such a situation the judge may find himself / herself trying to please those with power to confirm him/ her by deciding cases in their favour. The involvement of the head of state in the process of appointing judges intimidates against an independent judiciary. Due to this fact such appointment can not be free of political considerations. The constitution still rests arguably judicial powers on the president. In a situation where the appointing body is politically influenced one cannot hope for independent judiciary. People seeking judicial appointments might be lobby appointed. Thus such people would feel a sense of obligation to the executive and be inclined to favour the executive in the adjudicatory process.

Judicial tenure and remuneration

Article 98(1) provides a position holding the offices of a judge of the Supreme Court or the office of a judge of the high court shall vacate that office on attaining the age of 65 years. Provided that the president –(a) may appoint a judge of the supreme court, who has attained that age to continue in office for such further period, not exceeding seven years as the president may determine. Judges along with other specified officers such as attorney general, investigators-general solicitor- general director of public prosecutions are paid from the general revenues of the republic. Such salaries and or allowances may be presented by or under an act of parliament. Article 119(3) provides that the salary payable to the holder of any holder of office shall not be uttered to his disadvantage after his appointment. Note article 96.

Removal of judges from office

For additional analytical, business and investment opportunities information, please contact Global Investment & Business Center, USA at (202) 546-2103. Fax: (202) 546-3275. E-mail: rusric@erols.com

According to Article 98(2) a judge of the Supreme Court, high court chairman of deputy chairman of the industrial relations court may be removed from office only for inability to perform the functions of his office whether arising from infirmity of body or mind, incompetence or misbehavior and shall not be so removed except in accordance with the provisions of this article. Article 98(3) provides for the establishment of a tribunal which will investigate the case of a judge before removal in which the tribunal consists of a chairman and not less than the other members who hold or have held high judicial office. This tribunal can be biased in the sense that the judge whose perpetual removal has been influenced by the political motives can collude to remove him from offices in order to gain favour from the executive. The tribunal after a proper inquiry represents the matter to the president and advices the president whether the judge ought to be removed from office for inability or incompetence or for misbehavior for which the president has an obligation to remove such judge from office. Article 98 gives so much power on the president to remove and suspend judge and this compromises the independence of judiciary as narrated by article 91(2).

The Supreme Court

Article 92 establishes the supreme court of Zambia, which shall consist of: the chief justice, the deputy chief justice, seven Supreme Court judges or such greater number as may be prescribed by an act of parliament. The Supreme Court is a superior court of record.

The High Court

Article 97 establishes the high court of Zambia which shall have, except as to the proceedings in which the industrial relations court has exclusive jurisdiction under the industrial relations (act no.27 of 1993), unlimited or original jurisdiction to hear and determine any civil or criminal proceedings under any law and such jurisdiction and powers as may be conferred on it by this constitution or any other law. The high court shall be divided into such divisions as may be determined by an act of parliament 94(2). The chief justice shall be such an ex-offices judge of the high court (3). The other judges of the high court shall be such number of puisne judges as maybe prescribed by parliament.

Article 94(6) provides that the high court shall be a superior court of record. The high court has jurisdiction to supervise any civil or criminal proceedings before any subordinate court or any court martial and may such order issues such as writs and give such direction as it may consider appropriate for the purposes of ensuring that question as is duly administered by such court.

Specialist courts in Zambia

Apart from the Supreme Court and the High Court which are ordinary courts, Zambia also has specialist courts set up to deal with particular matters. These are creatures of statute, with limited jurisdiction as set out in the legislation establishing them. The Industrial Court and Local courts are examples of specialist courts in Zambia.

The Local Courts

The local courts play an important part in the settlement of disputes of the majority of the majority of the population the customary law itself is in a state of flux. The main thrust of the law governing the operation of the Local Courts, contained in Chapter 29 o the Laws of Zambia, is the administration of customary law. In reality the Local Courts are the focal point of varied societal claims. Customary law is the ambiguous expression in which are hidden many legal claims. It can be safely asserted that Local Courts are the clearing grounds for simple torts, contracts, and petty crimes. But the main workload of the courts is the law relating to non-statutory marriages. Divorce, reconciliation, custody of children, payment of mabolo or lobola, persons who die without

For additional analytical, business and investment opportunities information,
please contact Global Investment & Business Center, USA
at (202) 546-2103. Fax: (202) 546-3275. E-mail: rusric@erols.com

a will-these are areas which affect the legal rights of the majority of the population. The effective handling of these disputes and their fair and just resolution assure stability in the community.

There is no uniform formal educational qualification for adjudicators of local courts. They bring important innovation in the administration of community justice derived in part from their practical understanding of the workings of a post-traditional society. These justices are often fluent in more than four local languages.

Small Claims Courts

There is on the Zambian statute books the Small Claims Court Act. The objective of the Act is to provide for the establishment, of Small Claims Courts to be situated in areas to be designated by the Chief Justice. The Small Claims Courts adopt arbitration as a mode of resolving disputes. The choice of this mode of dispute resolution is questionable because arbitration is typically adjudicative and is quite formal. Mediation would probably have been a more apt mode of resolving disputes in the Small Claims Courts. The tragedy of the Small Claims Court legislation is that although the legislation has been on the statute books for over a decade, the Small Claims Courts have not yet been operationalized. However the idea of Small Claim Courts is a very good one. It depends on involvement of legal practitioners of 5 year standing with more personnel allocated to them. The Small Claims Court could utilize existing infrastructure such as school buildings, community halls and several others. If the existing mechanisms of resolving disputes in both rural and urban areas are adopted but also adapted to suit the needs of the poor the small claims court could work most effectively. Rules that normally apply to formalized courts should be more flexible to enable the poor.

The Legal Aid Board

The Legal Aid Act 70 was enacted on 20th November 1967. The objective of the Act is to provide for legal aid in civil and criminal matters and causes to persons whose means are inadequate to enable them to engage practitioners to represent them. The Directorate of Legal Aid Board operated as a department within the Ministry of Legal Affairs and consequently enjoyed limited autonomy. However, by the Legal Aid (Amendment) Act the Legal Aid department was transformed into a Legal Aid Board. The Legal Aid Board comprised the following part-time members appointed by the Minister: 73

(a) A person qualified to be a Judge of the High Court who shall be the Chairperson;

(b) A representative of the Law Association of Zambia;

(c) The Permanent Secretary in the Ministry responsible for legal affairs;

(d) A representative of the Ministry responsible for Home Affairs;

(e) The Director who shall be an ex officio member;

(f) A representative of a non-governmental organization active in the promotion of human rights; and

g) One other person

Furthermore, the Legal Aid (Amendment) Act defined the functions of the Board as being to:

> (a) Manage and administer the Legal Aid Fund; and
>
> (b) To carry out any other activities relating to the provision for legal aid which are necessary or conducive to the performance of its functions under the Act. There was

For additional analytical, business and investment opportunities information, please contact Global Investment & Business Center, USA at (202) 546-2103. Fax: (202) 546-3275. E-mail: rusric@erols.com

however a proviso placed on this function, namely, that the Board would not be responsible for the supervision and administration of the Directorate. It is difficult to fathom the intention of the legislature in this respect because it is usual for boards of corporate bodies to superintend secretariats or directorates. A further amendment was made to Legal Aid legislation in 2005. By the Legal Aid (Amendment) Act, the Legal Aid Board was re-constituted as a body corporate, with perpetual succession and legal capacity to sue and to be sued. The composition of the Board was enlarged to include representatives from the Ministries responsible for finance and national planning; community development and social welfare; labour and sport and child development.

Furthermore, the functions of the board were reformulated and enlarged. The functions of the Board are to:

(a) Administer and manage the Legal Aid Fund;

(b) Facilitate the representation of persons granted legal aid under the Act;

(c) Assign practitioners to persons granted legal aid under the Act;

(d) Advise the Minister on policies relating to the provision of legal aid and implement

Government policies relating to the same; and

(e) Undertake such other activities relating to the provision of legal aid and which are conducive or incidental to the performance of its functions under the Act.

Although the Legal Aid Board has been established as a body corporate, it has not been delinked from the Ministry of Justice. The Ministry still recruits, disciplines and determines the conditions of service for legal aid personnel. The Ministry is also still responsible for mobilizing and disbursing resources to the Board. The de-linkage is important in order to establish an independent body that can effectively plan for expansion, hiring and retention of staff as well as mobilize resources from either Government or cooperating partners. The formality surrounding the Legal Aid Board still makes it difficult for the ordinary person to easily approach the Board.

The Legal Aid Board has offices in Lusaka, Kitwe, Ndola, Kabwe and Livingstone. It has on its establishment a total of twenty-one lawyers, out of an establishment of thirty four. 79 the lawyers for the Board are faced with crashing case loads. Apart from facing a critical shortage of staff, the Board has inadequate transport and operational tend to suffer. In view of the preceding constraints, the Board tends to limit the grant of legal aid to accused persons facing serious criminal cases mostly in the High Court. The Board therefore handles a very limited number of civil cases. The woes of the Board are also worsened by the fact that the Board is unable to attract and retain lawyers due to the poor conditions of service. The failure to decentralize the Board and its myriad of administrative and logistical problems has resulted in denying many indigent persons especially in rural areas legal aid.

Law reports

Zambia has a law report series known as the Zambia Law Reports (ZLR). These Law reports are available online and they are obtainable at the high court. The statutes of Zambia are available online and are listed by name. Supreme Court, High Court, Industrial Relations Court, Land Tribunal, Revenue Tribunal rulings are also found online. The 'Zambian Law Journal' is found at the school of Law in the University of Zambia. The 'Laws of Zambia' is a 1996 compilation of 26 Volumes containing all the laws and the entire respective various Republican Constitutions since independence. Volume 1 Contains the Index of the Laws of Zambia. The Laws are in read only PDF format. Zambia law Reports can also be obtained at the University of

Pretoria. There is also 'Zambia Law Reports Consolidated Index' containing the cumulative indexes of cases reported, cases referred to, legislation referred to, and subject matter from 1963 to 1978 Published in 1984, Council of Law Reporting, and High Court for Zambia (Lusaka, Zambia).

The Zambia Legal Information Institute (ZamLII) was established by the Law School of the University of Zambia in 1996, in partnership with Zamnet. It has received important start-up assistance from the Legal Information Institute of Cornell Law School. The Institute's aim is to improve access to judgments, statutes and other legal materials of the Republic of Zambia both within Zambia and elsewhere and to connect lawyers, judges, academics, students and others within Zambia with the growing collection of legal information available around the globe via the Internet.

ZamLII provides on-line research of Zambian and foreign legal information and general information about Zambia. Our collection of legal information in Zambia includes The Constitution of the Greater Republic of Zambia, rules and selected decisions of the courts, selected acts,legal commentary, a legal directory, and finally, information about the University of Zambia School of Law. ZamLII also provides links toforeign legal information in and outside of Africa. You can also find general information about Zambia through our link with Zamnet.

Government Gazettes

The government of Zambia publishes a gazette that contains all relevant announcements and enactment or amendments of laws and regulations. It incorporates various government decisions, and once they feature in the Gazette, government decisions are deemed and laws and regulations are deemed to have been published and validly promulgated.

Gazettes are used by both the government and ordinary citizens to convey information to the public. The following are some of the normal uses of gazettes:

- Notices to creditors and debtors in administration of estates.
- Publication of amendments to existing laws, regulations and rules.
- Publications of newly enacted laws, regulations and rules.
- Invitation for tenders from government departments.
- Insurance of trading licenses for companies.
- Publication of title deeds and deed of transfer in respect of property.

POLITICAL PARTIES

Significant political developments have occurred in Zambia since the 2001 tripartite elections. After having had two previous elections in 1991 and 1996, the 2001 elections produced a multiparty Parliament for the first time since Zambia's independence in 1964. These elections seem to signal that the country has moved from a dominant one party political system to a competitive multi-party system. Despite these positive political developments, political parties and the party system in Zambia still remain relatively undeveloped. This trend in Zambian political culture may be partly due to the short time period in which political parties have had to organize, a lack of organizational funds, and a host of legal and political obstacles that have exacerbated political party fragmentation. Political parties play a vital and indispensable role in modern political systems and are the raison d'être of a multiparty system.

For additional analytical, business and investment opportunities information, please contact Global Investment & Business Center, USA at (202) 546-2103. Fax: (202) 546-3275. E-mail: rusric@erols.com

To its credit Zambia has been deemed an “oasis of peace” in Africa since its independence. Although the country experienced one-party rule for 27 years, there was not the degree of repression and social anarchy that characterized many other African countries. Because of this unique attribute, Zambia's political transition in 1991 was peaceful; Zambia successfully held presidential and parliamentary elections in 1996 and 2001. Despite disputes over the election results in 1996 and 2001, the country has been able to utilize constitutional provisions to resolve political differences.

The MMD government was elected in 1991 and within six months of assuming office; fragmentation began to surface within the ruling party. Several MPs resigned in the fracas. In 1993, several former cabinet ministers and notable MPs left MMD to form the National Party. Although several MPs successfully won their seats on the NP ticket, the party atrophied and failed to offer a serious challenge to the MMD government. Due to continued dissatisfaction with MMD, two other parties, the Zambia Democratic Congress (ZDC) and the Agenda for Zambia (AZ) were formed in 1995 and 1996 respectively.

Faced by a perceived threat from the political opposition, by 1996 the MMD government orchestrated a constitutional amendment to preclude the strongest challenger, UNIP's Kenneth Kaunda, from competing in the 1996 elections. Traditional tribal chiefs were also barred from standing as candidates. In a backlash attempt by supporters of UNIP, the 1996 elections were widely boycotted by civil society representatives, and supporters of UNIP, resulting in a consolidation of MMD's dominance in Parliament. That year, the MMD increased its parliamentary seats from 125 to 131, while the political opposition remained largely fragmented. Both parties were led by individuals who held senior positions in the first MMD National Executive Committee and were ministers in Chiluba's first cabinet.

With the combined opposition parties winning only nine seats and the independent candidates having won ten seats, this parliamentary result followed serious irregularities in the electoral process. The alleged irregularities included poor management of the voter registration process, resulting in a massive reduction in voters eligible to participate in the elections. The overwhelming evidence of widespread vote rigging and other forms of electoral fraud in the 1996 elections led to the elections result being challenged in the Courts.

Amid popular contestation, Chiluba announced in May 2001 that he would not seek a third presidential term on the MMD ticket. In late August 2001, Levy Mwanawasa emerged as the party's choice for its presidential candidate. The election date was announced at the end of November, in the middle of the rainy season and well after the MMD had commenced its election campaign. At the dissolution of Parliament, prior to the election, MMD held 89 seats as compared to 131 when elected in 1991. The opposition UPND, NP and UNIP held twenty seats in sum. Forty seats in Parliament were vacant. After a split within the MMD, forty seats that were occupied by that party were left vacant, as several MP's who left the government either joined the opposition or formed other parties.

The 2001 tripartite elections were also widely regarded as flawed by both domestic and international observers. There were serious doubts as to whether the results reflected the will of the people. The final results released by the Electoral Commission of Zambia indicated that about 70% of the registered electorate cast their votes for president. Of these votes the MMD party received 28.69%, while the UPND receiving 26.76%, a difference of 30,000 votes. Expressed as a percentage of registered voters, the MMD received less than 20% of the vote, which makes it the only party to win the government with such a narrow margin of victory since independence, in spite of allegations against the party over vote rigging and other alleged abuses of electoral fraud.

The 2001 elections seem to highlight the risks associated with transitioning from a dominant single party system to a non-authoritarian competitive party system. Of the seven political parties in Parliament, no party had an absolute majority. The MMD won less than 50 % of the seats (46%), while the UPND had just about a third (33%). Combined, MMD and UPND shared about 80% of seats in Parliament. Together, UNIP and FDD accounted for 17% of the seats while the remaining three opposition parties shared 5% of the seats. At the local government level, opposition parties controlled key city and municipal councils in about six provinces.

Movement for Multiparty Democracy (MMD)

The MMD originally formed during a planned referendum in July 1991 as a pressure group to campaign for the restoration of a multiparty system to contest the ruling party UNIP. In January 1991, MMD transformed itself into a political party with diverse representation, including trade unions, commercial farmers, the clergy,
students, academics, businesspersons and former UNIP politicians. Under the leadership of the former Zambia Congress of Trade Unions (ZCTU) chairman-general, Frederick Chiluba, the party united around a cohesive platform to remove UNIP from power. As MMD consolidated power in 1991 and 1996 elections, with the
party leadership garnering the majority vote, there were fears that the country was regressing back to a one-party state. As Although legislation severed the formal links between the party and government, MMD's priority position in government allowed it to use the incumbency to access state resources, especially during election campaigns. As a result of discord within the party over governance issues, between 1993 and 1996 the party experienced several defections and resignations leading to the formation of rival political parties.

In 2001, the MMD had an organizational presence in every province within the country. Consequently the party could boast of national structures and coverage and it held regular elections for its national leaders. However, as the 2001 elections drew nearer, the party was faced with the prospect of defeat, triggered by the desire of President Chiluba to run for a third term in office. As public pressure against the third term mounted and senior party leaders began denouncing the action, the party began to lose its popularity. Eventually, the president declared he would not seek a third term and the MMD went on to win its third mandate. However, MMD's electoral performance was very poor -having gained less than 30% of the national vote and winning less than three seats in four provinces. This was perhaps the lowest mandate won by any ruling party in Zambia since independence and posed serious challenges to the new leadership.

The MMD manifesto is based on the promotion of a free market economy and good governance. Since 1991 the party has implemented a very ambitious economic reform program. It has liberalized the economy and removed most of the controls that characterized the Zambian economy in the Second Republic. These policies have produced a serious social impact, which has contributed to deterioration in living standards and a high incidence of poverty. The party faces a number of challenges, as has been reflected in the party's declining representation in Parliament, considering that since the 2001 elections the MMD no longer commands an absolute majority.

The United Party for National Development

United Party for National Development (UPND) was formed the UPND in 1998. The party was established on a social democratic platform of providing free health and educational services to the Zambian people. It also articulated a commitment to providing agricultural subsidies to rural farmers to increase agricultural production. The UPND's performance in local government and parliamentary elections between 1998 and 2000 made it the main opposition party to the MMD.

For additional analytical, business and investment opportunities information, please contact Global Investment & Business Center, USA at (202) 546-2103. Fax: (202) 546-3275. E-mail: rusric@erols.com

The party won more than 60 local council seats in the 1998 local government elections and six parliamentary by-elections in Southern, Western and Central provinces. It also controlled one council in Northwestern province. Although the party claimed an organizational presence in almost all of Zambia's nine provinces, it was better organized in Central, Northwestern, Southern and Western provinces.

UPND finished second to the MMD presidential candidate in the 2001 elections. The party won the majority of local government seats in Western, Central, Northwestern, Southern and Lusaka provinces. With these 49 seats UPND was the second largest party in Parliament. Historically, UPND has strong ties to other opposition parties, with which it contested the results of the 2001 election in the Supreme Court. The party has encountered serious leadership and organizational challenges, including its level of dependency on the patronage of its party president. Although the party's national leadership is representative of all the ethnic groups, the electorate perceives it as a regional or ethnic party. Additionally, the party has had difficulty asserting itself as the main opposition party in the country. Without recognition as the official opposition, on account of falling short of the threshold of 53 seats, the party has been unable to systematically challenge government policy in Parliament and to initiate legislation. Notwithstanding these shortcomings, UPND has been internally cohesive and self-confident, as evidenced by very few defections among the senior leadership. Additionally, it is the only political party that successfully expelled its MP for accepting a ministerial appointment in the MMD government.

United National Independence Party (UNIP)

UNIP is the oldest African political party in Zambia. It was established in 1959. It was briefly involved governmentwiththeANCbetween1962-1964and it was the governing party in Zambia from 1964-1991.The leader of the party until 1992 was former President Kenneth Kaunda, who was the first president of the independent country of Zambia. He voluntarily stepped down in favour of Kebby Musokotwane, but returned to the party in 1995 to increase the party's chances of defeating the MMD in 1996. Kaunda was excluded from running on the party's ticket in 1996 due to a controversial constitutional amendment passed by the ruling MMD, which barred persons whose parents were not born in Zambia from contesting the presidency.

Between 1992 and 1998 UNIP suffered harassment under the government's rule, including arrests and detentions over allegations that the party conspired to overthrow the Government. The most controversial of these alleged conspiracy acts were the "Zero Option" and "Black Mamba" "plots" that resulted in a number of UNIP leaders being detained, including the party's vice president Chief Inyambo Yeta. Additionally, UNIP president Kenneth Kaunda was detained in connection with an alleged coup attempt to overthrow the MMD government in December 1997.

Although the party can legitimately claim to have countrywide organizational structures, the party has experienced serious organizational problems since leaving office in 1991. During the one-party era prior to 1991, UNIP benefited from the use of public funds because there was no distinction between the ruling party's purse and the government as evidenced by the fact that party officials were paid from the public treasury, the party used government vehicles and the State financed party offices. Since leaving office, UNIP has had to rely upon its own resources and properties, which has translated into a diminution of the party's organizational capacity. The Central Committee that was formerly full-time is now part-time and a number of staff have been laid off or have not been paid for a significant period of time. Due to financial problems the party has not been able to hold important party meetings.

In addition to organizational problems, the party has also experienced serious leadership problems since 1992. Internal bickering and factionalism has led to frequent leadership turnover, suspensions and sometimes expulsions. The influence of the party's founder and former president Kenneth Kaunda may have had a negative impact on party organization and

For additional analytical, business and investment opportunities information, please contact Global Investment & Business Center, USA at (202) 546-2103. Fax: (202) 546-3275. E-mail: rusric@erols.com

membership morale, as the party seems to be divided between two camps between supporters of the former president, and those who want fresh leadership without formal ties to Kaunda.

A leadership crisis in 2000 led to the ouster of party president Francis Nkhoma and his replacement by Kaunda's son and UNIP's secretary general, Tilyenji Kaunda, who later contested the 2001 presidential elections. There are concerns within the party over Tilyenji Kaunda's leadership ability, as he is perceived to be directing the affairs of the party from outside the country and lacking necessary organizational experience. UNIP espouses a distinct social-democratic ideology that calls for more state- involvement in the economy and the provision of state resources for social services. However, the perceived failure of its past policies, coupled with its serious leadership problems have contributed to the party's failure to offer a formidable opposition to the ruling MMD.

Forum for Democracy and Development (FDD)

This party was formed in July 2001 by senior party and government officials who were expelled from the MMD for opposing a third term of the country's president. The original founders included the former Vice President of Zambia, Christon Tembo, cabinet ministers, deputy ministers and MPs. In September 2001 Tembo was elected as the party's first president, with a similar manifesto as the MMD. In the 2001 elections the FDD won 12 MP seats in Lusaka and Eastern provinces. It also gained control of the Lusaka City Council. Additionally, its candidate in presidential elections finished third, managing to win 13% of the national vote. Additionally, the party fielded the largest number of councilors and MPs and won the mayoral ticket. Unsatisfied with the results, however, the FDD have joined in collaboration with other parties to contest the 2001 elections results in the Supreme Court. The party has an organizational presence in all nine provinces of the country. Although relatively well organized, lately a significant number of FDD party members have defected to the MMD government. Recently three of its MPs were appointed to governmental ministerial positions without party consultation. While the party supports a Government of National Unity (GNU), as it has sought to negotiate its involvement in the MMD government with the President to date it has been unable to reach a workable partnership.

Heritage Party (HP)

Godfrey Miyanda, former Zambian Vice President from 1994 to 1997 founded the HP. Like other opposition parties, the HP was formed in protest of the government's bid for a third presidential term. HP is committed to promoting integrity in public office, transparency and greater public accountability. The party's leader is a central force in the party's operation. Although the party contested the 2001 elections and finished fifth with about 8% of the national vote, it obtained only four MPs in the most recent elections. Since those elections two of these MPs have defected to the ruling party, while the remaining two HP MPs have both been appointed to Deputy Ministerial positions in the MMD government party approval. The party views this action as "poaching" and because there is no expulsion clause in the HP constitution, it has not challenged with the "erring" MPs. Currently HP is one of the parties challenging the election of the country's president in the Supreme Court

Zambia Republican Party (ZRP)

Many former MMD members claim that their only quarrel with the MMD was Chiluba's desire to run for a third term. This explains why a number of FDD members and officials have gravitated back to the MMD after Levy Mwanasa was elected President. The ZRP was formed in early 2001 through an alliance of four parties including the Republican Party. The ZRP presidential candidate in the 2001 elections did not perform well finishing sixth with less than five percent (4.8%) of the national vote. Although the party did win one Parliamentary seat in Lusaka Province, the MP has since been appointed by the government as Cabinet Minister. The party's policy direction does not differ fundamentally from the MMD. ZRP supports a free-market economy based on private entrepreneurship, good incentives to the private sector and a Government that is responsive and responsible to the citizens.

Patriotic Front (PF)

In September 2001 Michael Sata, a former Cabinet Minister and the MMD National Secretary, formed the PF. It was the last of the parties to be formed as a result of MMD succession problems. The party was organized quickly to contest the 2001 elections and consequently it did not perform well. The PF secured under 4% (3.3%) of the national vote and won only one MP seat. The party's main policy platform is the reduction in taxes and prudence in the management of public resources. The party's leader is a central force in the party's operation. However, the main problem the party faces is a public perception that its leader supported Chiluba's third term bid and was at the forefront of prosecuting those opposed to it through suspensions and expulsions. The are other political parties which have contested parliamentary seats and they include National Citizens Coalition (NCC), Social Democratic Party (SDP), Zambia Alliance for Progress (ZAP), National Leadership for Development (NLD) and the NCC (National Citizens Coalition).

Civil society

Zambia has a variety of non-governmental organizations working on issues of human rights and related fields. Despite the euphoria over the defeat of President-since-independence, Kenneth Kaunda's, United National Independence Party (UNIP) in Zambia's first ever multi-party elections, it has become clear that elections did not herald an end to the prominence of human rights issues in the political life of the country. The then ruling Movement for Multiparty Democracy (MMD has been beset by political scandal, defection, corruption and allegations of involvement in the traffic of illegal drugs. The new government has also demonstrated a certain degree of intolerance by declaring a state of emergency and detaining several opponents, following claims of a coup plot hatched by members of UNIP. At the same time, law enforcement agencies for the most part remain fixated on their erstwhile methods of operation, which were, to say the least, not human rights-sensitive. The press is often targeted for harassment.

Human rights organizations (HROs) in Zambia are, in the main, faced with extending the experience they gained in the monitoring of elections and civic education to other areas of human rights work. While the elections were an issue around which it was fairly easy to galvanize interest and attention, there is a need to aggressively promote knowledge of human rights among the general populace--broadly described as "apathetic". Some prominent cases from the past regime, such as the detention-without-trial of Katiza Cebekhulu (the key witness in the trial of Winnie Mandela, who was spirited away from South Africa in order not to give testimony expected to be potentially damaging), have been passed over to the new government, but the government has done little to address the concerns expressed by human rights groups about them. Torture is reported to take place on a regular basis. In addition, there have been reports of a number of incidents where police have detained the relatives of their intended victims, in order to flush them out of hiding--the case of opposition UNIP member, William Banda, being the most prominent. The new HROs that have come into existence are largely believed to be "elitist", and need to cooperate more effectively with the press and others involved in the human rights struggle.

Centre for Human Rights and Democracy (CHRD)

The Centre for Human Rights and Democracy (CHRD) has yet to make a significant impact on the human rights scene in Zambia, although it runs an office for *pro bono* counseling on legal and human rights matters. The Centre faced initial problems with registration, as the authorities suspected their motives. Although the registration matters were overcome, it continues to encounter problems with government obstruction of receipt of external funding granted to the organization. The Centre is nevertheless looking around for alternatives, and intends to organize a paralegal training course to be conducted in June 1994.

Christian Council of Zambia (CCZ)

The Christian Council of Zambia (CCZ) was part of the group that was active in the Foundation for Democratic Process (FODEP), but it has, in general, adopted a low profile with respect to advocacy on human rights issues in Zambia. Instead it deals with questions such as refugees and relief, some gender questions, ethics, development and unemployment. This activity is all conducted under the auspices of the Social Justice Committee of the CCZ.

Foundation for Democratic Process (FODEP)

Initially begun as a monitoring group prior to the 1991 general elections, FODEP is an umbrella organization comprised of several church groups, women's organizations, the Law Association and the Press Association. Today, FODEP has broadened its mandate to cover civic education for the purposes of enhancing the general awareness of the population. Drawing on its experience in the elections, FODEP intends to focus on civil and political rights at the local level, and to involve parliamentary and other elected representatives in the dissemination of knowledge and information about these rights.

Human Rights Committee of the Law Association of Zambia (LAZ)

The Law Association of Zambia (LAZ), a statutory body recognized by law in 1973, established a Human Rights Committee to function under its auspices. The Committee was heavily involved in civic education around the elections and produced a number of programs for the broadcast media on elections and civic rights. The Committee transcribed the notes from these seminars and circulated them as a further mechanism of sensitization. In conjunction with the Catholic Secretariat, it has also designed a program for the conduct of simultaneous seminars on human rights in all the provincial centres of the country, as a starting-point for the sensitization of the broad populace on general human rights issues. A series of seminars for the police force have also been designed, the first to commence in Lusaka. As a major human rights actor, the Committee has received several reports on police violence and prison conditions, and attempts to ensure that these issues are expeditiously addressed.

Inter-African Network for Human Rights (AFRONET)

AFRONET is billed as an organization designed to promote coordination and networking among African HROs. As yet, it has only begun to meet with various organizations within Zambia and to publicize its operations outside the country. Although it has observer status at the African Commission on Human and Peoples' Rights, it still has a long way to go, both in the conceptualization of its precise goals and programs, and in raising the consciousness of HROs throughout the continent on the need for coordination and networking. Its programs focus on communication, the promotion of good governance and sustainable development, human rights, and the interaction of law and society.

Legal Resources Foundation (LRF)

The Legal Resources Foundation (LRF) was established as a company limited by guarantee, in order to obviate the possibility of the authorities' exercising their powers to ban a society under the provisions of the Societies Act. The idea of the LRF was conceived in 1991 prior to the meeting of the Commonwealth Heads of Government (CHOGUM) in Harare. LRF has several objectives, including the promotion of an interest in human rights; the development of law (through the publication of cases, law reports and a monthly newsletter); and reform of the law.

For additional analytical, business and investment opportunities information, please contact Global Investment & Business Center, USA at (202) 546-2103. Fax: (202) 546-3275. E-mail: rusric@erols.com

So far, however, LRF has not commenced operations and has yet to formulate specific programs to actualize its objectives.

National Women's Lobby Group

Established on July 20, 1991, the National Women's Lobby Group (WLG) is a pressure group established to pursue the rights of women, children and minorities, especially in relation to the policy-making bodies in the country. It is headed by a Secretary General, who is presently assisted only by a secretary. WLG is composed of a number of women's NGOs and its approach is broad in ambit. It is involved in networking and is a resource base for information and policies about women. It also lobbies the President and informs the electorate about issues of women's rights. WLG has developed a three-year plan by which it will work towards a core budget to cover training in human rights and, especially, in lobbying and outreach.

Office of Social Education of the Zambian Episcopal Conference (ZEC)

Often working in collaboration with the other church groups in Zambia (the Christian Council and the Evangelical Fellowship); the Zambian Episcopal Conference (ZEC) has been more public and active in the arena of human rights, especially in the issuance of public statements or pastoral letters, than have its counterparts. ZEC statements have covered issues such as structural adjustment and its impact on human rights, a review of the Constitution, and problems with the transition to the third (present) republic. The ZEC has embarked on an active program of encouraging the formation of Justice and Peace Committees at the local level, building on the model of the Zimbabwean experience. To this end, it has conducted a total of five seminars over the past two years in order to sensitize its members on the spirituality of justice and peace, and the need for respect for human rights. The attendees at these seminars have then proceeded out into the countryside, and sought to disseminate the information they have culled to the broader populace. The results have varied, but are a significant beginning for a process that will invariably take some time to gel. Individual Justice and Peace Committees also identify areas of specific concern to their local communities. Among the issues that have been addressed are: the treatment of prisoners on remand, the payment and condition of domestic workers at large and within church institutions, the issue of allocation of places in schools, and the effect of the structural adjustment program. A national Justice and Peace Committee/Commission is yet to be established.

Women's Rights Committee of the Law Association of Zambia (WRC)

Established in 1988 as part of the LAZ, the Women's Rights Committee (WRC) gained impetus after the passing of the Intestate Succession Act. Following this, WRC established a National Legal Aid Clinic for Women in November 1990, which has been run in the main by volunteer lawyers. A full-time Coordinator for the Clinic was appointed in 1991, and continues to be assisted by volunteers. The clinic still has problems of recognition and has not been formally registered, but utilizes the framework of the Citizen's Advice Bureau of the LAZ in order to appear in court. The WRC functions like a private law firm and the majority of its cases are on inheritance, divorce, and custody and maintenance matters. The clientele are mainly the unemployed who are charged only a nominal fee.

Zambia Civic Education Association (ZCEA)

The Zambia Civic Education Association (ZCEA) initially commenced as a program of UNIP--the former ruling political party--as a mechanism in its "revival campaign" to meet the challenges following the general election, but the party was not extremely responsive to its overtures. Consequently, the group has attempted to distance itself from any direct political affiliation and claims to be wholly independent. The ZCEA is under the organizational control of a Chair, who is the only full-time worker, while all its programs are implemented by volunteers. One of its first

For additional analytical, business and investment opportunities information, please contact Global Investment & Business Center, USA at (202) 546-2103. Fax: (202) 546-3275. E-mail: rusric@erols.com

actions was to inaugurate what it calls "clinics", which are held every Saturday and Sunday, where ZCEA holds public information sessions, discussing the role of public officers, human rights education and issues such as health, hygiene and the environment, as the most "basic needs" of the community. The group has also targeted the police and attempted to implement a community-policing scheme in at least one area of peri-urban Lusaka. This has been approached as a pilot project, and an attempt has been made to deal with common problems in the relationship between police and the community. The scheme has also addressed conditions at the stations, related to the cells, women prisoners, and so on. The ZCEA has also designed a "right to shelter" project in Mapoloto Township.

National Assembly

The National Assembly is comprised of 150 directly elected members, up to eight presidentially-appointed members, and a speaker. Zambia is divided into nine provinces, each administered by an appointed deputy minister who essentially performs the duties of a governor. The Supreme Court is the highest court and the court of appeal; below it are the high court, magistrate's court, and local courts.

Voting in Parliament

Voting is done through simple majority. There are no reserved seats or quotas for women, ethnic minorities or other categories. Vacancies arising between general elections are filled through by-elections. Voting is not compulsory.

Voting is open to all people above 18 years and eligibility to stand for parliamentary is 21 years, of Zambian citizenship (including naturalized citizens), and resident in the country at the time of election. Also eligible are people who are able to speak and read in the official language of Zambia, as well as citizens overseas, who are not civil servants.

Disqualified are people who pay allegiance to a foreign State, insanity, sentence of death or imprisonment, conviction of a corrupt or illegal practice within five years preceding the elections, persons found guilty of such practice upon the trial of an election petition, lawful custody, persons who are not in possession of a national registration card, insanity, undischarged bankrupts, sentence of death or imprisonment, restriction in movement or detention pursuant to certain laws, etc.

For additional analytical, business and investment opportunities information,
please contact Global Investment & Business Center, USA
at (202) 546-2103. Fax: (202) 546-3275. E-mail: rusric@erols.com

STRATEGIC INFORMATION FOR CONDUCTING BUSINESS

TRADE REGULATIONS

IMPORTS

Zambia has two import categories:

- Goods paid for with funds remitted from the Bank of Zambia
- Goods paid for with funds held outside the country.

An import licence is required for both the categories of goods and should be obtained in advance by the Zambian importer.

EXPORT PROCEDURES AND DOCUMENTATION IN ZAMBIA

Zambia exports a wide range of products and the main, or traditional exports, are refined minerals Copper, lead, zinc and cobalt. Other exports, commonly referred to as Non Traditional copper semi manufactures, gemstones, fresh fruits and vegetables and timber and wood and wood products.
Zambia has one of the simplest and hurdle free export procedures in Southern Africa and the COMESA subregion. The documentation is basically the same with minor differences depending on whether the product is traditional, non traditional or personal effects.

EXPORT PERMITS

No export permits are required as these have been replaced by Export Declaration Forms. Mineral products (copper, zinc, lead and cobalt) are exported by use of Export Declaration Form Number one (Form EXD No. 1); Non traditional exports by use of Form EXD No. 2, while gifts, trade fair exhibits and personal effects for non residents and other persons leaving Zambia for good or for long periods are exported on Form EXD No.3.

Except for very few selected products, no other bank or customs documentation is required other than the usual accompanying documents, where necessary, like commercial invoices, road/rail consignment note or airway bill, which transporters/freight forwarders take care of anyway.

Grain exports are occasionally subject to seasonal regulation such as during drought years by the Ministry of Agriculture Food and Fisheries to forestall shortages on the domestic market. Gemstones are subject to pre export inspection and valuation by the Ministry of Mines and Minerals Development which issues a special permit.

VAT AND EXPORT TAXES

Export products do not attract Government VAT and there is no export tax on exports from Zambia, except on minerals and gemstones which are taxed at 5%.

EXPORT PROCEDURES (NON TRADITIONAL EXPORTS)

1. An exporter obtains and completes Form EXD in six copies from his commercial bank.

2. The commercial bank endorses/approves the form if payment for exports is by advance payment, cash or letter of credit. Other modes of payment require the form to be referred to the Bank of Zambia for approval and later payment reconciliation.

3. The commercial bank hands back all five copies of the approved form EXD as appropriate to the exporter who then proceeds to the point of exit with his product.

CERTIFICATES OF ORIGIN

To benefit from preferential entry to COMESA, EU and selected EFTA and other countries, an exporter needs to complete the appropriate certificate of origin, e.g. EUR Form 1 for exports to the EU, COMESA Certificate of Origin for exports to COMESA member states GSP Schemes for exports to USA, Canada and the Scandina vian countries.

SPECIAL TRADE ARRANGEMENTS

COMMON MARKET FOR EASTERN AND SOUTHERN AFRICA (COMESA)

Zambia is a member country and houses the headquarters of the Common Market for Eastern and Southern Africa Secretariat. Zambia extends to fellow member states any preferences mandated by current membership rules. Hence COMESA duty rates apply to the country's imports.

SOUTHERN AFRICA DEVELOPMENT COMMUNITY (SADC)

SADC was set up to liberalise trade and integrate economic devel opment of the 10 countries of which Zambia is one. The country is in the fore front in trying to achieve SADC's objectives.

TRADE FAIRS

ZAMBIA INTERNATIONAL TRADE FAIR

The Zambia international Trade Fair (ZITF) takes place annually at the end of June to beginning of July, in Ndola. The ZITF is a commercial show which attracts exhibitors of a wide range products from all over the world.

ZAMBIA AGRICULTURAL AND COMMERCIAL SHOW

The Zambia Agricultural and Commercial Show (ZACS) is an interna tional exhibition of agricultural produce and equipment and manufactured goods. It is an annual event held in Lusaka at the beginning of August. Like the ZITF, ZACS attracts large numbers of local and foreign exhibitors.
The main tenets of the current government economic policy are privatisation of over ninety (90) state owned Enterprises (SOEs), liberalisation of the economy and investment and export promo tion. Adequate policy instruments and relevant legislation have all been promulgated and enacted to facilitate implementation of these economic measures.

producers have penetrated the competitive European markets.

MANUFACTURING

Zambia has a vibrant public and private sector manufacturing industry. Zambia's main manufactured products include: edible oils, sugar, cigarettes, textiles, paper, rubber, chemicals, cement, automobiles assembling, shoes, light electrical and engineering equipment and a wide range of metal products. Many of the public sector manufacturing firms are slated for privatisation in line with the Government's Privatisation policy. Details are available from the Zambia Privatisation Agency.

FORESTS

Zambia is rich in forest. Good quality teak grows in the Western Province. Sawmills supply sawn and finished timber to railways for sleepers and flooring work. Timber based industries have considerable potential for domestic and export markets.

TOURISM

Zambia is endowed with magnificent natural wonders including the famous Victoria Falls and nineteen game reserves. The tourism industry is one of the country's foreign exchange earners. Several tourists visit Zambia every year and a few of these after discovering the vast potential for investment have come back to open tour travel operations and other related activities. In 1993 alone about 20 tour and travel companies were opened.

HANDICRAFTS

The handicraft industry has great potential to contribute signif icantly to the country's non-traditional export earnings. A variety of handicrafts are produced mainly in the rural areas. The Western and Southern provinces produce mostly basket◂ ware that is hand woven by women.

A variety of other crafts are produced and exported by men living in the urban and rural areas. These include: Tonga baskets, Makenge and Mukulwani baskets, wooden carvings, ebony household goods, wooden bracelets and traditional instruments.

INVESTMENT

The government of Zambia through the Zambia Investment Centre has embarked on an aggressive investment promotional campaign. The Centre was set up in 1991 when the Investment Act was passed. It facilitates, promotes and regulates domestic and foreign investment.

Investment opportunities exist in: agriculture, tourism and mining sectors, utilities and services such as transportation, distribution networks and generation and supply of electricity. Other opportunities exist in manufacturing such as transformation of agricultural produce, minerals and timber into finished products.

ECONOMY AND ECONOMIC DEVELOPMENT

Some 85% of Zambians work the country's relatively infertile soil as subsistence farmers; commercial agriculture is mostly confined to a small number of large farms. The leading crops are corn, sorghum, rice, peanuts, sunflower seeds, tobacco, sugarcane, and cotton. Cattle and other livestock are raised. There is a small fishing industry.

The mining and refining of copper constitutes by far the largest industry in the country and is concentrated in the cities of the Copperbelt. Cobalt, zinc, lead, gold, silver, gemstones, and coal are also mined. Manufactures include food products, beverages, textiles, construction materials, chemicals, and fertilizer. Most of Zambia's energy is supplied by hydroelectric plants, especially the one at Kariba Dam.

Copper accounts for over 80% of foreign exchange. The principal imports are machinery, transport equipment, consumer goods, petroleum and petroleum products, and foodstuffs. The leading trade partners are the European Union countries, South Africa, Japan, and the United States. Zambia is a member of the Southern African Development Community.

For additional analytical, business and investment opportunities information, please contact Global Investment & Business Center, USA at (202) 546-2103. Fax: (202) 546-3275. E-mail: rusric@erols.com

MAJOR TRENDS

Zambia's remarkable economic reform program is on track with business confidence domestically and internationally increasing as a result of the sale of the parastatal Zambia Consolidated Copper Mines (ZCCM) in 2000. The tremendous impact of that privatization is evident with the revitalization of the Copperbelt, and even though initial setbacks caused copper production to decline slightly in 2000, the outlook for the industry's recovery is positive. ZCCM had been the major impediment to Zambia's hard-won macroeconomic stability, and its privatization has opened the doors for foreign investment and donor cash injections by reiterating Zambia's commitment to serious reform.

Other companies slated to be privatized include the Zambian National Commercial Bank, the Zambian Telecommunications company, and Zambia Railways. The US government funded a feasibility study of the electricity supply company (Zesco) and a decision regarding the Zambian government's planned concession of it is expected in mid-2001. There have also been studies commissioned to look into the privatization of the postal service, and the national airports company.

Privatization of the economy in general allows quicker and more flexible responses to unforeseen economic developments. Governmental corruption and bureaucratic inefficiency are continuing problems that affect the business environment.

As was expected, in December 2000 international financial institutions supported interim debt relief for Zambia under the advanced Highly Indebted Poor Country (HIPC) initiative, which will reduce debt service obligations by about 45%. Total debt service relief from all of Zambia's creditors will be worth more than US$2.5 billion, with bilateral donors pledging 100% debt cancellation once HIPC conditions have been met. Total external debt is US$6.3 billion, a drop of 3.1% from the previous year. Zambia is expected to reach its HIPC Completion Point by late 2003.

Inflation stabilized in January 2001 after high oil prices, electricity tariffs, and monetary expansion contributed to inflation levels of 30.1% at year end 2000, which was well over the 2000 target of 14%. The year-end target for 2001 is 17.5%, but fuel prices will continue to create negative upward pressure. The reasonable harvests expected for this year and next will keep down food prices, the main component of the consumer price index. As a result of pressure from international financial institutions, Zambia will continue its tight fiscal and monetary policies, as well as stabilizing the exchange rate to mitigate inflationary pressures.

The target for foreign reserves for 2001—US$150 million—will be difficult to realize after the actions BoZ took to stabilize the Kwacha and will be greatly dependent on the amount of pledged donor support that is realized. In July 2000 the twelfth Consultative Group meeting was held in Lusaka, resulting in pledges worth US$1 billion, US$355 million of which is balance of payment support. Following the sale of ZCCM, disbursements resumed in 2000, totaling $158 million.

The Kwacha depreciated dramatically in the fourth quarter of 2000, with a December average of ZK4,108: US$1. Then in mid-January the Kwacha rapidly appreciated after a move by the BoZ and Ministry of Finance to tighten the monetary supply and to take precautionary exchange measures. Most notable was the use of US$25 million worth of foreign exchange reserves in an attempt to stabilize the currency. The sudden appreciation hurt exporters, particularly those in the non-traditional export (NTE) sector. The Kwacha is anticipated to depreciate further this year, but increased capital inflows should moderate its depreciation.

PRINCIPAL GROWTH SECTORS

The outlook for copper is still encouraging even with temporary production setbacks as the mining sector rehabilitates. In 2000, export earnings reached US$800 million, a 5.4% increase from the previous year. In 2000 Zambia produced 226,169 tons of copper compared to 257,111 in the previous year, an achievement given that the privatized companies took over on April 1, resulting in the loss of production during all of the first and most of the second quarter of FY2000.

Fuel prices, electricity tariffs, and economic troubles have all adversely affected the manufacturing sector. Many manufacturers complain that they have yet to gain from the Common Market for Eastern and Southern Africa (COMESA) Free Trade Area (FTA).

Agriculture continues to be a good performer for Zambia although many of the nation's resources are directed to producing maize, a non-cash crop. There is growing interest by small farmers to engage in more valuable crops such as coffee and tobacco, even though the highly charged issue of food security is equated with warehouses full of maize reserves and the government offers many incentives for farmers to continue producing the commodity.

Poor economic prospects for other countries in the region will continue to limit regional demand for non-traditional Zambian exports. Non-traditional exports declined by 13% in 2000. However, the non-reciprocal access offered by the AGOA and Cotonou agreements for the US and EU markets, respectively, should encourage growth. In 2000, Zambia qualified as an eligible country under the AGOA and is expected to gain access to the preferential treatment for apparel by fourth quarter 2001.

In June 2001, the World Bank signed an agreement with the African Trade Insurance Agency (ATI), of which Zambia is a member, extending credit to the group in an effort to improve terms of trade finance for exporters in the region.

The tourism industry in Zambia continues to grow. Construction of the Sun International, a large resort in Livingstone, has been completed. The Sun International marks a significant investment in the tourism industry in Zambia. Typically, the Zambia side has been overlooked relative to the Zimbabwe side of Victoria Falls, but as a result of the recent instability in Zimbabwe, Zambia's prospects are improving.

The social sector currently suffers from government's fiscal constraints and structural changes. Private sector incomes have not kept pace with inflation. The result is that people often do without basic social services. The HIV/AIDS pandemic continues to hamper development and depress productivity, as an estimated 19% of the working age population is infected.

GOVERNMENT ROLE IN THE ECONOMY

The 2001 budget continues to be dependent on donor support, which accounts for 53% of revenues. The primary source of additional income for the Zambian government would be the proceeds from the privatization of the remaining parastatal assets, and increased tourism and energy revenues. The 2001 budget speech leaned away from earlier statements by government that the remaining parastatals would not be privatized. The business community continues to closely monitor privatization, as backpedaling on commitments to privatization this year would negatively affect donor commitments.

Some of the expenditure headings are inflexible and it may well fall to the usually more flexible budget line items to absorb any shortfall. The more flexible items tend to include capital expenditure and payment of domestic arrears, the former being vital to the infrastructure development of the economy and the latter to the confidence and ability of the private sector to perform and contribute further to revenues.

BALANCE OF PAYMENTS SITUATION

The trade deficit will worsen in light of the mining-related imports that will be purchased to reform the privatized copper industry. However, improved official and commercial inflows, buoyed by the resumption of concessional donor support, should trigger a recovery, albeit in a very difficult foreign exchange position. Even with multilateral funding and disbursements resuming, the current account deficit in 2000 was US$578 million, up from US$483 in 1999. The World Bank continues to release Balance of Payment support (fiscal sustainability credit) which is aimed at helping Zambia sustain fiscal progress achieved in recent years by expanding fiscal adjustment beyond the central government to other public entities. It also aims to re-establish fiscal discipline through improvement in the predictability, accountability, and transparency of public spending. The government target for 2001 budget deficit is 75% of GDP.

INFRASTRUCTURE

Transport and communications infrastructures are fair by regional standards. Telecommunications is expensive and are expected to stay so, as they are one of the few sources of revenue left to the government. However assurances have been made that they will be privatized. A road maintenance board has been created, funded by a gasoline tax, to deal with Zambia's deteriorated roads, although financial accountability has been problematic resulting in unreliable rehabilitation. Health facilities are mostly of poor quality. Educational facilities vary greatly in quality and Zambia suffers from an acute shortage of teachers.

ECONOMIC DEVELOPMENT STRATEGY AND REFORMS[1]

I. RECENT ECONOMIC DEVELOPMENTS

2. **Zambia's economic performance during the first half of 2001 continued to improve.** Although growth in agriculture is projected to decline moderately, the targeted real GDP growth of 5 percent for 2001 should be achieved on the basis of a strong performance by the mining, manufacturing, and services sectors. In addition, the 12-month inflation rate through August was markedly lower than the indicative target, largely on account of tight financial policies and a greater-than-expected appreciation of the kwacha, and it is expected that the end-December target of at most 17.5 percent will be met.

3. **Following a substantial tightening of monetary policy in January 2001, broad money declined by 15.6 percent through end-March compared to the outstanding stock at end-December 2000.** Over the same period, the kwacha appreciated by 27 percent in local currency terms. Towards end-March, the BoZ eased monetary policy by lowering the minimum reserve ratio from 15 percent to 10 percent. Mainly as a result of this relaxation of the monetary stance, the exchange rate depreciated by 22 percent between end-March and end-June, and largely in response to this rapid depreciation, the BoZ again raised the cash reserve ratio to 12.5 percent. Through end-June, broad money declined by about 5 percent compared to the targeted increase of about 1.5 percent. In line with monetary developments, the yield on 91-day treasury bills rose from 34 percent at end-December 2000 to 53 percent in March 2001. However, with the moderation in inflationary pressures and larger-than-expected public sector net deposits, the yield

[1] IMF Materials

declined to 43 percent by end-June. Thus, real interest rates have remained very high, notwithstanding the deceleration of inflation.

4. **Fiscal performance through end-June was generally favorable.** In particular, revenue exceeded the program target by over 9 percent, despite the unexpected appreciation of the kwacha, mainly because of the strong performance of income tax and the VAT. Total government cash expenditures fell short of the program target by some 13 percent as overruns in domestic capital outlays and in RDCs were more than offset by lower-than-programmed expenditures on HIPC-related programs, elections, transfers to Zambia Consolidated Copper Mines (ZCCM), and contingency outlays. Consequently, net borrowing from the banking system was much lower than anticipated despite a significant shortfall in external program support. At the same time, domestic arrears at end-March and end-June were substantially higher than programmed. In addition, at end-June, cash releases for social sector outlays were below budgeted levels, and there was a delay of one quarter in commencing with HIPC Initiative financed expenditures.

5. **Balance of payments developments during the first half of 2001 were mixed.** Despite lower-than-expected copper and cobalt prices, exports receipts of these two products rose substantially on account of greater-than-expected volume increases from the newly privatized mines. However, growth of nontraditional exports was substantially lower-than-programmed largely because of the continuing civil strife in Zambia's key regional export markets. Nonfactor service receipts rose significantly, but external assistance fell short of the program target by US$56 million reflecting a substantial shortfall in disbursements from the World Bank and the European Union (EU). Nonetheless, the program's gross international reserves targets for end-March and end-June were met after taking account of the program adjustor for shortfalls in balance of payments support net of debt service and Fund disbursements.

6. **Regarding structural reforms, the government issued instructions in March 2001 to the Zambia Privatization Agency (ZPA) to proceed with the sale of a majority controlling interest in ZNCB, consistent with Zambia's commitments under the PRGF and the HIPC documents.** A full-scope inspection of the bank for the period ending December 2000 revealed that its financial position remains unsatisfactory. However, its position has been stabilized mainly as a result of repayments by RAMCOZ and by government on guarantees on loans to ZNOC. Going beyond ZNCB, the stability of the banking system has improved. Of the three problem banks, two have been put under liquidation and the third is now fully capitalized. Some members of the management of the fourth bank were found to be pursuing improper financial practices and this resulted in the bank being closed temporarily. The bank has since reopened under a new management team approved by the Bank of Zambia.

7. Actions to liberalize the oil sector have been delayed. However, we have been working closely with the World Bank and have taken the following measures: (i) issued a written notification that the private sector is free to import crude oil; (ii) amended the Energy Regulatory Board (ERB) license conditions to abolish the requirement for ex-ante price adjustment request; to monitor pump prices ex-post; to require display of pump prices; and to maintain a minimum stock of products; and (iii) began the process of forming a private consortium for importation of feedstock. Moreover, the Government has agreed that the import tariff on petroleum products will be lowered from 25 percent to 5 percent, by end-December 2001.

II. PROGRAM IMPLEMENTATION

8. **All quantitative performance criteria for end-March, and end-June 2001 were met[1] except that the domestic arrears ceiling was breached on both dates,[2] and the end-March ceiling on the net domestic assets of the BoZ of K 193 billion was missed by less than K 1 billion (Table 1).** Given that the verified stock of domestic arrears at end-June is now much larger than programmed, the performance criterion for end-September is unrealistic.

For additional analytical, business and investment opportunities information,
please contact Global Investment & Business Center, USA
at (202) 546-2103. Fax: (202) 546-3275. E-mail: rusric@erols.com

9. **The program's structural performance criterion on the abstention from new tax reductions was observed, as was the benchmark on the nonaccumulation of new tax arrears by ZESCO and ZNOC.** The benchmark for end-June for the BoZ to improve the treasury bill market was also observed, albeit with some delay on the issuance of auction guidelines.

III. THE PROGRAM

A. Macroeconomic Policies

10. The key macroeconomic objectives for 2001 remain to achieve GDP growth of 5 percent and limit the 12-month rate of inflation to at most 17.5 percent by year-end, within a financial framework that targets a substantial increase in gross international reserves while reducing poverty. Achieving these objectives will require implementing appropriate fiscal and monetary policies, strengthening structural reforms, and re-orienting government expenditures towards the social sectors and poverty reduction.

B. Fiscal Policies, External Resources, HIPC, and PRSP

11. **Notwithstanding the more appreciated exchange rate, total revenue is projected to exceed the program target by 0.6 percent of GDP.** The shortfall in domestic VAT will be largely offset by the VAT on imports as the impact of the Import VAT Deferment Scheme has been much smaller than expected, and as the delay in the operation of the Indeni refinery has required continued imports of refined petroleum. Income taxes are projected to perform strongly, reflecting increased activity in the mines. We will continue to abstain from new tax reductions, exemptions, rebates or any other preferential tax treatment, including for the mining sector, pending a thorough review of mining taxation policy in consultation with Fund staff.

12. **Expenditure pressures during the rest of the year are likely to remain strong, particularly in view of the upcoming elections.** The government recently concluded the lengthy process of reaching wage agreements with the civil service and public workers unions. The major agreement covers the period July 2001 to December 2002 with no retroactive increases for January-June 2001. The wage bill is now projected to reach 6.3 percent of GDP compared with the program estimate of 5.7 percent. There have also been overruns in recurrent departmental charges and in domestically financed capital expenditures. To offset these overruns, outlays for financial restructuring will be curtailed by agreeing on an appropriate repayment schedule with ZNCB for the remaining payments on the government guarantee on its loan to ZNOC. In any event these payments will need to be made in the context of concluding the privatization of the bank. No new financial commitments will be made on account of ZNOC by the government or BoZ other than those for which they are legally liable. Transfers to the former ZCCM's creditors will continue, but will be less than budgeted partly on account of an audit which has questioned the validity of some of these claims. Taking account of increased revenues, the domestic budget balance will be limited to 3.8 percent of GDP or 0.5 percentage points above the program target.

13. **While maintaining control on overall expenditures, the government will re-orient expenditures toward the social sectors.** Following the government's reestablishment of the "80 percent rule" in April, and the move to a "100 percent rule" in July for social sector ministries,[3] the cumulative share of social sector spending in discretionary expenditures during January-July (38 percent) is now broadly in line with targets agreed with the World Bank. In addition, since setting up the mechanism for channeling HIPC Initiative debt relief toward pro-poor activities, HIPC-financed spending has increased substantially as noted below.

For additional analytical, business and investment opportunities information, please contact Global Investment & Business Center, USA at (202) 546-2103. Fax: (202) 546-3275. E-mail: rusric@erols.com

14. **A significant problem for public finances that has emerged is the likelihood of a substantial shortfall in donor balance of payments support in 2001.** The 2001 budget was based on disbursements of US$79 million grants from the EU. However, it appears likely that actual disbursements will amount to only US$10 million because of complex conditionality, and a recently instituted historical audit of the use of EU funds since the mid-1990s. The budget also envisages highly concessional loans of US$95 million from the World Bank comprising two tranches. We believe that the policies and actions underlying the first of these tranches have been implemented. The last tranche is related to the reform of the oil sector. Substantial progress has already been made as noted above and we envisage taking all necessary remaining actions by end-December 2001. The government will continue to cooperate closely with its development partners.

15. **Total public sector debt service (including to the Fund) for 2001 is currently estimated at US$145 million, compared with the programmed US$160 million,**[4] mainly reflecting lower payments to Russia. Paris Club creditors are expected to agree to a flow rescheduling on Cologne terms shortly, and key multilateral institutions, including the Fund, World Bank, and the African Development Bank, are providing interim relief as envisaged. The government is also making best efforts to reach agreement with non-Paris Club bilateral and commercial creditors on terms comparable to those provided by Paris Club creditors.

16. **HIPC Initiative financed expenditures have been delayed by uncertainties about the timing and level of relief and how to set up a mechanism to register the inflows.** These issues have been resolved, and each month, estimated debt relief received (excluding from the Fund) will be credited to a HIPC account (account 49) from which disbursements will be made to the relevant projects.[5] The government deposited US$42 million to the HIPC account in June and an additional US$12 million per month will be deposited for the period July-December 2001. The government will inform the Fund staff of the monthly payments into account 49 and the cash releases to ministries. Given the delay in starting HIPC-financed poverty-reducing programs, spending the full amount programmed for the year would involve inefficiencies. In collaboration with line ministries, a revised disbursement profile was agreed which is expected to bring total HIPC-financed expenditures for the year to K 280 billion. Thus 80 percent of the original programmed K 352 billion will be spent during July-December. The Accountant General has drawn up guidelines for tracking and reporting on the disbursement of funds from the HIPC account, and issued them to Controlling Officers. The first summary report on HIPC resources and expenditures, which covered the first and second quarters, has been published in the newspapers. The second report will be published by end-November. The World Bank, UK, and others are planning to fund a public expenditure tracking survey in the education sector, and we will cooperate with donors in this regard.

17. **The system outlined above will enable the government to track the receipt and use of HIPC resources.** At the same time, the current system of budget classification makes it difficult to judge whether overall spending has taken on a more "pro-poor" orientation. As such, government has set up a committee charged with establishing an agreed set of anti-poverty expenditure items in the budget and, in this manner, hopes to be able to define an expenditure baseline for 2000 against which to compare the outturns for 2001 and beyond. Government intends to request technical assistance from the Fund in this regard.

18. **Regarding the PRSP, considerable progress has been made and a draft final document has been prepared, which has benefited from a country-wide participatory process involving local government officials, civil society groups, and local communities.** The government will hold a National Summit in mid-October involving all stakeholders, in order to reach a broad consensus on the PRSP.

C. Monetary Policies

For additional analytical, business and investment opportunities information, please contact Global Investment & Business Center, USA at (202) 546-2103. Fax: (202) 546-3275. E-mail: rusric@erols.com

19. Monetary policy during the second half of 2001 will aim to achieve the program's targets on growth, inflation and international reserves. In line with these objectives, growth of broad money will be targeted at about 13 percent during 2001 compared with 16.5 percent in the program. The BoZ has made substantial progress in improving the operations of the treasury bill market, including the issuance of the new auction guidelines, and the modification of the book entry system to enable the reintroduction of the multiple pricing format for treasury bills and the prorating of the marginal bids. The BoZ will adhere strictly to the new auction guidelines so that interest rates will reflect the prevailing market conditions. The recent introduction of repurchase agreements will enhance the BoZ's capacity to implement monetary policy. The government recognizes the need to recapitalize the BoZ in order to strengthen monetary policy implementation.

D. External Sector and Exchange Rate Policies

20. **Zambia's external current account deficit (excluding grants) is projected to be 18.5 percent of GDP in 2001, as a larger trade deficit is partially offset by a substantial improvement in the services account.** Total exports receipts are projected to increase by 14 percent, compared with the programmed 24 percent, reflecting lower copper and cobalt prices and lower-than-expected nonmetal exports. Total imports are envisaged to rise by 18 percent linked to higher project financing, foreign direct investment, and maize imports. The better-than-expected performance in services largely reflects increased tourist receipts, partly on account of the OAU conference and the solar eclipse. Reflecting mainly the shortfall in balance of payments assistance from the EU, gross international reserves are projected to increase by US$74 million to 1.5 months of imports, compared with the programmed increase of US$135 million to 1.9 months of imports.

21. **Since end-June 2001, the exchange rate has remained relatively stable.** The exchange rate will continue to be market-determined, with central bank intervention limited to meeting the international reserves target and to smoothing short-term fluctuations. Zambia continues to maintain a liberal trade regime, and as noted earlier, the government has agreed that the import tariff on petroleum products will be lowered to 5 percent by end-December 2001. The government will lift the recently imposed ban on the export of maize as soon as conditions return to normal.

E. Structural Reforms, Public Expenditure Management, and Governance

STRUCTURAL REFORMS

22. **Completing the privatization of ZNCB remains the government's top priority.** The recent full scope inspection of the Bank confirmed weaknesses in its financial condition. To address some of these weaknesses, the BoZ has issued instructions for ZNCB to properly account for the unrealized trading losses/gains on its foreign exchange holdings, and to write off all unreconciled inter-branch items of more than 90 days. A targeted inspection to review compliance with the instructions will be completed by end-October 2001.

23. **Following Cabinet approval of the proposal to privatize ZNCB, consultants began a due diligence study which is scheduled to be completed by October.** The study will assess the bank's current financial situation and valuation, and prepare international tender documents. The consultant will also identify options for privatization, including hiving off the nonviable rural branches of ZNCB and possibly combining them with the National Savings and Credit Bank as part of developing a rural financial entity that will provide services in small towns and rural areas. In any event the rural branches will be fully separated from the sale of the bank as a commercial undertaking, and the final decision on those branches will not delay the offer for sale of the bank. It is expected that the ZPA board will approve the privatization proposal and tender document,

For additional analytical, business and investment opportunities information, please contact Global Investment & Business Center, USA at (202) 546-2103. Fax: (202) 546-3275. E-mail: rusric@erols.com

and appoint a negotiating team, and we intend to issue the tender documents for sale of a majority controlling interest in the bank by end-November. In the interim, the government will strengthen oversight by appointing ZPA to the Board of ZNCB.

24. The BoZ has taken steps to strengthen the banking system and, in May 2001, it conducted a self assessment of Zambia's compliance with the Basel Core Principles. The assessment, however, focused more on laws and regulations as opposed to actual practice. In this context, the Financial Sector Assessment Program (FSAP) mission from the Fund and the World Bank planned for 2002 to conduct a comprehensive external assessment of the financial system will be useful.

25. **The government is moving as rapidly as feasible to implement the remaining actions agreed with the World Bank on the oil sector.** In this regard by end-December, government will (i) offer for sale its share in Indeni refinery in order to reduce its equity stake to below 50 percent; (ii) offer for sale or long-term concession the Ndola storage tank and TAZAMA pipeline to a private sector operator through a competitive bidding process; and (iii) restructure ZNOC to limit its role to that of maintenance of strategic stock of petroleum products.

PUBLIC EXPENDITURE MANAGEMENT

26. Public expenditure management requires further strengthening, as evidenced by the sharp increase in domestic payments arrears during the first half of the year. Recognizing the critical importance of improvements in this area, government has devised an action plan to deal with this problem. First, the Controller, Internal Audit has conducted an audit of arrears at end-June and the reasons for the large increase. Controlling officers will be required to sign off on these results, certifying that no other bills corresponding to this period will be unearthed at a later date. The line ministries should take the results of the internal audit as the base for reporting the monthly expenditure returns from September onwards. To verify the accuracy of the data for the Ministry of Works and Supplies, which accounts for 45 percent of total arrears, the Auditor General has commenced an independent audit of the ministry's arrears with its major contractors. The audit will be completed by end-November. At the same time we are taking urgent steps to strengthen the monthly reports from controlling officers that must form the basis of long-term improvement in financial management and control. In particular, we intend to modify the existing system of computerized monthly reporting to include information on commitment and arrears. Until then, the system of manual monthly reporting should continue and be strengthened. Once this system is more reliable, the quarterly reports of the Controller, Internal Audit could fulfill the normal function of quality control. In addition, we are taking a number of steps, as detailed in Annex I, to improve budget preparation and expenditure control.

27. With regard to the IFMIS, in September 2001 an EU-funded consultant, produced a "roadmap" of the development and implementation of the system, which has served as a useful input for the internal project management team in analyzing existing weaknesses and preparing user requirements for the IFMIS. The members of this team have recently been freed from their other duties in government to allow sufficient time for IFMIS. A World Bank-funded consultant is currently reviewing the work of the project management team. Government anticipates that the user requirements and timetable for implementation will be submitted to the IFMIS steering committee by end-October. The next steps will be clarified in the team's report, but it appears unlikely that a consultant for designing hardware and software requirements will be in place by December 2001, as initially envisaged.

28. **The accounts of government at the Bank of Zambia are being streamlined to improve information availability for monitoring government finances.** The government has requested technical assistance from the Fund to simplify the system of government accounts at the BoZ. In the meantime, the government plans to close all dormant accounts and will review the foreign

For additional analytical, business and investment opportunities information, please contact Global Investment & Business Center, USA at (202) 546-2103. Fax: (202) 546-3275. E-mail: rusric@erols.com

exchange bridge loan account at the Bank of Zambia. Government is moving to a system in which the general revenue account receives all inflows, including the kwacha value of external support, and is used to pay all outflows, including debt service, in order to strengthen the management of public finances. Credit to government would be provided by treasury bills and by a single ways and means account on which government would pay an appropriate rate of interest. The government will issue rules governing the terms and conditions for commercial bank accounts of all government agencies.

GOVERNANCE

29. **Given the importance for good governance and transparency of publishing the audited government accounts in a timely fashion,** the Financial Report for 2000, prepared by the Accountant General and verified by the Auditor General, was tabled in Parliament in September, and the Auditor General's report on the overall outturn should be completed by December, all as required under Zambian law. This represents a substantial improvement over recent years, when Financial Reports have been delayed by up to four years.

30. **In June 2001, the government completed the provision of all information and documents requested by the auditors as necessary to finalize the report on cobalt sales.** However, the Metal Resource Group (MRG), the apparent beneficiary of the below-market-price sales, questioned the findings of the draft report and has initiated legal action for libel against the auditors and the government. This has delayed the auditor's completion of the report, but we expect it to be finalised shortly. The report will be referred to Cabinet for appropriate follow-up actions under the law, and if feasible the government will publish the document.

IV. TECHNICAL ASSISTANCE AND DATA ISSUES

31. Zambia continues to require technical assistance in the areas of public expenditure management, monetary operations and liquidity management, and simplification of government accounts with the banking system. More critically, this year there has been a considerable delay in producing monetary statistics, particularly the monetary survey.[6] BoZ is making concerted efforts to ensure that this problem is resolved as soon as possible. Regarding national accounts, methodological weaknesses relating to the use of outdated weights, long delays, and frequent revision in the estimates undermine government's ability to monitor economic developments and formulate policies. The BoZ will also seek to improve the tourism and foreign direct investment statistics in the balance of payments. To address these weaknesses, the government will request technical assistance from the Fund and other donors.

V. PROGRAM MONITORING

32. For end-December 2001, the implementation of the program will be monitored on the basis of the quantitative and structural performance criteria and benchmarks indicated in Tables 1 and 2. Owing to difficulties in measuring and monitoring domestic arrears, the quantitative performance criterion on domestic arrears has been replaced by a structural performance criterion and benchmarks involving progress towards improving the monitoring and control of these arrears. The fourth review of the PRGF-supported program will be conducted based on performance through end-December 2001, and will include agreement on an appropriate macroeconomic and financial framework for 2002.

IMPROVING BUDGET PREPARATION AND EXPENDITURE CONTROL

For additional analytical, business and investment opportunities information, please contact Global Investment & Business Center, USA at (202) 546-2103. Fax: (202) 546-3275. E-mail: rusric@erols.com

Government efforts to **strengthen public expenditure management** focus both on budget preparation and on expenditure control. Regarding the former, if ministries are expected to carry out a certain set of programs but given unrealistic budget appropriations, the accumulation of arrears is inevitable. As such, government intends to narrow the scope of expenditure so as to allow an increase in budget allocations for key priorities. In particular, circulars have been issued to curtail motor vehicle allowances for government servants and education and housing allowances for foreign diplomats: savings from these two initiatives will be redirected toward road works and other areas in which arrears have typically arisen as a result of low budget allocations.

Government is also committed to ending the practice of entering projects and programs in the budget with only a token provision (usually one kwacha). This practice, intended to obtain parliamentary authority for items for which funding sources may emerge in the future, has often led to spending pressures from line ministries even in the absence of funding. Government will ensure that no item will be recorded in the Yellow Book without an adequate appropriation.

In terms of expenditure control, the procedures of the Zambia National Tender Board will be tightened. Current regulations state that a contract can only be approved if the project appears in the Yellow Book and if there are adequate funds, but in practice, it is difficult for the Tender Board to assess whether funds are, indeed, available. As such, it is proposed that endorsement of the Minister of Finance should be required for any project above K 500 million.

To eliminate any possible uncertainty regarding permissible virement, the 2002 Yellow Book will clarify budget regulations to state clearly that, without prior Treasury authority, a controlling officer may not apply funds released for a certain subhead toward expenditure under a different subhead. For instance, variations between grants and RDCs would be forbidden, as would variations between drugs and allowances within RDCs.

To reinforce financial discipline, permanent secretaries shall be made contractual employees. Terms of their contracts would include compliance with all financial regulations (including those governing virement and aggregate commitments), and any malfeasance would be regarded as grounds for sanctions, up to and including dismissal.

Finally, as a further boost to expenditure control, the personal responsibility of heads of accounting units shall be enhanced. Although it is recognized that the controlling officer bears ultimate financial responsibility for an expenditure head, chief accountants will be subject to disciplinary action by the Accountant General should they fail to report on all instances in which they have been requested to process transactions inconsistent with the Financial Regulations. Similarly, the responsibility of internal audit will be reiterated in a treasury circular.

---

[1] After applying the adjustor for the shortfall in balance of payments assistance net of debt service payments (US$42.6 million), the delay in Fund disbursements (SDR 24.94 million) related to the end-March performance criteria, and the reduction in the cash reserve ratio to 10 percent in March and the subsequent increase to 12.5 percent in June.

[2] The increase since December reflected the verification of old arrears on previously contracted road works, the impact of the exchange rate on dollar denominated arrears, and a build-up of penalties on outstanding arrears. It also reflected the accumulation of new arrears, which we estimate to amount to about K 40 billion. By comparison, over the same period, net credit to government was K 218 billion less than programmed.

[3] These rules require the Budget office to make cash releases to line ministries consistent with their budget appropriations.

[4] Pending agreement with the Paris Club on interim relief, Zambia has stopped paying to Paris Club creditors debt service that was expected to be subjected to interim relief under the HIPC initiative, to allow the resources freed by relief to be directed towards poverty-reducing expenditures rather than towards debt service. Once the Paris Club agreement is finalized, we

hope to recoup the overpayments made to Paris Club creditors during January-August 2001.
[5] Each month, the kwacha bridge loan will be debited for the kwacha equivalent of US$12 million and funds will flow first to account 99 and then to account 49. At the time of disbursement, funds will flow back through account 99 briefly so as to utilize current government cash release procedures. As for the amount of debt service remaining due after debt relief, the foreign exchange bridge loan will be debited for this amount, as payments fall due, and funds will be transferred to account 99 and then to account 63 before being paid.
[6] The BoZ has been having problems introducing a new accounting software package and has temporarily reverted to its previous software for generating monetary data.

For additional analytical, business and investment opportunities information,
please contact Global Investment & Business Center, USA
at (202) 546-2103. Fax: (202) 546-3275. E-mail: rusric@erols.com

PRACTICAL AND LEGAL INFORMATION FOR CONDUCTING BUSINESS

DOING BUSINESS IN ZAMBIA

MARKET OVERVIEW

* Zambia is a politically stable, multi-party democracy, rich in natural resources. Its relatively open economy has averaged more than six percent real GDP growth over the past five years and was ranked one of the fastest growing economies in the world in a recent report by *The Economist* magazine. Through market liberalization, fiscal discipline, and sound economic policies, the country has

brought down the annual inflation rate to less than 10 percent and attracted substantial foreign investment.

* Zambia's main export markets are Switzerland, South Africa, DR Congo, China, and Egypt. Imports come primarily from South Africa, India, Kuwait, China, DR Congo, and the United Arab Emirates.

* Zambia's main exports are non-ferrous metals (primarily copper and cobalt), non-metallic minerals, coffee, tea, spices, miscellaneous manufactured goods, and wood products.

* In 2010, 1.4% of Zambia's total imports were from the United States. These consisted primarily of cereals, telecommunications equipment, machinery, tractors, agricultural equipment and parts, medicaments, medical instruments, chemicals, and mining equipment.

* In 2010, less than one percent of Zambian exports went to the United States, consisting almost entirely of copper and cobalt. Other exports included precious and semi-precious stones, coffee, honey, spices, and handicrafts.

* As of December 2010, U.S. Foreign Direct Investment assets in Zambia were estimated to be USD 144.3million.

Real GDP Growth	6.6%
GDP per capita	USD 1,286
Zambia Total Exports	USD 6.9billion
Zambia Total Imports	USD 5.1billion
Total Imports through Nov 2010 from the U.S.	USD 50.8million
Total Exports through Nov 2010 to the U.S.	USD 25.8million
Zambia's total trade with the U.S	USD 76.6million

For additional analytical, business and investment opportunities information, please contact Global Investment & Business Center, USA at (202) 546-2103. Fax: (202) 546-3275. E-mail: rusric@erols.com

Trade balance with the U.S	USD 25.0million
Estimated Population	13.6million
Inflation December (annual rate)	7.9%

MARKET CHALLENGES

* The Zambian economy is heavily dependent on copper mining and rain-fed agricultural production, which exposes the economy to external vulnerabilities such as global copper prices and seasonal weather patterns.

* The Kwacha remained relatively stable in 2010 ranging from K 4,775 to K 4,720 per USD. Historically, the Kwacha's volatility has generally tracked closely with global copper price fluctuations. Some financial institutions offer derivatives and forward contracts to hedge against exchange rate movement.

* Although the year-on-year inflation rate closed at 7.9%, high food and non-food prices and perennial fuel shortages continue to pose challenges.

* Zambia has a relatively small domestic market that is spread across a country roughly the size of Texas. Its internal road infrastructure is generally adequate for the movement of goods between cities and towns. Outside of the main transportation arteries, however, the transportation network is largely undeveloped.

* Although improvements have been made at key entry points, including the opening of integrated customs services at the Zambia-Zimbabwe border at Chirundu, the cross-border movement of goods remains slow. This, combined with high fuel prices, translates to steep transportation costs to and from (as well as within) Zambia.

* Domestic economic growth is constrained by the limited availability of commercial credit (due to risk aversion, rather than lack of liquidity, in the banking sector) and high fees for financial services.

* Occasional government interference in the private sector, the continued government ownership of key public utilities, a weak court system, and inadequate law enforcement capacity tarnish Zambia's liberal investment environment in practice.

* Other challenges include pervasive corruption, complex permit requirements, unreliable and expensive communication costs, and low, but growing, Internet connectivity.

* Although hourly wages are low, actual labor costs are considered high for the region—driven up by stringent labor laws, a shortage of skilled labor, and health-related absenteeism. Life expectancy at birth is about 39 years. HIV prevalence is approximately 14%.

MARKET OPPORTUNITIES

These challenges notwithstanding, there are commercial opportunities in Zambia's emerging economy. A middle class has developed in Lusaka that has resulted in a proliferation of South African franchises, a construction boom, and a formidable (although mostly risk-averse) banking sector. In general, most sectors are uncompetitive and are dominated by a few large players, leaving plenty of room for new market entrants. There have been few cases of blatant discrimination against foreign investors.

Market opportunities abound in the following sectors:

* **Energy**
* **Mining**
* **Agriculture**
* **Food processing**
* **Telecommunications**
* **Construction**
* **Transportation**
* **Tourism**
* **Health**

MARKET ENTRY STRATEGY

* Only a few U.S. companies have a significant presence in Zambia. U.S. companies usually either license through local representatives, or export indirectly through (often South African) intermediaries.

* Franchising, direct exporting, and greenfield investments are uncommon.

* Whatever market entry strategy is chosen, businesses should bear in mind that entering the market will require local expertise on legal and regulatory issues.

Useful sources of information include:

Bank of Zambia: http://www.boz.zm

Zambia Central Statistical Office: http://www.zamstats.gov.zm

International Monetary Fund: http://www.imf.org/external/country/zmb

World Bank: http://www.worldbank.org/afr/zm

Zambia Association of Chambers, Commerce, and Industry: http://zambiachambers.org

SELLING U.S. PRODUCTS AND SERVICES

USING AN AGENT OR DISTRIBUTOR

* There is substantial local interest to represent and/or distribute on behalf of U.S. companies.

* Financing local inventories is often a problem, especially given high commercial loan rates. Few companies have sales or service networks that meet U.S. standards and expectations.

* The U.S. Embassy has the capacity to conduct limited agent/distributor searches or other services when requested through a U.S. Department of Commerce district office, or when contacted directly by a U.S. company.

* Local offices of international accounting and consulting firms can also assist in identifying qualified local business partners.

ESTABLISHING AN OFFICE

The legal requirements for establishing an office in Zambia are relatively simple.

* A prospective company must register with the Registrar of Companies at the Patents and Companies Registration Agency (PACRA), a semi-autonomous institution under the Ministry of Commerce, Trade, and Industry, by submitting the company charter and a registration fee. A local agent may be appointed to do this on behalf of the potential investor.

* After submission of the company charter and payment of registration fees, a Certificate of Incorporation is generally issued within 24 hours.

* Under the terms of the new Zambia Development Agency (ZDA) Act, foreign nationals who invest USD 250,000 and employ a minimum of 200 persons are entitled to self-employment or resident permits. With an approved investment

license, these investors are also eligible for up to five expatriate work/resident permits.

* Foreign companies that plan to invest in Zambia should obtain an investment license from the ZDA to take advantage of its services. The procedure is simple and licenses are approved or disapproved within 30 days. The ZDA may be contacted at the following address:

Zambia Development Agency

Privatization House
Nasser Road
PO Box 30819, Lusaka, Zambia
Tel: 260-211-220 177; Fax: 260-211-225 270
Email: zda@zda.org.zm
Website: www.zda.org.zm

FRANCHISING

Franchise business arrangements in Zambia are based on British contract law rather than more-binding U.S. franchising regulations. There is increased interest in franchising in Zambia generated by publicity and exposure to international franchise trade events in South Africa. Lack of financing options, however, remains a major obstacle to franchise business development in Zambia.

There may be opportunities for U.S. franchises in the following areas:

o Restaurants

o Retail (including pharmaceutical and hardware)

o Non-luxury hotels

o Internet Service Providers

DIRECT MARKETING

There are no restrictions on conducting direct marketing in Zambia. However, direct marketing companies may be constrained by inadequate postal services, high phone tariffs, and low Internet penetration.

JOINT VENTURES/LICENSING

The Zambian business community has a strong interest in joint ventures and licensing agreements. Local investors actively seek out these arrangements in order to overcome scarcity of domestic capital, technology, and expertise. There are no legal restrictions which define the terms of a joint venture arrangement. A suitable partnership should be established contractually and registered with the Patent and Company Registration Agency (PACRA). The registration certificate from PACRA should be submitted o the Zambia Development Agency (ZDA) for an investment license.

See chapter four for specific investment opportunities, all of which potentially could be undertaken through a joint venture operation.

SELLING TO THE GOVERNMENT

All government expenditure's above USD 100,000, as well as all government loan and credit agreements, must go through the Zambia Public Procurement Authority (until recently known as the Zambia National Tender Board). Government purchases below USD 100,000 are handled by institutional tender committees, and these are open to any company that meets the terms and conditions.

The Public Procurement Authority advertises tenders for procurement of goods and services through the print media and posts copies of all tenders on its website (www.tenderboard.gov.zm).

DISTRIBUTION AND SALES CHANNELS

Goods destined for Zambia arrive via South Africa (Durban, Port Elizabeth, and East London), Namibia (Walvis Bay), Mozambique (Beira), and Tanzania (Dar es Salaam). Durban, Walvis Bay and Dar es Salaam are the most commonly used sea ports. Virtually all imports are transported by truck, entering Zambia primarily through Chirundu and Livingstone (on the Zimbabwean border), Kazungula (on the Botswana border), Nakonde (on the Tanzanian border), and Sesheke (on the Namibian border). The Kasumbalesa border with DR Congo sees a great deal of mining sector-related traffic.

Imports coming through Durban, Walvis Bay, and Dar es Salaam can take up to two weeks to reach Zambia, due primarily to delays at border crossings. Transportation costs are high and are estimated to account for 60-70 percent of the cost of production for many goods in Zambia.

Wholesale trade and distribution is concentrated in Lusaka, Kitwe, Ndola, Livingstone, Kasama, and Chipata.

SELLING FACTORS/TECHNIQUES

Selling is normally done on a cash basis, due to scarce and expensive credit. Companies that can offer credit, or an extended payment schedule, have an edge even if their prices are higher. After-sales service is an important factor for technical products.

Imported food products must have English-language labels that detail ingredients and shelf life of products. Any food products failing to meet this requirement are confiscated by local authorities and destroyed without compensation.

Goods and services are advertised through flyers in the main daily newspapers such as *Times of Zambia*, *The Daily Mail* and *The Post Newspaper* for wider circulation at a fee. There are five private television stations including two public channels operated by the state-run Zambia

National Broadcasting Corporation. The television and community radio station provide advertising service.

ELECTRONIC COMMERCE

E-commerce is relatively new to Zambia. Very few firms have web sites or are equipped to conduct on-line transactions. Internet penetration is growing but still particularly low (estimated to be 816,000 users as of June 2010), due to lack of ICT investment, particularly in rural areas, and the high cost of an Internet Service Provider operating licenses (USD 25,000).

TRADE PROMOTION AND ADVERTISING

Zambia holds four annual trade fairs. The main trade events are:

* Zambia Mining, Agriculture, and Commercial Show, which is held during the last week of May in Kitwe (in the Copperbelt);

* Zambia International Trade Fair, which is held in Ndola (in the Copperbelt) during the last week of June;

* Zambia Agriculture and Commercial show, which takes place in Lusaka during first week of August; and

* Gemstone and Mining Exhibition, which is held in Livingstone and Lusaka.

http://www.cacss.co.zm

http://www.zitf.org.zm

Electronic Media: Zambia has two national channels and five private television stations and over 40 community radio stations. Radio broadcasts are in English as well as local languages and tend to reach a wider audience than television broadcasts. The contacts for the most important television and radio broadcasters are:

Zambia National Broadcasting Company (ZNBC)
TV 1 and TV2
Email: znbc@zamtel.zm
Website: www.znbc.co.zm
MUVI Television
Email: muvi@iconnect.zm
Website: www.muvitv.com

MOBI Television
Email: mobitel@zamtel.zm
Radio Phoenix
E-mail: rphoenix@zamnet.zm
Website: www.radiophoenic.co.zm

Print media: The *Times of Zambia* and the *Zambia Daily Mail* are state-owned daily newspapers. The only independent daily is *The Post.* Two monthly business publications, the Zambia National Farmers Union's *Zambian Farmer*, and *Profit Magazine*, published by the Zambia Association of Chambers of Commerce and Industry, are strong voices for private sector business in Zambia. The following are contact addresses for the major print media:

Times of Zambia
E-mail: times@zamtel.zm

Website: www.times.co.zm
Zambia Daily Mail
E-mail: zadama@zamnet.zm
Website: www.daily-mail.co.zm
The Post Newspaper
E-mail: post@post.co.zm
Website: www.postzambia.com
The U.S. advertising firm Young & Rubicam has offices in Zambia and may be contacted at the following address:
Young & Rubicam (Zambia) Limited
Email: yrubicam@coppernet.zm

PRICING

Local pricing formulas usually account for international and domestic transportation charges, customs duty, and value added tax (16 percent), all of which contribute to high local prices. In general, Zambian consumers are price conscious and place greater emphasis on price than quality. However, in many sectors Zambians still see the value for money in U.S. products and services compared to products and services from other countries.

SALES SERVICE/CUSTOMER SUPPORT

After-sales service and customer support are important factors to business, particularly for technical products such as computers and equipment. Nevertheless these are often lacking in Zambia.

PROTECTING YOUR INTELLECTUAL PROPERTY

The protection of Property rights has been addressed in chapter six – Investment Climate statement. However, a company entering the Zambian market should register its trademark with the Patent and Company Registration Agency (PACRA) and coordinate with the Intellectual Property Unit (IPU) of the Zambia Police Service. The IPU has the ability to enforce intellectual property rights in Zambia's major cities and border areas where counterfeit and pirated materials enter the country. Unless there is a complainant, police action cannot take action. Zambian intellectual property legislation is still undergoing review in order to remove archaic provisions, bring it to international standards, and stiffen punishments.

Protecting Your Intellectual Property in Zambia:

Several general principles are important for effective management of intellectual property (—IP‖) rights in Zambia. First, it is important to have an overall strategy to protect your IP. Second, IP is protected differently in Zambia than in the U.S. Third, rights must be registered and enforced in Zambia, under local laws. Your U.S. trademark and patent registrations will not protect you in Zambia. There is no such thing as an —international copyright‖ that will automatically protect an author's writings throughout the entire world. Protection against unauthorized use in a particular country depends, basically, on the national laws of that country. However, most countries do offer copyright protection to foreign works under certain conditions, and these conditions have been greatly simplified by international copyright treaties and conventions.

Registration of patents and trademarks is on a first-in-time, first-in-right basis, so you should consider applying for trademark and patent protection even before selling your products or services in the Zambia market. It is vital that companies understand that intellectual property is primarily a private right and that the U.S. government generally cannot enforce rights for private individuals in Zambia. It is the responsibility of the rights' holders to register, protect, and enforce their rights where relevant, retaining their own counsel and advisors. Companies may wish to seek advice from local attorneys or IP consultants who are experts in Zambian law. The U.S. Commercial Service can provide a list of local lawyers upon request or visit the website: http://zambia.usembassy.gov/zambia/attorney_information.html.

While the U.S. Government stands ready to assist, there is little we can do if the rights holders have not taken these fundamental steps necessary to securing and enforcing their IP in a timely fashion. Moreover, in many countries, rights holders who delay enforcing their rights on a mistaken belief that the USG can provide a political resolution to a legal problem may find that their rights have been eroded or abrogated due to legal doctrines such as statutes of limitations, laches, estoppel, or unreasonable delay in prosecuting a law suit. In no instance should U.S. Government advice be seen as a substitute for the obligation of a rights holder to promptly pursue its case.

It is always advisable to conduct due diligence on potential partners. Negotiate from the position of your partner and give your partner clear incentives to honor the contract. A good partner is an important ally in protecting IP rights. Consider carefully, however, whether to permit your partner to register your IP rights on your behalf. Doing so may create a risk that your partner will list itself as the IP owner and fail to transfer the rights should the partnership end. Keep an eye on your cost structure and reduce the margins (and the incentive) of would-be bad actors. Projects and sales in Zambia require constant attention. Work with legal counsel familiar with Zambian laws to create a solid contract that includes non-compete clauses, and confidentiality/non-disclosure provisions.

It is also recommended that small and medium-size companies understand the importance of working together with trade associations and organizations to support efforts to protect IP and stop counterfeiting. There are a number of these organizations, both Zambia or U.S.-based. These include:

* The U.S. Chamber and local American Chambers of Commerce

* National Association of Manufacturers (NAM)

* International Intellectual Property Alliance (IIPA)

* International Trademark Association (INTA)

* The Coalition Against Counterfeiting and Piracy

* International Anti-Counterfeiting Coalition (IACC)

* Pharmaceutical Research and Manufacturers of America (PhRMA)

* Biotechnology Industry Organization (BIO)

IP RESOURCES

A wealth of information on protecting IP is freely available to U.S. rights holders. Some excellent resources for companies regarding intellectual property include the following:

* For information about patent, trademark, or copyright issues -- including enforcement issues in the US and other countries -- call the STOP! Hotline: 1-866-999-HALT or register at www.StopFakes.gov .

* For more information about registering trademarks and patents (both in the U.S. as well as in foreign countries), contact the US Patent and Trademark Office (USPTO) at: 1-800-786-9199.

* For more information about registering for copyright protection in the US, contact the US Copyright Office at: 1-202-707-5959.

* For more information about how to evaluate, protect, and enforce intellectual property rights and how these rights may be important for businesses, a free online training program is available at www.stopfakes.gov .

* For US small and medium-size companies, the Department of Commerce offers a "SME IP Advisory Program" available through the American Bar Association that provides one hour of free IP legal advice for companies with concerns in Brazil, China, Egypt, India, Russia, and . For details and to register, visit: http://www.abanet.org/intlaw/intlproj/iprprogram_consultation.html

* For information on obtaining and enforcing intellectual property rights and market-specific IP Toolkits visit: www.StopFakes.gov This site is linked to the USPTO website for registering trademarks and patents (both in the U.S. as well as in foreign countries), the U.S. Customs & Border Protection website to record registered trademarks and copyrighted works (to assist customs in blocking imports of IP-infringing products) and allows you to register for Webinars on protecting IP.

DUE DILIGENCE

All U.S. companies are advised to exercise due diligence before doing business in Zambia. The Embassy has the capacity to provide limited information about local companies when requested through a U.S. Department of Commerce district office, or when contacted directly by a U.S. company. Local attorneys or business consultants can provide more comprehensive assistance in determining the bona fides of a prospective business partner.

LOCAL PROFESSIONAL SERVICES

A number of professional service providers are available to U.S. companies. A list of attorneys can be found on the Embassy website: http://zambia.usembassy.gov

Other resources are:

Zambia Institute of Chartered accountants: http:// www.zica.co.zm

Zambia Institute of Marketing: http:// www.zim.com.zm

National Construction Council of Zambia: http:// www.ncc.org.zm

WEB RESOURCES

Zambia Development Agency: http://www.zda.org.zm/
Zambia Institute of Chartered accountants: http:// www.zica.co.zm
Zambia Institute of Marketing: http:// www.zim.com.zm
National Construction Council of Zambia: http:// www.ncc.org.zm
Website: www.postzambia.com
Website: www.times.co.zm
Website: www.daily-mail.co.zm

Website: www.radiophoenic.co.zm
Website: www.muvitv.com
Website: www.znbc.co.zm
Website: www.cacss.co.zm
Website: www.zift.org.zm

LEADING SECTORS FOR U.S. EXPORT AND INVESTMENT

ELECTRICAL POWER GENERATION, DISTRIBUTION, AND TRANSPORTATION EQUIPMENT

Electricity generation in Zambia is currently dominated by ZESCO Limited, a state-owned company with an installed capacity of 1,760 MW, about 10,000 miles of transmission lines, and about 15,600 miles of distribution lines. ZESCO has national and regional control centers. There are three private entities in the sector; Lunsemfwa Hydro Power (48MW), Copperbelt Energy Corporation (80MW) and Northwestern Energy Company (10 MVA). Lunsemfwa sells into the grid and Copperbelt Energy supplies power to the mines and is building Zambia's second interconnect with DR Congo. Northwestern supplies electricity to Lumwana Mine in Northwest Province.

SUB-SECTOR BEST PROSPECTS

* Electrical power systems
* Electrical power transmission equipment
* Hydro electrical generators
* Turbines
* Alternative energy systems
* Conventional energy systems
* Engineering services
* Power plant personnel training equipment

OPPORTUNITIES

Given that a large portion of Sub-Saharan Africa's water resources pass through Zambia, there is significant untapped hydropower potential to not only meet domestic demand but to export to Eastern and Southern African countries. Zambia is connected to the Southern African Power Pool and has plans to connect to the East African Power Pool. Domestic demand often exceeds domestic production due to maintenance and upgrades at major hydropower facilities and brown outs are relatively common.

There may be opportunities for U.S. companies to invest in large and small-scale energy generation and distribution projects, particularly those that supply electricity to manufacturers, mining companies, and farming blocs. New projects at Itezhi Tezhi, Kalungwishi, Mambilima, and Batoka may present opportunities to U.S. exporters. There is also a market for small-scale power generating equipment, such as solar panels and diesel-powered generators for household or commercial use.

In 2010 the GRZ raised ZESCO's electricity rates 25.6 percent as part of a commitment to raise rates to long-term cost recovery levels by the end of 2010. This could make energy generation projects more attractive to private investors. New incentives for

investors in energy sector also include provisions to carry forward tax losses for ten years instead of the five-year limit given to other companies.

Web Resources

Website: www.zda .org.zm

MINING AND MINERAL PROCESSING EQUIPMENT

The mining sector has played a leading role in the development of the economy. Zambia's mining sector suffered from the decline in world metals prices in 2008/early 2009. During this period, several mining companies shut down operations and others scaled back their investments. However, the sharp increase in global copper prices in mid-2009 resulted in the re-opening some closed mines and substantial new investment in the sector. Although the closure created unemployment, there remains a shortage of locally available skilled labor in the sector.

Sub-Sector Best Prospects

* Mining equipment
* Mineral exploration
* Operations/maintenance services
* Transportation services
* Security/safety equipment
* Trucks
* Pollution control

Opportunities

All mining companies are required by law to upgrade their mining equipment, particularly smelters, to conform Zambia's mining sector to international regulations and UK and U.S. environmental standards by 2015.

Despite problems within the sector, U.S. companies may find ample local interest in environmentally friendly smelting equipment as well as tunneling and haulage systems. Companies are also likely to continue with plans to replace machinery, equipment, and vehicles. Opportunities also exist for uranium production.

Given global mineral price volatility, the timing may be appropriate for mineral exploration activities, particularly technologies that bring down the cost of extraction.

Mine operators, especially of semi-precious and precious stone mines, continue to report that theft is a constraint to profitability. In this regard, there may be demand for more effective security equipment.

Web Resources

http://www.zda.org.zm

FOOD PROCESSING AND PACKAGING

The Zambian Government has several investment zones (Multi-Facility Economic Zones) to stimulate the manufacturing sector, including food processing.

Sub-Sector Best Prospects

* Foods – processed

* Food processing/packaging equipment

* Used/Reconditioned equipment

Opportunities

Local production is currently small and regional demand for processed food is being met mostly by South African firms. Zambia's landlocked location may not make it an ideal candidate for export to the United States or Europe, but may present export opportunities to neighboring DR Congo, Tanzania, Malawi, Mozambique, Namibia, Zimbabwe, and Angola. Demand is likely to increase for food processing equipment such as boilers, chillers, refrigerators, evaporative condensers, and processors, and for packaging and labeling equipment.

Web Resources

http:// www.zda .org.zm

TOURISM INFRASTRUCTURE SERVICES

Tourism opportunities abound with Zambia's 19 national parks and 34 game management areas as well as the 23 million hectares devoted to the conservation of animals. After significant growth in the past few years, the sector recorded a 23 percent

decline in tourist arrivals in 2009 due to the global economic crisis Tourism infrastructure investment has concentrated on the town of Livingstone, home of Victoria Falls, which now receives direct flights from Johannesburg. Tourism picked up in 2010, although final figures are not yet available.

Government has identified tourism development as a central pillar in its strategy to diversify the economy away from an over-reliance on the extractive industries. However, the sector remains constrained by inadequate road infrastructure, limited and costly domestic transportation, relatively high cost of labor and running a business, and insufficient marketing and promotional activities. The country's efforts to market itself as a high-end tourist destination do not always succeed, given its frequent inability to provide services on par with its steep prices. Potential investors are often deterred by the high costs (in terms of time and money) of compliance with government regulations, including operating licenses.

Sub-Sector Best Prospects

* Travel/tourism services

* Tourism infrastructure services

* Hotel/restaurant equipment

* Transportation services

* Architectural/construction/engineering services

* Advertising services

* Franchising

* Management consulting services

OPPORTUNITIES

Prospects exist for investments in (or franchising of) mid-range accommodation, restaurants, car rental, recreational activities, and organized tours. Adventure and ecotourism also present opportunities. There may also be a demand for additional sporting and recreational facilities in Livingstone.

The Zambian Government intends to develop further the tourism sector in Livingstone, which already enjoys VAT free status. The GRZ also plans to develop the —Northern Circuitll of waterfalls as well as the Kasaba Bay area of Lake Tanganyika in Northern Zambia into a full-service tourist destination. The GRZ has also expressed an interest in further developing Kafue National Park to make it more accessible to visitors to Livingstone. Lusaka and Livingstone have become popular conference destinations in recent years. There are many investment opportunities for reasonably priced conference facilities, services, and accommodation. There is also demand for corporate, short-term housing that meets international standards.

To promote Zambia abroad, Government will refund up to 15 percent of expenses related to filming movies in Zambia.

WEB RESOURCES

http:// www.zda .org.zm

TELECOMMUNICATIONS EQUIPMENT

Although more than 97 percent of the telephone exchanges are automatic, telecommunication infrastructure remains inadequate especially in rural areas. The Information and Communications Technology (ICT) Bill of 2009 repealed the Telecommunications Act 1994 and the Radio Communications Act 1994 to which transformed the Communications Authority of Zambia (CAZ) to the Zambia Information and Communications Technology Authority (ZICTA). The GRZ privatized 75 percent of government-owned ZAMTEL and liberalized the international gateway in 2010.

SUB-SECTOR BEST PROSPECTS

* Telecommunications equipment

* Telecommunications services

* Telecommunications distribution equipment

* Satellite/microwave equipment

* Broadcasting/receiving equipment

* Audio/video equipment

OPPORTUNITIES

Given high costs as well as unreliable and slow bandwidths associated with Internet connectivity in Zambia, 3G mobile phone technology that provides reasonably priced and efficient Internet access is likely to be well received in both urban and rural areas, particularly if coverage could be expanded utilizing new CDMA technology or something comparable.

WEB RESOURCES

Website: www.zda.org.zm

ROAD, RAIL CONSTRUCTION

Zambia has weak transportation infrastructure, which significantly increases the cost of doing business in Zambia. The railway has the potential to be a dominant mode of transport for heavy goods but is in need of substantial upgrades and improvements in efficiency.

SUB-SECTOR BEST PROSPECTS

Architectural/construction/engineering services

Building products

Construction equipment

Railroad equipment

Used/reconditioned equipment

OPPORTUNITIES

Export opportunities exist for the sale of railway wagons, road construction equipment, and engineering services. Investment opportunities may exist for the establishment of a reliable local construction company that has a reputation for accountability and quality. Changes to the Zambian procurement system may entail greater transparency and efficiency, leveling the playing field in an area that had been marred by allegations of corruption. There is a 60 percent increase in the 2011 national budget allocation to road building compared to 2010.

WEB RESOURCES

Website: www.zda.org.zm

TRANSPORTATION SERVICES AND EQUIPMENT

SUB-SECTOR BEST PROSPECTS

* Aviation services
* Insurance services
* Leasing services
* Operations/maintenance services
* Transportation services
* Aircraft/parts
* Airport/ground support equipment
* Trucks, trailers, busses
* Vehicles

OPPORTUNITIES

New entrants to the commercial airline industry, including Zambezi Airlines, may entail leasing opportunities in Zambia for U.S. companies.

The railway sector is run down and undergoing restructuring. Passenger train travel is unreliable and uncomfortable. The GRZ commissioned the 27 kilometer Chipata-Mchinji Railway, connecting the eastern border with Malawi through Nacala Port in Mozambique in August 2010. Other projects include new railway lines from the mining town of Chingola to Solwezi in Northwestern and from Solwezi connecting to the Benguela Railway Line in Angola through to Lobito Bay and a railway line from the farming and mining district of Mumbwa of Central Province connecting to Lusaka.

There are investment opportunities in providing transportation services to the mining, manufacturing, and tourism sectors.

WEB RESOURCES

http://www.zda.org.zm

HEALTH CARE SERVICES

Weak health care service delivery, poor infrastructure, and a lack of specialized equipment are some of the major problems facing public hospitals and clinics countrywide. The GRZ has increased its budget for purchasing essential drugs and medical supplies. Patients are sometimes evacuated to South Africa or India even for treatable ailments due to lack of equipment and high quality health care services.

The government purchases drugs through the Health Ministry's procurement office and the Zambia Public Procurement Authority (ZPPA). The ZPPA issues tenders for supply and delivery of drugs in bulk. Successful bidders deliver the drugs to Medical Stores Limited, a government owned entity, which stores and distributes the products. Some medications are procured by donors directly, in consultation with Ministry of Health.

Sub-Sector Best Prospects

* Healthcare services

* Insurance services

* Dental equipment

* Pharmaceuticals

* Medical equipment

Opportunities

There are few companies providing international medical insurance. This may be an area where U.S. companies can participate. Export opportunities abound for affordable medical equipment, supplies, and medicine.

Web Resources

http:// www.zda.org.zm

http://www.moh.gov.zom

AGRICULTURAL SECTORS OPPORTUNITIES

AGRICULTURAL EQUIPMENT

Agriculture is at the core of the Zambian Government's strategy for rural development and poverty reduction. Only about 15% of Zambia's arable land is currently cultivated. GRZ investment in the national road network and rural feeder roads could create additional opportunities for agricultural growth. Rising global food and commodity prices, as well as Zambia's relatively weak Kwacha, make Zambian exports more competitive and create opportunities for investment and trade. As part of its agricultural development plan, the government is setting aside significant tracts of land to develop commercial farm blocks to attract large-scale private investment into the industry. The Nansanga Block in Central Province was the first block to be put out for tender in December 2010.

Investment and export opportunities are hampered by the GRZ's intervention in the market through export and import bans on specific crops from time to time, a restrictive policy environment on genetically modified crops, and inefficient fertilizer subsidy programs.

Sub-Sector Best Prospects

* Agricultural machinery and equipment

* Autos/light trucks

* Commercial fishing equipment

* Forestry/woodworking machinery

* Automotive parts/service equipment

* Leasing services

OPPORTUNITIES

There is increasing demand for agricultural equipment, ranging from new and used tractors, harvesters, land clearing equipment, and irrigation devices. New farming blocks such as the proposed 155,000 hectare Nansanga Farming Block in Serenje District will create opportunities for exports of U.S. agricultural equipment. Currently, several USAID projects focus on strengthening links within Zambia's agricultural value chain by improving private sector delivery of extension services.

WEB RESOURCES

http://www.znfu.org.zm

http:// www.zda.org.zm

AGRICULTURAL CHEMICALS

In previous years the Zambian Government has directed much of its agricultural budget to a highly politicized and inefficient fertilizer support program, utilizing two companies for distribution. The GRZ is piloting a new system whereby the government provides eligible farmers with vouchers with which to purchase fertilizer from any vendor. This should introduce a measure of competition into the market and stimulate growth in an otherwise undeveloped sector.

SUB-SECTOR BEST PROSPECTS

* Synthetic fertilizers and other growth agents

* Pesticides

* Fertilizer components

OPPORTUNITIES

U.S. companies could supply fertilizers and agriculture chemicals to commercial farmers as well as to local fertilizer producers and retailers. Given high transportation costs, it might be difficult to remain competitive with South African importers on direct exports for fertilizer. U.S. investors may wish to consider investing in local production and/or distribution.

WEB RESOURCES

http://www.zda.org.zm

AGRICULTURAL EXTENSION SERVICES

The Zambian Government provides extension services to farmers, but this program has been constrained by inadequate funding levels. There continues to be strong need for technical advice on inputs, soil maintenance, crop management, marketing, and storage.

Currently most cooperatives do not provide extension services, but only serve as a purchasing agent for government subsidized fertilizer.

SUB-SECTOR BEST PROSPECTS

* Agricultural services
* Marketing services
* Education/training
* Veterinary services

OPPORTUNITIES

There are investment opportunities for affordable extension services in virtually every agricultural sub-sector, particularly given the interest in diversifying the economy, improving productivity, and expanding into more complicated crops, livestock, and fisheries.

WEB RESOURCES

http://www.zda.org.zm

SEED

As the Zambian Government introduces greater openness to its fertilizer support program and decreases its presence in the inputs area of the agricultural value chain, industry experts anticipate increased competition and investment within the seed sector.

SUB-SECTOR BEST PROSPECTS

* Agricultural seed
* Agricultural services
* Marketing services
* Education/training

OPPORTUNITIES

Due to rigid import requirements for agricultural seed (including the very restrictive regulatory environment in place for genetically modified organisms), the Zambian Government encourages potential investors to engage in local seed production. Local seed producers have export opportunities within the region.

WEB RESOURCES

http://www.zda.org.zm

AQUACULTURE

This sector is largely undeveloped in Zambia, although there is growing interest due to reports of overfishing in Zambia's rivers and lakes. Currently, small-scale traders export fish to neighboring countries.

SUB-SECTOR BEST PROSPECTS

* Commercial fishing equipment

* Agricultural services

OPPORTUNITIES

With an abundance of water resources and excess market demand for fish and fish protein, there is no shortage of opportunities within this sector, particularly with regard to commercial fish farming. To be profitable, it must be approached intensively, with heavy stocking densities, sophisticated management, specialized (imported) feeds, and reliable sources of electricity. U.S. companies not interested in investing locally may choose instead to provide professional services and/or inputs.

WEB RESOURCES

http://www.zda.org.zm

TRADE REGULATIONS, CUSTOMS AND STANDARDS

IMPORT TARIFFS

Customs valuation is ad valorem on a Cost Insurance and Freight (CIF) basis. A small number of goods may be imported duty-free. These include medicines, pharmaceuticals, veterinary supplies, medical equipment, computer parts, chemicals in bulk, fertilizers, and seeds. Most goods fall into one of three tariff bands: 5 percent (selected raw materials, and capital equipment); 15 percent (intermediate goods); or 25 percent (final products). Duty on productive machinery for agriculture and mining is zero percent.

TRADE BARRIERS

The Zambian Government frequently pronounces import and export bans on agricultural staples in its efforts to ensure domestic supply. It also maintains a de facto ban on agricultural products with genetically modified content through very restrictive legislation and regulations, and places additional import duties on selected items, including vegetable cooking oils and soaps, and export taxes on copper concentrates and cotton seed.

In its Sixth National Development Plan (2011-2015) released in February, the GRZ commits to adhering to rules-based and predictable trade policies, and some government ministries have expressed a new openness to exploring agricultural biotechnology as a way to increase agricultural production, food security, and rural economic growth.

Administrative corruption may be the most serious non-tariff barrier, particularly as it relates to government procurement. Other non-trade barriers include intellectual property infringement, preferential treatment of state-owned enterprises, and an overly cumbersome—and often arbitrary and non-transparent—regulatory environment.

For additional analytical, business and investment opportunities information, please contact Global Investment & Business Center, USA at (202) 546-2103. Fax: (202) 546-3275. E-mail: rusric@erols.com

IMPORT REQUIREMENTS AND DOCUMENTATION

In general, the Zambian Government does not require import licenses. Certification, however, is required to import meat (certification available from the Veterinary Department), plants and seeds (Mount Makulu Research Station), food and drugs (Ministry of Health), and firearms and ammunition (Zambia Police).

U.S. EXPORT CONTROLS

There are no sanctions against Zambia. The U.S. Government requires export licenses for products related to national security, particularly dual-use technology that has commercial and military or proliferation application. Other items that the U.S. Government regulates for export include defense articles, nuclear materials, and

controlled substances. The U.S. Government controls exports on a case-by-case basis, examining the following factors: the destination, the end-user, the product, and its end-use. The majority of exports which do require a license are either controlled on the Commerce Control List (CCL), administered by the Commerce Department, or the U.S. Munitions List (USML), administered by the State Department.

For more information on export controls, please visit the following sites:

http://www.dtic.mil/dtic/stinfo/exportcontrol.html

http://www.export.gov/regulation/exp_001498.asp

http://www.export.gov/regulation/exp_defense_trade_controls.asp

http://www.bis.doc.gov/licensing/exportingbasics.htm

http://www.treas.gov/offices/enforcement/ofac/articles/ticupdt.pdf

http://www.access.gpo.gov/bis/ear/ear_data.html#ccl

http://www.pmddtc.state.gov/

TEMPORARY ENTRY

Visitors are generally permitted to enter the country with goods for their own use. When a visitor's motor vehicle is not covered by a valid carnet, Customs will issue a customs import permit (CIP). For goods not intended for the visitor's own use, permission must be acquired from the Commissioner of Customs. Prior to importation, persons intending to import such goods should seek authority in writing, detailing the goods, value, purposes for importing, and duration of stay in Zambia. The Commissioner will in turn indicate the conditions for importation, which may include a refundable monetary security pending exportation after expiry.

LABELING AND MARKING REQUIREMENTS

Imported food products must have English-language labels that detail ingredients and shelf life of products. If inadequately labeled, these products may be confiscated and destroyed. Pharmaceutical products must also be labeled in English, detailing ingredients, recommended dosage, shelf life, and any cautionary notes.

PROHIBITED AND RESTRICTED IMPORTS

Zambian law prohibits the importation of indecent, obscene, or objectionable material, as well as goods produced wholly or in part by prison labor. Regulations related to the importation and transportation of pharmaceuticals are relatively strict. Travelers are strongly encouraged to carry their prescription drugs and medications in original labeled containers, as well as the written prescription from their physician. Travelers who cannot get a doctor's note for their over-the-counter medications, including some cold medicines, must leave them behind or risk arrest.

CUSTOMS REGULATIONS AND CONTACT INFORMATION

It is against both Zambian and U.S. law to buy, possess or transport animals or animal products, such as warthog tusks, tortoise shell, rhino horn, elephant ivory or any items made out of these materials. In Zambia, penalties range from large fines to mandatory five-year prison sentences. The Zambian Wildlife Authority has screeners at international ports of entry and will prosecute offenders to the fullest extent of the law. While many of these items are sold in open markets particularly aimed at foreign tourists, it remains the responsibility of the customer to ensure that he/she is not purchasing a prohibited item.

Mr. Muyangwa Muyangwa

Commissioner – Customs

Zambia Revenue Authority

Kalambo Road

Revenue House

P. O. Box 35710

Lusaka, Zambia

Tel: 260-211-223760

Fax: 260-211-221923

STANDARDS

STANDARDS ORGANIZATIONS

The Zambia Bureau of Standards (ZABS) intends to renew its standards legislation, which is generally outdated. Several companies are attempting to become ISO 9000 certified.

NIST NOTIFY U.S. SERVICE

Member countries of the World Trade Organization (WTO) are required under the Agreement on Technical Barriers to Trade (TBT Agreement) to report to the WTO all proposed technical regulations that could affect trade with other Member countries. Notify U.S. is a free, web-based e-mail subscription service that offers an opportunity to review and comment on proposed foreign technical regulations that can affect your access to international markets. Register online at: http://www.nist.gov/notifyus/

CONFORMITY ASSESSMENT

ZABS has acquired modern equipment with support from the European Union for the Metrology Laboratory that provides calibration services.

PRODUCT CERTIFICATION

Manufacturing companies use in-house laboratories to certify products according to standards set by ZABS. ZABS utilizes portable electronic equipment to clear electronic goods at some ports of entry.

ZABS has signed memorandums of understanding with ASTM International (2004), Malawi Bureau of Standards, and the Standards of Association of Zimbabwe.

ACCREDITATION

ZABS is the accreditation body in Zambia.

PUBLICATION OF TECHNICAL REGULATIONS

The Zambia Development Agency issues a monthly publication, "ZDA Newsletter," containing updates on technical regulations, in collaboration with ZABS. The —Zambia Gazettell also provides information related to new legislation.

LABELING AND MARKING

English-language labeling is required for all imported food and pharmaceutical products.

CONTACTS

Mr. Mataa Mukelabai,

Director

Zambia Bureau of Standards (ZABS)

Lechwe House, Freedom Way

P. O. Box 50259

Lusaka, Zambia

Tel: 260-211 231 385

Fax: 260-211 238 483

Email: zabs@zamnet.zm

Mr. Anthony Bwembya

Acting Registrar and Chief Executive Officer

Patents and Companies Registration Agency

Mwayi House, Haile Selassie Avenue

P. O. Box 32075

Lusaka, Zambia

Tel: 260-211 255 151

Fax: 260-211 255 426

Ms. Esnat Mwape

Director General

Pharmaceutical Regulatory Authority

Plot 6903, Tuleteka Road

P. O. Box 31890

Lusaka, Zambia

Tel: 260-211 220 429

Fax: 260-211 230 458

Email: pharmacy@pra.gov.zm

TRADE AGREEMENTS

Zambia belongs to the 19-member Common Market for Eastern and Southern Africa (COMESA), which allows for preferential tariff duties between member states. In 2008, COMESA agreed to harmonize its FTA with that of the East African Community (EAC) and the Southern African Development Community (SADC). In June 2009, COMESA launched a customs union. Zambia also belongs to the 14-member SADC, which established an FTA in 2008.

Negotiations with the European Union over the Economic Partnership Agreement are ongoing. To ensure that there is no disruption in trade, the European Commission devised interim bilateral agreements, known as Framework Economic Partnership Agreements, which Zambia initialed on December 5, 2007.

Zambia is also eligible for trade benefits under the African Growth and Opportunity Act (AGOA), which provides duty-free/quota-free access to the U.S. market for most goods, including textile and apparel.

WEB RESOURCES

COMESA: http://www.comesa.int

SADC: http://www.sadc.int

U.S. Embassy Consular website: http://zambia.usembassy.gov/zambia/consular.html

INVESTMENT CLIMATE

OPENNESS TO FOREIGN INVESTMENT

The GRZ actively seeks foreign investment through the Zambia Development Agency (ZDA), which was established in January 2007 through the consolidation of a number of trade and investment promotion entities into a one-stop resource for international investors interested in investing in Zambia.

The major laws affecting investment include:

--The Zambia Development Agency Act of 2006, which offers a wide range of incentives in the form of allowances, exemptions and concessions to companies. The Act also provides for investment threshold that investors have to meet to qualify for fiscal and non-fiscal incentives.

--The Companies Act of 1994, which governs the registration of companies in Zambia.

--General incentives to investors in various sectors are provided in various legislations that govern the Zambia Revenue Authority (ZRA), including the Customs and Excise Act, Income Tax Act of 1966 and the Value Added Tax Act of 1995.

--The Employment Act Cap 268 is Zambia's basic employment law and provides for required minimum employment contractual terms.

--The Immigration and Deportation Act Cap 123 regulates the entry into and residency in Zambia of visitors, expatriates, and immigrants.

The Zambian judicial system has a mixed record in upholding the sanctity of contracts. The judicial process is lengthy and inefficient. Many magistrates lack experience in commercial matters.

There is no distinction in Zambian law between foreign and domestic investors. Investors are free to invest in any sector of the economy and are entitled to incentives per the ZDA Act of 2006 (discussed later in this report). In the privatization process, foreign investors are eligible to bid on state-owned companies. Non-Zambians may also invest in the Lusaka Stock Exchange without restriction and on terms comparable to those Zambians receive. Companies seeking licenses or concessions or investors bidding for privatized companies are encouraged to seek local partners, although it is not clear how such commitments are weighed when decisions are made by the ZDA.

The ZDA board screens all investments for which incentives are requested and usually makes its decision within 30 days. The reviews appear routine and non-discriminatory, and applicants have the right to appeal investment board decisions. The ZDA board is comprised of sixteen members, including representatives from various government and private sector stakeholders

An investment can be subject to review for determination of sector or value and filing is mandatory. An investment application is subjected to screening mechanism, among other things, to determine the extent to which the proposed investment will lead to the creation of employment opportunities and the development of human resources; the degree to which the project is export oriented; the impact the proposed investment is likely to have on the environment and, where necessary, the measures proposed to deal with an adverse environmental consequence in accordance with the Environmental Protection and Pollution Control Act; the possibility of the transfer of technology; and any other considerations that the Board considers appropriate.

The possible outcome of the review could be prohibition or imposition of additional requirements, especially where adverse environmental issues arise. The reviews are generally completed in a timely manner.

An investor may, within 14 days of receiving a Board decision, can appeal the decision to the Minister of Finance and National Planning. Within 30 days of receiving the appeal, the Minister may confirm, set aside or amend the decision of the Board. An investor dissatisfied with the decision of the Minister, may within 30 days appeal to the High Court of Zambia against the decision. No negative reports have been received from U.S. firms concerning this process.

The ZDA Act does not discriminate against foreign investors, and all sectors are open to both local and foreign investors. The GRZ plans to issue a Statutory Instrument in the first quarter of 2011 that will give preference of procurement of Government contracts to Zambian-owned companies. The Citizens Economic Empowerment Commission is working with the Zambia Public Procurement Authority to implement preferential procurement that would support Zambian-owned based firms.

Measure	Year	Index/Ranking
TI Corruption Index	2010	3.0
Heritage Economic Freedom	2010	58.0
World Bank Doing Business	2011	76
MCC Gov't Effectiveness	2011	0.23 / 69%
MCC Rule of Law	2011	0.45 / 77%
MCC Control of Corruption	2011	0.27 / 77%
MCC Fiscal Policy	2011	-2.0 / 58%
MCC Trade Policy	2011	82.4 / 95%
MCC Regulatory Quality	2011	0.24 / 69%
MCC Business Start Up	2011	0.969 / 81%
MCC Land Rights Access	2011	0.631 / 55%
MCC Natural Resource Mgmt	2011	64.40 / 58%

CONVERSION AND TRANSFER POLICIES

There are no restrictions on converting or transferring funds associated with an investment (including remittances of investment capital, earnings, loan repayments, lease payments) into freely usable currency and at a legal market clearing rate.

Investors are free to repatriate capital investments as well as dividends, management fees, interest, profit, technical fees, and royalties. Foreign nationals can also transfer and/or remit wages earned in Zambia without difficulty. There is no exchange control in Zambia for anyone doing business as either a resident or non-resident. Additionally, there are no restrictions on non-cash transactions.

Over-the-counter cash conversion of the local currency, the Kwacha, into foreign currency is restricted to a USD 5,000 maximum per transaction for account holders and USD 1,000 for non-account holders. There are no changes or plans to change remittance policies affecting foreign exchange for investment remittance.

EXPROPRIATION AND COMPENSATION

Investments may only be expropriated by an act of Parliament relating to the specific property expropriated. Although the ZDA Act states that compensation must be at a fair market value, the method for determining fair market value is ill-defined. Compensation is convertible at the current exchange rate. The ZDA Act also protects investors from being adversely affected by any subsequent changes to the Investment Act of 1993 for seven years after initial investment.

Leasehold land, which is granted under 99-year leases, may revert to the government if it is ruled to be undeveloped after a certain amount of time (generally five years). Land title is sometimes questioned and land is re-titled to other owners.

There has been no expropriatory action in the recent past or policy shifts which would lead the Mission to believe there may be expropriatory actions in the near future. The GRZ does not discriminate against investors or U.S. investments, companies or representatives in expropriation.

DISPUTE SETTLEMENT

There have been relatively few investment disputes involving U.S. companies since the Movement for Multi-party Democracy (MMD) government took office in 1991. The Zambian Investment Code stipulates that claimants must first file internal dispute settlements with the Zambian High Court. Failing that, the parties may go to international arbitration, which the state recognizes as binding. Zambia is a member of the International Center for the Settlement of Investment Disputes (ICSID) and the United Nations Commission of International Trade Law (UNCITRAL).

Previous disputes involved delayed payments to U.S. companies from state-owned enterprises for goods and services and the delayed deregistration of a U.S.-owned aircraft that was leased to a Zambian airline company that went bankrupt.

The courts in Zambia are somewhat independent, but contractual and property rights enforcement is weak, and final court decisions can take a prohibitively long time. The Foreign Judgments (Reciprocal Enforcement) Act Chapter 76 of the Laws of Zambia (cited as the Act) makes provision for the enforcement in Zambia of judgments given in foreign countries which accord reciprocal treatment. The registration of a foreign judgment is not automatic. In 2010 a Lusaka High Court Judge ruled that a London civil

judgment against former president Chiluba could not be registered in a Zambian court despite precedent.

There is no bankruptcy law in Zambia. Secured interests in property are possible and recognized but fairly rare.

The Zambian Arbitration Act No. 19 of 2000 applies to both domestic and international arbitration and is based on the UNCITRAL Model Law. Arbitration agreements must be in writing. Parties may appoint an arbitrator of any nationality, gender or professional qualifications. Foreign lawyers

For additional analytical, business and investment opportunities information, please contact Global Investment & Business Center, USA at (202) 546-2103. Fax: (202) 546-3275. E-mail: rusric@erols.com

cannot be used to represent parties in domestic or international arbitrations taking place in Zambia. There are no facilities that provide online arbitration, although there is an arbitral institution, the Zambia Institute of Arbitrators. Arbitration awards are enforced in the High Court of Zambia, and judgments enforcing or denying enforcement of an award can be appealed to the Supreme Court. On average, it takes about 14 weeks to enforce an arbitration award rendered in Zambia, from filing an application to a writ of execution attaching assets. It takes about 18 weeks to enforce a foreign award. Contracts involving state entities commonly rely upon arbitration as a dispute resolution tool.

Zambia is Party to the Convention on the Recognition and Enforcement of Foreign Arbitral Awards of 1958, which entered into force on 7th June 1959 and Party to the Convention of the Settlement of Investment Disputes between States and Nationals of Other States of other States of 1965 and entered into force on 14 October 1966. These are being enforced through the Investment Disputes Convention Act Cap 42 of the Laws of Zambia.

PERFORMANCE REQUIREMENTS AND INCENTIVES

The GRZ strives to be consistent with Trade Related Investment Measures (TRIMs) requirements and generally abides by the WTO's TRIMs obligation.

The ZDA Act of 2006 offers a wide range of incentives in the form of allowances, exemptions and concessions for companies, which are applied uniformly to both local and foreign investments. Investors who invest at least USD 10 million in an identified sector or product are entitled to negotiation with the government for additional incentives other than what they might already qualify for under the ZDA Act.

Investors who invest at least USD500,000 in a Multi Facility Economic Zone (MFEZ) and /or in a sector or product provided as for as a priority sector or product under the ZDA Act, in addition to being entitled to the general incentives, are entitled to:

--Zero percent tax rate on dividends for five years from year of first declaration of dividends

--Zero percent tax on profits for five years from the first year profits are made. For year six to eight, only 50 percent of profits are taxable and year nine and ten, only 75 percent of profits are taxable.

--Zero percent import duty on raw materials, capital goods, machinery including trucks and specialized motor vehicles for five years.

--Deferment of VAT on machinery and equipment including trucks and specialized motor vehicles.

Priority sectors and products under the ZDA Act include:

--Agriculture

--Manufacturing

--Mining

--Tourism

Priority products are:

--Floriculture

--Horticulture

--Processed foods

--Beverages and stimulants

--Production and processing of textiles

--Manufacturing of engineering products

--Mini-hydro stations

--Education and skills training

--Production of fertilizers, cement, leather and timber products

General Incentives and Taxation: Foreign investors receive national treatment under Zambia's tax system. Income from farming is taxed at a rate of 15 percent, below the standard corporate tax rate of 35 percent. In addition, that portion of income determined by the Commissioner of Taxes to originate from the export of non-traditional products is taxed at a rate of 15 percent (traditional exports include copper, cobalt, lead, zinc, gold, and silver).

Capital Allowances: Manufacturing, mining, and hotel structures qualify for a depreciation allowance of five percent per year plus an initial allowance of ten percent of the cost in the year in which the building was first used. Equipment, machinery, and plants used exclusively for farming, manufacturing, and tourism qualify for a depreciation allowance of 50 percent. Capital expenditures on farm improvements qualify for a farm improvement allowance of 20 percent per year for the first five years after improvement. Capital expenditure allowance on the growing of coffee, tea, bananas, citrus fruits, or similar plants qualifies for a development allowance of ten percent per year through the first year of production. A farm work allowance of 100 percent applies to farmland expenditures such as stumping; clearing; preventing soil erosion; drilling boreholes, wells, and water conservation; and aerial or geographical surveys. The depreciation allowance for non-commercial vehicles is 20 percent (straight-line depreciation). Expenditure on other assets used in creating income qualifies for a depreciation allowance of 25 percent (straight-line depreciation).

Although performance requirements are not imposed, authorities expect commitments made in applications for investment licenses to be fulfilled. No requirements currently exist for local content, equity, financing, employment, or technology transfers. Government does not impose ‗offset' requirements or impose conditions on permission to invest in specific geographical area or local content, but investors are encouraged to employ local nationals.

Government requires that all international firms licensed operating a domestic cellular telephone network offer ten percent of shares on the Lusaka Stock Exchange, per commitments made by agreement prior to entering the market. Investors are required to disclose proprietary information to ZDA as part of the regulatory approval process.

Work Permit Requirements: Notwithstanding the provisions of the Immigration and Deportation Act of 1994, a foreign national who invests a minimum of USD 250 thousand or equivalent in convertible currency is entitled to a self-employment permit and employment permits for up to five (5) expatriates. However, in practice some foreign companies have had difficulty securing these permits, especially smaller-scale investors.

Import restrictions are in force on poultry products and genetically modified products for environmental, health and security reasons. Import licensing is required for most agricultural products and Zambia does not currently apply trade sanctions. Food imports must satisfy the provisions of the Food and Drugs Act of September 1978 which requires packaging and labeling requirement to be in English. A consignment of assorted food products which were labeled in

Chinese were destroyed at Chirundu Border post for not meeting the packaging and labeling requirements.

RIGHT TO PRIVATE OWNERSHIP AND ESTABLISHMENT

Foreign and domestic private entities have a right to establish and own business enterprises and engage in all forms of remunerative activities, and no business ventures are reserved solely for the government. Although private entities may freely establish and dispose of interests in business enterprises, investment board approval is required to transfer an investment license for a given enterprise to a new owner. Private enterprises have occasionally complained that the playing field is not level when they compete with public enterprises for licenses or concessions.

PROTECTION OF PROPERTY RIGHTS

The ZDA Act assures investors that property rights shall be respected. Secured interests in property, both movable and real are recognized and enforced.

The ZDA Act provides for legal protection and facilitates acquisition and disposition of all property rights such as land, buildings and mortgages. Currently the ZDA is working with the Commissioner of Lands to develop a fast tracking system for identifying land for investment in the priority sectors.

The legal framework for trademark protection in Zambia is adequate. There are fines for revealing business proprietary information; however, they are not large enough to penalize disclosure adequately. Copyright protection is limited and does not cover computer applications. Enforcement of intellectual property rights is weak in Zambia, and courts have little experience with commercial litigation.

Zambia's patent laws conform to the requirements of the Paris Convention for the Protection of Industrial Property, to which Zambia is a signatory. It takes a minimum of four months to patent an item or process. Duplicative searches are not done, but patent awards may be appealed on grounds of infringement.

Zambia is a signatory to a number of international agreements on patents and intellectual property, including the World Intellectual Property Organization (WIPO), Paris Union, Bern Union, African Regional Industrial Property Organization (ARIPO), and the

Universal Copyright Convention of UNESCO. National laws are generally adequate in protecting intellectual property rights, and there recently has been effective enforcement against pirated musical and video recordings, cosmetics, as well as software. Small-scale trademark infringement occurs for some packaged goods through copied or deceptive packaging.

TRANSPARENCY OF REGULATORY SYSTEM

The government has made strides toward introducing transparent policies to foster competition, although complaints arise from time to time. Questions have arisen in recent years regarding the process of awarding Game Management Areas by the Zambia Wildlife Authority, the enforceability of existing mine development agreements, which gave mine owners the right to compensation if government failed to comply with agreed tax stability guarantees, and the fairness of competition between state-owned enterprises and private firms. In the agricultural sector, Zambian government interventions, through the purchase of maize (corn) at subsidized prices and the distribution of subsidized fertilizer, undercut the private sector's capacity to enter these markets. The unpredictability of import and export bans on commodities, especially maize, is a deterrent to private sector participation in commodity markets.

Labor laws provide for extremely generous severance pay, leave, and other benefits to workers, which can impede investment. Such rules do not apply to personnel hired on a short-term basis. As such, the vast majority of Zambian employees are hired on an informal or short-term basis.

Although the ZDA seeks to serve as a "one-stop shop" for investors, in practice red tape associated with licenses and permits presents problems for potential investors. In some cases, dozens of licenses are required to establish and run a business. The GRZ is working to streamline numerous licensing requirements and administrative procedures. The 2011 World Bank Doing Business Report ranked Zambia 76th out of 183 countries.

Proposed laws are usually not published in draft form for public comment. Opportunities for comment on proposed laws and regulations exist through trade associations such as the Zambia Chamber of Commerce and Industry (ZACCI), Zambia Association of Manufacturers (ZAM), Zambia Chamber of Mines and Zambia Business Forum.

Although the underpinnings of an efficient system to handle court disputes exist, Zambian courts are relatively inexperienced in the area of commercial litigation. This, coupled with the large number of pending commercial cases, keeps the regulatory system from being prompt and transparent. Some measures to promote resolution of disputes by mediation have been implemented in an attempt to clear the case backlog. The courts support alternative dispute resolution, including a mechanism for binding arbitration. In 2004, the High Court established a commercial division to adjudicate high-value claims. This fee-based system has accelerated resolution of such cases.

EFFICIENT CAPITAL MARKETS AND PORTFOLIO INVESTMENT

Government policies generally facilitate the free flow of financial resources to support the flow of resources in the product and factor market. Banking supervision and regulation by the Bank of Zambia (BoZ), the central bank, has improved over the past few years.

Improvements include revoking licenses of some insolvent banks, denying bailouts, limiting deposit protection, strengthening loan recovery efforts, and upgrading the training and incentives of bank supervisors. In 2010, the BoZ instituted overnight lending facilities to inject further liquidity into the market.

Although some improvements have been registered in recent years, credit to the private sector is expensive and readily available only for low-risk investments. One factor inhibiting lending is a culture of tolerating loan default, which many borrowers view as a minor transgression. In addition, high returns on government securities have historically encouraged commercial banks to invest heavily in government debt, to the exclusion of financing productive private sector investments. Banking officials acknowledge that they need to upgrade the risk assessment and credit management skills within their institutions in order to better serve borrowers. At the same time, they argue that widespread financial illiteracy limits borrowers‘ ability to access credit. Banks provide credit denominated in foreign currency only for investments aimed at producing goods for export. Banks provide services on a fee-based model, and banking charges are generally high. Home mortgages are available from several leading Zambian banks, although interest rates are still very high.

The 15-year old Lusaka Stock Exchange (LuSE) is structured to meet international recommendations for clearing and settlement system design and operations. The LuSE has offered trading in equity securities since its inception, and in March 1998, the LuSE became the official market for selling Zambian Government bonds. Investors intending to trade in a listed security or government bond are now mandated to trade via the LuSE. The market is regulated by the Securities Act of 1993 and enforced by the Securities and Exchange Commission of Zambia. The secondary trading of financial instruments in the market is very low or non-existent in some areas. At the end of 2010, 21 companies were listed on the LuSE.

There are no restrictions on foreign participation in the LuSE and foreigners may invest in stocks on the same terms as Zambians.

Zambia's largest banks include Zambia National Commercial Bank (Zanaco), Barclays Bank Zambia, Standard Chartered Bank Zambia, and Stanbic Zambia Limited. In 2009, Barclays Bank estimated total assets were USD 926,261with 450,611 depositors. The bank's loan portfolio has continued to grow and accounted for 36.6 percent of the total loans in the sector. Zanaco estimated total assets are USD 638,286 with 482,160 depositors. Zanaco's loan portfolio accounted for 44 percent of the total loans in the banking sector. The third largest bank, Stanbic Bank Zambia's estimated total assets are USD 396,164 with 344,257 depositors while loans accounted for 13.8 percent of the sector's total loans.

Although the banking system is generally sound, sector officials estimate that about 15 percent of the total sector loan portfolio is non-performing. In December 2010, the Bank of Zambia took possession of Zambia's sixth largest bank, Finance Bank Limited Zambia, the first time the BOZ has intervened in more than a decade. The Governor of the Central Bank announced that take-over was necessary due to serious breaches of the provisions of the Banking and Financial services Act and ongoing unsafe and unsound banking practices that compromised the viability of the bank and threatened to destabilize the sector.

Private firms are open to foreign investment through mergers and acquisitions. The Competition Consumer Protection Commission (CCPC) reviewed and handled 43 mergers and acquisitions in 2010, including Bharti Airtel's purchase of Zain/Celtel Zambia, the purchase through privatization of Zamtel by LAP Green, and the acquisition of Chevron's assets in Zambia by Engen Petroleum.

COMPETITION FROM STATE OWNED ENTERPRISES

There are few state-owned enterprises (SOEs) remaining in Zambia, and all have serious operational and management challenges. ZESCO Ltd is responsible for generation, transmission, and distribution of electricity in Zambia. Two private entities are contracted to supply electricity to some mines. Copperbelt Energy Corporation supplies electricity to mining companies on the Copperbelt while North-Western Energy Company supplies power to Lumwana (Equinox) Mine in Solwezi.

Private enterprises are allowed to compete with public enterprises under the same terms and conditions with respect to access to markets, credit and other business operations, such as licenses and supplies. Zambia has a pipeline of privately developed hydro-power projects, but few have attracted financing.

The SOEs are governed by Boards of Directors that are appointed by Government with consultations and participation of the private sector. The chief executive of the SOE reports to the Board Chairperson. In the event that the SOE declares dividends, these are paid to Ministry of Finance and National Planning. The Board Chairperson is informally obligated to consult with government officials before making decisions. Zambia does not have a Sovereign Wealth Fund.

Zambian SOE's are audited by the Auditor General's Office as required by law and using international reporting standards. The audited reports are submitted to the President for tabling in the National Assembly in accordance with the provisions of Article 121 of the Constitution of

Zambia and the Public Audit Act Cap 378 of the Laws of Zambia. The audits are carried annually, but delays in finalizing and publishing results are common.

CORPORATE SOCIAL RESPONSIBILITY

The concept of corporate social responsibility (CRS) has recently gained traction in Zambia. There is a general awareness of corporate social responsibility among both producers and consumers. Some local and foreign enterprises tend to follow generally accepted CSR principles, such as the OECD Guidelines for multinational enterprises while other foreign firms ignore complex issues such as labor rights, environmental protection, bribery, corruption and human rights. The firms who pursue CSR are viewed favorably by the government and the communities.

POLITICAL VIOLENCE

Zambia does not have a history of significant political violence. Infrequent student protests sometimes turn violent, but they are generally confined to small areas in and

around universities. The presidential by-election in October 2008 following the death of President Levy Mwanawasa was carried out peacefully and in accordance with the constitution. In December, a Lusaka High Court nullified a parliamentary by-election held Mufumbwe, Northwestern Province in April 2010 citing extreme violence, intimidation and destruction of property. Recent upticks in violence during by-elections are becoming a source of concern for the government and the general public. Presidential and parliamentary elections are scheduled to be held in 2011.

CORRUPTION

Corruption, including bribery, raises the costs and risks of doing business. Corruption has a corrosive impact on both market opportunities overseas for U.S. companies and the broader business climate. It also deters international investment, stifles economic growth and development, distorts prices, and undermines the rule of law.

It is important for U.S. companies, irrespective of their size, to assess the business climate in the relevant market in which they will be operating or investing, and to have an effective compliance program or measures to prevent and detect corruption, including foreign bribery. U.S. individuals and firms operating or investing in foreign markets should take the time to become familiar with the relevant anticorruption laws of both the foreign country and the United States in order to properly comply with them, and where appropriate, they should seek the advice of legal counsel.

The U.S. Government seeks to level the global playing field for U.S. businesses by encouraging other countries to take steps to criminalize their own companies' acts of corruption, including bribery of foreign public officials, by requiring them to uphold their obligations under relevant international conventions. A U. S. firm that believes a competitor is seeking to use bribery of a foreign public official to secure a contract should bring this to the attention of appropriate U.S. agencies, as noted below.

U.S. Foreign Corrupt Practices Act: In 1977, the United States enacted the Foreign Corrupt Practices Act (FCPA), which makes it unlawful for a U.S. person, and certain foreign issuers of securities, to make a corrupt payment to foreign public officials for the purpose of obtaining or retaining business for or with, or directing business to, any person. The FCPA also applies to foreign firms and persons who take any act in furtherance of such a corrupt payment while in the United States. For more detailed information on the FCPA, see the FCPA Lay-Person's Guide at: http://www.justice.gov/criminal/fraud/

Other Instruments: It is U.S. Government policy to promote good governance, including host country implementation and enforcement of anti-corruption laws and policies pursuant to their obligations under international agreements. Since enactment of the FCPA, the United States has been instrumental to the expansion of the international framework to fight corruption. Several significant components of this framework are the OECD Convention on Combating Bribery of Foreign Public Officials in International Business Transactions (OECD Antibribery Convention), the United Nations Convention against Corruption (UN Convention), the Inter-American Convention against Corruption (OAS Convention), the Council of Europe Criminal and Civil Law Conventions, and a growing list of U.S. free trade agreements. This country is party to [add instrument to which this country is party], but generally all countries prohibit the bribery and solicitation of their public officials.

OECD Antibribery Convention: The OECD Antibribery Convention entered into force in February 1999. As of December 2009, there are 38 parties to the Convention including the United States (see http://www.oecd.org/dataoecd/59/13/40272933.pdf). Major exporters China, India, and Russia are not parties, although the U.S. Government strongly endorses their eventual accession to the Convention. The Convention obligates the Parties to criminalize bribery of foreign public officials in the conduct of international business. The United States meets its international obligations under the OECD Antibribery Convention through the U.S. FCPA. Zambia is Party to the OECD Convention on Combating Bribery of Foreign Public Officials in International Business Transactions.

UN Convention: The UN Anticorruption Convention entered into force on December 14, 2005, and there are 143 parties to it as of December 2009 (see http://www.unodc.org/unodc/en/treaties/CAC/signatories.html). The UN Convention is the first global comprehensive international anticorruption agreement. The UN Convention requires countries to establish criminal and other offences to cover a wide range of acts of corruption. The UN Convention goes beyond previous anticorruption instruments, covering a broad range of issues ranging from basic forms of corruption such as bribery and solicitation, embezzlement, trading in influence to the concealment and laundering of the proceeds of corruption. The Convention contains transnational business bribery provisions that are functionally similar to those in the OECD Antibribery Convention and contains provisions on private sector auditing and books and records requirements. Other provisions address matters such as prevention, international cooperation, and asset recovery. Zambia is a Party to the Anticorruption Convention.

OAS Convention: In 1996, the Member States of the Organization of American States (OAS) adopted the first international anticorruption legal instrument, the Inter-American Convention against Corruption (OAS Convention), which entered into force in March 1997. The OAS Convention, among other things, establishes a set of preventive measures against corruption, provides for the criminalization of certain acts of corruption, including transnational bribery and illicit enrichment, and contains a series of provisions to strengthen the cooperation between its States Parties in areas such as mutual legal assistance and technical cooperation. As of December 2009, the OAS Convention has 33 parties (see http://www.oas.org/juridico/english/Sigs/b-58.html). Zambia is not Party to the OAS Convention.

Council of Europe Criminal Law and Civil Law Conventions: Many European countries are parties to either the Council of Europe (CoE) Criminal Law Convention on Corruption, the Civil Law Convention, or both. The Criminal Law Convention requires criminalization of a wide range of national and transnational conduct, including bribery, money-laundering, and account offenses. It also incorporates provisions on liability of legal persons and witness protection. The Civil Law Convention includes provisions on compensation for damage relating to corrupt acts, whistleblower protection, and validity of contracts, inter alia. The Group of States against Corruption (GRECO) was established in 1999 by the CoE to monitor compliance with these and related anti-corruption standards. Currently, GRECO comprises 46 member States (45 European countries and the United States). As of December 2009, the Criminal Law Convention has 42 parties and the Civil Law Convention has 34 (see www.coe.int/greco.) Zambia is not Party to the Council of Europe Conventions.

Free Trade Agreements: While it is U.S. Government policy to include anticorruption provisions in free trade agreements (FTAs) that it negotiates with its trading partners, the anticorruption provisions have evolved over time. The most recent FTAs negotiated now require trading partners to criminalize —active briberyll of public officials (offering bribes to any public official must be made a criminal offense, both domestically and trans-nationally) as well as domestic —passive briberyll (solicitation of a bribe by a domestic official). All U.S. FTAs may be found at the U.S. Trade Representative Website: http://www.ustr.gov/trade-agreements/free-trade-agreements . Zambia does not have a free trade agreement (FTA) with the United States.

Local Laws: U.S. firms should familiarize themselves with local anticorruption laws, and, where appropriate, seek legal counsel. While the U.S. Department of Commerce cannot provide legal advice on local laws, the Department's U.S. and Foreign Commercial Service can provide assistance with navigating the host country's legal system and obtaining a list of local legal counsel.

Assistance for U.S. Businesses: The U.S. Department of Commerce offers several services to aid U.S. businesses seeking to address business-related corruption issues. For example, the U.S. and Foreign Commercial Service can provide services that may assist U.S. companies in conducting their due diligence as part of the company's overarching compliance program when choosing business partners or agents overseas. The U.S. Foreign and Commercial Service can be reached directly through its offices in every major U.S. and foreign city, or through its Website at www.trade.gov/cs .

The Departments of Commerce and State provide worldwide support for qualified U.S. companies bidding on foreign government contracts through the Commerce Department's Advocacy Center and State's Office of Commercial and Business Affairs. Problems, including alleged corruption by foreign governments or competitors, encountered by U.S. companies in seeking such foreign business opportunities can be brought to the attention of appropriate U.S. government officials, including local embassy personnel and through the Department of Commerce Trade Compliance Center —Report A Trade Barrierll Website at tcc.export.gov/Report_a_Barrier/index.asp .

Guidance on the U.S. FCPA: The Department of Justice's (DOJ) FCPA Opinion Procedure enables U.S. firms and individuals to request a statement of the Justice Department's present enforcement intentions under the anti-bribery provisions of the FCPA regarding any proposed business conduct. The details of the opinion procedure are available on DOJ's Fraud Section Website at www.justice.gov/criminal/fraud/fcpa . Although the Department of Commerce has no enforcement role with respect to the FCPA, it supplies general guidance to U.S. exporters who have questions about the FCPA and about international developments concerning the FCPA. For further information, see the Office of the Chief Counsel for International Counsel, U.S. Department of Commerce, Website, at http://www.ogc.doc.gov/trans_anti_bribery.html . More general information on the FCPA is available at the Websites listed below.

Exporters and investors should be aware that generally all countries prohibit the bribery of their public officials, and prohibit their officials from soliciting bribes under domestic laws. Most countries are required to criminalize such bribery and other acts of corruption by virtue of being parties to various international conventions discussed above.

Public sector corruption, including bribery of public officials, remains a major challenge for U.S. firms operating in Zambia. Insert country specific corruption climate, enforcement, commitment and information about relevant anticorruption legislation.

Anti-Corruption Resources

Some useful resources for individuals and companies regarding combating corruption in global markets include the following:

* Information about the U.S. Foreign Corrupt Practices Act (FCPA), including a —Lay-Person's Guide to the FCPA‖ is available at the U.S. Department of Justice's Website at: http://www.justice.gov/criminal/fraud/fcpa .

* Information about the OECD Antibribery Convention including links to national implementing legislation and country monitoring reports is available at: http://www.oecd.org/department/0,3355,en_2649_34859_1_1_1_1_1,00.html . See also new Antibribery Recommendation and Good Practice Guidance Annex for companies: http://www.oecd.org/dataoecd/11/40/44176910.pdf

* General information about anticorruption initiatives, such as the OECD Convention and the FCPA, including translations of the statute into several languages, is available at the Department of Commerce Office of the Chief Counsel for International Commerce Website: http://www.ogc.doc.gov/trans_anti_bribery.html .

* Transparency International (TI) publishes an annual Corruption Perceptions Index (CPI). The CPI measures the perceived level of public-sector corruption in 180 countries and territories around the world. The CPI is available at: http://www.transparency.org/policy_research/surveys_indices/cpi/2009 . TI also publishes an annual *Global Corruption Report* which provides a systematic evaluation of the state of corruption around the world. It includes an in-depth analysis of a focal theme, a series of country reports that document major corruption related events and developments from all continents and an overview of the latest research findings on anti-corruption diagnostics and tools. See http://www.transparency.org/publications/gcr .

* The World Bank Institute publishes Worldwide Governance Indicators (WGI). These indicators assess six dimensions of governance in 212 countries, including Voice and Accountability, Political Stability and Absence of Violence, Government Effectiveness, Regulatory Quality, Rule of Law and Control of Corruption. See http://info.worldbank.org/governance/wgi/sc_country.asp . The World Bank Business Environment and Enterprise Performance Surveys may also be of interest and are available at: http://go.worldbank.org/RQQXYJ6210 .

* The World Economic Forum publishes the *Global Enabling Trade Report*, which presents the rankings of the Enabling Trade Index, and includes an assessment of the transparency of border administration (focused on bribe payments and corruption) and a separate segment on corruption and the regulatory environment. See http://www.weforum.org/en/initiatives/gcp/GlobalEnablingTradeReport/index.htm .

* Additional country information related to corruption can be found in the U.S. State Department's annual *Human Rights Report* available at http://www.state.gov/g/drl/rls/hrrpt/ .

* Global Integrity, a nonprofit organization, publishes its annual *Global Integrity Report*, which provides indicators for 92 countries with respect to governance and anti-corruption. The report highlights the strengths and weaknesses of national level anti-corruption systems. The report is available at: http://report.globalintegrity.org/ .

BILATERAL INVESTMENT AGREEMENTS

Zambia has signed bilateral reciprocal promotional and protection of investment protocols with most of the Common Market for Eastern and Southern Africa (COMESA) and the SADC member states. In November 2001, COMESA signed a Trade and Investment Framework Agreement with the United States. On October 2, 2000, Zambia became a beneficiary of the African Growth and Opportunity Act (AGOA). Zambia has initialed market access offer through the Eastern and Southern Africa (ESA) interim Economic Partnership Agreement (IEPA) with the European Union on September 30, 2008. In completing these negotiations, the provisions of trade in goods chapter and related annexes of the ESA IEPA now apply to Zambia. Zambia has signed protective agreements with Chinese investors, Nigerian, Libyan and Indian investors.

Zambia does not have a bilateral investment treaty or a bilateral taxation treaty with the United States.

OPIC AND OTHER INVESTMENT INSURANCE PROGRAMS

An OPIC/Zambia agreement was signed in June 1999. Zambia is also a signatory to the Multilateral Investment Guarantee Agency (MIGA), which guarantees foreign investment protection in cases of war, strife, disasters, other disturbances, or expropriation. In June 2001, the World Bank extended credit in the amount of USD five million for starting the African Trade Insurance Agency (ATI). This institution, which is open to all African states that are members of the AU, provides exporters with insurance against receivables on export trade deals and political risk insurance for trade transactions.

The Embassy uses approximately USD 8.6 million in Zambian Kwacha per year. Kwacha was purchased at the average market exchange rate of K4,830 to the U.S. dollar in 2010. Zambia's foreign exchange rates track closely with international copper prices. As such, when copper prices rise, the Kwacha generally appreciates in value.

LABOR

Although there is an abundance of unskilled labor in Zambia, investors complain that there is an inadequate supply of skilled and semi-skilled labor. The government adheres closely to International Labor Organization (ILO) conventions. Labor-management relations vary by sector. Strikes are not uncommon in the public sector and often are related to the government's failure to pay salaries or allowances on time. The minimum

monthly entitlement for any permanent employee including general workers is approximately Kwacha 419,000 (USD 84).

FOREIGN-TRADE ZONES/FREE PORTS

An investor may apply to be appointed and licensed by the Commissioner General to establish and operate a bonded factory under Section 65 of the Customs and Excise Act. In early 2007, the GRZ announced the creation of multi-facility economic zones (MFEZ) where investors enjoy waivers on customs duty on imported equipment, excise duty and value added tax, among other concessions.

On October 31, 2000, the COMESA Free Trade Area (FTA) was launched. COMESA launched a customs union in June 2009, during the 13th Summit of the COMESA Heads of State and Government. The top five intra-COMESA exports from Zambia include tobacco, raw sugarcane, wire, refined copper and cement.

The SADC Trade Protocol Member States Southern African Development Community (SADC), a regional grouping of 13 African states came into force in 2008. The protocol promotes regional integration through trade development and to develop their natural and human resources for the mutual benefit of their people. Trade between the SADC member states is being conducted on reciprocal preferential terms and Rules of Origin define the conditions for products to qualify for preferential trade in the SADC region. Products have to be ‗wholly produced' or ‗sufficiently processed' in the SADC region to be considered compliant with Rules of Origin. The Rules of Origin for SADC are product specific and not generic like the ones for COMESA.

FOREIGN DIRECT INVESTMENT STATISTICS

The ZDA compiles data on investment commitments from investors who obtain investment licenses at the ZDA. Investors in mining projects do not invest through the ZDA but instead work with the Ministry of Mines and Mineral Development. The ZDA data are therefore incomplete and should not be considered a complete measure of investment. However, these are the only FDI data available in Zambia.

Below are U.S. Investment Pledges by Sector for 2009 and 2010.

Sector	2009 (USD)	January/November 2010 (USD)
Agriculture	251,125,000	
Construction	3,422,999	550,000
Education	2,500,000	
Manufacturing	1,756,000	30,585,000
Real Estate		2,000,000
Service	1,000,000	
Tourism	500,000	1,024,850
Total	260,303,999	34,159,850

Investment Pledges by Sector and Nationality in USD for the period January-November 2010.

Investment by Country	Sector	Value in USD
American	Construction	550,000
	Manufacturing	30,000,000
	Real Estate	500,000
American British	Tourism	1,024,850
American/British/South Africa	Manufacturing	585,000
American/Zambian	Real Estate	1,500,000

Australian/Zambian	Manufacturing	553,000
Brazilian/South African	Mining	350,000,000
British	Agriculture	5,900,000
	Energy	5,000,000
	Manufacturing	4,300,000
	Service	10,500,000
	Tourism	1,241,000
	Transport	500,000
British/Italian	Service	500,000
	Tourism	90,277,500
British/Italian/Zambian	Service	2,100,000
British/Kenyan	Manufacturing	3,000,000
British/Kenyan/Zambian	Real Estate	20,000,000
British/Namibian	Real Estate	570,000
British/South African/Botswana	Manufacturing	921,000
British/South African/Zambian	Manufacturing	3,000,000
British/Swedish	ICT	500,000
	Mining	6,000,000
British/Zambian	Agriculture	4,920,000
BVI/Israeli	Real Estate	25,250,000
Canadian	Tourism	750,000
	Transport	500,000
Canadian/Mauritian/Senegalese	Agriculture	1,000,000
Canadian/Zambian	Manufacturing	554,690,000
	Service	1,000,000
Chinese	Construction	20,410,000

	Manufacturing	628,400,000
	Mining	477,780,000
	Service	4,800,000
	Tourism	500,000
	Transport	500,000
Cypriot	Manufacturing	1,470,000
Danish	Tourism	2,500,000
Djibouti/Kenyan	Construction	700,000
Dutch	Manufacturing	742,500
Dutch/Zambian	Tourism	2,950,000
Egyptian	ICT	1,350,000
Eritrean	Tourism	1,500,000
Eritrean/Italian/Zambian	Tourism	2,100,000
Eritrean/Zambian	Manufacturing	7,000,000
	Mining	20,000,000
Ethiopian	Transport	600,000
Ethiopian/Somalian	Manufacturing	500,000
Greek/Thai	Construction	1,100,000
	Manufacturing	2,100,000
Greek/Zambian	Mining	5,000,000
Indian	Agriculture	15,520,000
	Construction	2,200,000
	Energy	550,000,000
	Health	10,918,000
	ICT	700,000
	Manufacturing	159,670,000

	Mining	101,000,000
	Service	5,830,000
	Tourism	3,250,000
	Transport	1,500,000
Indian/Zambian	Tourism	880,000
Irish/Zambian	Tourism	1,950,000
Italian	Manufacturing	11,000,000
Italian/Zambian	Manufacturing	40,000,000
	Transport	500,000
Japanese	Manufacturing	15,844,000
Jersey	Construction	32,500,000
Kenyan/Zambian	Real Estate	57,200,000
Lebanese	ICT	1,900,000
	Manufacturing	3,700,000
Lebanese/Sierra Leon/Zambian	Construction	1,200,000
Lebanese/Zambian	Manufacturing	6,400,000
Libyan/Zambian	ICT	147,000,000
Mauritian/Zambian	ICT	1,000,000
New Zealand/Zambian	Real Estate	1,500,000
Nigerian/Zambian	Energy	15,200,000
Norwegian	Mining	1,200,000
Omani	Mining	30,000,000
Palestinian	Manufacturing	1,100,000
Peruvian/Zambian	Construction	1,950,000
Russian	Agriculture	3,200,000

For additional analytical, business and investment opportunities information, please contact Global Investment & Business Center, USA at (202) 546-2103. Fax: (202) 546-3275. E-mail: rusric@erols.com

Russian/Zambian	Manufacturing	20,000,000
Singaporean	Mining	17,000,000
Slovenia	Service	956,000
South African	Agriculture	13,050,000
	Construction	12,000,000
	Health	572,000
	Manufacturing	6,560,000
	Service	3,247,000
	Tourism	1,000,000
South Africa/British/Zambian	Tourism	923,000
South African/Trinidad	Tourism	1,432,000
South African/Zambian	ICT	8,779,000
	Tourism	2,500,000
South African/Zimbabwean	Construction	1,000,000
	Manufacturing	1,000,000
South Korean	Tourism	1,000,000
Sri Lankan	Real Estate	2,060,000
Swiss	Service	1,977,000
Swiss/Zambian	Education	600,000
Tanzanian	Service	10,000,000
Botswana	Tourism	10,000,000
Ugandan	ICT	500,000
Ugandan/Zambian	Real Estate	16,000,000
Zambian	Education	214,000,000
	Manufacturing	294,657,350
	Real Estate	126,864,000

	Service	1,000,000
	Tourism	1,000,000
Zambian/Dutch	Tourism	1,058,000
Zambian/South Africa	Construction	866,630
	Service	1,000,000
Zambian/Zimbabwean	Manufacturing	500,000
	Service	10,000,000
Zimbabwean	Agriculture	564,000
TOTAL		4,333,612,830

Source: Zambia Development Agency

Investment by U.S. Companies in Zambia	Value in USD
Cargill Cotton Ginners Ltd	USD 18 million
National Milling Corporation *(Seaboard Corporation)*	USD 20 million.
Pioneer DuPont Zambia *(Pioneer Hi-Bred International Inc)*	USD 4 million

Actual Investment by other Nationals in Zambia	Value in USD
Albidon Zambia *(Chinese)*	USD 37 m
Pick N Pay (Woodlands, Lusaka) *(South African)*	USD 25 m
Zambia-China Economic and Trade Cooperation Zone (Chambishi MFEZ) *(Chinese)*	USD 780 million
Lafarge Cement *(French)*	USD 737.5 million

Maamba Collieries USD 600 million

(Singaporean)

Protea Hotel Arcades Limited USD 1.8 million

(Zambian)

WEB RESOURCES

Http://www.zda.org.zm

TRADE AND PROJECT FINANCING

METHODS OF PAYMENT

Credit is the most common method of payment used for Zambian imports. In general, Zambian companies find it difficult to finance their own imports and seek credit arrangements, but businesses considering offering their exports on credit should make a very careful check of the bona fides and finances of Zambian companies before doing so. Delinquent payments (even from government-owned companies) to suppliers are a common problem in Zambia. The cash-in-advance payment method may be advisable, especially when dealing with small companies.

HOW DOES THE BANKING SYSTEM OPERATE

Zambia's commercial banking sector is composed of 18 international and local banks. All banks operating in Zambia must incorporate locally. As a result, there are no local branches of foreign (including U.S.) banks or financial institutions. However, Citibank Zambia Limited, a wholly-owned subsidiary of Citicorp NY, provides corporate banking services in Zambia.

The banking sector is supervised by the central bank, the Bank of Zambia (BoZ), which reports to the Ministry of Finance and National Planning. The sector is governed by the Banking and Financial Services Act of 1994. Industry observers generally credit the BoZ with making large strides in improving bank oversight over the past several years.

Legislation is being drafted which will provide for the establishment of a deposit insurance system.

While Zambia currently lacks an anti-money laundering regime that meets international standards, it has passed legislation to create an independent financial intelligence unit (FIU). The FIU has yet to take over investigative authority from the Drug Enforcement Commission (DEC), and remains hampered by a lack of funding.

FOREIGN-EXCHANGE CONTROLS

There are no controls on the movement of capital in or out of Zambia. Bank accounts may be held in local or foreign currency, and funds are easily transferred out of the country or held offshore. Amounts over 5,000 U.S. Dollars, carried in or out in cash or travelers checks, must be declared. Commercial banks and bureau de change operators restrict issuance of over-the-counter cash to USD 5,000 per transaction.

The BoZ is responsible for the management of the country's foreign exchange reserves and participates in open market operations to either build up reserves or to smooth exchange rate volatility.

U.S. BANKS AND LOCAL CORRESPONDENT BANKS

Zambia has one U.S. owned bank:

Citibank Zambia Limited

Citibank House

Cha Cha Cha Road

P.O. Box 30037

Lusaka, Zambia

Tel: 260-211-22 0913

Fax: 260-211-22 6258

Contact: Mr. Amedoe Anniciello

Managing Director

PROJECT FINANCING

The availability of project financing, particularly for export-oriented projects, is improving. Besides bilateral and multilateral government agencies, commercial banks and venture capital funds are playing an increasing role. Both the U.S. and European Union (EU) have established enterprise development funds, which can be accessed for projects in Zambia. U.S. enterprise development funds include the Southern African Enterprise Development Fund and the United States African Development Foundation. The International Finance Corporation (IFC) and Commonwealth Development Corporation (CDC) both offer financial assistance for projects in Zambia. There are no restrictions for U.S. companies to participate in bids and tenders floated by the Zambia Public Procurement Authority (ZPPA) and funded by the international institutions such as the World Bank, Africa Development Bank and other. After selection of successful bidder,

the relevant government ministry will supervise the project while payments are made from the financing institution. However, channels for remittance of project funds will differ according to the financing institution.

http://www.saedf.com

http://www.usadf.gov

WEB RESOURCES

Export-Import Bank of the United States: http://www.exim.gov
Country Limitation Schedule: http://www.exim.gov/tools/country/country_limits.html
OPIC: http://www.opic.gov

Trade and Development Agency: http://www.tda.gov/
SBA's Office of International Trade: http://www.sba.gov/oit/
USDA Commodity Credit Corporation: http://www.fsa.usda.gov/ccc/default.htm
U.S. Agency for International Development: http://www.usaid.gov

IMPORTANT CONTACTS

U.S. Embassy Lusaka
Ambassador – Mark C. Storella
Deputy Chief of Mission – Stephen Schwartz
Political/Economic Chief - Pamela Tremont
Commercial Specialist - Vedruna Santana
U.S. mailing address: 2310 Lusaka Pl., Washington DC 20521-2310.
International mailing address: United States Embassy, PO Box 31617, Lusaka, Zambia.
Street address: Subdivision 694/Stand 100, Ibex Hill Road, Lusaka, Zambia.
Telephone: 260-211-357 000
Fax: 260-211-357 224
Email: CommercialLusaka@state.gov

Zambian Government and Industry:

Ministry of Commerce, Trade and Industry, Permanent Secretary, Dr. Buleti Nsemukila, P.O. Box 31968, Lusaka, Zambia. Tel: 260-211 223 617.

Ministry of Finance and National Planning, Permanent Secretary, Mr. Emmanuel Ngulube, P.O. Box RW 50062, Lusaka, Zambia. Tel: 260-211 250 657 and

260-211 251 843.

Zambia Development Agency (ZDA), Director General, Mr. Andrew Chipwende, P.O Box 30819, Lusaka, Zambia. Tel: 260-211 221 417.

Zambia Association of Chambers of Commerce and Industry (ZACCI), Chairman, Mr. Geoffrey Sakulanda, P.O. Box 30844, Lusaka, Zambia. Tel: 260-211 252 369.

ZAMBIA FINANCIAL SYSTEM

LIQUIDITY

An evaluation of liquidity risk management mainly involves an assessment of the level of compliance with the statutory liquid asset requirements, an analysis of the short-term liquidity mismatch in terms of its size and trend and an assessment of the sources and volatility of liquid funds available for funding such mismatches.

In Zambia, there are two statutory liquid asset requirements which are used as monetary policy instruments and also serve as prudential supervisory tools; these are the core liquid asset ratio (CLR) and the statutory reserve ratio (SRR).

During 1996, the core liquid asset ratio was adjusted twice from 30% to 40% and again to 43.5%.\With the exception of two banks whose accounts remained overdrawn at Bank of Zambia during the year, the banks in the industry were able to meet the core liquidity requirement of the Central Bank. There was, however, notable strain on the industry liquidity towards the end of 1996 when the ratio was raised to 43.5%. At the end of the year, the average core liquid assets ratio was 27.5%, which was well below the minimum requirement above.

The statutory reserve ratio was also adjusted twice during the year, from 3% to 5% and again to 8%. With the exception of two commercial banks, the rest were able to meet this requirement.

The industry ratio of liquid assets to deposits and short-term liabilities averaged 68% during the year. The average ratio does not include two banks whose aggregate ratio was 30%. Also excluded is one bank which operates as a discount house and had an average ratio of 889%. If these banks were to be included a distorted average ratio of 329% would be reflected.

NEW REGULATIONS ISSUED

Five new regulations and a guideline were passed as law during the year. These are:

(a) **Foreign exchange management and risk exposure regulations (effective 21 March** 1996). The suspension of the Exchange Control Act led to an increased level of activity in the foreign exchange market. This contributed positively to banks' earnings. However, the Department has recognized the potential impact that adverse movements in exchange rates (the exchange risk) can have on the banks' financial condition.

Therefore, in order to address such risks and ensure that banks' exposures are minimized, these ,egulations were issued, among other things, to limit individual banks' e~osure to exchange rate risk to 20% and 25% of regulatory capital for single currency and overall exposures respectively.

(b) **Large loans regulations (effective 21 June** 1996). The financial 'sickness' of a bank borrower or group of related borrowers can have serious impact on g a bank if that borrower or group of related borrowers represent a large concentration of risk to the bank. Recognizing this, the large loans regulations were issued with the primary aim of limiting concentration of loans to a single borrower or a group of related borrowers, thereby minimizing the effect of loss to the bank in the event of failure of such borrowers.

The regulations limit a bank's large loans exposures (exposures of 10% or more of regulatory capital) to 25% and 600% of regulatory capital for single borrower and total large loans exposures respectively.

(c) Insider loans regulations (effective 31 March 1996). The Department also recognized that loan exposures to directors, shareholders and others concerned in the ownership and management of banks either directly or indirectly can be quite problematic as these loans easily drift into non-performing status and their terms do not usually reflect arm's length dealing. In this regard the insider loans regulations were issued with the objective of limiting a bank's loan exposures to insiders to 5% and 100% of regulatory capital for single and overall exposures respectively.

(d) **Fixed assets investment regulations (effective 31 March** 1996). The aim of these regulations is to control investment in fixed assets by banks. The regulations are in response to the need to restrict banks from making excessive investments in fixed assets as these do not directly contribute to the core business of banking.

(e) **Classification and provisioning of loans regulations (effective 1 January** 1997). The primary aim of these regulations includes among other things; to standardise the loans classification process and give guidance on minimum provisioning levels. However, because of the likely adverse impact of the

For additional analytical, business and investment opportunities information, please contact Global Investment & Business Center, USA at (202) 546-2103. Fax: (202) 546-3275. E-mail: rusric@erols.com

classification an provisioning of loans regulations particularly on the earnings and consequently on regulatory capital, some

REGULATORY MATTERS

banks have been given until 31 December 1997 to fully comply with the regulation. This exemption was given under Section 18(4) of the Banking and Financial Services Act 1994 (BFSA).

(f) **Capital and Money Market Instruments Guideline No.** 1/96. In 1995 some non-bank financial institutions started accepting money from the public through issuance of instruments called debentures. These instruments had maturity periods ranging from thirty days to twelve months.

In order to regulate the issuance of debentures, the Bank of Zambia issued the Banking and Financial Services (Capital and Money Market Instruments) Guideline No. 1/96. This Guideline defmes money market instruments and explains how they should be accounted for in the issuers' books.

DEPOSIT INSURANCE SCHEME

It is evident from past experience, particularly the failure of three banks in 1995, that banking instability can have serious adverse effects on a nation's economy because it can impair a nation's payments mechanism, reduce the nation's savings rate, diminish the financial intermediation process, and inflict serious harm on small savers. To prevent these adverse effects, the Government has created a variety of institutional arrangements designed to preserve banking stability. These arrangements have included banking laws and regulations that set the ground rules for bank operations and attempt to constrain undue bank risk-taking; the laws and regulations are intended to provide a framework for the supervision and examination of banks to ensure compliance with laws and regulations and lender of last resort facilities designed to prevent temporary bank liquidity problems from turning into insolvency.

In addition to these more traditional arrangements, the Government is in the process of developing and setting up a deposit insurance scheme. The primary purpose of the scheme is to preserve public confidence in the banking system, provide the Government with a formal mechanism for dealing with failing banks, and ensure that small depositors are protected in the event of bank failures.

MONEY LAUNDERING

There is a growing global concern over money laundering, and Zambia is no exception. Explained in simple terms, money laundering is the "washing of dirty money" into the financial system thereby legitimising proceeds of illegal activities such as drug trafficking. Money laundering not only undermines public confidence in the financial system, it also causes distortions in the economy in terms of significant influence on key economic variables such as money supply which do not derive from economic activity.

As there is no law against money laundering at present, a committee (on which the Bank of Zambia has a representation) has been established with the objective of drafting legislation to outlaw money laundering.

Licensing activities New licences were issued to the following institutions; (a) Access Leasing Limited (b) Cavmont Bureau de Change, kapiri Mposhi (c) Credit Management Services Limited

For additional analytical, business and investment opportunities information, please contact Global Investment & Business Center, USA at (202) 546-2103. Fax: (202) 546-3275. E-mail: rusric@erols.com

(d) Gemini Bureau de Change, Chingola (e) Investrust Merchant Bank Limited and (f) The United Bank of Zambia Limited.

Licences for the following institutions were revoked; (a) Continental Bank (Z) Limited (b) Goldmark Bureau de Change Limited (c) Mercantile Bank (Z) Limited, (d) Meridien Leasing Limited and (e) Royalty Bank of Zambia Limited.

PENALTIES INTRODUCED

In January, penalties were introduced for late submission of prudential returns. This was with a view to ensure timely supervision in terms of early identification of problems in the system and also to make early corrective action possible and enhance the capacity of our newly created off-site analysis division.

The effect has been an improvement in the timely submission of returns by banks thus enhancing the general ability of the Bank of Zambia to detect problems in banks and institute corrective measures on a timely basis.

LITIGATION

The following litigation cases, for and against the Bank of Zambia, involve financial institutions under our control:

SS **Kakoma and others vs Wilfred Mwanza, Meridien BIAO Bank (in liquidation), the Bank of Zambia and the Attorney General**

This matter has been brought under the BFSA and the Companies Act. The Applicants are requesting the court for leave to be heard on an application for an order to form a committee of inspection in the liquidation of MBBZ (in liquidation). A ruling is awaited.

Simeza Sangwa, Legal Resources Foundation vs Bank of Zambia, Ronald Yenza and the Attorney General

This case is brought under the BFSA. The Applicants are claiming to be paid their deposits totalling K30 million. These deposits have been locked up in MBBZ (in liquidation). Hearing commences on 12 June 1997.

REGULATORY MATTERS

PROMISE SHINONDO AND KABOMPO LIMITED VS BANK OF ZAMBIA

In February 1996, the Bank of Zambia placed African Commercial Bank (Z) Limited (ACB) in liquidation. This followed the end of the ninety (90) day receivership period. However, in April 1996, P Shinondo and Kabompo Limited obtained an injunction to restrain the Bank of Zambia against liquidating ACB. The Applicant is alleging that the Bank of Zambia decision was made in bad faith. The case is awaiting judgement.

ROYALTY BANK (Z) LIMITED VS BANK OF ZAMBIA

In November 1994, Royalty Bank was licensed as a Bank **under the Banking** Act (CAP 700) which required that banks commence operations with a minimum regulatory capital of K20 million.

For additional analytical, business and investment opportunities information, please contact Global Investment & Business Center, USA at (202) 546-2103. Fax: (202) 546-3275. E-mail: rusric@erols.com

A month later, in December 1994, the BFSA was enacted. The new requirement was that banks maintain a minimum regulatory capital of K2 billion.

Royalty Bank took out an interim injunction (ex parse) to restrain the Bank of Zambia from effecting the requirements of the BFSA 1994. The court discharged the interim injunction granted ex parse and no further steps to prosecute the action have been taken. In the year under review, the Bank of Zambia revoked its banking licence.

ZAMBIA NATIONAL BUILDING SOCIETY (ZNBS) VS BANK OF ZAMBIA

that;

In June 1996 ZNBS sued the Bank of Zambia seekin~ an order of the co1lrt

(a) S.47 of the Bank of Zambia Act and Part B(10) of the Clearing House Rules permit financial institutions and not just commercial banks to be members of the clearing house.

(b) The Applicant being a financial institution and upon meeting the requirements of the respondent be eligible to membership of the clearing house.

The application was dismissed and the court ruled that though ZNBS is a financial institution in its own right, it is not a commercial bank. Therefore it was not eligible for membership in the Clearing House for Zambia Payment System rules of 1996.

ON-SITE INSPECTIONS

The two main pillars of the supervisory activity are the off-site monitoring and on-site inspections. In the practice of various countries the supervisors put different emphasis on these two pillars. In South Africa and some European countries the supervision is clearly based on off-site monitoring, whereas in the United States of America (USA) it is a combination of the two with perhaps a higher inclination towards on-site inspections.

The development of the Zambian financial system supervision initially emphasised on on-site inspection of commercial banks and this was further enhanced during 1996. Financial System Supervision carried out inspections of twelve banks out of a total of nineteen operating in 1996. The inspections evaluated capital, asset quality, management, earnings and liquidity. In some cases the biggest problems were related to the lack of regulations on the quality of loan portfolio, risk assessment and classification. The low quality of management in certain instances was highlighted.

Nine NBFI out of a total of eighteen registered with the Registrar of Banks and Non-Bank Financial Institutions were inspected during the year. Additionally, though not registered with the Registrar, four were inspected. These included a building society, a cooperative society, a development bank and a social security institution.

NBFI are a heterogenous group which include leasing companies, finance houses, agricultural lending institutions and building societies and consequently engage in varied financial activities with the degree and nature of risks they face being different. The risks they pose to customers and the stability of the financial system will therefore be varied. Additionally these NBFI are incorporated under various Acts, implying that they are supposed to be supervised and regulated by the supervisory authorities stipulated in those Acts. The Bank of Zambia could therefore not legally impose its prudential regulations on these institutions.

For additional analytical, business and investment opportunities information, please contact Global Investment & Business Center, USA at (202) 546-2103. Fax: (202) 546-3275. E-mail: rusric@erols.com

The above problems necessitated the Bank of Zambia requesting the Least Developed Countries (LDC) Division of the United Nations Conference on Trade and Development (UNCTAD) to carry out a study on the nature of the non-bank financial sector to determine supervisory implications. Recommendations of the study will be implemented during 1997.

It is now felt that appropriate prudential regulations and supervisory strategies for the effective supervision of these institutions need to be formulated.

OFF-SITE MONITORING

The off-site monitoring system commenced in January 1996 and involves continuous monitoring of compliance with laws and regulations. In addition, monthly analysis is made based on the CAMEL (capital, asset, management, earnings and liquidity) method developed in the USA.

SUPERVISORY ACTIVITIES THE DEPARTMENT

The system is currently manual utilising basic spreadsheet packages for analysis. Plans are under way to develop a software which will be used to record, store and analyse the data submitted by the banks monthly, quarterly and annually. This will further strengthen our monitoring of compliance with laws and regulations.

The off-site monitoring system is also being modified so that it could be used as an early warning system and improve on the management information requirements. The system should also allow for deeper and more comprehensive analysis about the banking system as well as faster and more flexible changes in the regulatory system.

The off-site monitoring of NBFI did not take off in 1996 because of the above-mentioned problems. It was also felt that NBFI activities and types of assets and liabilities on their balance sheets are so diversified that appropriate prudential regulations need to be put in place to take into account the specific risks facing particular types of institutions.

INSPECTION OF MANAGEMENT INFORMATION SYSTEMS

Technological advances in computer and telecommunications have led to an increased reliance on automated accounting systems by banks and financial institutions worldwide. In response to the risks associated with Information Technology, the Department has started inspecting management information system facilities of supervised institutions.

BANK MERGER

During the year, the industry witnessed the first bank merger in history. First Merchant Bank (Z) Limited and Safe Deposit Bank, both indigenous banks, merged to become First Merchant Bank (Z) Limited.

BANKS PLACED IN RECEIVERSHIP AND LIQUIDATION

Currently, there is one bank in compulsory liquidation namely Meridien BIAO Bank Zambia Limited (MBBZ). Two banks have been placed in receivership, these are African Commercial Bank Zambia Limited (ACB) and Commerce Bank Zambia Limited.

In the event of a bank failure, the law prescribes that depositors be paid amounts not exceeding K500 000.

For additional analytical, business and investment opportunities information, please contact Global Investment & Business Center, USA at (202) 546-2103. Fax: (202) 546-3275. E-mail: rusric@erols.com

Therefore in the case of MBBZ, an amount of K4.6 billion was made available to the Liquidation Manager to pay the 40 000 depositors. At the end of the year, K750 million was still outstanding to pay the remaining 15 000 depositors.

The Receivers of ACB and Commerce Bank were availed of K867 million and K518 million respectively to pay 6,878 and 3,700 depositors respectively.

MERIDIEN BIAO BANK ZAMBIA LIMITED (IN LIQUIDATION) (MBBZ)

As at 31 December 1996, close to K3 billion had been realised from the disposal of assets. Methods of selling the assets included; tender sales, public auctions and private treaty sales.

By the end of the year, the liquidation exercise had reached a stage where the Bank of Zambia was almost ready to make partial distributions to the depositors and creditors. The dividend payments will be made in the course of 1997 and the pay-out ratio will be determined by the available funds at the time of payment.

(B) AFRICAN COMMERCIAL BANK (IN RECEIVERSHIP)

ACB was placed in liquidation in February 1996. Two months later, on April 22 1996 the former ACB Managing Director obtained an injunction to restrain Bank of Zambia against liquidating the bank. Bank of Zambia is contesting this stay and by the end of the year judgement had not been passed as yet.

Against this background, there has not been much work going on at the bank. The major activity has been loan recoveries and debt collection.

(C) COMMERCE BANK ZAMBIA LIMITED (IN RECEIVERSHIP)

In February 1996, after the ninety-day period of receivership, the Receiver in accordance with Section 100 of the BFSA formulated a plan to restructure and reorganise the bank. The plan focuses on sourcing fresh investment for recapitalising the bank and restructuring the shareholding of the bank.

The document has been submitted to the Bank of Zambia and the Department is currently studying the proposals. If in our opinion the proposals are viable, the Bank of Zambia will endorse the plan to allow the bank to recommence operations.

LIST OF REGISTERED COMMERCIAL BANKS

1. African Commercial Bank Limited ***
2. Barclays Bank (Z) Limited
3. Cavmont Merchant Bank (Z) Limited
4. Chase Trust Bank (Z) Limited
5. Citibank (Z) Limited
6. Commerce Bank (Z) Limited ***
7. Credit Africa Bank (Z) Limited
8. Finance Bank (Z) Limited ~
9. First Alliance Bank (Z) Limited

For additional analytical, business and investment opportunities information, please contact Global Investment & Business Center, USA at (202) 546-2103. Fax: (202) 546-3275. E-mail: rusric@erols.com

10. First Merchant Bank (Z) Limited
11. Indo Zambia Bank Limited
12. Intermarket Discount House (Z) Limited *****
13. Investrust Merchant Bank (Z) Limited
14. Manifold Investment Bank (Z) Limited
15. Meridien Bank (Z) Limited *******
16. New Capital Bank Plc
17. Prudence Bank (Z) Limited
18. Stanbic Bank (Z) Limited
19. Standard Chartered Bank (Z) Limited
20. Union Bank (Z) Limited
21. Zambia National Commercial Bank

in receivership

***** *operates as a discount house*

#****** *in liquidation*

RECOGNISED AND SUPERVISEDI NON-BANK FINANCIAL INSTITUTIONS

1. Access Financial Services Limited
2. Access Leasing
3. Anglo Leasing Company Limited
4. C&S Small Enterprises Development Fund
5. Civil Servants Pension Fund
6. Cooperative Bank Limited***
7. Credit Union and Savings Association
8. Credit Management Services Limited
9. Development Bank of Zambia
10. Emerging Markets Leasing Limited
11. Executive Card
12. Finance Building Society
13. First Alliance Financial Services Limited
14. IMS Financial Services Limited
15. Industrial Credit Company Limited
16. Integro Finance Company Limited
17. Leasing Finance Company Limited
18. Local Authorities Superannuation Fund

19. Lima Bank Limited*****
20. National Savings and Credit Bank of Zambia
21. Pan African Building Society
22. Prudential Finance Company ~
23. Small Scale Enterprises Promotion Limited
24. Stanbic Leasing Zambia Limited
25. Unifinance Zambia Limited -
26. Union Leasing Zambia Limited
27. Workmen's Compensation Fund ~Board
28. ZCF Finance Services -
29. ZANACO Leasing _
30. Zambia Export and Import Bank
31. Zambia National Building Society
32. Zambia National Provident Fund
33. Zambia State Financing Company Limited

~ Some of the institutions may not be supervised by the Bank of Zambia

because they are enacted under different legislation.

#*# *closed*

LIST OF REGISTERED BUREAUX

1. ABC Bureau de Change, Lusaka
2. Africa Direct Bureau de Change, Lusaka
3. Atics Bureau de Change, Lusaka
4. C & A Bureau de Change, Lusaka
5. Cavmont Bureau de Change, Kapiri Mposhi
6. Cavmont Bureau de Change, Lusaka
7. Continental Bureau de Change, Livingstone
8. DK Bureau de Change, Lusaka
9. Delta Bureau de Change, Lusaka
10. ERZ Bureau de Change, Lusaka
11. Express Bureau de Change, Lusaka
12. Finance Bureau de Change, Lusaka
13. Funfair Bureau de Change, Lusaka
14. Gemini Bureau de Change, Chingola
15. Hazida Bureau de Change, Lusaka

**For additional analytical, business and investment opportunities information,
please contact Global Investment & Business Center, USA
at (202) 546-2103. Fax: (202) 546-3275. E-mail: rusric@erols.com**

16. Imperial Bureau de Change, Lusaka
17. IMS Bureau de Change, Lusaka
18. Kapiri Bureau de Change, Kapiri Mposhi
19. Manifold Bureau de Change, Lusaka
20. Mill Bureau de Change, Lusaka
21. Monex Bureau de Change, Ndola
22. Prime Bureau de Change, Lusaka
23. Professional Bureau de Change, Ndola
24. Prudence Bureau de Change, Lusaka
25. Quick Services Bureau de Change, Lusaka
26. South-end Bureau de Change, Livingstone
27. Sterling Bureau de Change, Kabwe
28. Sterling Bureau de Change, Ndola
29. Tops Bureau de Change, Chingola
30. Unifinance Bureau de Change, Lusaka
31. Unifinance Bureau de Change, Ndola
32. Valour Bureau de Change, Lusaka
33. Valour Bureau de Change, Northmead Lusaka
34. YMF Bureau de Change, Lusaka
35. Zamforex Bureau de Change, Kitwe
36. Zamforex Bureau de Change, Lusaka

LIST OF ABBREVIATIONS

ACB African Commercial Bank
BAZ Bankers Association of Zambia
BFSA Banking and Financial Services Act 1994
CAP Caption
CLR Core Liquid Assets Ratio
DIS Deposit Insurance Scheme
ESAF East and Southern African Banking Supervisors
FDIC Federal Deposit Insurance Corporation
FSS Financial System Supervision
GRZ Government Republic of Zambia
LDC Least Developed Countries
MBBZ Meridien BIAO Bank (Z) Limited
NBFI Non-Bank Financial Institutions
SEC Securities and Exchange Commission
SRR Statutory Reserve Ratio
TB Treasury Bills
UNCTAD United Nations Conference on Trade and Development
Exchange rate US$1 = ZMK 1 216.27 (average exchange rate)

For additional analytical, business and investment opportunities information, please contact Global Investment & Business Center, USA at (202) 546-2103. Fax: (202) 546-3275. E-mail: rusric@erols.com

SETTING UP A COMPANY IN ZAMBIA

- The basic requirement is to register a business name or incorporate a company through the Registrar of Companies. This involves name clearance and submission of articles of association with details of directors in triplicate.

  A limited company must have a minimum of two directors, above the age of18 and one of whom must be a resident in Zambia. If the company has more than two local directors, at least half of them must be resident in Zambia.

  A company incorporated outside Zambia can establish a place of business in Zambia and must within 28 days of setting up, file a certified copy of the memorandum and articles of association and the list of the company directors with the Registrar of Companies.

  Corporate tax is 35% and 30% for companies listed on the Lusaka Stock Exchange. The rate for farming enterprises is 15% while rural based and exporting enterprises pay tax reduced by one seventh of the normal tax.

  Foreign companies setting up in Zambia are advised to apply for an investment certificate. The certificate guarantees your right of repatriation of profits, dividends, royalties etc. It also protects your investment from nationaling action by the state. With the certificate a foreign investor can acquire immigration status and purchase land in Zambia.

  Application for the certificate is made by completing a standard form available from the Investment Centre.

  The applicant is also required to submit a copy of the Certificate of Incorporation in Zambia, the business plan and the official list of directors.

  Minimum investment per share holder is US$50,000, this can be in the form of capital or assets or both. This only applies to foreign shareholders that will be living in the Country.

  The other requirements are as follows

- Name clearance fees - K5,000
- Purchase of the set of form for company registration - K8,000
- Share capital form - K15,000
- The forms must be filled in duplicate (typed)
- The applicant should also prepare at least four copies of Articles of Association
- Company Incorporation fee - K95,000 for minimum nominal share capital of K2,000,000
- Otherwise the incorporation fee increases as the nominal share capital increases (we will get the pro rata fees from PACRO in this regard)
- Another aspect to be included under setting up a company in Zambia is the duration it takes from name clearance, lodging of completed forms to issuance of the Certificate of Incorporation.
- Name search and clearance is 3 days

- Issuance of Certificates of Incorparation, Share capital etc is?????? (I will find out this)
- Details requires are
- Three proposed names
- Principal business of the company
- Other business
- Physical address of the company
- Postal address of the company
- Nominal share capital (minimum is K2,000,000)
- Details of the Shareholders/Directors

  (i) Full names

  (ii) Nationality

  (iii) Passport Number

  (iv) Residential address of each shareholder/director

  (v) Postal address of each shareholder/director

  (vi) Occupation of each shareholder/director
- Number of shares held by each shareholder/director

CONSULTING FIRMS

Grant Thornton Associates
P.O Box 30885,
Lusaka 10101
Tel: +260-1-22 77 22
gt@gt.com.zm
Website:www.grantthornton.com.zm

KPMG
Box 31014
Lusaka
Tel: +260-1-22 88 74/8
Fax: +260-1-22 28 61
kpmg@zamnet.zm

Renco Associates (Ernest Young)
P O Box 34223
Lusaka
Tel: +260-1-22 70 22
Fax: +260-1-22 70 22

Deloitte & Touche
P O Box 30030

Lusaka
Tel: +260-1-22 86 77/9
Fax: +260-1-22 69 15
dtt@deloite.co.zm

Price Waterhouse Coopers
P O Box 30942
Lusaka 10101
Tel: +260-1-22 88 89
Fax: +260-1-22 07 68

ZAMBIA TEXTILE INDUSTRY: STRATEGIC INFORMATION

Despite the disadvantage of being land-locked, Zambia was once one of the wealthiest countries in sub-Saharan Africa. This began to change in the early 1970s. After the oil crisis (increasing the price of imports) and relative commodity price collapse (reducing the revenue from exports), Zambia had to turn to the International Monetary Fund (IMF) and World Bank for assistance. So began some thirty years of Bank and Fund intervention in the Zambian economy. In return for loans, Zambia was required to implement Bank and Fund endorsed economic policies over three decades. Unfortunately, this period is a sad story of increasing debt, economic stagnation or collapse, and social crisis.

After the external economic shocks suffered in the early 1970s, Zambia's total external debt rose from US$814 million to US$3,244 million by the end of the decade. The situation then further deteriorated with Zambia's external debt more than doubling to US$6,916 million by the end of the 1980s. By the late 1990s the debt crisis in countries such as Zambia led to the creation of the much vaunted Heavily Indebted Poor Countries (HIPC) initiative.

Unfortunately, the relief that Zambia is getting under the HIPC initiative is proving to be inadequate in removing its debt burden. By the start of 2003, Zambia had received only 5 per cent of the debt service reduction committed to it under HIPC. Even when it has reached completion point, Zambia's debt service will continue to rise. As Zambian Finance Minister Peter Magande has pointed out, "Zambia's current levels of debt even after it receives its full quota of debt relief as defined in the decision point document under HIPC initiative will continue to be unsustainable."

Since 1991, in order to qualify for debt relief, Zambia has implemented such economic policies as privatisation, trade liberalisation, subsidy cuts and public sector wage freezes.

Just as worrying as Zambia's continuing debt crisis is the fact that the HIPC initiative is being used as another lever with which the IMF and World Bank can wield influence over Zambia's economy. In return for debt relief, Zambia must implement economic policies, such as privatisation and cuts in public spending, that meet with Bank and Fund approval. The conditions tied to the HIPC initiative are just the latest in a long line of 'free market' policy interventions that have included: trade liberalisation; investment deregulation; privatisation; cutting or abolishing subsidies; laying-off civil service staff; public sector wage cuts or freezes and reduced state intervention in the agricultural sector.

Yet a close examination of economic and social indicators suggests the kind of policies being foisted on Zambia by these institutions over the past twenty years have been a dismal failure.

For example, trade liberalisation, a key plank of Bank and Fund economic orthodoxy, has been disastrous for Zambia's manufacturing sector. Textile manufacturing has been one sector particularly badly hit. The lowering of tariffs on textile products, and particularly the removal of all tariffs on used clothes, led to large increases in imports of cheap, second-hand clothing from industrialised countries. The Zambian textile industry could not compete with these imports, and the sector has all but vanished. There were more than 140 textile manufacturing firms in 1991, but this had fallen to just eight by 2002. Ramesh Patel, director of SWAPP Ltd commented, "We used to have factories everywhere, but Ndola is a ghost town now. We are one of the lucky ones who have managed to survive, but there's no comparison. We used to supply retailers with 3.5 thousand tons of clothing annually; we're down to less than 500 tons now. We had 250 employees eight years ago; we're down to 25 now."

Agricultural liberalisation has had a similarly poor record. A 2000 World Bank study acknowledged that the removal of all subsidies on maize and fertilizer under World Bank/IMF structural adjustment loans led to "stagnation and regression instead of helping Zambia's agricultural sector." And the United Nations Conference on Trade and Development (UNCTAD) concluded that, in Zambia, "Agricultural credit and marketing by the private sector turned out to be uneven and unpredictable, and once market forces had eliminated the implicit subsidies to remote and small farmers, many farmers were left worse off."

Privatisation was one of the strongest features of IMF and World Bank conditionality from 1992 onwards. But despite attracting praise from the Bank for the 'success' of its privatisation programme, the reality is that privatisation has had a very mixed record in Zambia. Although some failing state run enterprises have been transferred into private hands and are now operating more effectively; post-privatisation, many companies have collapsed, jobs have been lost and welfare programmes originally performed through a parastatal have not been continued by private companies.

The patchy record of past sell-offs has resulted in the one-size-fits-all privatisation programme being doubted even at the highest levels. In 2003, the Zambian President, Levy Mwanawasa, said, "[The IMF's privatisation programme] has been of no significant benefit to the country - privatisation of crucial state enterprises has led to poverty, asset stripping and job losses."

The real impact of these core IMF and World Bank policies: trade liberalisation, agricultural liberalisation and privatisation, can clearly be seen in Zambia's economic and social performance.

Zambia's economic record since the oil price shocks of the 1970s has been woeful. Real GDP per capita fell from US$1455 in 1976 to US$1037 by 1987, an average of -3.6 per cent per year. This decline stabilised or even reversed from 1987 to 1991, before the economy entered a massive recession again in 1992, the year an extensive reform programme began. By 2000, real GDP per capita had fallen to US$892.

The IMF has even failed to achieve one of its core aims for intervention - to stem temporary balance of payments problems. Statistics from the United Nations Development Programme (UNDP) suggest that Zambia's trade deficit has actually increased through the 1990s. At the start of the decade the difference between imports and exports was around -5 per cent of GDP, but since 1994 its range has tended to be between -9 and -15 per cent.

Not surprisingly, employment has suffered. Formal manufacturing employment fell from 75,400 in 1991 to 43,320 in 1998. Paid employment in mining and manufacturing fell from 140,000 in 1991 to 83,000 in 2000. Paid employment in agriculture fell from 78,000 in 1990 to 50,000 in 2000 and employment in textile manufacturing fell from 34,000 in the early 1990s to 4,000 in 2001.

Economic decline has been mirrored by a social decline. For example, the proportion of the population classed as undernourished, having a calorie consumption below their minimum energy requirement, has increased from 45 per cent in 1990 to 50 per cent in 2001. Without radical change, it looks increasingly unlikely that Zambia will achieve most of the Millennium Development Goals (MDGs) by the globally agreed target date of 2015. In fact, the indicators for

For additional analytical, business and investment opportunities information, please contact Global Investment & Business Center, USA at (202) 546-2103. Fax: (202) 546-3275. E-mail: rusric@erols.com

eradicating hunger, achieving universal primary education and reducing child mortality are actually in reverse, so, if current trends continue, these goals will never be met.

Overall, Zambia's level of human development has been in freefall in comparison to other countries. In 1990 it was ranked 130 on the UNDP's Human Development Index, falling to 163 in 2001. Although very poor in 1990, Zambia was ranked as one of the most developed countries in sub-Saharan Africa. It is now one of the poorest.

Such a dismal performance has led to widespread dissatisfaction with Bank and Fund policies. Yet time and again public protest has simply been ignored while 'more of the same medicine' has been prescribed. This exposes the fundamental lack of democracy in World Bank and IMF intervention in Zambia.

A recent example of this democratic deficit is the required privatisation of Zambia's state electricity company (ZESCO) and state bank (ZNCB) in return for debt relief. The Government initially agreed to implement these measures, but the prospect of these privatisations provoked large scale public resistance. Following a major protest march in Lusaka, the Zambian Parliament voted for a motion urging the government to rescind their decision to privatise ZNCB.

Following this opposition the Government decided to reverse its earlier commitment to sell off these companies. The IMF responded immediately by announcing that Zambia risked forfeiting US$1 billion in debt relief if it did not go ahead with the privatisation. IMF resident representative Mark Ellyne said, "If they [the government] don't sell, they will not get the money." The Government was forced to ignore its own Parliament and go back on its decision not to privatise ZNCB.

Another condition for receiving debt relief has been to curb public spending. This has forced the Government to abandon plans to provide a living wage to public sector workers. The IMF will not let the Government increase its budget deficit from 1.55 per cent to 3 per cent.

By way of comparison, the projected 3 per cent Zambian budget deficit contrasts with a 2003 US budget deficit of 3.4 per cent (projected to rise to 4.1 per cent in 2004) and a projected UK budget deficit of 3.4 per cent. In fact the IMF recently criticised the UK government for planning to increase its budget deficit to this level, which met with a curt response. A UK Treasury spokesman said, "We are not going to accept a stability pact from the IMF, the European Commission or anybody else" and that the IMF had an "ideological opposition" to public spending. Unfortunately, Zambia does not have the same luxury of being able to ignore the IMF.

Recent criticism of the undemocratic nature of IMF and World Bank policies has been met - both by these institutions and the UK government alike - with the response that the Zambian people chose these policies through their 'participatory' Poverty Reduction Strategy Paper (PRSP) process.

But the incorporation of civil society viewpoints in the final PRSP did not extend to the macroeconomic policies in the PRSP. Despite its poor record, the IMF and World Bank were unwilling to backtrack or renegotiate the macroeconomic framework that had been imposed on Zambia throughout the 1980s and 90s. The IMF's existing Poverty Reduction Growth Facility (PRGF) programme formed the basis of this aspect of the PRSP, and so in effect overrode any macroeconomic discussions within the PRSP process. The result was the so-called 'participatory' PRSP 'endorsing' a predictable mixture of wholesale privatisation, trade liberalisation and fiscal stringency.

Despite the relatively receptive attitude from civil society regarding the PRSP process in Zambia, it is still clearly influenced by donors in its inception and development and by the fact that the Bank and Fund Boards have the final sign-off to 'approve' it. Also, the PRSP is not the only document that defines conditionality. Zambia cannot access the HIPC initiative unless its government has negotiated a 'Decision Point' document with the IMF and World Bank and has agreed a 'Letter of Intent' for an IMF PRGF programme.

The undemocratic imposition of policies on Zambia has also undermined its ability to engage effectively in multilateral fora such as the World Trade Organisation (WTO). As the WTO was being created in 1994 through the Uruguay Round of the General Agreement on Tariffs and Trade (GATT), Zambia was already being required to unilaterally reduce its tariff barriers, rendering meaningless some of the results of the WTO process.

Zambia's bound rates on goods at the WTO, agreed as part of the Uruguay round, are all in the range of 35 to 60 per cent. The vast majority are 40 to 45 per cent. Yet the actual tariffs practised since the Bank and Fund required trade liberalisation in the early 1990s are: 0, 5, 15 and 25 per cent, well below what was negotiated in the WTO. Most of this liberalisation happened before 1994, and none as part of a multilateral process. None of the WTO negotiated rates will ever be applied under the four tariff line system devised with the IMF.

In contrast to industrialised countries, which wait for trade rounds to reduce their tariffs as part of a multilateral process, the IMF and World Bank require poor countries such as Zambia to liberalise unilaterally. This effectively takes away their bargaining chips in any subsequent negotiations. So there is little point in developed country Ministers - such as the UK Trade Secretary or the UK Development Secretary - telling poor countries such as Zambia to make the most of the multilateral system and stand up for their rights in the WTO when, through the IMF and World Bank, these same developed countries are unfairly pushing poor countries into unilateral liberalisation.

In conclusion, while there is no doubt that pre-IMF/World Bank Zambian economic policy would have had its flaws, and while it is possible to lay some of the blame for Zambia's post-IMF/World Bank economic and social problems at the door of government corruption, there is no escaping the responsibility the IMF and World Bank, and their political masters, must shoulder for their interventions.

This report clearly demonstrates that the IMF and World Bank's involvement in Zambia has been unsuccessful, undemocratic and unfair. The evidence suggests that the past twenty years of IMF and World Bank intervention have exacerbated rather than ameliorated Zambia's debt crisis. Ironically, in return for debt relief, Zambia is required to do more of the same. The country has been condemned to debt.

If the downward spiral is to be broken, and the MDGs are to be achieved, radical action must be taken. The evidence presented in this report points to two obvious conclusions. It is time to cancel Zambia's debt. And it is time to fundamentally rethink the role of the IMF and World Bank. It is not acceptable that these institutions have effective control over policy-making in countries like Zambia. Policies need to be developed which are genuinely home grown alternatives that put the Zambian people, especially the poor, first.

The responsibility for this change lies with industrialised country governments such as the UK. The UK Development Secretary (Hilary Benn) sits on the Board of the World Bank and the UK Chancellor of the Exchequer (Gordon Brown) sits on the Board, and Chairs the Finance Committee, of the IMF. Fundamental change in these institutions can only come from these political decision-makers. As the holders of power in the IMF and World Bank, it is the industrialised countries who must take action if they are to turn their development rhetoric into meaningful results.

COMESA TEXTILE PROGRAM

1. INVESTOR DESCRIPTION

ABC Clothing is a Mauritian clothing manufacturer. They are primarily in the business of making shirts and pants, although they have made uniforms to order for local businesses. ABC has considered options of exporting to the United States under AGOA, however its production facilities are capable of producing only a tenth of what a typical American buyer would require.

2. OPPORTUNITIES

ABC sees an opportunity to supply countries in Southern Africa including Zambia, Zimbabwe, Botswana, Malawi and Namibia with its clothing. There are few local manufacturers with the exception of Zimbabwe, and while the clothing must be made at a low cost to accommodate the income levels of the market, clothing remains a basic necessity item.

ABC understands that competition will come primarily from within the region from South Africa and Zimbabwe. It also knows that foreign goods sourced from Asia are plentiful in the countries. Finally, the company has great concerns of competing with used clothing that is present in some of the target countries.

3. INVESTMENT PROCESS

ABC is unfamiliar with the marketplace and the rules of doing business in its targeted countries. Little information is available to them, however some individual buyers have come to Mauritius to buy goods from Zambia and Zimbabwe for resale in their countries.

ABC would likely send management to trade fairs and exhibitions typically during August and September with the intent of making contacts with local distributors to find a partner. ABC would prefer to sell its goods into the market for at least one year before deciding on an investment destination. Because Mauritius' labor market is almost at capacity, it will be very difficult for ABC to expand its operations to serve these markets. It does have the option of expanding production to Madagascar, which is what many Mauritian firms have done.

4. DECISION PROCESS

Cost of Investment: ABC is concerned about the time that management must take away from the factory to establish marketplaces. From speaking to other clothing manufacturers, it is extremely difficult to establish relationships with reputable local distributorships. It is likely that they will have to work on a cash basis until strong relationships are built, and this can stunt the growth of the business.

ABC is unsure about available land and/or existing facilities into which it can expand its operations. There is little information available to them in Mauritius on labor laws, productivity rates, and infrastructure rates (although Mauritian firms are better off than their counterparts in Namibia, Zambia, and Malawi due to the presence of the Mauritian Export Development and Investment Authority). ABC anticipates a lengthy process in investigating these costs.

Revenues: ABC is currently unsure as to the level of competition, although it feels that it can competitively price its goods with Zimbabwe and South Africa, particularly with duty-free access to the marketplace. It understands that many local competitors, particularly in Zambia and Malawi, have gone out of business, and it believes that this is due to foreign competition and the presence of used clothing. It also understands that local wages are low and in some of the envisaged marketplaces stagnant. Nonetheless it feels it can compete, although the products it will manufacture will be of a considerably lower quality that what it delivers to Europe.

Cost of Doing Business: Clothing does not have a high transport component, although the lower quality clothing does, by its nature, have a relatively higher cost component. What concerns ABC in some respects is the access to currency. Several of its target markets have experienced shortages in hard currency, and in some cases significant devaluations have taken place in short periods of time. ABC can initially work around this problem by pricing in dollars and demanding payment in cash, but eventually if it intends to expand, it will be forced to become more immersed in the market's currencies.

ABC does not anticipate heavy bureaucracy. There are positive stories of firms working in Madagascar, and they believe that the integration of economies that comes from COMESA (more so than SADC) will allow them choose a site and open a facility fairly easily. ABC does not perceive these countries as being very corrupt and feels it can do business without making payments and bribes to officials.

Risk: For the most part, ABC does not fear nationalization of its facilities so it does not feel this form of risk. It feels a greater risk lies in its ability to repatriate profits, make payments for raw materials, and collect from debtors. ABC does not believe that the court systems in these countries will protect their interests, and they worry about changing policies towards profits and overseas remittances.

It has encountered a number of stories of unscrupulous business people and this is of great concern to them. ABC will seek to ameliorate this risk by seeking out business partners with whom other Mauritian firms have dealt.

5. ANALYSIS

The scenario of ABC clothing emphasizes the barriers inherent in sales and revenues. Competition has all but eliminated clothing manufacturing in Zambia and Malawi, and it threatens Zimbabwean firms. Some of this competition comes through legal channels, a considerable amount is smuggled in duty free. The question that will face ABC is whether they will be able to sell enough to justify the investment.

In this scenario, it is likely that ABC will move very slowly, learning the ropes via marketing its goods for cash through various contacts. Many other firms from Zimbabwe and Mauritius have gone this route, and have sometimes had the misfortune of selling goods on terms to distributors that are either unscrupulous or unable to pay. Doing business on a cash basis makes it very difficult to expand the operations, so in this case growth comes very slowly.

Some of the firms interviewed have proceeded directly on these lines. Firms mainly from Zimbabwe and Mauritius, and, to a lesser degree Malawi have been encouraged by sales to individual traders that have purchased items with cash. They have traveled to marketplaces, sometimes using the exhibitions, other times trying to make local contacts through telephone books and word of mouth. Both are slow and often unrewarding processes. In most cases, the company owners themselves are traveling. This puts a heavy burden on the management of the facility because the owners often play a major role in the factory's day-to-day operations. Communications are difficult and very expensive between member states, and travelers feel cut-off from their facilities.

Assuming ABC makes it past the stage of merely trading in the nations and chooses an investment destination, it must turn to some of the government imposed processes. For the most part, clothing manufacturers do not have a heavy bureaucracy burden imposed on them. They are often labor-intensive operations with low environmental impact, and most governments are very welcoming to this type of operation. However, ABC will likely face very difficult problems when it comes to exporting management, particularly in the startup stages.

High unemployment in the target countries make it difficult for immigration departments to understand why operations managers, many of them with fewer academic qualifications than some of the local unemployed, must be imported. It is likely that ABC will fight a pitched battle for every non-senior executive it wishes to import. Even countries that permit a base number of expatriates (such as Zambia's allowance of 5 expatriates) still create problems if they feel that local talent is available.

It is important to note at this time that this investment can range from anywhere between 40 and 150 percent of the firm's investment already in Mauritius, making it, for this investment, an extremely high-risk investment. This investor's inability to import management will scare off many investors completely from investing. Investors in Mauritius suggest that in Madagascar, there has been little or no interference by government in allowing Mauritian firms to import labor to Madagascar.

All these points may be made moot if ABC is unable to sell its goods. No bureaucracy, magnificent relationships with distributors, stable currencies and other factors mean nothing if the typical garment is sold for less than ABC's cost of manufacture.

The first concern for ABC will be used clothing. Surprisingly, some Malawi manufacturers do not attribute the import of used clothing to the downfall of the Malawian and Zambian clothing manufacturing industries. However, it is clear that goods, some of which are of higher quality than goods sold as new, are available for a fraction of the price and with wide distribution.

National governments are faced with a dilemma: despite claims by the above-mentioned Malawi firms, Zimbabwean and Zambian clothing manufacturers claim that there is little market for new goods. A once thriving Zambian clothing manufacturing industry, albeit well protected by tariffs in the past, has been decimated, putting thousands out of work. Neighboring countries Botswana, Namibia, and Zimbabwe, have either strictly curtailed access or prohibited them altogether.

However, used clothing provides a sometimes high quality basic necessity to low-income and unemployed individuals at affordable prices. Clearly there is a consumer benefit as the marketplace is more open and free.

This issue will magnify and may become a significant source of disagreement when the common external tariff is negotiated. Zimbabwe has a great deal of jobs in the clothing industry, and while it has the capability of exporting, a great deal of the work is dependent on the local marketplace. Should Zimbabwe open its borders to used clothing, it could possibly close a number of small manufacturers. Alternatively, Zambia and Malawi have provided citizens the opportunity to purchase used clothing at a significant discount to new.

ABC, like many manufacturers, is not very familiar with COMESA, the Secretariat, or its policies. It has heard of the free trade area through newspapers and announcements, and feels that it provides it with an advantage, particularly with competitors from South Africa and the Far East. Many firms do not understand the difference between SADC and COMESA, and are skeptical that real changes are taking place. Some have noticed lowered duties, but the duties have lowered very gradually. This left many interviewees indifferent about the announcement of a duty-free area. None of the firms interviewed had not heard of a Common Investment Area.

ABC will soon learn that a large number of goods enter the region completely duty-free through payoffs and bribery. This study was not intended to collect the percentage of goods that enter COMESA through these means or to identify ports of entry. However, several firms interviewed that have exported to neighboring countries have been disappointed that their advantage is not as great as first thought.

A complete analysis of imported goods was not done, but interviewees suggested that the goods that enter local markets are taken from batches of clothing destined for Western countries and are seconds and of lower quality. Their costs are minimal for these goods, as they have nowhere else to send them. When duties are not paid, these goods come into countries at a significant cost advantage.

The bottom line is this: If ABC cannot sell its goods at a price that allows it to be profitable because of competition, it will not expand its operations to other COMESA countries.

6. WHAT COMESA CAN DO

There is an ideological battle to be waged in thinking this process through. This report suggests that governments be concerned that manufacturers be able to acquire the price at which they can profitably sell their goods. This is not a new concept as manufacturers have, seemingly since the beginning of time, argued for more protection and more tariffs. On the other hand, the people that elect the government must buy these goods. Giving the population access to affordable basics necessities such as clothing is a must.

On the one front is the issue of used clothing. Its cost is minimal, not much more than the cost of shipping. Its quality is sometimes very good. Its distribution network in countries that allow it is extremely strong. Yet clearly it tremendously narrows the market to producers of new clothing and reduces the opportunity to engage this labor-intensive industry.

The other front involves the avoidance of paying duties by unscrupulous business people and customs officials. Long recognized as a drain on national economies, economic integration means that corruption in one country becomes another's loss. COMESA has not, to a large degree, addressed corruption as a regional issue. It has primarily left it as national. Indeed, degrees of corruption vary greatly from country to country. However, it is recommended that COMESA raise the issue of corruption as a regional issue.

Some textile firms that operate in markets that have used clothing continue to sell to the local market, indicating that opportunities do exist. However, the lack of information available has plagued firms, which was mentioned during the interviews. The trade fairs and exhibitions have provided firms with good opportunities to make contacts, but the costs are high. This goes beyond the cost of the plane fare and accommodation, but extends to the absences from the office.

By providing firms with more information, COMESA can decrease the cost of investment and ensure that textile and clothing firms can achieve the revenue levels that are required to invest in exporting.

Another point that was addressed in interviews was the American Growth and Opportunity Act (AGOA), which promised duty-free access to a massive marketplace. However, the vast majority of local manufacturers do not have even a small percentage of the required capacities to satisfy American firms. Some of the larger Zimbabwean and Mauritian firms either have the capacity or the resources to sell into the market. Mauritian firms, lacking the available labor pool to expand, have tapped labor resources in Madagascar, through bi-lateral accords.

However, it is difficult to see where COMESA will have an impact on AGOA. While Zambia and Zimbabwe produce cotton, it is sold at world market prices as a commodity. Most countries in the region already either have incentives for raw material import or are duty free. Textiles are often imported from countries with comparative advantages (typically the Far East). AGOA allows certain countries to source raw materials from outside the region, but it is likely that companies based in those countries that are not eligible for this exemption will simply shift production to countries that are eligible (e.g., Mauritian firms in Madagascar).

AGOA has already had an impact on production in some firms. This impact is not the result of COMESA integration, but comes from the need of these firms to tap into other markets to increase their benefits, whether through export or through moving their production. COMESA could possibly have an impact if it can assist small producers in given regions to connect with each other across borders in order to meet the scale for the demands of the U.S. Market. This will only be successful, however, if private sector investors find this profitable by standardizing the quality of the small producers to meet export demand.

SELECTED TEXTILE EXPORTERS

GARMENTS AND ACCESSORIES

Bonar Colwyn Ltd
P O Box 70431
Ndola, Zambia
Tel: 613097
Telex: 33180
Fax: 613090

Industrial wear, Protective clothing, bermuda shorts jeans trousers

Contact: Mr Harris

Serioes International
P O Box 90830
Luanshya,Zambia
Tel: 510754
Telex: 6563
Fax: 511616

Suits, trousers, overalls protective clothing, combat uniforms, accessories

Contact: Mr J Zulu

HANDICRAFTS AND CURIOS

AFZU Crafts Ltd - Bushcraft
P O Box 31045
Lusaka, Zambia
Tel: 221116 Telex: 44860
Fax: 291134

Basketware, costume jewellery, wooden carvings, malachiteware

Contact: Ms K Kotze

Makishi Crafts Limited
P O Box 32930
Lusaka,Zambia
Tel/Fax: 226200

Basketware, costume, jewellery, wooden carvings, wooden carvings, malachiteware

Contact: Mrs D M Mulombwe

Medusa Arts Limited
P O Box 22874
Kitwe,Zambia

Contact: Julia Summons

Zintu Ltd
P O Box 31190
Lusaka, Zambia
Tel/Fax: 254463

Basketware, carvings, Costume Jewellery

Contact: Mrs G F Chongwe

HORTICULTURAL PRODUCTS

Agribeef Limited
P O Box CH 30
Lusaka, Zambia

Tel: 281717
Fax: 281501

Vegetables

Contact: Mr N Slade

Amanita Zambia Limited
P O Box 30131

Mushrooms

Lusaka, Zambia Contact: Mr D Cassilli

Cheetah Zambia Limited Vegetables, spices, paprika,
P O Box 36666 natural colours
Lusaka, Zambia
Tel: 287630/1
Fax: 286665 Contact: Mr M Terken

Framkos Limited Grapes
P O Box 840040
Mkushi,Zambia Contact: Mr F Arnautovic

Galaunia Farms Vegetables
P O Box 30089
Lusaka, Zambia
Tel: 229556 Telex: 42850
Fax: 221428 Contact: Mr P Clapp

J Y Estates Limited Vegetables
P O Box CH 30
Lusaka,Zambia
Tel: 230888
Fax: 230888 Contact: Mr Jones

Littleford Enterprises Grapes
P O Box 31830
Lusaka,Zambia
Tel: 230142 Contact: Mr D Littleford

Watergreen Farms Vegetables
P O Box 31111
Lusaka, Zambia
Tel: 227824-8
Telex: 41850 Contact: Mr G Narder

York Farm Vegetables
P O Box 30829
Lusaka, Zambia
Tel: 274080
Telex: 40637
Fax: 272357 Contact: Mr P Barker

Zambia Export Growers Association Horticultural Products
P O Box 31705
Lusaka,Zambia
Tel: 271166/271472-4
Fax: 271504
Tlx: ZA 40559 Contact: Chief Executive

LEATHER AND LEATHER PRODUCTS

Asaria Leather Industries Ltd Wetblue leather,
P O Box 36050 crust leather

For additional analytical, business and investment opportunities information, please contact Global Investment & Business Center, USA at (202) 546-2103. Fax: (202) 546-3275. E-mail: rusric@erols.com

Lusaka, Zambia
Tel: 241519/240966
Telex: 40008
Fax: 242860/240982 Contact: Mr K R Mehta

Bimzi Limited — Exclusive leather garments, Footballs, Handbags, Conference bags, etc.
P O Box 50514
Lusaka,Zambia
Tel: 247353/242985/242993
Fax: 245558 Contact: Sales Manager

Copperbelt Shoes Limited — Industrial footwear, PVC footwear
P O Box 71644
Ndola,Zambia
Tel: 650156/650327
Fax: 650215 Mr P Dawson

Kembe Estates Ltd — Waterblue leather, crust leather, leather splits
P O Box 32922
Lusaka, Zambia
Tel: 221580 Fax: 223035 Contact: Mr C A Spyron

SIDO Tnning and Leather — Wetblue leather, crust leather
P O Box 80831
Kabwe,Zambia
Tel: 221937
Fax: 813952
Tlx: 813952 Contact: General Manager

TEXTILE, YARN AND FABRICS

Copperbelt Weaving Ltd — Medical Bandages
P O Box 71101
Ndola, Zambia
Tel: 650398 Telex: 30062
Fax: 650170 Contact: Mr R C Desai

Deetex Ltd — Knitted grey fabric
P O Box 30015
Lusaka, Zambia
Tel: 247549 Telex: 43230
Fax: 243029 Contact: Mr Gordhino

Excel Textile Mills — Cotton yarn, Tarpaulins, canvas fabric
P O Box 71406
Ndola,Zambia
Tel: 655234
Fax: 655372 Contact: Mr R Patel

Kafue Textiles (Z) Ltd — Loomstate cotton fabric
P O Box 360131
Kafue, Zambia
Tel: 311501 Telex: 70020
Fax: 311514 Contact: J P Bondaz

For additional analytical, business and investment opportunities information, please contact Global Investment & Business Center, USA at (202) 546-2103. Fax: (202) 546-3275. E-mail: rusric@erols.com

Mukuba Textiles Ltd Cotton yarn
P O Box 70358
Ndola, Zambia
Tel: 655397 Telex: 30550
Fax: 655813 Contact: Mr M S Naik

Mulungushi Textiles Ltd African prints, dress prints P O Box 81091
cotton yarn,loomstate fabric
Lusaka, Zambia
Tel: 224407 Telex: 81330
Fax: 224916 Contact: Marketing Manager

Ndola Knitting Mills Ltd Knitted grey fabric, single and
P O Box 72097 double cotton jersey
Ndola, Zambia
Tel: 650139 Telex: 34640 Contact: General Manager

Ndola Weaving Textiles Ltd Suiting fabric
P O Box 72160
Ndola, Zambia
Tel: 655578 Telex: 34830
Fax: 655247 Contact: Mr N K Patel

Nkwazi Manufacturing Company Twin & Fishing nets
P O Box 360106
Kafue,Zambia
Tel: 311447/247549
Telex: 70070/43230
Fax: 311432 Contact Mr Bwanali

Sakiza Spinning Mills Acrylic Yarn
P O Box 23156
Kitwe, Zambia
Tel: 210865 Telex: 51023
Fax: 210041 Contact: Mr Mehta

Swarp Spinning Mills Ltd Cotton yarn, polycot sewing
P O Box 71846 threads
Ndola, Zambia
Tel: 650296 Telex: 30060
Fax: 650172 Contact: Mr R J Patel

Starflex Textiles Ltd Cotton yarn
P O Box 70813
Ndola, Zambia
Tel: 655735 Telex: 34640
Fax: 650216 Contact: Mr C Q Mtonga

Towel Textiles Ltd Terry Towelling
P O Box 22354
Kitwe, Zambia
Tel: 223109 Telex: 53450

Fax: 228862 Contact: Mr D L Crawford

Townap Textiles Limited
P O Box 60039
Livingstone,Zambia
Tel: 320574
Fax: 320461
Bedsheets, towelling suiting
Contact: Technical Manager

Agribusiness Development Corp
P.O Box 320171
Lusaka
Tel:611154
Fax:611154
Sawn Timber, Hardwood
Contact: Mr John Castle

Appolo Enterprises Limited
P O Box 10610
Chingola,Zambia
Tel: 313225
Tlx: 54330
Sawn mukwa boards
Railway sleepers and knocked down furniture
Contact: Mr J H Steyn

Chivas Limited
P O Box 33467
Lusaka,Zambia
Tel: 272351
Sawn Timber
Contact: Mr N Holloway

Fallsway Timbers Ltd
P O Box 60010
Livingstone, Zambia
Tel: 320175 Telex: 24420
Fax: 323286
Sawn timber, mining timber and parquet battens
Contact: Mr S B Vora

Supersonic International
P O Box 60497
Livingstone, Zambia
Tel: 320301 Telex: 24170
Fax: 322130
Email:kkmal@zamnet.zm
Railway sleepers, planks, parquet battens, wooden doors, sawn boards.
Contact: Mr Malani

Wood Processing Industries
P O Box 71415
Ndola, Zambia
Tel: 650396 Telex: 34780
Fax: 650109
Email:wpi@zamnet.zm
Chipboards, particle boards, pine timber and knocked down furniture.
Contact: Mr R N Patel

Zambia Forests & Forestry Industries Corp. (ZAFFICO)
P O Box 71566
Ndola, Zambia
Tel: 613867 Telex: 30000
Fax: 613867
Eucalyptus poles and pine sawn timber, transmission poles and telephone poles - all treated
Contact: Mr C T Mwale

KAFUE TEXTILES OF ZAMBIA

KTZ is a vertically integrated textile mill with the capacity to produce 20 million metres/year of fabrics in a wide range of finished goods (including African Print and Drills). It is located on a 21.044 hectares (52 acres) site in the Industrial Area of Kafue, which is approximately 40 kilometres south of Lusaka and is well serviced by roads, utilities and rail.

The large and versatile textile manufacturing complex comprises spinning/weaving and textile processing factories, warehouses/storage buildings, training centre with canteen and kitchen, clinic, boiler house and customer sales office. It is served by a skilled and committed workforce. The company is jointly owned by Government (99.33%), Maurer Textiles/Amenital (0.33%), Commonwealth Development Corporation (0.19%) and Barclays Bank of Zambia Limited Staff Pension Fund (0.15%). The shareholders have waived their rights of preemptions, to facilitate this sale.

PRODUCTS AND MARKET
In recent years, KTZ's dominant position in the domestic textile market (ie sales of African prints, drills, cotton/polyester poplin, averaging US$ 6 million/year), has been eroded by increased competition from imported textiles and liquidity problems. The company has responded by producing 100% grey cloth for export.
The textile industry in Zambia appears poised for an exciting period of prolonged growth. This is underscored by the 154% rise recorded in textile export sales to Zambia's largest single market, Germany, which rose by 70% from US$ 8.1 million in 1994 to US$ 13.8 million in 1995. The rise is reflective of:

The benefits of tariff and quota free access to Europe Community Markets, as a result of the Lome IV convention.

The relatively low cost of power (less than three cents/KWH) and affordable & skilled workforce.
Success of export enhancement programmes funded by bilateral/multilateral agencies.
Domestically, a market exists for a wide range of fabrics including industrial clothing, drills and African print, which are currently being imported.

Therefore, the opportunity exists (with the right kind of leadership, marketing and level of resource) for KTZ to be transformed into a regionally competitive company.

SUPPLY AND PRODUCTION
The availability of cotton has been enhanced by the recent privatisation of Zambia's state cotton ginnery, resulting in a sector characterised by rapid expansion and quality cotton at competitive prices.
Major equipment includes the blowroom, spinning and weaving plants, which incorporate Platt and Reiter spinning machinery and Sultzer-Ruti looms.
Presently the company's mainstay is the yarn preparation and weaving section, which was augmented in 1984 with the addition of new Rieter plant.

Privatisation Process
The Zambia Privatisation Agency is inviting offers for the immediate sale of KTZ.
Contact:
The Chief Executive
Zambia Privatisation Agency
Privatisation House
Nasser Road
P.O. Box 30819
LUSAKA, ZAMBIA
Fax: + 260 1 225270
Tel: + 260 1 222858, 220177, 227791

For additional analytical, business and investment opportunities information, please contact Global Investment & Business Center, USA at (202) 546-2103. Fax: (202) 546-3275. E-mail: rusric@erols.com

E Mail: zpa@zpa.org.zm

SEMI-PRECIOUS STONES

Allied Metals Ltd — Lapidary Products
P.O Box 35579
Lusaka
Tel:227946
Fax:228065 — Contact: Mr O Makungo

Chinole Mining Company — Aquamarine
P.O Box 33315
Lusaka
Tel:272959
Tel\Fax:241107 — Contact:Mr Grey Zulu

Chipazuba Company Ltd — Amethyst
P.O Box 310265
Lusaka
Tel:283161 — Contact: Mrs P Mundia

E Kayaya Enterprises Ltd — Lapidary Products
P O Box 37527
Lusaka,Zambia
Tel:222736 — Mr E Kayaya

Gramiraj Investments Ltd — Amethyst
P O Box 34393
Lusaka, Zambia
Tel: 223641
Fax: 223641 — Contact: Mrs M Lubemba

JACE Enterprises — Amethyst
P O Box 30304
Lusaka,Zambia
Tel: 221165 — Mr B C Wightman

Fax: 221003
Jagoda Gems Ltd — Various Stones
P.O Box 33373
Lusaka
Tel:223131
Fax:263764 — Contact: Mr Ross Walker

Kagem Mining Ltd — Emeralds - rough
P O Box 21657
Kitwe, Zambia

Tel: 216477/226919/216049
Fax: 216324 Telex: 52032 Contact: The General Manager

Kariba Amethyst Marketing Ltd Amethyst, rough
P O Box 32568
Lusaka, Zambia
Tel: 287043/287041 Contact: Mr K Fey
Telex: 42230
Fax: 22696

Klenan Investment Ltd Various Stones
P.O Box 23453
Kitwe
Tel:226342 Contact: Mr Jason Stephenson

Livingstone Lapidaries Ltd Lapidary Products
P.O Box 60005
Livingstone
Tel:322484
Fax:322484 Contact: Mr R S Nayee

Lumpuma Mines Ltd
P.O Box 40956
Mufulira
Tel:412638\222877 Contact: Mr F. C.Katele

Makoye Gemstones Ltd Various Stones
P.O Box 37561
Lusaka,Zambia
Contact: Mr Christopher Musako

Makunga Investment Ltd Amethyst
P.O Box 37387
Lusaka,Zambia
Tel:225565
Fax:225564 Contact: Mr Philemon Kalaba

Montana Mining Zambia Ltd Emeralds
P.O Box 260024
Kalulushi
Tel:733254
Fax:733254 Contact:Mr Jack Grobler

Nkuralu Gem Prospecting Emeralds - rough
P O Box 21672
Kitwe, Zambia
Tel: 212735 Contact: Mr P Nkhata

Norodom Mines Ltd Emeralds - rough
P O Box 28059
Kitwe, Zambia

Tel: 228436/227295 Contact: Mr M Kabwe

Pan-Afro Gem Lapidary — Precious and semi-precious stones
P O Box 70016
Ndola,Zambia
Tel: 613171/613385
Fax: 615685 Contact: Shirley Dechnik

Reserved Minerals Corp. Ltd — Aquamarine, beryl, tourmaline garnet, rough emerald
P O Box 35175
Lusaka, Zambia
Tel: 229459/227050
Telex: 40094
Fax: 223652 Contact: Mr CM Chitambo

Sachin Mines — Emeralds
P.O Box 90826
Kalulushi
Tel:731133
Fax:731122 Contact: Mr H K Kastner

Sitonia Limited — Amethyst
P O Box 337167
Lusaka,Zambia
Tel: 287167
Fax: 272540

Southern Stream Enterprises Ltd — Various Stones
Lima Hall, Showgrounds
P.O Box 33342
Lusaka
Tel: 251333
Fax: 246281 Contact: Mrs Rita Mittal

Zambia Emerald Industries Ltd — Emeralds, cut and polished
P O Box 73717
Ndola, Zambia
Tel: 655661-2/655824/655204
Fax: 655802 Telex: 34320 Contact: Marketing Manager

USEFUL BUSINESS CONTACTS

TRADE RELATED ORGANISATIONS AND MINISTRIES

Ministry of Commerce Trade and Industry Cairo Road	Export Board of Zambia 3rd Floor Lotti House P.O. Box 30064 Lusaka	Investment Centre Ndeke House P.O. Box 34580 Lusaka

P.O. Box 31968 Lusaka Tel: 228301-9 Tlx: 45630 Fax: 226673	Tel: 228106/7 Tlx: 40309 Fax: 222509	Tel: 252130, 252133, 252152 Tlx: 40596 Fax: 252150
Zambia Privatisation Agency P.O. Box 30189 Lusaka Tel: 223859 Tlx: 406641 Fax: 225270	Lusaka Stock Exchange P.O. Box 34523 Lusaka Tel: 228537 Fax: 225969/228608	Ministry of Finance Headquarters P.O. Box RW 50062 Lusaka Tel: 250544
Zambia Revenue Authority Profund House P.O. Box 35710 Lusaka Tel: 223754/229214-8	National Commission for Development Planning (NCDP) P.O. Box 50268 Lusaka Tel: 227649	Zambia Bureau of Standards P.O. Box 50259 Lusaka Tel: 227171
Zambia Association of Chambers of Commerce and Industry (ZACCI) P.O. Box 30844 Lusaka Tel: 252369 Fax: 252483 Tlx: ZA 40124	Common Market for Eastern and Southern Africa (COMESA) P.O. Box 30051 Lusaka Tel: 229725 Fax: 224961 Tlx: 40456	SGS Lusaka Liaison Office Cairo Road P.O. Box 33673 Lusaka Tel: 225323/225137 Tlx: 45300 Fax: 227394/227176
Zambia International Trade Fair (ZITF) P.O. Box 71058 Ndola Tel: 655514-6 Fax: 655704 Tlx: 34260	Zambia Agricultural & Commercial Show Society P.O. Box 30333 Lusaka	

CENTRAL BANK

Bank of Zambia
P.O. Box 30080
Lusaka
Tel: 228888/229885
Fax: 221791
Tlx: ZA 42999

COMERCIAL BANKS

Barclays Bank of Zambia Ltd Cairo Road P.O. Box 31936 Lusaka Tel: 228858 66 Tlx: 43500 Fax: 222519	Citi Bank (Z) Ltd Katunjila Road P.O. Box 30037 Lusaka Tel: 229025/227592 Tlx: 45610	Credit Africa Bank Ltd Anchor House Cairo Rd P.O. Box 36245 Lusaka Tel: 220201 4 Fax: 220196 Tlx: ZA 40707
Finance Bank Ltd P.O. Box 37102	Indo Zambia Bank Limited 686 Cairo Road	New Capital Bank Ltd 1st Floor.Lotti Hse

Lusaka Tel: 229739/229742 Fax: 227544 Tlx: ZA 40338	P.O. Box 35411 Lusaka Tel: 225080/222622 Tlx: 40613 Fax: 225090	Cairo road P.O. Box 36452 Lusaka Tel: 229508/11 229569 Tlx: 43830 Fax: 224055
Stanbic Bank (Z) Ltd (formerly ANZ Grindlays Bank International) Cairo Road Woodgate House P.O. Box 31955 Lusaka Tel: 229071/3 229285 Tlx: 42461 Fax: 221152	Standard Chartered Bank (Z) Ltd P.O. Box 32238 Lusaka Tel: 229242 Tlx: 41660/45420 Fax: 222092	Union Bank Ltd Zimco House P.O. Box 34940 Lusaka Tel: 229397/8 Tlx: 45150/40112 Fax: 221866
Zambia Export and Import Bank Ltd P.O. Box 33046 Lusaka Tel: 229504/222304/229486/88 Fax: 222313	Zambia National Commercial Bank Ltd Cairo Road P.O. Box 33611 Lusaka Tel: 221377/221584 Tlx: 42360	

DEVELOPMENT BANKS

Development Bank of Zambia P.O. Box 33955 Lusaka Tel: 228576/224072	Cavmont Merchant Bank Tazara House P.O. Box 35476 Lusaka Tel: 224316 Fax: 224304	Zambia National Building Society Society House, Cairo Road P.O. Box 30420 Lusaka Tel: 229191 Fax: 225510 Tlx: ZA 41880

INSURANCE FIRMS

Zambia State Insurance Corporation Limited Premium House P.O. Box 30894 Lusaka Tel: 229343/57 Fax: 222263 Tlx: 42521	Professional Insurance Company Findeco House 2nd Floor P.O. Box 37782 Lusaka Tel: 224388/227509/227334 Fax: 222151 Tlx: 40338	Madison Insurance Company P/B E810 Lusaka Tel: 228340 Fax: 236532
ZCF Insurance Limited P.O. Box 32613 Lusaka Tel: 222663/222665/222706 Fax: 222762 Tlx: 40670	Zambia National Insurance Brokers P.O. Box 30699 Lusaka Tel: 228360/5 Fax: 222913 Tlx: 44630	

CAR HIRE FIRMS

Germins Car Hire & Tours Ltd P.O. Box 35257 Lusaka Tel: 220146/283310	Ridgeway Car Hire services P.O. Box 30929 Lusaka Tel: 225209	Rute Car Hire P.O. Box 31651 Lusaka Tel: 225018 Fax: 225025/221858
Taiwo Transport Ltd P.O. Box 36224 Lusaka Tel: 29183/291248/294043 Fax: 291248	Zungulila Zambia P.O. Box 31475 Lusaka Tel: 227730/223234/227790 Fax: 227729	

CLEARING AND FORWARDING AGENTS

AMI Zambia Ltd P.O. Box 30131 Lusaka Tel: 228988 Fax: 243146	Hill & Delamain (Z) Ltd P.O. Box 30899 Lusaka Tel: 228412/222218/271155 Fax: 271439	Kariba Freight Ltd P.O. Box 37080 Lusaka Tel: 244704/248233/224975 Fax: 223351
Manica Freight Services Ltd P.O. Box 31895 Lusaka Tel: 228707/292557/271025	Walford Meadows Ltd P.O. Box 31280 Lusaka Tel: 287804/287502 Fax: 286747/271183	Zamcargo (Z) Ltd P.O. Box 31055 Lusaka Tel: 289692 7 Fax: 271373 Tlx: 45590/40142

THE CHAMBERS OF COMMERCE & INDUSTRY

Most of the Chambers of Commerce and Industry in Zambia exist along an active business zone known as *the line of rail.*

This area runs from Chingola town in the Northern part of the Copperbelt to Livingstone in the Southern most part of the country.

Currently, there are only seven (7) Chambers that are affiliated to ZACCI. These Chambers are : Lusaka Chamber, Ndola Chamber, Kitwe Chamber, Kabwe Chamber, Chingola Chamber, Livingstone Chamber and the Eastern Province Chamber.

The Eastern Province Chamber is the only regional Chamber in the country at the moment.

It is expected that the list of Chambers will grow in the next few years owing largely to the increasing awareness by the local business sector that they need to be properly organised in order to develop.

The following are the full contact details for the Chambers of Commerce and Industry in Zambia :

NAME	ADDRESS	TEL	FAX	E-MAIL
ZAMBIA ASSOCIATION OF CHAMBERS	Showgrounds, Great East Road, Box 30844. Lusaka.	Tel: 255046/ 253020/ 252369	253007/ 252483	zacci@zamnet.zm

OF COMMERCE & INDUSTRY	Zambia			
LUSAKA CHAMBER	1st Floor, Farmers House, Room 126 Cairo Road, Box 37997, Lusaka Zambia	221266	224114	luschamb@zamnet.zm
NDOLA CHAMBER	C/O Shymans Services Box 210241, Ndola, Zambia	Tel: 619296	619297	shymans@zamnet.zm
KITWE CHAMBER	C/O INOVA Limited Box 21662, Kitwe, Zambia	222025	221360	inova@coppernet.zm
KABWE CHAMBER	Box 80914, Kabwe	221008/229350	229347/225776	.
CHINGOLA CHAMBER	C/O ZNCB Chingola Branch Box 10795, Chingola, Zambia	312957	313891	rotex@zamnet.zm
LIVINGSTONE CHAMBER	29 Airport Road, Box 60648 Livingstone, Zambia	Tel/Fax: 323656		denmar@zamtel.zm
EASTERN PROVINCE CHAMBER	C/O Box 510953, Chipata	062- 22925/ 22306/ 21447/ 21509	062-21210/ 21509	ais@zamnet.zm

HOTELS AND TRANSPORT IN ZAMBIA

HOTELS

There is a number of hotels in Zambia of international standards especially in Lusaka. Advance booking and reconfirmation imme diately prior to arrival is therefore essential. The following are the most commonly used by International travelers.

TRANSPORT

RAIL AND ROAD TRANSPORT

Being a landlocked country, transshipping is inevitable for Zambia. Ports usually used for imports and exports are Durban in South Africa and Dar es Salaam in Tanzania.
From all ports, goods may be transported by rail or by road. The infrastructure is in good condition.

The route from the port of Beira is fairly safe now with the improvement/cessation of civil hostilities in Mozambique and so, it too, offers an option to the southern route.
Covered, refrigerated as well as open wagons are available on the northern route on the Tanzania Zambia Railway, and the southern route through Zimbabwe or Botswana on Zambia Railways.

AIR TRANSPORT

Zambia has one international airport at Lusaka with a capacity to park twelve (12) large aircraft Airbus, Boeing 747, DC 10 etc. Smaller air ports are at Ndola, Kitwe and Livingstone. International passenger as well as cargo planes take off at Lusaka. Flights to London, Rome, Frankfurt, Amsterdam, Bombay, Johannesburg, Nairobi, Harare and Gaborone are available from Lusaka on airlines flying into Lusaka.

WATERWAYS

There are no major inland waterways in Zambia. Mpulungu Port on lake Tanganyika is an inland water port linking Zambia and Burun di. Some of Zambia's exports to Burundi and Rwanda, especially cement and sugar, go through this port. It is however a small port.

For additional analytical, business and investment opportunities information, please contact Global Investment & Business Center, USA at (202) 546-2103. Fax: (202) 546-3275. E-mail: rusric@erols.com

IMPORTANT LAWS AND REGULATIONS

THE CONSTITUTION OF ZAMBIA ACT, 1996

Date of assent: 28th May, 1996.

An Act to provide for the printing and publication of the amended Constitution; to provide for the savings and transitional provisions of existing offices, institutions and laws; to provide for the savings of succession of property and assets, rights, liabilities, obligations and legal proceedings; and to provide for matters connected with or incidental to the foregoing.

28th May, 1996
ENACTED by the Parliament of Zambia.

1. SHORT TITLE

This Act may be cited as the Constitution of Zambia Act, 1996.

2. INTERPRETATION

(1) In this Act, unless the context otherwise requires --

- "Constitution" means the Constitution of Zambia, 1991 Act No. 1 of 1991;
- "existing law" means all law, whether a rule of law or a provision of an Act of Parliament or of any other enactment or instrument whatsoever (including any Act of Parliament of the United Kingdom or Order of Her Majesty in Council), having effect as part of the law of Zambia or party thereof immediately before the commencement of this Act, and includes any Act of Parliament or statutory instrument made before such commencement and coming into force on such commencement or thereafter.

(2) Except where the context requires, words and expressions used in this Act have the same meaning as in the Constitution.

3. AMENDMENT OF CONSTITUTION OF ZAMBIA ACT, 1991 AND SCHEDULE THERETO

Except as provided under this Act, the Constitution of Zambia Act, 1991, and the Consitution in the Schedule thereto, are amended in so far as they form Part of the laws of Zambia.

4. COMMENCEMENT

Subject to the other provisions of this Act, the Constitution as amended under Act No. 18 of 1996, shall come into operation on the commencement of this Act.

5. PRINTING AND PUBLICATION OF THE CONSTITUTION

The Constitution may be printed and published by the Government Printer separately from this Act, and the production of a copy of the Constitution as amended purporting to be so printed shall be *prima facie* in all courts and for all purposes whatsoever of the Constitution and its provisions.

6. EXISTING LAWS

(1) Subject to the other provisions of this Act, and so far as they are not inconsistent with the Constitution as amended, the existing laws shall continue in force after the commencement of this Act as they had been made in pursuance of the Constitution as amended, but shall be construed with such modifications, adaptations, qualifications and exceptions as may be necessary to bring them into conformity with the Constitution as amended.

(2) The President may, by statutory instrument at any time within two years of the commencement of this Act, make such amendment to any existing law as may appear to him to be necessary or expedient for bringing that law into conformity with the provisions of this Act or the Constitution as amended or otherwise for giving effect or enabling effect to be given to those provisions.

(3) Where any matter that fails to be prescribed or otherwise provided for under the Constitution by Parliament or by any other authority or person is prescribed or provided for by or under any existing law, including any amendment to any such law made under this section, or is otherwise prescribed or provided immediately before the commencement of the Act by or under the law amended by section three, that prescription or provision shall, as from the commencement of this Act, have effect as if it had been made under the Constitution by Parliament or, as the case may be, the other authority or person.

(4) This section shall be without prejudice to any powers conferred by this Act or the Constitution upon any person or authority to make provision for any matter, including the amendment or repeal of any existing law.

7. PREROGATIVES AND PRIVILEGES OF THE PRESIDENT

Where under the existing law any prerogatives or privileges are vested in the President these prerogatives or privileges shall, after the announcement of this Act, continue to vest in the President.

8. CONTINUATION IN OFFICE OF PRESIDENT

The person holding the office of President immediately before the commencement of this Act shall, unless he ceases to hold office by virtue of the provisions of Article 34 or 35 of the Constitution or resigns, continue in office and shall exercise the executive powers of the President under the Constitution as amended until the person elected at the first election to the office of President under the Constitution as amended assumes office.

9. EXISTING OFFICES

(1) Where any office has been established by or under the law as amended repealed by section three and the Constitution as amended establishes a similar or an equivalent office, any person who immediately before the commencement of this Act holds or is acting in the former office shall, so far as is consistent with the Constitution as amended, be deemed to have been appointed, elected or designated as from the commencement of this Act to hold or to act in the latter office in accordance with the Constitution as amended and to have taken the oath of allegiance and any other necessary oath under the Constitution:

Provided that any person who, under the law amended under section three or any other existing law, would have been required to vacate his office at the expiration of any period or on the attainment of any age shall vacate his office at the expiration of that period or upon the attainment of that age.

(2) Any person holding the office of Vice-President, Minister and Deputy Minister under the Constitution immediately before the commencement of the Constitution shall continue in office and shall exercise the powers conferred on them by the existing Constitution as amended.

(3) Subject to the provision of the Constitution relating to persons in public employment, any person who is a public officer and who immediately before the commencement of this Act holds any public office shall continue to be a public officer of the Government after the commencement of this Act.

(4) The President may, at any time after the commencement of this Act, require any person who continues in office by virtue of this section to take an oath of allegiance and any oath for the due execution of his office that is prescribed by or under any Act of Parliament.

(5) This section shall be without prejudice to --

- (a) the provisions of section ten; and
- (b) any powers conferred by or under the Constitution upon any person or authority to make provision for the abolition of offices or the removal of any person holding or acting in any office.

10. THE NATIONAL ASSEMBLY

(1) Subject to subsection (2), the National Assembly constituted under the law amended by section three (hereinafter referred to as "the existing National Assembly") shall be the National Assembly during the period beginning on the commencement of this Act and ending on the date set for the holding of elections to the office of President and the National Assembly under the Constitution as amended.

(2) The persons who immediately before the commencement of this Act are the elected or nominated members of the existing National Assembly shall continue to be members of the National Assembly during the period beginning on the commencement of this Act and ending on the date set for the holding of elections to the office of President and the National Assembly under the Constitution as amended, and, in the case of elected members, shall be deemed to have been elected to the National Assembly to represent the same constituencies as the constituencies for which they were respectively elected.

(3) The persons who immediately before the commencement of this Act are the Speaker and the Deputy Speaker of the existing National Assembly shall continue to be respectively the Speaker and the Deputy Speaker of the National Assembly during the period beginning on the commencement of this Act and ending on the date set for the holding of elections to the office of the National Assembly under the Constitution as amended.

(4) As the functions and powers vested in Parliament by the Constitution shall be exercised, during the period beginning on the commencement of this Act and ending on the date set for the holding of elections to the office of President and National Assembly, by the Parliament in accordance with the existing Constitution as amended.

(5) The rules and orders of the existing National Assembly as in force immediately before the commencement of this Act, shall, until it is otherwise provided for under Article 86 of the Constitution as amended, be the rules of procedure of the National Assembly but shall be

For additional analytical, business and investment opportunities information, please contact Global Investment & Business Center, USA at (202) 546-2103. Fax: (202) 546-3275. E-mail: rusric@erols.com

construed with such modifications, adaptations, qualifications and exceptions as may be necessary to bring them into conformity with the Constitution as amended.

(6) Any person who under this section continued to be the Speaker, Deputy Speaker or a member of the National Assembly after the commencement of this Act shall be deemed to have taken the necessary oath under the Constitution as amended.

(7) All moneys granted, voted or appropriated by the existing National Assembly in respect of the services of the Republic for the current financial year shall be deemed to have been granted, voted or appropriated by the National Assembly and in accordance with the Constitution as amended.

11. SUCCESSION TO PROPERTY AND ASSETS

(1) Subject to this Act and the Constitution as amended, all property of every nature and kind whatsoever and all assets that immediately before the commencement of this Act were vested in, or held in trust for, the President or in any other person in right of or for the purposes of the Government of Zambia shall after the commencement of this Act continue to be so vested or held in trust, as the case may be.

(2) Any property which, immediately before the commencement of this Act, was liable to escheat or to be forfeited to the President for the purposes of the Government of Zambia, after the commencement of this Act, be liable to escheat or to be forfeited to the President on behalf of the Government of Zambia.

12. RIGHTS, LIABILITIES AND OBLIGATIONS

All rights, liabilities and obligations of the President or any public officer on behalf of the Government of Zambia before the commencement of this Act shall, on and after the commencement of this Act, be rights, liabilities and obligations of the President or such public officer, as the case may be, on behalf of the Government of Zambia.

13. LEGAL PROCEEDINGS

(1) All proceedings that, immediately before the commencement of this Act, are pending before any court established by or under the law amended by section three may be continued and concluded before the corresponding court established by or under the Constitution.

(2) Any proceedings that immediately before the commencement of this Act are pending before any Commissioner of the High Court appointed by or under the law amended by section three shall be continued and concluded before such Commissioner, notwithstanding the abolition of the office of Commissioner of the High Court.

14. TRANSITIONAL PROVISIONS

(1) All rights and obligations under conventions, treaties or agreements which were exercisable by or binding upon the Government of Zambia immediately before the commencement of this Act shall continue to be so exercisable and binding.

(2) All functions which immediately before the commencement of this Act were vested in the President or in any other authority shall, as far as the same continue in existence and are capable of being exercised after the commencement of this Act, be vested in the President or the authority

For additional analytical, business and investment opportunities information, please contact Global Investment & Business Center, USA at (202) 546-2103. Fax: (202) 546-3275. E-mail: rusric@erols.com

exercising similar functions under the Constitution as amended, as the case may be, except such functions as are by this Act or any other law vested in some other authority.

15. APPEALS IN RESPECT OF CERTAIN DECISIONS AFFECTING PENSIONS AND LIKE BENEFITS

(1) The following provisions of this section shall have effect for the purpose of enabling any officer to whom this section applies or his personal representatives to appeal against a decision to which this section applies, that is to say a decision within the following clauses:

- (a) a decision of the Service Commission to give such concurrence as is required by Article 124 of the existing Constitution as amended in relation to the refusal, withholding, reduction in amount or suspension of any benefits in respect of such an officer's service as a public officer;
- (b) a decision by any authority to remove such an officer from office if the consequence of the removal is that benefits cannot be granted in respect of the officer's service as a public officer;
- (c) a decision by any authority to take some other disciplinary action in relation to such an officer if the consequence of the action is to reduce the amount of any benefits that may be granted in respect of the officer's service as a public officer.

(2) Where any decision such as is referred to in subsection (1) is taken by any authority, the authority shall cause to be delivered to the officer concerned, or his personal representatives, a written notice of that decision stating the time, not being less than twenty-eight days from the date on which the notice is delivered, within which he, or his personal representatives, may apply to the authority for the case to be referred to an Appeals Board.

(3) If application is duly made to an authority within the time stated in such a notice as is mentioned in subsection (2) for a case to be referred to an Appeals Board, the authority shall notify the President in writing of that application and the President shall appoint an Appeals Board for that purpose consisting of --

- (a) one member selected by the President;
- (b) one member selected by an association representative of public officers or a professional body, nominated in either case by the applicant; and
- (c) one member selected by the two other members jointly (or, in default of agreement between those members, by the Chief Justice) who shall be the Chairman of the Board.

(4) Such an Appeals Board shall inquire into the facts of the case that is referred to it, and for that purpose the Board --

- (a) shall, if the applicant so requests in writing, hear the applicant either in person or by a legal representative of his choice, according to the terms of the request;
- (b) may hear any other person who, in the opinion of the Board, is able to give the Board information on the case; and
- (c) shall have access to, and shall consider, all documents that were available to the authority concerned and shall also consider any further document relating to the case that may be produced by or on behalf of the applicant or the authority.

For additional analytical, business and investment opportunities information,
please contact Global Investment & Business Center, USA
at (202) 546-2103. Fax: (202) 546-3275. E-mail: rusric@erols.com

(5) When such an Appeals Board has completed its consideration of the case, then --

- (a) if the decision that is the subject of the reference to the Board is a decision such as is mentioned in paragraph (a) of subsection (1), the Board shall advise the appropriate Commission whether the decision should be affirmed, reversed or modified and the Commission shall act in accordance with that advice;
- (b) if the decision that is the subject of the reference to the Board is a decision such as is mentioned in paragraph (b) or (c) of subsection (1), the Board shall not have power to advise the authority responsible for making the decision to affirm, reverse or notify the decision but the Board may advise the authority responsible for granting the benefits in question --
    - (i) where the officer has been removed from office, to grant all or part of the benefits for which the officer concerned would have been eligible under any law if he had retired voluntarily at the date of the dismissal; or
    - (ii) where some other disciplinary action has been taken in relation to the officer, that on the grant of any benefits under any law in respect of the officer's service such benefits shall be increased in such manner, as the Board may specify in order to offset all or any part of the reduction in the amount of such benefits that, in the opinion of the Board, would or might otherwise be a consequence of the action;
- and that authority shall act in accordance with that advice the provisions of that law shall have effect accordingly.

(6) In this section --

- "pensions benefits" has the meaning assigned to it in clause (5) of Article 124 of the Constitution as amended;
- "Service Commission" has the meaning assigned to it in clause (2) of Article 123 of the Constitution as amended.

(7) This section applies to any officer who on the 24th October, 1964, was on pensionable conditions of service and --

- (a) was designated under the Overseas Service Aid Scheme, or
- (b) was immediately before the 24th October, 1964, a member of Her Majesty's Overseas Civil Service or Her Majesty's Overseas Judiciary; or
- (c) whose conditions of service included an entitlement to free overseas passages from Zambia for the purpose of leave of absence upon the completion of a tour of duty; or
- (d) was not a citizen of Zambia.

16. COMPULSORY RETIREMENT OF NON-CITIZENS

Notwithstanding anything to the contrary contained in this Act or the Constitution the President may, with a view to securing the appointment of citizens of Zambia to public offices direct retirement from public office of any person who is not a citizen of Zambia.

For additional analytical, business and investment opportunities information, please contact Global Investment & Business Center, USA at (202) 546-2103. Fax: (202) 546-3275. E-mail: rusric@erols.com

Provided that no person shall be retired under the provisions of this section unless notice in writing is given to him specifying the date of retirement which shall not be earlier than six months from the date on which such notice is received by him.

THE INVESTMENT ACT, 1993

1. [SHORT TITLE]

This Act may be cited as the Investment Act, 1993.

2. [INTERPRETATION]

In this Act, unless the context otherwise requires--

- " Board" means the Investment Board of the Centre established by section six;
- " bonded factory " means a factory which is a warehouse, bonded and licensed in terms of section fifty-five of the Customs and Excise Act, in which goods may be lodged, kept and secured without the payment of duty or until the requirements of that Act have been satisfied, and includes any store, house, shed, yard, or other place in which goods are so lodged;
- " business enterprise " includes any undertaking, carrying on business in the field of manufacturing, agriculture, transport, communications, construction tourism and services or know-how; [*As amended by Act No. 26 of 1995*]
- " Centre" means the Investment Centre constituted under
- " Commissioner " means the Commissioner of Taxes appointed under the Income Tax Act;
- " Controller " means the Controller of Customs and Excise appointed under the Customs and Excise Act;
- " Director-General" means the chief executive officer of the Centre appointed by the Board;
- " economic development zone or export processing zone " means any area declared to be an economic development zone or export processing zone under section twenty-eight,
- " foreign investment " means investment brought in by an investor from outside, and invested in Zambia;
- " investment " means contribution of capital, in cash or in kind, by an investor, to a new business enterprise, to the expansion or rehabilitation of an existing business enterprise or to the purchase of an existing business enterprise from the State;
- " investor " means any person, natural or juridical, whether a Zambian citizen or not, investing in Zambia in accordance with the provisions of this Act;
- " Investment Certificate " means a certificate issued by the Board under section ten;
- " manufacturing " means the transforming, on a commercial scale, of raw materials into finished or semi-finished products, and includes the assembling of inputs into finished or semi-finished products, but does not include mining;

- " member " means a member of the Board;
- " mineral " shall be construed in its general, extensive and comprehensive sense and shall include ore and mineral products, any substance whether in solid, liquid or gaseous form occurring naturally in or on the earth but shall not include public and private water when used for a primary, secondary or tertiary use as defined in the Water Act;
- " mining " means the winning of any mineral;
- " non-traditional products " means products other than raw copper, lead, zinc or cobalt;
- " rural area " means any area in Zambia other than Kabwe Urban District, Kafue Township, Livingstone District, Lusaka Urban District and the Copperbelt Province excluding therefrom Ndola Rural District;
- " Secretary " means the Secretary to the Board.

3. [NON-DEROGATION FROM ANY OTHER LAW]

This Act shall be cumulative and in addition to, and not in derogation from, any other written law

PART II INVESTMENT CENTRE AND BOARD

4. [CONSTITUTION OF INVESTMENT CENTRE]

Notwithstanding section thirty-nine, the Investment Centre as constituted under the Investment Act, 1991, shall continue to exist as if constituted under this Act.

5. [FUNCTIONS OF CENTRE]

(1) The functions of the Centre shall be to promote, co-ordinate Government policies on, and facilitate, investment in Zambia, so as to provide a one-stop support facility to investors.
(2) Notwithstanding the generality of subsection (2) the functions of the Centre shall be to --

- (a) promote investment in Zambia;
- (b) monitor the performance of enterprises approved by it and enforce compliance with the terms and conditions of investment certificates approved under this Act;
- (c) establish and maintain institutional liaison arrangements;
- (d) assist in securing from any Ministry, government department, local authority or other relevant body any permission, exemption, authorisation, licence, bonded status, land and any other thing required for the purpose of establishing or operating a business enterprise;
- (e) keep records of all technology transfer agreements relating to investments under this Act;
- (f) provide consultancy services to investors;
- (g) collect and disseminate information on relevant laws and regulations, and technical matters, including applicable standards, specifications and quality control procedures;
- (h) undertake economic and sector studies, including market surveys, with a view to identifying investment opportunities;

- (i) register investors;
- (j) implement decisions made by the Board;
- (k) exercise all functions and powers and perform all duties which under or by virtue of this Act or any other written law are, or may be, vested or delegated to it; and
- (l) do all such things as are necessary or incidental or conducive to the functions specified in this Act.

6. [Establishment of Board]

(1) There is hereby established the Investment Board of the Centre which shall be a body corporate with perpetual succession and a common seal, capable of suing and of being sued in its corporate name and with power, subject to the provisions of this Act, to do all such acts and things as a body corporate may by law do or perform.
(2) The provisions of the First Schedule shall apply as to the constitution of the Board and otherwise in relation thereto.

7. [Functions of Board]

(1) Subject to the other provisions of this Act, the Board shall be responsible for the affairs of the Centre.
(2) Notwithstanding the generality of subsection (1) the Board shall--

- (a) implement investment policies;
- (b) formulate investment promotion strategies;
- (c) establish investment guidelines for the Centre;
- (d) issue investment certificates; and
- (e) do all such things as are necessary or incidental to the better carrying out of the functions specified in this Act.

PART III PROCEDURES FOR INVESTMENT IN ZAMBIA

8. [Investment Certificate]

Any person investing in a business enterprise may apply for an Investment Certificate under this Part:
Provided that in respect of the industries specified in the Second Schedule, the Board shall not issue an Investment Certificate to an investor until the investor obtains the necessary licences, authorisations, or permits from the relevant ministry or body.

9. [Application for Investment Certificate]

(1) An application for an Investment Certificate in the form set out in the Third Schedule shall be made to the Director-General and shall be accompanied by a non-refundable fee determined by the Board.
(2) The Director-General shall, on receipt of an application for an Investment Certificate, submit the application to the Board for its consideration at the next meeting of the Board.

10. [Issue of Investment Certificate]

For additional analytical, business and investment opportunities information, please contact Global Investment & Business Center, USA at (202) 546-2103. Fax: (202) 546-3275. E-mail: rusric@erols.com

(1) The Board shall, within six weeks of receipt of an application for an Investment Certificate issue an Investment Certificate, with general or special incentives, as the case may be, in the form set out in the Fourth Schedule, if--

- (a) the application is in accordance with the provisions of this Act; and
- (b) the activity planned to be undertaken by the business enterprise does not contravene any laws and regulations in force in Zambia.

(2) A decision of the Board in respect of an application for an Investment Certificate shall be communicated to the applicant, in writing, within fourteen days of the Board's decision: Provided that a decision of the Board rejecting an application shall be accompanied by the reasons for the rejection.

11. [Appeal from decision of Board]

Any applicant for an Investment Certificate who is aggrieved by a decision of the Board rejecting the application may appeal to the Minister subject to a further appeal to the High Court.

12. [Condition of Investment Certificate]

An Investment Certificate issued under section ten shall--

- (a) authorise the holder thereof to make all necessary arrangements for the commencement of the business enterprise described therein;
- (b) contain terms and conditions of the certificate and any general or special incentives given; and
- (c) have unlimited period of validity, subject to it being utilised within twelve months from the date of issue.

13. [Variation of Investment Certificate]

(1) The holder of an Investment Certificate may at any time during the validity of the certificate, of the terms and conditions of the certificate, the incentives granted thereunder or any matter relating to the certificate.
(2) The Board shall consider the application referred to in subsection (1) and may after negotiations, if any, grant or refuse such application.

14. [Extension and surrender of Investment Certificate]

(1) Where the holder of an Investment Certificate is unable to commence operations within twelve months from the date of issue, he shall, at least sixty days before the expiry of his certificate, apply to the Board for an extension of that period, giving reasons thereof; and the Board shall, if satisfied with the reasons, extend the validity for such period as he may consider reasonable.
(2) Where the holder of an Investment Certificate decides not to continue with any project to which the certificate relates, he shall so notify the Board in writing and shall agree with the Board the terms and conditions of the surrender of the certificate with particular reference to anything done or any benefit obtained under the certificate.
(3) Where the period of twelve months from the date of issue of an Investment Certificate has expired without the holder of the certificate commencing business operations and no application for its extension has been made in accordance with subsection (2) the certificate shall lapse and shall, subject to section seventeen, be cancelled and the holder of the licence shall cease to be entitled to any benefits obtainable under the certificate.

15. [Transfer of Investment Certificate]

(1) An Investment Certificate shall not be transferred to a third party without the prior approval of the Board but such approval shall not be unreasonably withheld.
(2) Every application for approval to transfer an Investment Certificate shall be made to the Board and the Board may, within thirty days of the application, approve the application, in accordance with this Act.

16. [AMENDMENT OF INVESTMENT CERTIFICATE]

The Board may amend an Investment Certificate --

- (a) where some other person has succeeded to the interest in the business enterprise belonging to the holder of the Investment Certificate, by substituting for the name of the holder the name of the successor; or
- (b) where the name of the business is altered, by substituting the name so altered.

17. [SUSPENSION OR CANCELLATION OF INVESTMENT CERTIFICATE]

(1) Subject to the other provisions of this suspend or cancel any Investment Certificate if the investor --

- (a) obtained the Investment Certificate by fraud, deliberate or negligent submission of false information or statements;
- (b) transfers or otherwise assigns an Investment Certificate without the prior approval of the Board;
- (c) contravenes this Act or any terms and conditions of the certificate issued to him; or
- (d) fails without reasonable cause to establish the business enterprise within the time stipulated in the certificate or any extension thereof.

(2) The Board shall, before suspending or cancelling an Investment Certificate in accordance with subsection (1), give its written notice to the investor of its intention to suspend or cancel the Investment Certificate and the grounds for the suspension or cancellation and require the investor to show cause within a period of not more than thirty days why the certificate should not be suspended or cancelled.
(3) The Board shall not suspend or cancel and Investment Certificate under this section if the investor takes remedial measures to the satisfaction of the Board within the period of thirty days referred to in subsection (2).
(4) If the Investor notified under subsection (2) fails to show cause to the satisfaction of the Board or does not take remedial measures to the satisfaction of the Board within the time specified in that subsection, the Board may suspend or cancel the Investment Certificate.
(5) Where an Investment Certificate is suspended, the holder of the certificate shall cease to be entitled to the rights and benefits conferred under this Act for the period of the suspension.
(6) Where an Investment Certificate is cancelled the holder of the certificate shall cease to be entitled to the benefits conferred under this Act with effect from the date of such cancellation and shall return the licence to the Director-General.
(7) Any person who is aggrieved by any decision of the Board under this section may appeal to the Minister subject to further appeal to the High Court.

PART IV
GENERAL INCENTIVES

Section:

18. [QUALIFICATIONS FOR GENERAL INCENTIVES]

The general incentives provided in this Part shall apply to any investor investing in a business enterprise under this Act.

19. [INCOME TAX FOR FARMING]

An investor shall be taxed on income received from farming at a rate of fifteen per centum.

20. [INCOME TAX ON NON-TRADITIONAL PRODUCTS]

An investor shall be taxed on that portion of income which is determined by the Commissioner as originating from the export of non-traditional products at a rate of fifteen per centum.

21. [INCOME TAX ON RURAL ENTERPRISES]

An investor shall be taxed on income received from a rural enterprise for each of the first five charge years for which such business enterprise is carried on, reduced by such amount as is equal to one-seventh of that tax which would otherwise be so chargeable on such income.

22. [INCOME TAX ALLOWANCES]

(1) An Investor shall be entitled to capital allowances which shall be deducted in ascertaining the gains or profits at the following special rates:

- (a) buildings used for manufacturing or hotels qualify for a wear and tear allowance of five per centum per year of the cost, plus an initial allowance of ten per centum of the cost in the year in which the building is first used; [*As amended by Act No. 26 of 1995*]
- (b) implements, machinery and plant used exclusively for farming, manufacturing or tourism qualify for a wear and tear allowance of fifty per centum per year of the costs in each of the first two years;
- (c) capital expenditure on farm improvements qualify for a farm improvement allowance of twenty per centum of such expenditure for each of the first five years.

(2) An Investor who incurs capital expenditure on the growing of tea, coffee, or banana plants, citrus fruit trees or other similar plants or trees, shall be entitled to a development allowance of ten per centum of such expenditure which shall be deducted in ascertaining the gains or profits of that business enterprise for the charge year up to the first year of production.
(3) An Investor is entitled to a farm works allowance of one hundred per centum in respect of expend ownership or occupation, and for the purposes of farming, or stumping and clearing, works for the prevention of soil erosion, boreholes, wells, aerial and geophysical surveys, and water conservation.

23. [INCOME TAX DEDUCTIONS]

An Investor shall be entitled to the following deductions in ascertaining gains or profits:

- (a) any loss incurred by an investor, in any charge year shall be deducted only from the income of the investor from the same source as that in which the loss was incurred; such loss shall be deducted from his income of the following charge year, and so on from year to year; [*As amended by Act No. 26 of 1995*]

For additional analytical, business and investment opportunities information, please contact Global Investment & Business Center, USA at (202) 546-2103. Fax: (202) 546-3275. E-mail: rusric@erols.com

- (b) any payments made for the purpose of technical education relating to a business enterprise or for the purposes of obtaining further experience, training or qualifications, relating to that business enterprise;
- (c) any expenditure, not being expenditure of a capital nature, incurred by a business enterprise during a charge year on experiments or research relating to that business enterprise.

24. [INCOME TAX EXEMPTION ON DIVIDEND FROM FARMING]

Income received by way of a dividend declared from farming shall be exempt from tax for the first five years of operations.

25. [DOUBLE TAXATION AGREEMENTS]

Where a double taxation agreement exists between Zambia and another country, foreign tax payable by an investor to the other country in respect of any foreign income shall be allowed as a credit for that investor against Zambian tax in respect of that foreign income.

26. [INCOME TAX ON MINING]

[*Repealed by Act No. 26 of 1995*]

27. [BONDED FACTORY]

An Investor may apply to be appointed and licensed by the Controller to establish and operate a bonded factory under section fifty-five of the Customs and Excise Act.

28. [ECONOMIC DEVELOPMENT ZONE OR EXPORT PROCESSING ZONE]

The Controller shall, after consultation With the Minister, licence an area as an economic development zone or export processing zone under section fifty-five of the Customs and Excise Act.

29. [SMALL SCALE AND VILLAGE ENTERPRISES]

A small scale enterprise or a village enterprise registered under the Small Industries Development Act, 1981, shall be entitled to the following incentives:

- (a) exemptions from payment of tax on income for--
  - (i) the first three years of operations for an enterprise operating in an urban area;
  - (ii) the first five years of operations for an enterprise in a rural area;
- (b) operation of a manufacturing enterprise for the first five years without a manufacturing licence required for such an enterprise under any law;
- (c) for an enterprise with an investment in plant and machinery of less than five million kwacha, exemption from the payment of licensing fees required for such an enterprise under any law; and
- (d) exemption from the payment of rates on factory premises for the first five years.

[As amended by Act No. 5 of 1996]

30. [IMMIGRATION CAP. 122]

(1) Notwithstanding the provisions of the Immigration and Deportation Act, an investor who invests a minimum of two hundred and fifty thousand United States Dollars or the equivalent in convertible currency and who employs a minimum of ten persons shall be entitled to a self employment permit or resident permit.
(2) The Centre shall assist an investor who meets the requirements of subsection (1) to obtain work permits for up to five expatriate employees.
(3) The Centre shall assist an investor who meets the requirements of subsection (1) to obtain work permits for up to five expatriate employees.

PART V
SPECIAL INCENTIVES

Section:

30A. [QUALIFICATION FOR SPECIAL INCENTIVES]

[As amended by Act No. 5 of 1996]

31. [SAVINGS FOR HOLDERS OF INVESTMENT CERTIFICATE ISSUED BEFORE 27/01/96 AND SMALL SCALE ENTERPRISES]

(1) Any investor who has been issued with an investment certificate with special incentives before the 27th of January, 1996 shall continue to enjoy such incentives.
(2) A small scale enterprise or a village enterprise registered under the Small Industries Development Act, 1981 (No. 18 of 1981), before the 27th January, 1996, shall be entitled to exemption from customs duties and value added tax payable on imported equipment to be used in the enterprise is such equipment was ordered but not imported before the 27th January, 1996.

PART VI
SERVICES

Section:

32. [LAND]

(1) The Centre shall assist an investor in identifying suitable land for investment and shall assist the investor in applying to the responsible authorities for the land in accordance with established procedures.
(2) Where an application is made under subsection (1) and the land has been demarcated for the purpose applied for and such land has not been allocated to any other person, body or authority, the authority responsible for the allocation of land shall, upon payment, by the investor, of the prescribed fees, charges, or rates, allocate the land to the investor and the officer responsible for the registration of such land shall make such entries in the appropriate register and shall issue to the investor a certificate of title in respect of the said land.

33. [WATER, ELECTRICITY, TRANSPORT, ETC.]

The Centre shall assist an investor in obtaining water, electric power, transport and communication services and facilities required for the investment.

34. [REGISTRATION AND LICENSING]

The Centre shall assist an investor in obtaining any licence permit, registration or authorisation for the purpose of commencing or operating the business enterprise.

PART VII
INVESTMENT GUARANTEES AND GENERAL

Section:

35. [PROTECTION FROM ACQUISITION]

(1) No property of any description shall be compulsorily acquired, and no interest in or right over property of any description of an investor shall be compulsorily acquired, except for public purposes under an Act of Parliament relating to the compulsory acquisition of property which provides for payment of compensation in respect thereof.
(2) Any compensation payable under this section shall be made promptly at the market value and shall be fully transferable at the applicable exchange rate in the currency in which the investment was originally made, without deductions for taxes, levies, and other duties except where those are due.

36. [TRANSFER OF FUNDS]

Notwithstanding the provisions of any other written law relating to externalisation of funds, a foreign investor who has registered foreign capital with the Bank of Zambia, shall be entitled, in respect of a business enterprise to which the Investment Certificate relates, to transfer out of Zambia in foreign currency and after payment of the relevant taxes--

- (a) dividends or after-tax income;
- (b) the principal and interest of any foreign loan;
- (c) management fees, royalties, and other charges in respect of any agreement; or
- (d) the net proceeds of sale or liquidation of the business enterprise.

37. [TRANSITIONAL PROVISIONS]

An investor who, immediately prior to the commencement of this Act, holds--

- (a) a valid investment licence or permit, certificate of incentives or certificate of registration under the Investment Act, 1991; or
- (b) any other valid certificate or licence issued under any other written law with respect to a business enterprise recognised by the Board;

shall give written notice to that effect to the Board within six months after the commencement of this Act with a certified copy of the licence, permit or certificate, as the case may be, and the rights and benefits accruing to the holder of such licence, permit or certificate shall continue in accordance with the provisions of the Investment Act, 1991.

38. [REGULATIONS]

(1) After consultation with the Board, the Minister may, by statutory instrument, provide for--

- (a) anything which by this Act is required or permitted to be prescribed;
- (b) the collection of industrial data and the procedure for such collection; and
- (c) such other matters as are necessary or conducive to the better carrying out of the purposes of this Act.

(2) The Minister may, upon recommendation by the Board, by statutory instrument, amend any form set out in the Schedules to this Act.

39. [REPEAL OF ACT NO. 19 OF 1991 AND SAVINGS]

(1) Subject to subsection (2), the Investment Act, 1991 is thereby repealed.
(2) Notwithstanding the repeal of the Investment Act, 1991--

- (a) any agreement executed under that Act shall continue in force as if made under this Act;
- (b) any applications pending before the Investment Board under that Act shall be deemed to have been made to the Board under this Act;
- (c) any registration done, any other right or benefits accruing, or any liabilities suffered under that Act, other than those specified in section thirty-seven, shall continue in accordance with this Act;
- (d) any regulations made or directions given under that Act shall, unless contrary to this Act, continue in force until revoked, as if made or given under this Act.

SCHEDULE I
INVESTMENT BOARD

1. [Composition of Board]

(1) The Board shall consist of--

- (a) a representative of a senior rank from responsible for finance, commerce and industry, legal affairs land, home affairs, tourism and agriculture;
- (b) a representative of the National Environmental Council;
- (c) four persons, one each from--
    - (i) the chambers of commerce and industry;
    - (ii) the farmers;
    - (iii) Non-governmental Organisation Coordinating Committee; and
    - (iv) the agencies promoting small Scale industries.
- (d) three reputable private businessmen appointed by the Minister:

Provided that, notwithstanding section thirty, the persons appointed as members of the Investment Board under the Investment Act, 1991, except the Director-General, shall continue to hold office as members of the Board until the Minister appoints the members under this Act.
(2) The members referred to in items (a), (b), and (c) shall be nominated by their respective institutions and the Minister shall appoint those nominated persons as members of the Board.
(3) The Chairman and the Vice-Chairman shall be elected by the Board from amongst its members:
Provided that the members appointed under items (a) shall not be elected as Chairman or Vice-Chairman.

2. [Tenure of office and vacancy]

(1) The members referred to in paragraph 1 shall hold office for a period of three years from the date of appointment and may be re-appointed upon the expiration of that term.

For additional analytical, business and investment opportunities information, please contact Global Investment & Business Center, USA at (202) 546-2103. Fax: (202) 546-3275. E-mail: rusric@erols.com

(2) A member referred to in items (b), (c), and (d) of sub-paragraph (1) of paragraph 1 may resign upon giving one month's notice in writing to the institution which nominated him and to the Minister.
(3) The office of a member shall become vacant --

- (a) upon his death;
- (b) if he is absent without reasonable excuse from three consecutive meetings of the Board of which he has had notice;
- (c) on ceasing to be a representative of the organisation which nominated him;
- (d) if he is an undischarged bankrupt; or
- (e) if he fails to disclose his interest as required by paragraph 7.

3. [SEAL OF BOARD]

(1) The seal of the Board shall be such device as may be determined by the Board and shall be kept by the Secretary.
(2) The Board may use a wafer or rubber stamp in lieu of the seal.
(3) The affixing of the seal shall be authenticated by the Chairman or the Vice-Chairman and the Secretary or one other person authorised in that behalf by a resolution of the Board.
(4) Any contract or instrument which, if entered into or executed, by a person not being a body corporate, would not be required to be under seal, may be entered into or executed without seal on behalf of the Board by the Secretary or any other person generally or specifically authorised by the Board in that behalf.
(5) Any document purporting to be a document with the seal of the Board or issued on behalf of the Board shall be received in evidence and shall be deemed to be so executed or issued, as the case may be, without further proof, unless the contrary is proved.

4. [REMUNERATION AND ALLOWANCE]

A member of the Board or any committee of the Board shall be paid such remuneration and allowances as the Board may determine.

5. [PROCEEDING OF BOARD]

(1) Subject to the other provisions of this Act, the Board may regulate its own procedure.
(2) The Board shall meet for the transaction of business at least once in very three months at such places and at such times as the Chairman may decide.
(3) Upon giving notice of not less than fourteen days, a meeting of the Board may be called by the Chairman; and shall be called if not less than five members so request in writing:
Provided that if the urgency of any particular matter does not permit the giving of such notice, a special meeting may be called by the Chairman, upon giving a shorter notice.
(4) Nine members shall form a quorum at any meeting of the Board.
(5) There shall preside at any meeting of the Board--

- (a) the Chairman; or
- (b) in the absence of the Chairman, the Vice-Chairman; or
- (c) in the absence of the Chairman and the Vice-Chairman such member as the members present ma elect for the purpose of that meeting.

(6) The Board may invite any person, whose presence is in its opinion desirable, to attend and to participate in the deliberations of a meeting of the Board but such person shall have no vote.

For additional analytical, business and investment opportunities information, please contact Global Investment & Business Center, USA at (202) 546-2103. Fax: (202) 546-3275. E-mail: rusric@erols.com

(7) A decision of the Board on any question shall be by a majority of the member present and voting at the meeting and, in the event of an equality of votes, the person presiding at the meeting shall have a casting vote in addition to his deliberative vote.
(8) The validity of any proceedings , act or decision of the Board shall not be affected by any vacancy in the membership of the Board or by any defect in the appointment of any member or by reason that any person not entitled so to do took part in the proceedings.
(9) The Board shall cause minutes to be kept of the proceeding of every meeting of the Board and of every meeting of any committee established by the Board.

6. [Committees of Board]

(1) The Board may, for the purpose of performing its functions under this Act, establish committees of members of the Board and delegate to any such committee such of its functions as it thinks fit.
(2) The Board may appoint the Director-General as a member of a committee established under subsection (1).
(3) Subject to any specific or general direction of the Board any committee established under subsection (1) may regulate its own procedure.
(4) A committee may invite any person, whose presence is in its opinion desirable, to attend and to participate in the deliberations of a meeting of the committee but such person shall have no vote.

7. [Disclosure of interest]

(1) If any person is present at a meeting of the Board or any committee of the Board at which any matter is the subject of consideration and in which matter that person or his spouse is directly or indirectly interested in a private capacity that person shall, as soon as practicable after the commencement of the meeting, disclose such interest and shall not, unless the Board otherwise directs, take part in any consideration or discussion of, or vote on, any question touching such matter.
(2) A disclosure of interest made under this section shall be recorded in the minutes of the meeting at which it is made.

8. [Immunity of members]

No action or other proceedings shall lie, or be instituted against any member or member of a committee for or in respect of any act or thing done or omitted to be done in good faith in the exercise or purported exercise of his functions under this Act.

9. [Director-General]

(1) The Board shall appoint, on such terms and conditions as it may determine, a Director-General who shall be the chief executive officer of the Centre, and who shall be responsible for the administration of the Centre and the implementation of the decisions of the Board.
(2) The Director-General may, subject to the approval of the Board, establish such organisational structures for the Centre as he may consider necessary for the discharge of the functions of the Centre.
(3) The Director-General shall attend meetings of the Board and may address such meetings, but shall not vote on any matter:
Provided that the person presiding at any meeting of the Board, may for good cause, require the Director-General to withdraw from such meeting.
(4) Paragraph 7 shall apply, with the necessary modifications, to the Director-General.

10. [Secretary and other staff]

For additional analytical, business and investment opportunities information, please contact Global Investment & Business Center, USA at (202) 546-2103. Fax: (202) 546-3275. E-mail: rusric@erols.com

(1) There shall be a Secretary to the Board who shall be appointed by the Board on such terms and conditions as the Board may determine.
(2) The Secretary shall be responsible for the day-to-day affairs of the Board under the general supervision of the Director-General.
(3) The Board may appoint, on such terms and conditions as it may determine, such other staff for the Centre as it considers necessary.

11. [PROHIBITION OF PUBLICATION OR DISCLOSURE OF INFORMATION]

(1) No member of the Board or employee of the person invited to attend a meeting of the Board or committee shall, without the consent in writing given by or on behalf of the Board, publish or disclose to any person, other wise than in the course of his duties, the contents of any document, communication or information whatsoever, which relates to, and which has come to his knowledge in the course of, his duties under this Act.
(2) Any person who knowingly contravenes the provisions of sub-paragraph (1) shall be guilty of an offence and shall be liable, upon conviction, to a fine not exceeding five hundred thousand kwacha or to imprisonment for a term not exceeding three years, or to both.
(3) If any person having information which to his knowledge has been published or disclosed in contravention of sub-paragraph (1) unlawfully publishes or communicates any such information to any other person, he shall be guilty of an offence and shall be liable, upon conviction, to a fine not exceeding five hundred thousand kwacha or to imprisonment for a term not exceeding three years, or to both.

12. [FUNDS OF BOARD]

(1) The funds of the Board shall consist of such moneys as may--

- (a) be appropriated by Parliament for the purposes of the Board;
- (b) be paid to the Board by way of grants or donations;
- (c) be paid to the Board by way of certificate fees; and
- (d) vest in or accrue to the Board.

(2) The Board may--

- (a) accept money by way of grants or donations from any source in Zambia;
- (b) raise money by way of loans or otherwise from any source in Zambia and, subject to the approval of the Minister, from any source outside Zambia, such moneys as it may require for the discharge of its functions; and
- (c) charge and collect fees in respect of programmes, publications, seminars, consultancy services, and other services provided by the Centre.

(3) There shall be paid from the funds of the Board --

- (a) the salaries, allowances and loans of the staff of the Board;
- (b) such reasonable travelling, transport and subsistence allowance for members or members of any committee of the Board when engaged on the business of the Board at such rates as the Board may determine; and
- (c) any other expenses incurred by the Board in the performance of its functions.

(4) The Board may invest in such manner as it thinks fit such of its funds as it does not immediately require for the performance of its functions.

For additional analytical, business and investment opportunities information, please contact Global Investment & Business Center, USA at (202) 546-2103. Fax: (202) 546-3275. E-mail: rusric@erols.com

13. [FINANCIAL YEAR]

The financial year of the Board shall be the period of twelve months ending on 31st December, in each year.

14. [ACCOUNTS]

(1) The Board shall cause to be kept proper books of account and other records relating to its accounts.
(2) The accounts of the Board shall be audited annually by independent auditors appointed by the Board.
(3) The auditor's fees shall be paid by the Board.

15. [ANNUAL REPORT]

(1) As soon as practicable, but not later than six months after the expiry of the financial year, the Board shall submit to the Minister a report concerning its activities during that financial year.
(2) The report referred to in subsection (1) shall include information on the financial affairs of the Board and there shall be appended to the report--

- (a) an audited balance sheet;
- (b) an audited statement of income and expenditure; and
- (c) such other information as the Minister may require.

(3) The Minister shall, not later than seven days after the first sitting of the National Assembly next after the receipt referred to in sub-paragraph (1), lay it before the National Assembly.

THIRD SCHEDULE

(Section 9)

INVESTMENT (NO.___) OF 1993

APPLICATION FOR AN INVESTMENT CERTIFICATE

The Director-General
Investment Centre
P.O. Box 34580
Lusaka

Application is hereby made under the provisions of the Investment Act for the grant and issuance of and Investment Certificate and the following information is submitted in support thereof:

1.

(a) Full name of enterprise..

(b) Plot No..**Street/Road**..
......

(c) Address..
....

(d) Province:.......................................District.......................................Telephone No...................................

(e) Date of incorporation or registration of business name..
....
....

2. State whether your enterprise is: Mark 'X' where applicable.

(a) Sole ownership...
....

(b) Partnership...
....

(c) Private Company...
..

(d) Co-operative Society...

(e) Public Company...
....

(f) Parastatal...
....

(g) Other...
....

3. Particulars of Ownership/Directors:

Name and Full Address	Nationality	Equity %	Amount K	Foreign equity contribution	Foreign investment

4. Brief details of the:

(a) Project:...
..

(b)
Products:..
...

5. Finance:

	Foreign	Local	Total
Equity Capital................			
Loans and Banks..........			
Suppliers credit............			

6. Employment and Training:

	Number to be employed	
Category	Zambian	Non-Zambian
Management		
Technical		
Operatives		
Other (Specify)		
TOTAL		

7. List all technological and management agreements.
Please give brief details:

1.
....

2.
....

3.
....

4.
....

5.
....

6.
....

(You may use a separate sheet)

---

8. The applicants are reminded that any person who fraudulently gives false information or conceals any material in his application risks the revocation of such certificate as provided under the Act. Where any certificate, incentive or other benefit has been granted in consequence of such false statement or concealment, the Investment Board may revoke or cancel any such certificate, incentive or benefit.

I, ... declare that information given above is to the best of my knowledge and belief correct. I further declare that I have not previously submitted any application in respect of the same project.

... Date: ....

...

...

...

INVESTMENT CERTIFICATE

This is to certify that the investors in this certificate has/have been duly registered under the Investment Act, 1993, in the business enterprise specified hereunder:

Name of Investor...

Business Enterprise..

Investment Certificate number:...

Date....................................day of.. 19....................

OFFICIAL STAMP:

THE PRIVATIZATION ACT

PART I
PRELIMINARY

Section:

1. [SHORT TITLE]

This Act may be cited as the Privatisation Act, 1992.

2. [INTERPRETATION]

In this Act, unless the context otherwise requires--

For additional analytical, business and investment opportunities information,
please contact Global Investment & Business Center, USA
at (202) 546-2103. Fax: (202) 546-3275. E-mail: rusric@erols.com

- "Agency" means the Zambian Privatisation Agency established under section three;
- "bank" means a commercial bank registered under the Banking Act [Cap. 700];
- "commercialisation" means the reorganisation of specified Government departments into commercialised enterprises which shall operate as profit making commercial ventures without the subvention of the Government and "commercialise" shall be construed accordingly;
- "consultant" means any person employed by the Agency to undertake any work of a specialized nature connected with the privatisation programme in Zambia and shall include merchant banks, public accountants, lawyers and valuers;
- "current value" means the market value of a State owned enterprise within three months of the completion of sale;
- "divestiture" means the disposing of the whole or part of the assets and shares of a State owned enterprise;
- "divestiture sequence plan" means a list of State owned enterprises, as approved by Cabinet, categorised according to the sequence in which the whole or part of their shares will be disposed of over the period of the privatisation programme;
- "established fund" includes pension funds, contributory social security schemes, compensation funds and superannuation funds;
- "financial institution" means a company, or body not being a bank, which carries on financial business and which is registered under any other law;
- "foreign investor" means a person, being a citizen of Zambia or not, who brings into Zambia foreign exchange for the purchase of shares in a State owned enterprise or for additional investment in a State owned enterprise;
- "golden share" means a share with special rights to enable the Government in the national interest to intervene in the operations of a company which intervention is caused by specific actions undertaken by the company;
- "investor" means an individual, company, established fund, mutual fund, financial institution or foreign government intending to invest in a State owned enterprise under this Act but does not include the Local Government, the Government of the Republic of Zambia and a State owned enterprise;
- "mutual fund" means an investment fund which purchases shares in a portfolio of companies and subdivides such portfolio into individual units for sale of such units to investors;
- "privatisation" means the transferring to the private sector of part or the whole of the equity or other interest held by the Government, directly or indirectly, in a State owned enterprise wholly or partly owned by the Government and "privatise" shall be construed accordingly;
- "Privatisation Revenue Account" means an account established under section thirty-nine;
- "Privatisation Trust Fund" means a fund established under section twenty-nine;

For additional analytical, business and investment opportunities information, please contact Global Investment & Business Center, USA at (202) 546-2103. Fax: (202) 546-3275. E-mail: rusric@erols.com

- "property" means all property movable or immovable, and all estates, interests, easements, and rights, whether legal or equitable into or out of property, choses-in-action, money and good-will;
- "specified Government department" means a department specified by the Minister under section thirty-seven;
- "State owned enterprise" means a corporation, board, company, parastatal or body in which the Government has direct or indirect ownership, equity or interest and includes partnerships, joint ventures or any other form of business arrangement or organisation in which the Government has direct or indirect interest but does not include a Government department;
- "stocks and shares" includes loans, stocks, debentures and debenture stocks and options on any stocks, shares, loan, stock, debentures or debenture stock and rights, in relation to State owned enterprises;
- "stock broker" means a person who carries on the business of buying and selling stocks or shares for and on behalf of other persons.

PART II
THE ZAMBIA PRIVATISATION AGENCY

Section:

3. [Establishment of Agency]

There is hereby established the Zambia Privatisation Agency which shall be a body corporate with perpetual succession and a common seal capable of suing and of being sued in its corporate name, and with power, subject to the provisions of this Act, to do all such acts and things as a body corporate may by law do or perform.

4. [Seal of Agency]

(1) The seal of the Agency shall be such device as may be determined by the Agency and shall be kept by the Director.
(2) The Agency may use a wafer or rubber stamp in lieu of the seal.
(3) The affixing of the seal shall be authenticated by the Chairman or the Vice-Chairman and the Secretary or any other person authorised in that behalf by a resolution of the Agency.
(4) Any contract or instrument which, if entered into or executed by a person not being a corporate, would not be required to be under seal, may be entered into or executed without seal on behalf of the Agency by the Secretary or any other person generally or specifically authorised by the Agency in that behalf.
(5) Any document purporting to be a document under the seal of the Agency or issued on behalf of the Agency shall be received in evidence and shall be deemed to be executed or issued, as the case may be, without further proof, unless the contrary is proved.

5. [Composition of the Agency]

(1) The Agency shall consist of the following members who shall, subject to scrutiny by a Select Committee of the National Assembly and ratification by the National Assembly, be appointed by the President:

- (a) the Permanent Secretary in the Ministry responsible for commerce, trade and industry;

For additional analytical, business and investment opportunities information, please contact Global Investment & Business Center, USA at (202) 546-2103. Fax: (202) 546-3275. E-mail: rusric@erols.com

- (b) the Permanent Secretary in the Ministry responsible for finance;
- (c) the Attorney-General;
- (d) a representative of the Zambia Confederation of Chambers of Commerce and Industry;
- (e) a representative of the Zambia Congress of Trade Unions;
- (f) a representative of the Zambia Federation of Employers;
- (g) a representative of the Law Association of Zambia;
- (h) a representative of the Zambia Institute of Certified Accountants;
- (i) the Dean of the School of Business of the Copperbelt University;
- (j) a representative of the churches of Zambia;
- (k) a representative of the Bankers Association of Zambia; and
- (l) a representative of the farmers.

(2) The Chairman and the Vice-Chairman shall be elected by the Agency from amongst its members:
Provided that the Permanent Secretary in the Ministry responsible for finance and the Permanent Secretary responsible for commerce, trade and industry shall not be elected as Chairman and Vice-Chairman.

6. [TENURE OF OFFICE AND VACANCY]

(1) The members, except ex-officio members, referred to in section five shall hold office for a period of three years from the date of nomination and shall be eligible for further nomination upon the expiration of that term.
(2) A member, except an ex-officio member, referred to in section five may resign upon giving one month's notice, in writing, to the organisation which nominated him and to the Minister.
(3) The office of a member, except an ex-officio member, shall become vacant--

- (a) upon his death;
- (b) if he is absent without reasonable excuse from three consecutive meetings of the Agency of which he has had notice;
- (c) on ceasing to be a representative of the organisation which nominated him; or
- (d) if he is an undischarged bankrupt.

7. [REMUNERATION AND ALLOWANCES OF MEMBERS]

A member shall be paid such remuneration and allowances as the Agency may, with the approval of the Minister, determine.

8. [FUNCTIONS OF AGENCY]

(1) It shall be the function of the Agency to plan, manage, implement and control the privatisation of State owned enterprises in Zambia.
(2) Not withstanding the generality of subsection (1) the functions of the Agency shall be to--

- (a) recommend privatisation policy guidelines to the Cabinet;
- (b) implement the privatisation programme according to the policy guidelines issued by the Cabinet;
- (c) oversee all aspects of the implementation of the privatisation programme in Zambia;
- (d) monitor progress of the privatisation programme in Zambia;
- (e) prepare the long term divestiture sequence plan and submit such plan to the Cabinet for approval;
- (f) recommend to the Cabinet the most appropriate method of sale for each State owned enterprise to be privatised;
- (g) carry out or cause to be carried out a valuation of a State owned enterprise that is to be privatised;
- (h) set prequalification criteria for the selection of potential buyers or investors of a State owned enterprise to be privatised;
- (i) evaluate offers from potential buyers with regard to the--
    - (i) price;
    - (ii) ability and commitment of buyers to develop the enterprise; and
    - (iii) track record of buyers and their expertise in the type of enterprise on offer;
- (j) ensure that monopolies are not created in the process of privatisation;
- (k) prepare or cause to be prepared the relevant documentation necessary to effect the privatisation of any state owned enterprise;
- (l) seek potential investors for State owned enterprises;
- (m) maintain records, safeguard information and establish administrative procedures to ensure confidentiality of information;
- (n) maintain close liason with all relevant institutions in the process of privatisation;
- (o) publicise the activities of the privatisation programme; and
- (p) do all such things as are necessary or incidental or conducive to the better carrying out of the functions specified in this Act.

9. [PROCEEDINGS OF AGENCY]

(1) Subject to the other provisions of this Act, the Agency may regulate its own procedure.
(2) The Agency shall meet for the transaction of business at least once every two months at such places and at such times as the Chairman may decide.
(3) Upon giving notice of not less than fourteen days, the meeting of the Agency may be called by the Chairman and shall be called if not less than four members so request in writing:
Provided that if the urgency of any particular matter does not permit the giving of such notice, a special meeting may be called upon giving a shorter notice.

For additional analytical, business and investment opportunities information, please contact Global Investment & Business Center, USA at (202) 546-2103. Fax: (202) 546-3275. E-mail: rusric@erols.com

(4) Five members shall form a quorum at any meeting of the Agency.
(5) There shall preside at any meeting of the Agency--

- (a) The Chairman;
- (b) in the absence of the Chairman, the Vice-Chairman; or
- (c) in the absence of both the Chairman and the Vice-Chairman such member as the members present may elect or the purpose of the meeting.

(6) A decision of the Agency on any question shall be by a majority of the members present and voting at the meeting and, in the event of an equality of votes, the person presiding at the meeting shall have the casting vote in addition to his deliberative vote.
(7) The Agency may invite any person, whose presence is in its opinion desirable, to attend and to participate in the deliberations of the meeting of the Agency but such person shall have no vote.
(8) The validity of any proceedings or decision of the Agency shall not be affected by an vacancy in the membership of the Agency or by any defect in the appointment of any member.
(9) The Agency shall cause minutes to be kept of the proceedings of every meeting of the Agency and of every meeting of any committee established by the Agency.

10. [COMMITTEES OF AGENCY]

(1) The Agency may for the purpose of performing its functions under this Act establish Committees and delegate to any such committee such of its functions as it considers necessary.
(2) The Agency may appoint as members of a committee established under subsection (1) persons who are or are not members of the Agency and such persons shall hold office for such period as the Agency may determine.
(3) Subject to any specific or general direction of the Agency any committee established under subsection (1) may regulate its own procedure.

11. [DISCLOSURE OF INTEREST]

If any person is present at a meeting of the Agency or any committee of the Agency at which any matter is the subject of consideration and in which matter that person or his immediate family or his professional and business partners, is directly or indirectly interested in a private or professional capacity, he shall, as soon as is practicable after the commencement of the meeting disclose such interest and shall not, unless the Agency or the committee otherwise directs, take part in any consideration or discussion of or vote on, any question touching on such matter.

PART III
ADMINISTRATION

Section:

12. [DIRECTOR OF AGENCY]

(1) The Agency shall appoint, on such terms and conditions as it may determine, a Director who shall be the Chief Executive Officer of the Agency.
(2) The Agency may appoint, on such terms and conditions as it may determine, a Deputy Director to assist the Director.
(3) The Director or in his absence the Deputy Director, shall attend meetings of the Agency and may address such meetings, but shall not vote on any matter:
Provided that the person presiding at any meeting of the Agency, may for good cause, require the Director or Deputy Director to withdraw from such meeting.
(4)Section eleven shall apply, with the necessary modifications, to the Director and the Deputy Director.

For additional analytical, business and investment opportunities information, please contact Global Investment & Business Center, USA at (202) 546-2103. Fax: (202) 546-3275. E-mail: rusric@erols.com

13. [SECRETARY AND OTHER STAFF]

(1) There shall be a Secretary to the Agency who shall be appointed by the Agency on such terms and conditions as the Agency may determine.
(2) The Secretary shall be responsible for the administration of the day-to-day affairs of the Agency under the general supervision of the Agency.
(3) The Agency may appoint, on such terms and conditions as it may determine, such other staff as it considers necessary for the performance of its functions.

14. [DISCLOSURE OF INTEREST BY EMPLOYEES]

(1) An employee of the Agency, or a consultant to the Agency who is, or whose spouse is, directly or indirectly interested in a private or professional capacity, in any matter relating to the privatisation programme shall be required to disclose such interests.
(2) A disclosure of interest made under this section shall be made to the Director who shall take such decision as he considers appropriate in each case.

15. [OATH OF SECRECY]

(1) The employees of the Agency, consultants, members of the Agency and members of a committee of the Agency shall take an oath of secrecy as prescribed under this Act.
(2) Any person who contravenes the provisions of subsection (1) shall be guilty of an offence and shall be liable upon conviction to a fine not exceeding twenty thousand penalty units or to a term of imprisonment for a period not exceeding two years, or to both.
[As amended by Act No. 9 of 1996]

16. [PROHIBITION OF PUBLICATION OR DISCLOSURE OF INFORMATION BY UNAUTHORISED PERSONS]

(1) No person shall, without the consent in writing given by, or on behalf of, the Agency, publish or disclose to any person, otherwise than in the course of his duties, the contents of any documents, communication or information, which relates to, and which has come to his knowledge in the course of his duties under this Act.
(2) Any person who knowingly contravenes the provisions of subsection (1) shall be guilty of an offence and shall be liable upon conviction to a fine not exceeding one hundred thousand kwacha or to a term of imprisonment not exceeding five years, or to both.
(3) If any person having information which to his knowledge has been published or disclosed in contravention of subsection (1) unlawfully publishes or communicates any such information to any person he shall be guilty of an offence and shall be liable upon conviction to a fine not exceeding one hundred thousand kwacha or to a term of imprisonment not exceeding five years, or to both

PART IV
PROCEDURE FOR PRIVATISATION AND COMMERCIALISATION

Section:

17. [PRIVATISATION OF STATE OWNED ENTERPRISES]

A State owned enterprise shall be privatised in accordance with the divestiture sequence plan.

18. [GOLDEN SHARE]

The Minister responsible for finance may, on the advice of the National Assembly, retain a share in a State owned enterprise and convert such share into a golden share.

19. [ALLOTMENT OF SHARES]

The shares of a State owned enterprise shall be alloted by the Agency.

For additional analytical, business and investment opportunities information, please contact Global Investment & Business Center, USA at (202) 546-2103. Fax: (202) 546-3275. E-mail: rusric@erols.com

20. [OBLIGATIONS OF SHARE HOLDERS]

The share holders in any State owned enterprise, when requested by the Agency, shall provide to the Agency such information as the Agency may require.

21. [OBLIGATIONS OF STATE OWNED ENTERPRISES]

(1) A State owned enterprise scheduled for the privatisation shall--

- (a) carry out any recommendations, made by the Agency, for preparing the company for privatisation;
- (b) keep up to date all business records and books of account;
- (c) prepare a two to three years' investment and financing plan and a manpower development plan;
- (d) prepare statutory accounts and cause them to be audited not later than four months after each financial year;
- (e) maintain a fixed asset register which shall be reconciled with the financial statement;
- (f) not perform any action or actions that would result in the assets of the company being dissipated;
- (g) not undertake any new capital investment programmes, unless a project appraisal document approved by the Agency, is prepared showing that--
    - (i) routine plant, equipment and vehicle renewal is required;
    - (ii) rehabilitation expenditure is essential to keep the operations of the State owned enterprise running or to improve the marketability of the enterprise;
    - (iii) new capital investment has a pay back period of less than two years;
    - (iv) capital investment will contribute to the promotion of export-import substitution;
    - (v) the State owned enterprise is not earmarked for divestiture within two years of the investment being completed; or
    - (vi) the State owned enterprise demonstrates that the investment will not allow a deterioration of the company's operations;
- (h) clear as far as possible all contractual, legal and other obligations;
- (i) not give any person information which might give undue advantage to that person or any potential investor;
- (j) pay all costs incidental to the privatisation of an enterprise relating to--
    - (i) valuation fees;
    - (ii) legal costs;
    - (iii) advertising charges;

For additional analytical, business and investment opportunities information, please contact Global Investment & Business Center, USA at (202) 546-2103. Fax: (202) 546-3275. E-mail: rusric@erols.com

- (iv) marketing expenses; and
- (v) any other expense;

- (k) when requested by the Agency, disclose all or any information about the enterprise; and
- (l) refrain from taking any action or actions which may cause industrial unrest.

(2) Any person or officer of a State owned enterprise who knowingly contravenes subsection (1) shall be guilty of an offence and shall be liable upon conviction to a fine not exceeding fifty-five thousand, five hundred and fifty-six penalty units or to a term of imprisonment not exceeding five years, or to both. *[As amended by Act No. 9 of 1996]*

22. [Modes of privatisation]

(1) The Agency may employ the following modes of privatisation:

- (a) public offering of shares;
- (b) private sale of shares through negotiated or competitive bids;
- (c) offer of additional shares in a State owned enterprise to reduce Government share holding;
- (d) sale of the assets and business of the State owned enterprise;
- (e) reorganisation of the State owned enterprise before the sale of the whole or any part of the State owned enterprise;
- (f) management or employee buyouts by management or employees in that State owned enterprise;
- (g) lease and management contracts; or
- (h) any other method the Agency may consider appropriate.

[As amended by Act No. 9 of 1996]

23. [Valuation of state owned enterprise]

(1) The valuation of State owned enterprises shall be performed by independent valuers who shall issue a certificate of valuation.
(2) The valuation of a State owned enterprise shall be done in accordance with the following:

- (a) the valuation shall be based on the current value of the State owned enterprise;
- (b) where the enterprise is not operational or the assets do not form part of a core of the business, the valuation shall be based on the net asset value of the State owned enterprise; or
- (c) any other prudent and acceptable valuation method.

(3) The net asset value shall be based on the--

- (a) valuation certificate of the market value of the real property valued by a real estate valuer;

- (b) valuation certificate of the depreciated replacement value of tangible assets other than real property, or
- (c) a fair value of other assets and liabilities valued by a consultant.

(4) The Agency shall ensure that each State owned enterprise is sold for its market value. *[As amended by Act No. 9 of 1996]*

24. [ELIGIBLE BUYER]

The shares in a State owned enterprise shall be sold to a citizen of Zambia or a person who is not a citizen of Zambia.

25. [SALE OS SHARES TO EMPLOYEES AND CONSULTANTS]

No member or members of a committee or any employee or consultant of the Agency or the spouse, child, mother, father, brother, sister or a professional business partner as the case may be, of the employee or consultant shall purchase shares unless the sale is by public offer of shares.

26. [POLITICAL LEADERS]

Political leaders and public officers shall publicly disclose their intention to bid for the purchase of shares in a State owned enterprise.

27. [DECLARATION BY POTENTIAL INVESTOR]

A potential investor shall disclose his bid in a State owned enterprise, his direct personal interest and his indirect interest, either through share holding or through a nominee or otherwise, in a State owned enterprise.

28. [ESTABLISHED FUND]

An established fund may, with a consent of the contributors, purchase shares in a State owned enterprise on behalf of the contributors.

29. [PURCHASE OF SHARES BY CITIZENS OF ZAMBIA]

(1) The Minister responsible for finance shall establish a Privatisation Trust Fund in which the Government shall hold shares in trust for citizens of Zambia for divesture. *[As amended by Act No. 9 of 1996]*
(2) The following shall apply to citizens of Zambia--

- (a) shares may be offered at a discount to persons who purchase a small number of shares;
- (b) a share bonus shall be given at the end of a prescribed period to small shareholders who hold onto shares;
- (c) individuals, management and employees of the State owned enterprise may pay for shares in instalments; or
- (d) individuals may participate in the acquisition of shares which have been transferred in a State owned enterprise to a Privatisation Trust Fund which shall be established under this Act.

30. [FOREIGN INVESTORS ACT NO. 19 OF 1991]

Foreign investors shall be entitled to incentives under the Investment Act if such investor acquires shares in a State owned enterprise where--

- (a) expertise is needed to upgrade efficiency of that State owned enterprise;
- (b) participation is necessary to promote the export market;
- (c) the nature of business requires global linkages and international exposure; or
- (d) capital investment or foreign technology is required to expand the capacity of the business operations.

31. [MODE OF PAYMENT FOR SHARES]

Subject to provisions of section twenty-nine or any other written law, the shares of a State owned enterprise shall not be sold on credit.

32. [NEGOTIATIONS FOR OFFER OF SALE]

(1) The Agency shall appoint an independent negotiating team for each sale.
(2) A person appointed on the negotiating team shall--

- (a) have proper professional qualifications, experience and good business standing;
- (b) take an oath of secrecy; and
- (c) disclose any personal or professional interest before accepting the appointment.

33. [CONVERSION OF PRIVATE COMPANIES TO PUBLIC COMPANIES]

The Agency may convert a State owned enterprise scheduled for privatisation, which is not a public company, into a public company in accordance with the provisions of the Companies Act [Cap. 686].

34. [TRADING IN SHARES]

Notwithstanding any provision in any other written law and for purposes of this Act, a bank or financial institution may carry on the business of a stock broker or a dealer in stocks and shares.

35. [LIQUIDATION]

The Agency may liquidate a State owned enterprise in accordance with the provisions of the Companies Act [Cap. 686].

35A. [APPOINTMENT OF RECEIVER]

The Agency may appoint a receiver to manage a State owned enterprise in financial difficulties or whose assets are being dissipated so as to enable the Agency to restructure or wind up the company in the interests of the greater community of creditors:
Provided that nothing in this section shall interfere with the rights under any written law of a debenture or mortgage holder.
[As amended by Act No. 9 of 1996]

36. [CONSUMMATION OF SALE]

(1) The Minister responsible for finance shall sign the final Sales Agreement to transfer shares to the selected bidder.

For additional analytical, business and investment opportunities information, please contact Global Investment & Business Center, USA at (202) 546-2103. Fax: (202) 546-3275. E-mail: rusric@erols.com

(2) The transfer of shares shall be in accordance with the provisions of the Companies Act [Cap. 686].

37. [Commercialisation of specified Government departments]

(1) The Minister, in consultation with the Ministry responsible for the department to be commercialised, may specify, by notice in the *Gazette*, any Government department for purposes of commercialisation under this Act.
(2) A specified Government department may be incorporated under the Companies Act [Cap. 686]. *[As amended by Act No. 9 of 1996]*
(3) A Government department specified under this section may--

- (a) fix its own rates, prices and charges for goods and services provided;
- (b) capitalise assets; and
- (c) borrow debenture stocks.

38. [Publication of information]

(1) The Agency shall publish by notice in the *Gazette*--

- (a) the names of the approved State owned enterprises to be privatised;
- (b) the registered consultants, valuers, lawyers, public accountants and merchant banks dealing with the privatisation process;
- (c) the bidders and bid prices;
- (d) the successful bidders and the reason for selecting such the bidders.
- (e) the price of shares and any other special conditions of the sale of shares; and
- (f) any other matters deemed appropriate.

(2) Any person with an interest in a State owned enterprise to be privatised, shall make a claim to the Agency within a period of thirty days after the notice referred to in subsection (1) is published.
(3) Any person having an interest in a State owned enterprise and who does not make a claim within thirty days of the notice referred to in subsection (1) shall be deemed to have relinquished all interests in the State owned enterprise. *[As amended by Act No. 9 of 1996]*

PART V
FINANCIAL AND OTHER PROVISIONS

Section:

39. [Use of proceeds]

(1) Net proceeds from completed sales and assets shall be paid into a Privatisation Revenue Account established by the Minister responsible for finance and held at the Bank of Zambia. *[As amended by Act No. 9 of 1996]*
(2) With the prior approval of the Minister responsible for finance the proceeds of sale referred to in subsection (1) may be used for--

- (a) funding the cost of privatisation and the Privatisation Trust Fund;
- (b) initial financing of mutual funds;

For additional analytical, business and investment opportunities information, please contact Global Investment & Business Center, USA at (202) 546-2103. Fax: (202) 546-3275. E-mail: rusric@erols.com

- (c) expanding existing productive capacities;
- (d) financing credit creation by the Government for Zambian investors;
- (e) rehabilitating existing plants;
- (f) supporting new capital investments;
- (g) funding the restructuring of State owned enterprises to be privatised;
- (h) supporting redundancy payment schemes in consultation with the Ministry responsible for labour;
- (i) supporting alternative income generating projects; or
- (j) funding of any social project that will be in the public interest.

40. [FUNDS OF AGENCY]

(1) Subject to section thirty-nine the funds of the Agency shall consist of such moneys as may--

- (a) be appropriated by Parliament, for the purposes of the Agency;
- (b) be paid to the Agency by way of grants or donations;
- (c) be retained by the Agency from the proceeds of sale as may be approved by the Minister responsible for finance; and
- (d) vest in or accrue to the Agency.

(2) The Agency may--

- (a) accept money by way of grants or donations from any source in Zambia;
- (b) raise money by way of loans from any source in Zambia and, subject to the approval of the Minister, from any source outside Zambia, such moneys as it may require for the discharge of its functions; and
- (c) charge and collect fees in respect of programmes, publications, seminars, documents, consultancy services and other services provides by the Agency.

(3) There shall be paid from the funds of the Agency--

- (a) the salaries and allowances of the staff of the Agency;
- (b) such loans to members of staff as may be approved by the Agency;
- (c) such reasonable travelling, transport and other allowances for the members of the Agency or a committee of the Agency when engaged on the business of the Agency at such rates as the Agency may, with the approval of the Minister, determine; and
- (d) any other expenses incurred by the Agency in the performance of its functions.

(4) The Agency may invest in such manner as it thinks fit such of its funds as it does not immediately require for the performance of its functions.

41. [FINANCIAL YEAR]

The financial year of the Agency shall be the period of twelve months ending 31st December, in each year.

42. [ACCOUNTS]

(1) The Agency shall cause to be kept proper books of account and other records relating to its accounts.
(2) The accounts of the Agency shall be audited annually by independent auditors appointed by the Agency.
(3) The auditors' fees shall be paid by the Agency.

43. [ANNUAL REPORTS]

(1) As soon as practicable, but not later than six months after the expiry of the financial year, the Agency shall submit to the Minister a report concerning its activities during the financial year.
(2) The report referred to in subsection (1) shall include information on the financial affairs of the Agency and there shall be appended to the report--

- (a) an audited balance sheet;
- (b) an audited statement of income and expenditure; and
- (c) such other information as the Agency may consider appropriate.

(3) The Minister shall, not later than seven days after the first sitting of the National Assembly next, after receipt of the report referred to in subsection (1), lay it before the National Assembly.
(4) The report shall be published for sale to the public.

44. [PROGRESS REPORT]

(1) The Agency shall submit a report, at the end of June and at the end of December of each year, on its activities to the Minister giving details of bids received and reasons for preferring the successful bid.
(2) The Agency shall publish the report for sale to the public.
(3) The Minister shall, not later than seven days after the first sitting of the national Assembly next, after receipt of the report referred to in subsection (1), lay it before the National Assembly.

45. [VESTING OF PROPERTY OF THE AGENCY]

Any property, real or personal procured or acquired for the purposes of the privatisation programme shall, after the commencement of this Act, vest in the Agency.

46. [PROCUREMENT OF GOODS AND SERVICES]

(1) The procurement of goods and services of the Agency shall not be subject to the provisions of the Zambia National Audit Corporation Act [Act No. 32 of 1982] and the Zambia National Tender Board Act [Act No. 30 of 1982]:
Provided that the procurement of goods and services above two million kwacha or ten thousand United States Dollars shall be approved by a committee of the Agency and the procurement of goods and services below two million kwacha or ten thousand United States Dollars shall be approved by a management tender committee of the Agency.
(2) The Agency shall, in procuring the goods and services, approve increases to the kwacha amount based on the percentage of the official rate of inflation.

47. [ARBITRATION]

Any dispute arising from the privatisation process shall be settled by arbitration in accordance with the Arbitration Act [Cap. 180].

For additional analytical, business and investment opportunities information, please contact Global Investment & Business Center, USA at (202) 546-2103. Fax: (202) 546-3275. E-mail: rusric@erols.com

48. [PENALTIES FOR FALSIFICATION OF INFORMATION]

(1) A person who knowingly falsifies any information of knowingly does not disclose any material facts or solicits for his own use or as agent of any other person any confidential information relating to the privatisation of a State owned enterprise shall be guilty of an offence and shall be liable on conviction to a fine not exceeding two hundred and fifty thousand kwacha or to imprisonment for a term not exceeding five years, or to both.
(2) A person found guilty under subsection (1) shall not thereafter participate in the purchase of shares in any State owned enterprise.

49. [REGULATIONS]

The Minister, on the advice of the Agency, may by Statutory Instrument prescribe the--

- (a) sale tender procedures;
- (b) public flotation procedures;
- (c) pre-qualification and registration of bidders procedures;
- (d) public announcement requirements;
- (e) tender evaluation procedures;
- (f) tender selection procedures;
- (g) negotiation guidelines;
- (h) final sale monitoring guidelines;
- (i) pre and post sale audit requirements;
- (j) any forms for the purpose of this Act;
- (k) any fees payable in respect of any service provided by the Agency; and
- (l) such other matters as are necessary or conducive to the better carrying out of the purposes of this Act.

50. [PRIOR LEASES AND AGREEMENTS]

All leases and agreements entered into in relation to enterprises to be privatised under this Act and in anticipation of the coming into force of this Act are hereby nullified.

THE LANDS ACT

PART I
PRELIMINARY

Section:

1. [SHORT TITLE]

This Act may be cited as the Lands Act, 1995.

2. [INTERPRETATION]

In this Act, unless the context otherwise requires -

- "Certificate of Title" means a Certificate of Title to land issued in accordance with the Lands and Deeds Registry Act; [Cap. 287]
- "customary area" means, notwithstanding section thirty-two, the area described in the Schedules to the Zambia (State Lands and Reserves) Orders, 1928 to 1964 and the Zambia (Trust Land) Orders, 1947 to 1964; [Appendix 4 of the Laws of Zambia]
- "Fund" means the Land Development Fund established by section sixteen;
- "improvements" means anything resulting from expenditure of capital and labour and includes carrying out of any building, engineering or other operations in, on, over, or underland, or the making of any material change in the use of any building or land charges for services provided and other expenses incurred in the development or towards the development of land;
- "land" means any interest in land whether the land is virgin, bare or has improvements, but does not include any mining right as defined by the Mines and Minerals Act in respect of any land; [Act No. of 1995]
- "lease" means a lease granted by the President or a lease that was converted from a freehold title under the repealed Act and "lessee" shall be construed accordingly;
- "Permanent Resident" means an established resident or a person holding an entry permit in accordance with the Immigration and Deportation Act; [Cap. 122]
- "Provisional Certificate of Title" means a Provisional Certificate of Title to land issued in accordance with the Lands and Deeds Registry Act; [Cap. 287]
- "Registrar" has the meaning assigned to it in the Lands and Deeds Registry Act; [Cap. 287]
- "Repealed Act" means the Land (Conversion of Titles) Act; [Cap. 289]
- "State Land" means land which is not situated in a customary area;
- "Tribunal" mean the Lands Tribunal established by section nineteen.

PART II
ADMINISTRATION OF LAND

Section:

3. [ALL LAND TO VEST IN THE PRESIDENT]

(1) Notwithstanding anything to the contrary contained in any other law, instrument or document, but subject to this Act, all land in Zambia shall vest absolutely in the President and shall be held by him in perpetuity for and on behalf of the people of Zambia.
(2) Subject to subsection (4) and to any other law, the President may alienate land vested in him to any Zambian.
(3) Subject to any other provisions and procedures relating to alienation of land, the President may alienate land to a non-Zambian under the following circumstances:

- (a) where the non-Zambian is a permanent resident in the Republic of Zambia;

For additional analytical, business and investment opportunities information, please contact Global Investment & Business Center, USA at (202) 546-2103. Fax: (202) 546-3275. E-mail: rusric@erols.com

- (b) where the non-Zambian is an investor within the meaning of the Investment Act or any other law relating to the promotion of investment in Zambia; [Act No. 39 of 1993]
- (c) where the non-Zambian has obtained the President's consent in writing under his hand;
- (d) where the non-Zambian is a company registered under the Companies Act, and less than twenty-five per centum of the issued shares are owned by non-Zambians; [Act No. 26 of 1994]
- (e) where the non-Zambian is a statutory corporation created by an Act of Parliament;
- (f) where the non-Zambian is a co-operative society registered under the Co-operative Societies Act and less than twenty-five per centum of the members are non-Zambians; [Cap. 689]
- (g) where the non-Zambian is a body registered under the Land (Perpetual Succession) Act and is a non-profit making, charitable, religious, educational or philanthropic organisation or institution which is registered and is approved by the Minister for the purposes of this section; [Cap. 288]
- (h) where the interest or right in question arises out of a lease, sub-lease, or under-lease, for a period not to exceed five years, or a tenancy agreement;
- (i) where the interest or right in land is being inherited upon death or is being transferred under a right of survivorship or by operation of law;
- (j) where the non-Zambian is a Commercial Bank registered under the Companies Act and the Banking and Financial Services Act; or [Act No. 26 of 1994, Act No. 21 of 1994]
- (k) where the non-Zambian is granted a concession or right under the National Parks and Wildlife Act. [Act No. 10 of 1991]

(4) Notwithstanding subsection (3), the President shall not alienate any land situated in a district or an area where land is held under customary tenure--

- (a) without taking into consideration the local customary law on land tenure which is not in conflict with this Act;
- (b) without consulting the Chief and the local authority in the area in which the land to be alienated is situated, and in the case of a game management area, and the Director of National Parks and Wildlife Service, who shall identify the piece of land to be alienated;
- (c) without consulting any other person or body whose interest might be affected by the grant; and
- (d) if an appellant for a leasehold title has not obtained the prior approval of the chief and the local authority within whose area the land is situated.

(5) All land in Zambia shall, subject to this Act, or any other law be administered and controlled by the President for the use or common benefit, direct or indirect, of the people of Zambia.
(6) The President shall not alienate any land under subsection (2) or (3) for a term exceeding ninety-nine years unless--

- (a) the President considers it necessary in the national interest or in the fulfilment of any obligations of the Republic; and

For additional analytical, business and investment opportunities information, please contact Global Investment & Business Center, USA at (202) 546-2103. Fax: (202) 546-3275. E-mail: rusric@erols.com

- (b) it is approved by a two-thirds majority of the members of the National Assembly.

(7) In alienating land the President shall take such measures as shall be necessary to--

- (a) control settlements, methods of cultivation and utilisation of land as may be necessary for the preservation of the natural resources on that land; and
- (b) set aside land for forest reserves and game management areas and national parks and for the development and control of such reserves, game management areas and national parks.

4. [CONDITIONS ON ALIENATION OF LAND]

(1) The President shall not alienate any land under subsection (2) or (3) of section three without receiving any consideration, in money for such alienation and ground rent for such land except where the alienation is for a public purpose:
Provided that where a person has the right of use and occupation of land under customary law and wishes to convert such right into leasehold tenure, no consideration shall be paid for such conversion.
(2) In this section "public purpose" includes the following:

- (a) for the exclusive use of Government or for the general benefit of the people of Zambia;
- (b) for or in connection with sanitary improvements of any kind including reclamations;
- (c) for or in connection with the laying out of any new township or the extension or improvement of any existing township;
- (d) for or in connection with aviation;
- (e) for the construction of any railway authorised by legislation;
- (f) for obtaining control over land contiguous to any railway, road or other public works constructed or intended at any time to be constructed by Government;
- (g) for obtaining control over land required for or in connection with hydro-electric or other electricity generation and supply purposes;
- (h) for or in connection with the preservation, conservation, development or control of forest produce, fauna, flora, soil, water and other natural resources.

5. [CONSENT OF PRESIDENT]

(1) A person shall not sell, transfer or assign any land without the consent of the President and shall accordingly apply for that consent before doing so.
(2) Where a person applies for consent under subsection (1) and the consent is not granted within forty-five days of filing the application, the consent shall be deemed to have been granted.
(3) Where the President refuses to grant consent within thirty days, he shall give reasons for the refusal.
(4) A person aggrieved with the decision of the President to refuse consent may within thirty days of such refusal appeal to the Lands Tribunal for redress.

6. [SURRENDER OF LAND HELD BY A COUNCIL]

(1) Subject to subsection (2), all land held by a Council on a lease including that which has been subleased, for a period of ninety-nine years or less shall, by virtue of this Act and without further

For additional analytical, business and investment opportunities information, please contact Global Investment & Business Center, USA at (202) 546-2103. Fax: (202) 546-3275. E-mail: rusric@erols.com

assurance or conveyance, be deemed to have been surrendered to the President and the sub-lessee be deemed to hold that land, as if a direct lease had been granted by the President.
(2) Subject to subsection (3) the sublessee referred to in subsection (1) shall be deemed to hold land on the conditions and convenants of the lease granted to the Council, except that the lessee shall pay such annual ground rent to the President as may be prescribed by statutory instrument.
(3) Subsection (1) shall not apply to land held by the Councils for their own use or held under the Housing (Statutory Improvement Areas) Act. [Cap. 441]
(4) On the commencement of this Act, and on the payment of a prescribed fee, the Registrar shall endorse on the relevant folio of the register, the effect of this section.

7. [CUSTOMARY HOLDINGS TO BE RECOGNISED AND TO CONTINUE]

(1) Notwithstanding subsection (2) of section thirty-two but subject to section nine, every piece of land in a customary area which immediately before the commencement of this Act was vested in or held by any person under customary tenure shall continue to be so held and recognised and any provision of this Act or any other law shall not be so construed as to infringe any customary right enjoyed by that person before the commencement of this Act.
(2) Notwithstanding section thirty-two, the rights and privileges of any person to hold land under customary tenure shall be recognised and such holding under the customary law applicable to the area in which a person has settled or intends to settle shall not be construed as an infringement of any provision of this Act or any other law except for a right or obligation which may arise under any other law.

8. [CONVERSION OF CUSTOMARY TENURE INTO LEASEHOLD TENURE]

(1) Notwithstanding section seven, after the commencement of this Act, any person who holds land under customary tenure may convert it into a leasehold tenure not exceeding ninety-nine years on application, in the manner prescribed, by way of -

- (a) a grant of leasehold by the President;
- (b) any other title that the President may grant;
- (c) any other law.

(2) The conversion of rights from a customary tenure to a leasehold tenure shall have effect only after the approval of the chief and the local authorities in whose area the land to be converted is situated, and in the case of a game management area, and the Director of National Parks and Wildlife Service, the land to be converted shall have been identified by a plan showing the exact extent of the land to be converted.
(3) Except for a right which may arise under any other law in Zambia, no title, other than a right to the use and occupation of any land under customary tenure claimed by a person, shall be valid unless it has been confirmed by the chief, and a lease granted by, the President.

9. [PROHIBITION OF UNAUTHORISED OCCUPATION OF LAND]

(1) A person shall not without lawful authority occupy or continue to occupy vacant land.
(2) Any person who occupies land in contravention of subsection (1) is liable to be evicted.

10. [RENEWAL OF LEASES]

(1) The President shall renew a lease, upon expiry, for a further term not exceeding ninety-nine years if he is satisfied that the lessee has complied with or observed the terms, conditions or covenants of the lease and the lease is not liable to forfeiture.
(2) If the President does not renew a lease the lessee shall be entitled to compensation for the improvements made on the land in accordance with the procedure laid down in the Lands (Acquisition) Act. [Cap. 296]

For additional analytical, business and investment opportunities information, please contact Global Investment & Business Center, USA at (202) 546-2103. Fax: (202) 546-3275. E-mail: rusric@erols.com

11. [GROUND RENT AND BENEFIT OF LEASEE'S COVENANTS AND CONDITIONS]

(1) Notwithstanding severance of a reversionary estate, ground rent and the benefit of every covenant or provision contained in a lease or any Act of Parliament having reference to the subject matter of the lease shall be annexed and incidental to, and shall go with, the reversionary estate in the land or in any part of the estate immediately expectant on the term granted by the lease.
(2) The obligation under a condition of a covenant entered into by the President or contained in any Act of Parliament having reference to the subject matter of the lease shall be annexed and incidental to and shall go with the reversionary estate, or the several parts of that estate, notwithstanding severance of that estate and may be enforced by the person in whom the term is vested by assignment, transfer, devolution in law or otherwise.
(3) Subsection (1) shall be without prejudice to any covenant, lease or Act of Parliament which imposes a duty on a lessee to observe or perform the covenant and to every condition of re-entry.

12. [APPORTIONMENT OF CONDITIONS ON SEVERANCE]

(1) Every condition or right of re-entry and every other condition contained in the lease except for ground rent fixed in the grant shall be apportioned, in like manner as if the land comprised in each several part, or the land as to which the term remains subsisting, as the case may be, had alone originally been comprised in the lease, notwithstanding -

- (a) the severance by assignment, transfer, surrender, or otherwise of the reversionary estate in any land comprised in a lease or any other grant of land; and
- (b) the avoidance or cesser in any other manner of the term granted by a lease as to part only of the land comprised in the lease.

(2) Every condition or right of re-entry referred to in subsection (1), shall remain annexed to the severed parts of the reversionary estate as the term where each several part is reversionary, or the term in part of the land as to which the term has not been surrendered or has been avoided or has not ceased in the manner as if the land comprised in each several part, or the land as to which the term remains subsisting, as the case may be, had alone originally been comprised in the lease.
(3) This section applies to leases or any other grant subsisting before or made after the commencement of this Act and whether the severance of the reversionary estate was effected before or after the commencement of this Act.

13. [CERTIFICATE OF RE-ENTRY TO BE ENTERED ON REGISTER]

(1) Where a lessee breaches a term or a condition of a covenant under this Act the President shall give the lessee three months notice of his intention to cause a certificate of re-entry to be entered in the register in respect of the land held by the lessee and requesting him to make representations as to why a certificate or re-entry should not be entered in the register.
(2) If the lessee does not within three months make the representations required under subsection (1), or if after making representations the President is not satisfied that a breach of a term or a condition of a covenant by the lessee was not intentional or was beyond the control of the lessee, he may cause the certificate of re-entry to be entered in the register.
(3) A lessee aggrieved with the decision of the President to cause a certificate of re-entry to be entered in the register may within thirty days appeal to the Lands Tribunal for an order that the register be rectified.

14. [PAYMENT AND PENALTY FOR LATE PAYMENT OF RENT]

(1) A lessee shall pay such ground rent as may be prescribed by the President, by statutory instrument.

For additional analytical, business and investment opportunities information, please contact Global Investment & Business Center, USA at (202) 546-2103. Fax: (202) 546-3275. E-mail: rusric@erols.com

(2) Subject to subsection (3) where any amount of ground rent unpaid after the day on which it became payable under subsection (1) remains unpaid after the day on which it became payable, the lessee shall be liable to pay a penalty of twenty-five per centum of the rent due.

15. [APPLICATION OF TRIBUNAL ON LAND DISPUTES]

(1) Any person aggrieved with a direction or decision of a person in authority may apply to the Lands Tribunal for determination.
(2) In this section "person in authority" means the President, the Minister or the Registrar.

PART III
THE LAND DEVELOPMENT FUND

Section:

16. [LAND DEVELOPMENT FUND]

(1) There is hereby established a Land Development Fund.
* (2) The Fund shall consist of -

- (a) all moneys appropriated by Parliament for the purposes of the Fund;
- (b) seventy-five per centum of the consideration paid under section four; and
- (c) fifty per centum of ground rent collected from land.

17. [ADMINISTRATION OF THE FUND]

The Fund shall be vested in the Minister responsible for finance and shall be managed and administered by the Minister responsible for land.

18. [APPLICATION OF MONEYS OF THE FUND]

(1) The Ministers referred to in section seventeen shall apply the moneys of the Fund to the opening up of new areas for development of land.
(2) A council that wishes to develop any area in its locality may apply to the Fund for money to develop the area.

19. [STATEMENT OF INCOME AND EXPENDITURE]

The Ministers referred to in section seventeen shall cause an annual statement of the income and expenditure to be prepared and laid before the National Assembly.

PART IV
THE LANDS TRIBUNAL

Section:

20. [LANDS TRIBUNAL]

(1) There is hereby established a Lands Tribunal.
(2) The Tribunal shall consist of the following members who shall be appointed by the Minister:

- (a) a Chairman who shall be qualified to be a judge of the High Court;

For additional analytical, business and investment opportunities information, please contact Global Investment & Business Center, USA at (202) 546-2103. Fax: (202) 546-3275. E-mail: rusric@erols.com

- (b) a Deputy Chairman who shall be qualified to be appointed as a judge of the High Court;
- (c) an advocate from the Attorney-General's Chambers;
- (d) a registered town planner;
- (e) a registered land surveyor;
- (f) a registered valuation surveyor; and
- (g) not more than three persons from the public and private sectors.

(3) The members referred to in paragraph (a) and (b) of subsection (2) shall be appointed after consultation with the Judicial Service Commission.
(4) The members of the Tribunal shall be appointed on such terms and conditions as may be specified in their letters of appointment.

21. [ASSESSORS]

The Tribunal may appoint persons who have ability and experience in land, agriculture, commerce or other relevant professional qualifications as assessors for purposes of assisting it in the determination of any matter under this Act.

22. [JURISDICTION OF TRIBUNAL]

The Tribunal shall have jurisdiction to -

- (a) inquire into and make awards and decisions in any dispute relating to land under this Act;
- (b) to inquire into, and make awards and decisions relating to any dispute of compensation to be paid under this Act;
- (c) generally to inquire and adjudicate upon any matter affecting the land rights and obligations, under this Act, of any person or the Government; and
- (d) to perform such acts and carry out such duties as may be prescribed under this Act or any other written law.

23. [PROCEEDINGS OF TRIBUNAL]

(1) The Chairman or the Deputy Chairman shall preside over the sittings of the Tribunal.
(2) The Tribunal, when hearing any matter, shall be duly constituted if it consists of five members which number shall include either the Chairman or the Deputy Chairman.
(3) The determination of any matter before the Tribunal shall be according to the opinion of the majority of the members considering the matter.
(4) A member of the Tribunal or an assessor shall not sit at a hearing of the Tribunal if he has any interest, direct or indirect, personal or pecuniary, in any matter before the Tribunal.
(5) The Tribunal shall not be bound by the rules of evidence applied in civil proceedings.

24. [RULES]

The Chief Justice may, by statutory instrument, make rules -

- (a) regulating the procedure of the Tribunal; and

For additional analytical, business and investment opportunities information, please contact Global Investment & Business Center, USA at (202) 546-2103. Fax: (202) 546-3275. E-mail: rusric@erols.com

- (b) prescribing the procedure for the summoning and appearance of witnesses and the production of any document or other evidence before the Tribunal.

25. [LEGAL REPRESENTATION]

A person appearing as a party before the Tribunal may appear in person or through a legal practitioner at his own expense.

26. [FRIVOLOUS AND VEXATIOUS PROCEEDINGS]

If the Tribunal is satisfied that any application to the Tribunal is frivolous or vexatious, it may order the applicant to pay his costs, that of the other party and that of the Government in connection with the proceedings.

27. [EXPENSE OF TRIBUNAL]

The expenses and costs of the Tribunal shall be paid out of funds appropriated by Parliament for the performance of the Tribunal's functions under this Act.

28. [SECRETARIAL AND ACCOUNTING]

The Ministry responsible for legal affairs shall provide the necessary secretarial and accounting assistance to the Tribunal to enable the Tribunal to perform its functions under this Act.

29. [APPEALS]

Any person aggrieved by any award, declaration or decision of the tribunal may within thirty days appeal to the Supreme Court.

PART V
GENERAL

Section:

30. [SAVING OF EXISTING INTERESTS AND RIGHTS]

Subject to the other provisions of this Act, nothing in this Act shall affect any estate, right or interest legal or equitable, in or over any land which was at any time before the commencement of this Act created, granted, recognised or acknowledged.

31. [REGULATIONS]

(1) The Minister may, by statutory instrument, make regulations for the better carrying out of the provisions of this Act. [Regulations]
(2) In particular, but without prejudice to the generality of subsection (1), such regulations may prescribe -

- (a) the terms, conditions and covenants of leases;
- (b) the procedure for applying for the President's consent to any transaction relating to or affecting land;
- (c) the procedure for converting customary tenure to leasehold tenure;
- (d) the procedure for applying for the renewal of a lease;
- (e) the ground rent for land;

For additional analytical, business and investment opportunities information, please contact Global Investment & Business Center, USA at (202) 546-2103. Fax: (202) 546-3275. E-mail: rusric@erols.com

- (f) fees for transactions in land; and
- (g) any other matter which is to be or may be prescribed under this Act.

[As amended by Act No. 20 of 1996]

32. [REPEAL OF CAP. 289 AND LAWS IN SCHEDULE]

(1) The Land (Conversion of Titles) Act is hereby repealed.
(2) The Laws set out in the Schedule are hereby repealed.
SCHEDULE
(Section 32)
REPEALED LAWS

- 1. The Zambia (State Lands and Reserves) Orders, 1928 to 1964.
- 2. The Zambia (Trust Land) Orders, 1947 to 1964.
- 3. The Zambia (Gwembe District) Orders, 1959 to 1964.
- 4. The Western Province (Land and Miscellaneous Provisions) Act, 1970.

TAX REGISTRATION AND REPORTING

Zambian taxes include individual and corporate income tax, import tariffs, excise taxes, and value-added tax (VAT). The Zambia Revenue Authority handles administration of the tax system.

PROCESS FOR REGISTERING DIRECT TAX

To register with ZRA to pay corporate income tax,
· A company must first register with the Registrar of Companies.
· Companies must complete a tax registration form and submit it to the local ZRA office, care of the Commissioner of Direct Taxes, along with a copy of the Zambian certificate of incorporation and a copy of the company's Memorandum of Association.
Except for employees covered by a Pay As You Earn (PAYE) scheme, all individuals and entities receiving taxable income in Zambia must notify the ZRA within 30 days of receiving compensation.

TYPES OF TAXES

Zambia has several schemes for the collection and assessment of income taxes. Outlined below are some of the taxes used:

Pay As You Earn (PAYE)

PAYE is a method of collecting taxes at the source of an individual's employment. The employer is responsible for deducting a certain amount of tax from his or her employee's salary or wages each payday and then remitting the tax to ZRA. Depending on the annual revenue of the company, the ZRA collects PAYE taxes monthly or quarterly. Currently, companies with an annual turnover of more than 2 million (US$1 081) must remit their employees' taxes monthly within 14 days of a month's end. The ZRA requires that companies complete a CF/P16 Card monthly for each employee and return it along with a cheque to the collector of taxes. Employee income tax payments are audited annually, and companies must submit an annual certificate of pay and tax deducted, Form ITF/P22.

Individual income tax rates are assessed based on four bands of income. Individuals earning K1, 920, 000.00 (US$ 45) per year or less do not pay taxes, and the first K70, 000.00 earned counts as a tax credit to everyone. At K1.2 million (US$324) is assessed at a rate of 20%, and the balance therefore is assessed at 30 percent.

COMPANY TAX

Company tax is a form of income tax levied on companies with limited liability. Companies are required to remit an estimated tax payment on a quarterly basis to the ZRA using form CF270C. To avoid paying fines, companies must adjust these estimated payments over the course of the year so that each quarter, estimating payments are at least 80 percent of the total due. Once per year corporations are audited for actual tax due and required to file Form ITF/2a. Three general tax rates apply to companies in Zambia. The basic tax rate is currently 35 percent of corporate profits, adjusted for tax purposes. Companies listed on the Lusaka stock exchange pay 33 percent. Banks earning less than K100 million (US$54 054) per year pay tax at a rate of 35percent, and banking institutions with annual turnover in excess of K100 million annually pay 45 percent. Business loses can generally be curried forward for five years. A self- employed person pays tax at a rate of 30 percent.

Exemptions to these tax rates include income earned from farming by any person or company and fertilizer manufactures, which incur a maximum of 15 percent tax. Mining enterprises pay a maximum corporate tax of 10 percent and can curry business losses forward for ten years. Income from the export of non- traditional products that are defined as any good or service unrelated to mining is taxed a rate of 15 percent. Exporting companies are required to record clearly which goods are exported and to keep supporting documentation, including commercial invoices, proofs of sale, and copies of all export documentation (EXD Forms).
Provisional tax payments are demanded by ZRA four times a year with an annual filing of exact tax returns. Officially, the direct tax department pledges to issue any rebates within 14 days of filing. Issuing returns can take up to three months. This mainly due to cash shortages within the ministry of finance, which allocates whatever monies the ZRA pledges to rebate. While the time in which VAT rebates are to be paid is mandated by law, direct taxes and customs and excise refunds are dependent on the availability of cash within the Zambian Government.

WITHHOLDING TAX (WHT)

Withholding tax (WHT) is deducted from the following sources of income:
. Rents
. Interest
. Dividends
. Royalties
. Management fees and payments made either to non-resident contractors engaged in construction and haulage, or resident consultants

The current rate of WHT on all types of income is 15 percent, except on interest and dividends paid by successor companies to ZCCM, for which the rate is 10%.
In the case of rental in come, the tenant is required to deduct WHT from the gross rental charge and remit the tax to the ZRA on behalf of the landlord. The landlord is also liable to pay the tax due on the gross rent (less allowable expenses) with no relief granted for WHT. Thus, the landlord is responsible for ensuring that his tenants remit tax payments to the ZRA.
The first K20 000 (US$11) in dividend earnings is tax-free. For holders of a valid investment certificate, dividends earned from farming are exempt for the first five years. Monthly tax payments are to be filed by the ZRA using Form CF.82.A, and an annual audit of these payments is completed-using Form CF/182A.

BASE TAX

This is a presumptive tax levied on small-scale businesses that cannot manage to maintain adequate business records on which to base a correct tax assessment at the end of the charge year. Currently base tax is fixed at 266 penalty units (1 penalty unit equals 180 Kwacha, or US$0.10), which is equivalent to K47 880 (US$ 26) per year.

MINERAL ROYALTY TAX

Mineral royalty is a tax on all holders of a large-scale mining license on the net back value at 2 %. The net back value is the market value of minerals free on board at the point of export from Zambia or, in the case of consumption within Zambia, at the point of delivery within Zambia, less: the cost of transport, including insurance and handling charges, from the mining area to the point of delivery or export, and the cost of smelting and refinery and refining or any other processing costs, except on the processing costs as related to processing normally carried out in Zambia in the mining area

PROPERTY TRANSFER TAX.

There is no capital gains tax in Zambia per se, but there is a capital transfer tax charged on the realizable value of the property being transferred at a rate of 3 percent of the gross sale amount. The tax is payable by the transferor.

Property in this case means any land (including any buildings, structures, or additions) and any share issued by a company in Zambia that is not listed on the Lusaka stock exchange. The personal sale of a car is not taxed.

Note: all persons or companies are required by law to submit their returns, accompanied by the balance of tax payable, to the ZRA. Failure to comply may result in statutory pernulties being charged, which may include fines and imprisonment

VALUE ADDED TAX [VAT](REGISTRATION)

Since July 1995, all companies operating in Zambia above a certain revenue threshold need to register with the ZRA to pay VAT. The VAT is intended to collect revenue at each stage of a product or service life cycle at which value is added. Currently the rate of VAT charged is 17.5 percent. Businesses are required by law to register as VAT traders if they supply taxable goods or services and their taxable turnover exceeds one of the following mandated threshold requirements:

. K100 million (US$ 16 216) in any 12 consecutive months.
. K7.5 million in any consecutive 3 months.

. Taxable turnover is expected to exceed either of the amounts stipulated above within the subsequent 12 or 3 months, respectively.

A trader must register within one moth of commencing operations or surpassing the revenue thresholds stated above.
To register for VAT, a company must submit the following to the commissioner of VAT:
. For corporate entities, a certificate of corporation issued by the registrar of companies
. For individuals, a valid business or trading licenses
. VAT application form (VAT Form 1)

A company or trader can register for VAT prior to operating by submitting VAT Form 1 and an investor's license issued by the Zambia investment center. Once an application ahs been filed with the ZRA, a dated vat certificate, which includes an official VAT tracking number, is issued within 14 days. VAT registration is free.

Firms than earn less than the amounts specified above can register for VAT on voluntary basis. Once registered the trader has the same obligations to abide by the same rules that apply to statutory registered traders. To enable the Vat department to locate voluntary registrants, typically small traders, who do not work from fixed addresses, submit the documents listed above plus a site or business plan specifying where they operate.

VAT RATES AND ASSESSMENT

Businesses earning more than K300 million (US$162 162) per year are required to pay an actual VAT amount monthly; firms earning less than K300 million annually may opt to file quarterly. In each filing period companies are granted a 21 day grace period the actual amount of VAT owed, but if a trader does not pay the amount owed within this period, penalties and fines may be assessed. VAT refunds are assessed based on the difference between the VAT a company pays on inputs (input tax) and the VAT it charges its customers (output tax). Officially, the ZRA says it refunds all VAT within a calendar month of receiving an application for rebate. A trader with a taxable turnover not exceeding k300 million per year can apply for the accounting or payment basis. This method requires the traders to account for the VAT charged on their sales on amounts actually received and claim VAT only on the purchases that have been paid.
Some items are zero-rated (no VAT is charged on their sale), but a supplier can deduct the VAT on the inputs used to make these items. Items that are classified as exempts are also not assessed VAT, but suppliers of these items cannot deduct VAT on the goods and services needed to make these supplies.

To claim VAT, a company must keep tax invoices or certified copies of VAT Forms 200, 202, or 203 for each item purchased. Claims for VAT refunds are assessed for accuracy and approximately 50 percent of them pass the credibility test. Almost 25 percent of VAT refund claims require an on site inspection of business records. Valid tax invoices must contain the following:

The words tax invoice clearly printed on the form Company's name, address, and VAT registration number Name and address of the purchaser of the goods in question.
Companies seeking VAT input tax credits must present a certified copy of VAT Form 200, which in indicates the amount of import VAT paid to customs during importation. Zambia's 17.5 VAT is assessed on all other costs, fees, and taxes, including customs and excise duties, involved in importing. VAT form 203 is used for goods cleared at bonded warehouses.

The standard tax period commences on the first day and ends on the last day of each calendar month. Traders are expected to submit their returns by the 21st day of the following month. Traders are free to apply for extended accounting period to three months, subject to satisfying certain conditions. As of July 1998, the maximum annual taxable turnover limit for qualifying for the three-month tax period was raised to K200 million.
The Zambian VAT tax year runes from July 1st to June 31st. Tax records are to be maintained in the English language and kept for six years.

VAT TAX EXEMPTIONS

Other products are exempt from VAT, which means they do not need to be charged output tax, but cannot reclaim any VAT already paid on inputs. Major items exempt from VAT include:

. Water supply and sewerage service provided by a local authority
. Health supply services
. Educational services from nursery school to university
. Books and newspapers
. Passenger transport services by air, road, rail and boat

. Certain financial services, funeral services
. Domestic kerosene (paraffin)
. Trade union subscriptions
. Mosquito nets
. Road construction agreements entered prior to 1st July 1995
Certain item do not have to pay VAT for specific reasons-for example there is no VAT on agricultural produce. These are zero-rated. They do not have to pay VAT on their output and they can also reclaim VAT that has already been paid on their inputs. Major zero rated items include:
. Basic foods and agricultural products
. Exports
. Medical suppliers and drugs
. Hotel accommodation in the Livingstone district

LOCAL AND OTHER TAXES

Local councils are granted limited authority to tax and to charge fees under Zambian registration, including the ground rent and site development approval fees. Officially the local council is entitled to tax 3 percent of local businesses' turnover, and the taxes are to be paid annually. The local council has the right to inspect a business' accounts
Several other government entities have the right to charge levies and fees. For example, companies engaged in the fuel are assessed special levies, and some local authorities assess transportation charges for goods moving through their jurisdictions.

SELECTED LAWS

A - E

- **The Affiliation and Maintenance of Children Act**
- **The Constitution of Zambia Act**
- **The Constitution of Zambia (Amendment) Act**
- **Copyright and Performance Rights Act**
- **The Electoral Commission Act**
- **The Electoral (Amendment) Act**
- **The Energy Regulation Act**
- **The English Law (Extent of Application) Act, Cap. 4**

F - I

- **The Food Reserve Act**
- **The Intestate Succession Act**
- **The Investment Act**

J - M

- **The Judges (Conditions of Service) Act**
- **The Lands Act**

N - Q

- **The Preferential Claims in Bankruptcy Act**
- **The Privatisation Act**
- **The Public Order (Amendment) Act**

R - U

- **The Securities Act**
- **The Supreme and High Court (Number of Judges)(Amendment) Act**

V - Z

- **The Value Added Tax Act**
- **The Zambia Institute of Advanced Legal Education Act**
- **The Zambia Law Development Commission Act**
- **The Zambia Revenue Authority Act**

LARGEST LAW FIRMS

A

AA Tickley & Co
PO Box 32953
LUSAKA
Tel: 271308
Mr.Tickley Abdul Aziz

Achimota Chambers
Chachacha House
Chachacha Road
PO Box 36608
LUSAKA
Tel: 223485
Fax: 223495
Mr. Mensah Joe Frank

AD Adams & Co
1st Floor, Farmers House
Cairo Road
PO Box 33143
LUSAKA
Tel: 228660
Fax: 228661
Email: adaco@zamnet.zm, adaco@zamnet.zm
Adam Aziz HD, SC
Chaane George
Gani Abdul Ebrahim
Mitchley Anthony Owen Richard
Yousuf Musa Ahmed Adam

For additional analytical, business and investment opportunities information,
please contact Global Investment & Business Center, USA
at (202) 546-2103. Fax: (202) 546-3275. E-mail: rusric@erols.com

AJM & Associates
Carousel Shopping Centre
Rooms 28-30-32
2nd Floor
LUSAKA
PO Box 50540
Tel: 237725
Fax: 237743
Mr. Mumba John Alex

Ali M Hamir & Co
Westavia House
Plot No: 9214
Off Los Angeles Boulevard
PO Box 36475
LUSAKA
Tel: 288578/9
Fax: 288009
Hamir Ali Mohamed, S.C.
Hamir Osman Mohammed

AM Wood & Co
Advocates & Notaries
3rd Floor Godfrey House
PO Box 30028
LUSAKA
Tel: 237957
Fax: 237963 Email: markwood@zamnet.zm
Mr. Wood M Albert

AN Chambers
Makishi Road,
PO Box 30851,
PO Box 30851
LUSAKA
Tel: 231767/224548/ 97 797855/ 097 778196
Cell: 778196
Mr. Ngoma Nkalimo Agness
Mr. Mosha Billingtone

Andrea Masiye & Co
Lex House
PO Box 30757
LUSAKA
Tel: 254842
Mr.Lungu Chagwa Edgar
Mr. Masiye Sylvester Andrea
Mr. Gondwe Lameck

Asmal & Co
Plot 9249 Delhi Street
Fidelity Building
2nd Class Trading Area

PO Box 36626
LUSAKA
Tel: 244025 / 226210
Fax: 236538
Mr. Patel Younus Asmal

Atlas Partners
PO Box 34630
Lusaka Showgrounds
LUSAKA
Tel: 251246
Fax: 251245
Ms Zulu Lekiwe Angela

B

Banda Watae Advocates
"The House"
PO Box 33939
LUSAKA
Tel: 254678
Fax: 254678
Mr. Banda Micheal Chauba
Mr. Watae Sidney
Bango Associates
Plot 9686 Chudleigh
PO Box 50072
LUSAKA
Tel: 294013
Mr. Siakalima Zunga

Batoka Chambers
1st Floor Insurance House
PO Box 35858
LUSAKA
Tel: 234650
Fax: 228227
Mr. Hamakando Maambo Hamuzwe Fred
Ben Ngenda Advocates
Westavia House
Lumumba Road
PO Box 34844
LUSAKA
Tel: 097 - 771854
Email:BNgenda@excite.com
Mr. Ngenda Lubinda Benjamin

Beta Legal Consult Chambers
6 Nyati Close
PO Box 50742
LUSAKA
Tel: 250312

For additional analytical, business and investment opportunities information, please contact Global Investment & Business Center, USA at (202) 546-2103. Fax: (202) 546-3275. E-mail: rusric@erols.com

Fax: 250293
Ms. Mulamfu Beatrice Mukumbwa

C

Cave Malik & Co
Mambilima House
Kabelenga Road
PO Box 34204
LUSAKA
Tel: 235486/231964/096 766321
Mr. Mittal Rajesh Chandra

CC Mwansa Associates
PO Box 50235
LUSAKA
Mrs. Mwansa Charity Achuime Chola

Central Chambers
Lex House
Addis Ababa Roundabout
PO Box 50465
LUSAKA
Tel: 254610
Fax: 254815
E-mail: cclaw@zamnet.zm <mailto:cclaw@zamnet.zm>
Ms Mapara Rita
Mr. Han'gandu Kelvin
Mr. Ndhlovu Matiya
Mr. Sikota Sakwiba

Chaiwila & Chaiwila Associates
2nd Floor Permanent House
"T Wing" No. 253
Cairo Road
PO Box 34750
LUSAKA
Tel: 097 795621 /096431479
Chaiwila Mwango Maurice
Chaiwila Towa Silweya

Charles & Charles
3rd Floor Development House
PO Box 37619
LUSAKA
Tel: 231541 / 225510
Muneku Charles Nathaniel

Chifumu Banda & Associates
Godfrey House, Longolongo Rd
PO Box 31025
LUSAKA
Tel: 233395/233059

For additional analytical, business and investment opportunities information, please contact Global Investment & Business Center, USA at (202) 546-2103. Fax: (202) 546-3275. E-mail: rusric@erols.com

Fax: 232203
Email: chifumu@zamtel.zm <mailto:chifumu@zamtel.zm>
Mr. Banda Chifumu Kingdom SC
Mr. Chisi Prince
Mr. Lungu Bubile Grace
Mr. Ndhlovu Masauso Nelson

Chilembo & Co.
Plot 2796 Chempro Building
PO Box 30584
LUSAKA
Mr. Chilembo Oliver Bangala

Chilupe & Co
1st Floor, Superannuation House
Ben Bella Road
PO Box 30819
LUSAKA
Tel: 227879/227880
Fax: 222769 / 222768
Mr. Chilupe Kabwe George
Gen Gilbert Chewe Chileshe

Chimungu & Co
Ground Floor Permanent House
PO Box 33693
LUSAKA
Tel: 235845/096 760901
Mr. Chimungu Chewe Tarsisius

Chintu & Co
Plot 685, 4th Floor Lotti House
PO Box 30446
LUSAKA
Tel: 237576/237548/223448
Mr. Chintu Mulenga Hubert
Christopher Russell Cook & Co
Woodgate House
Cairo Road
PO Box 34091
LUSAKA
Tel: 229366-70
Fax: 225158/225713
Mr. Njobvu Alick Jonathan Corinth
Mr. Patel Kanti Kanjimbhai

CKM & Associates
Chester House
Cairo Road,
PO Box 38288
LUSAKA
Cell: 097 792172
Ms Kapatamoyo Maudy Chama

For additional analytical, business and investment opportunities information, please contact Global Investment & Business Center, USA at (202) 546-2103. Fax: (202) 546-3275. E-mail: rusric@erols.com

CL Mundia & Co
1st Floor Bible House
Freedom Way
PO Box 35492
LUSAKA
Tel: 220272 / 220267 / 220288
Fax: 294093
Mr. Mundia Lubasi Christopher

CM Sampa & Co
Esco Building
Kabelenga Avenue
PO Box 38209
LUSAKA
Tel: 233052
Mr. Sampa Mofu Christopher

Corpus Globe
Stand No. 2386
Growell Building
Longolongo Road
PO Box 32115
LUSAKA
Tel: 235480/1
Fax: 238657
Email: corpus@zamnet.zm corpus@zamnet.zm
Mr. Chibesakunda Mwelwa
Mr. Chipimo Chileshe Elias
Mr. Kunda Christine
Mr. Machila Bradford
Mr. Musyani Gertrude
Mr. Sabi Mwape Samuel
Mrs. Young Pio Amilha

D

DH Kemp & Co
Plot 6941 Suez Road
Off Church Road
PO Box 31000
LUSAKA
Tel: 255081/252381
Fax: 255225
Email: dhkemp@zamnet.zm
Locha Godfrey
Mubonda Kabanda Newton
Zaheeda Essa

Dindi & Co
Plot 1B, Room 115, 1st Floor,
Western Wing, Above Cairo Chemist
Chiparamba Road
PO Box 34871

LUSAKA
Tel: 231446
Fax: 229875
Mr. Dindi Kaponda Noah

Dove Chambers
Plot 106/7, E W Tarry Building
Cairo Road
PO Box 39538
LUSAKA
Tel: 221030
Cell: 097 789579
Mrs Zaloumis Mwangala Frances
Mr. S M J Zaloumis

Dzekedzeke & Co
Dzekedzeke & Co.
Findeco House 14th Floor
Cnr Independence/Cairo Rds
PO Box 30685
LUSAKA
Tel: 225582/232584
Mr. Dzekedzeke Ostoph (Deceased)
Mr. Muyawala Moses Patrick

E

EBM Chambers
Former Sheriff's Yard
Jacaranda Road
PO Box 32081
LUSAKA
Tel: 252185
Cell:703476
Mr. Chanda Priscilla
Mr. Mwansa Bupe Emmanuel

Echo Temple & Chambers
Indeco House
Cairo Road,
RW 51258
LUSAKA
Tel: 228561
Email: echo@zamnet.zm <mailto:echo@zamnet.zm>
Mr. Kapilikisha Francis Chowa
Mrs. Munsaka Maudy Manda

Ellis & Co
No 8 Tito Road, Off Church Road
Phillip Ellis House, O
PO Box 31902
LUSAKA
Tel: 252709/738/809

Fax: 250802
Email: elisanco@zamnet.zm <mailto:elisanco@zamnet.zm>
Mr. Chonta Chileshe Charles
Mr. Chimuka Haangala Constatine
Mr. Lwatula Mwenya
Mr. Nyembele Lagos
Mr. Mutale Bonaventure Chibamba

Ernst & Young
PO Box 32385
LUSAKA
Tel: 237785/58/56/220080
Fax: 227022/229008
Celine Nair

Equity Chambers
4th Floor Kulima Tower
Katunjila Road
PO Box RW 51052
LUSAKA
Tel: 224045/Cell: 097 705022
Mr. Miaze Sibuba Bornfree

Ernest Mwansa & Partners
PO Box 35868
LUSAKA
Tel/Fax: 225661
Mr. Elita P Mwikisa
Mr. Mwansa Chitumwa Ernest

F

Fidelity Chambers
9th Floor
Premium House
PO Box 38906
LUSAKA
Tel: 231823
Email: gscom@zamnet.zm
Mr. Cornhill Gregory

Finance Management Services
PO Box 37012
LUSAKA
Tel: 224276/223586
Mr. Roberts Alfred

Finsbury Investment Ltd
PO Box 37012
LUSAKA
Tel: 229733-42
Fax: 227544
Chanda Joan Lubasi

Fraser Associates
1st Floor Fintex House
Dar-es-Salaam Place, Sapele Rd
PO Box 35641
LUSAKA
Tel: 227563/229387
Fax: 236893
Chishimba Fraser
Malata Mwenya Flavia

G

Gideon & Partners
2nd Floor Impala House
Cha Cha Cha Road
PO Box RW 50347
LUSAKA
Tel: 231278
Cell: 096 766413
Mr. Mwewa Gideon Kateba

Global Partners
5th Floor, Zimco House
Chainda Place, Cairo Road
PO Box 32018
LUSAKA
Tel: 227974
Mr. Muhyila Hinyungwe Austin

GW Simukoko & Co
Plot 11994 off Lake Road
Woodlands
PO Box 38247
LUSAKA
Tel: 264403/255733
Fax: 255533
Mr. Simukoko Wamusula Geoffrey

H

Hakasenke & Co
1st Floor Insurance House
Plot 4432 Cairo Road
PO Box 35858
LUSAKA
Tel: 238810/238811
Fax: 228814
Mr. Hakasenke Claydon
Mr. Mudenda S Frederick

Hamanyanga & Co
Grosvenor Court, Cairo Road

For additional analytical, business and investment opportunities information, please contact Global Investment & Business Center, USA at (202) 546-2103. Fax: (202) 546-3275. E-mail: rusric@erols.com

PO Box 34417
LUSAKA
Tel: 225642
Mr. Hamanyanga Hamalala George
Mrs Ngónomo FM Beatrice

H C Mubashi & Co
Plot 5430 Kasangula Road Kalundu
PO Box 35981
LUSAKA
Tel: 290188
Cell: 095 702346
Mr. Mubashi Chomba Hugo

H Chanda & Co
First Floor Sitwe Plaza,
Opp. Kulima Bus Stop
Cha Cha Cha Road
PO Box 35364
LUSAKA
Tel: 220085
Mr. Chanda Henry

HH Ndhlovu & Co
3rd Floor Rm 307
Woodgate House, Cairo Road
PO Box 35789
LUSAKA
Tel: 220541
Fax: 250184
Mr.Ndhlovu Hlazo Humphrey

I

IC Ngónga & Co
Muyuni House, Plot 8116
1st Floor Room 3 Bombay Street
Kamwala
PO Box 36309
LUSAKA
Tel: 220254/56
Mr. Chiwale Vincent McRobby
Mr. Ngónga Chifumbe Isaiah

Ituna Partners
PO Box 32314
LUSAKA
Tel: 223796/237882
Fax: 222977
Mr. Mulwila Mubanga John Dr
Ms. Mwamba Emmah

For additional analytical, business and investment opportunities information, please contact Global Investment & Business Center, USA at (202) 546-2103. Fax: (202) 546-3275. E-mail: rusric@erols.com

IZ Mbewe Associates
Ground Floor Kambemdekela House
PO Box 30123
LUSAKA
Tel: 237529/237528
Ms Zeko Inonge Ireen Mbewe

I. M. Zulu & Associates
2nd Floor Eagle House
Former Chuundu House
PO Box
LUSAKA
Tel: 234440
Cell: 097 776024 / 096 767598
Email: ianmz@coppernet.zm <mailto:ianmz@coppernet.zm>
Mr. Ian M. Zulu

J

Jacob & Partners
Zimco House 8th Floor
PO Box
LUSAKA
Tel: 223917
Fax: 223916
Mr. Keith Akakelwa Mukata (Cell: 096 766131)
Mr. Kearns Andrew (Cell: 095 702389)

Jaques & Partners
4th Floor Anchor House
Cairo Road,
PO Box 30275
LUSAKA
Tel: 228081/1 222543
Fax: 226173
Email: jaques@zamnet.zm jaques@zamnet.zm
Mr. Sakala Chimbeka K.
Mr. Katongo Chindeni Damson

JB Sakala & Co
Permanent House, Wing A
Ground Floor
PO Box 34279
LUSAKA
Tel: 226885
Fax: 224443
Email: chiyak@yahoo.com
Ms. Sakala Kondwa Emily
Mr. Ngulube Anderson

Jitesh Naik Advocates
PO Box 31176

LUSAKA
Tel: 227216/17
Fax: 226928
Email: jnaikadv@zamnet.zm jnaikadv@zamnet.zm
Mr. Jitesh Naik
Mr. Chuula Chikosola Patrick
Mr. Munakopa Lloyd

JMC & Co
2nd Floor CUSA House
Stand 628 Cairo Road
PO Box 34855
LUSAKA
Tel: 238496
Mr. Chimembe Mwila Joseph

JMM Consultants
PO Box 30481
LUSAKA
Tel: 222201
Fax: 220126
Mr. Mwanakatwe Chipampe Paul
Mr. Mwanakatwe Mupanga John

K

Kajimanga & Co
5th Floor & 2nd Floor
Godfrey House
PO Box 50794
LUSAKA
Tel: 234451
Fax: 234436
Cell: 700595
E-mail: ckajima@zamnet.zm <mailto:ckajima@zamnetzm>
Mr. Kajimanga Charles

Kalima Chambers
Kulima House
Plot/Stand No. 1 Addis Ababa Avenue
PO Box 51209
LUSAKA
Tel/Fax: 255216/700927
Mr. Mebeelo Kalima

Kasonde & Co
PO Box 37458
LUSAKA
Mr.Kasonde Mutale Andrew

Katayi & Co.
First Alliance Bank Premises
Cha Cha Cha Road,

For additional analytical, business and investment opportunities information, please contact Global Investment & Business Center, USA at (202) 546-2103. Fax: (202) 546-3275. E-mail: rusric@erols.com

PO Box RW 50022
LUSAKA
Tel: 096 759551
Mr. Katayi Kabwe

Katuta & Company
4th Floor Cusa House
PO Box FW 110
LUSAKA
Tel: 235134
Fax: 235843
Mr. Nsemukila Katuta Kosta

KBF & Partners
1st Floor, E W Tarry Building
Cairo Road
PO Box 34444
LUSAKA
Tel: 236450
Mr. Bwalya Kelvin Fube

Kongwa & Co
Lusaka Polytechnic Building
Lumumba Road
PO Box 34512
LUSAKA
Tel: 226390
Kongwa S Francis

L

Lai-Loi Chambers
Plot 317 3rd Floor Kulima House
Plot 317, Cha Cha Cha Road
PO Box 35981
LUSAKA
Tel: 236674
Mr. Katuta Chituampyana Bruno

Law Bank
Attorneys at Law
Permanent House
P/B 442X
Ridgeway
LUSAKA
Tel: 231490
Fax: 231096
Mr. Musaba Keith K.
Mr. Mwananshiku Slyvester Chibangu

LC & Co
Plot No. 5997
Vintage Building, Great East Road
PO Box 37221

For additional analytical, business and investment opportunities information,
please contact Global Investment & Business Center, USA
at (202) 546-2103. Fax: (202) 546-3275. E-mail: rusric@erols.com

LUSAKA
Tel: 290195/295151
Fax: 295176
Mr. Chiti Kambole Lannette
Mr. Chiti Stanley Kasonde Bwalya

LC Zulu & Company
AMI Head Office Building
3535 Lumumba/Malambo Roads
PO Box 30131
Lusaka
Tel: 246191/6
Fax: 246192
Cell: 096 762110
Mr. Leslie Chembe Zulu

Levy Mwanawasa & Co
Plot 6798 Chiwalamabwe Road,
Olympia Extension,
PO Box 31283
LUSAKA
Tel: 292880
Fax: 224034
Email: mwaka@coppernet.zm
Mr. Mwanawasa Patrick Levy
Mrs. Mwanawasa Kakubo Maureen
Mr. Kasote Kirk Donald

Libertas Legal Practitioners
Plot 4833 Los Angeles Boulevard
PO Box 50843
LUSAKA
Tel: 251784
Mr. Nkonde Bwalya Sunday
Mr. Ngwira William
Ms.Lungu Helen

Light House Chambers
Villa Elizabetha
Musonda Ngosa Road
PO Box 37072
LUSAKA
Tel: 242527 / 096 758002/96 763140
Fax: 292958
Mr. Sitwala Sachika

Lincoln Chambers
1st Floor Salvation Army house
Cairo Road
PO Box 37489
LUSAKA
Tel: 220476/220749
Mr. Mwape Darlington

Lisimba & Co
PO Box 35929
LUSAKA
Tel: 221140/224674
Mr. Lisimba Munalula Vernon

Lisulo & Co
Opp. UNZA Gate
Plot 5839 Nanshila Road, Kalundu
PO Box 32259
LUSAKA
Tel: 294970
Cell: 097 794969
Mrs. Haimbe Njolomba Nama Dilys
Mr. Musonda Edward

Lloyd Siame & Co
Cusa House
PO Box 37418
LUSAKA
Tel: 237241
Fax: 237242
Mr. Chongo Ireen
Mr. Phiri Jack

Luangeni Chambers
Stand 12500 Kafue/Lumumba Road Junction
Caroussel Building
PO Box 37493
LUSAKA
Tel: 234650
Cell: 096 762043
Zulu Mangani Lucas

Lukona Chambers
Lex House, Addis Ababa Roundabout
PO Box 31160
LUSAKA
Tel: 254748
Fax: 253166
e-mail: lukona@zamnet.zm <mailto:lukona@zamnet.zm>
Mrs. Mutti Butete Kashumba Nellie
Mrs Chibale Agness Nonde
Ms. Kwenda Inonge
Ms Ndhlovu Hope Mukatimui

M

M.C. Kayuma Associates
5th Floor Anchor House
PO Box 33955
LUSAKA
Tel: 231849

Ms Kayuma Mary Natchihulu Chitebe

M Makasa & Co
21st Floor, Findeco House
PO Box 310263
LUSAKA
Tel: 237563
Fax: 282321
Mr.Makasa Mukula Robinson

M Musonda & Co
3rd Floor Permanent House
PO Box 36470
Tel: 221382
Fax: 221383
LUSAKA
Email: mmusonda@zamnet.zm
Mr. Bukali Domingo
Mr. Musonda Micheal

M Phiri & Partners
Plot 4749 Lubwa Rd/Beit Road
Rhodespark
PO Box 38582
LUSAKA
Tel: 250017
Fax: 250027
Mr. Phiri Moses

Mabutwe Associates
Plot No. 37 Ngumbo Road
Prospect Hill
PO Box 37991
LUSAKA
Tel: 253384
Mr. Mabutwe Clement
Mr. Sakala David O.

Mahachi Chambers
6th Floor Findeco House
PO Box 51093
LUSAKA
Tel: 225063
Fax: 225063
Mr. Chona Mainza Mathias, SC

Mainza & Company
4th Floor Chester House
Cairo Road
PO Box 34143
LUSAKA
Tel/Fax: 223126

Ms Kapita Astridah Kangwa
Mr. Mainza Remmy

Makala & Co
Plot 2103, 5th Floor, Woodgate House
Nairobi Place
PO Box 33431
LUSAKA
Tel: 237461/223895
Fax: 226312
Mr. Makala Hachuka Kenny
Mr. Ngenda Akalemwa
Ms Haimbe H. Mulambo

Malambo & Silwamba Advocates & Notaries
6th Floor Kwacha House
Cairo Road
PO Box E 342
LUSAKA
Tel/Fax: 238601
Malambo Blackskin Vincent
Silwamba Suwilanji Eric
Wright Andy Henry Jonathan
Ms Mwiche Kafula

Marshall Chambers
Suite 406/7 Anchor House
Plot 1369-71
Cairo Road
PO Box 51230
LUSAKA
Tel: 097 780256
Mr. Kaulung'ombe Germand Mutale

Mayowe & Co
Plot No. 2516
Cha Cha Cha Road
PO Box 31916
LUSAKA
Tel: 235292
Mr. Mayowe Christopher

MB Kamuwanga & Co
5th Floor Zimco House
PO Box 33713
LUSAKA
Tel: 221502
Fax: 223534
Dr.Kamuwanga M. Beatrice
(Also at Zambia Law Dev. Commission)

MG Johnson-Mwenda & Co
Plot No. 628
1st Floor CUSA House

PO Box 33645
LUSAKA
Tel: 223261
Fax: 224692
Mr. Mwenda Grace Marjorie

Miyanda Associates
3rd Floor, Cusa House
PO Box 35600
LUSAKA
Tel: 238474 / 96 766417
Fax: 221441
Miyanda S Samuel
Samulela Maureen

MNB Legal Practitioners
Stand 6131, 3rd & 4th Floor
Godfrey House, Longolongo Road
PO Box 34207
LUSAKA
Tel: 236920
Fax: 236134 / 234019
Email: mnb@zamnet.zm
Mr. Matibini Patrick
Mr. Siampwili Patrick
Mr. Nchito Mutembo
Mr. Nchito Nchima
Mr. Norman Sampa
Mr. Philimon Songolo

MMW & Co.
Electra House
PO Box 31619
LUSAKA
Tel: 097 786737
Mr. Willombe Bevin Chansa

Mofya Chambers
Stand 20,21,22Central Arcade Annex, Behind Society House
PO Box 31593
LUSAKA
Tel: 235723
Mr. Mofya Letford Nigel

Mukande & Co
Stand 685 Salvation Army House
PO Box 30134
LUSAKA
Tel: 220489
Fax: 239756
Mr. Mukande Mwikisa Louis

Mulenga Mundashi & Co
3rd Floor Development House

Katondo Street
PO Box 34972
LUSAKA
Tel: 235846 / 225886
Fax: 238547
Mr. Chanda Mumbi Nicolas
Mr. Chibundi Kafusha Phillip
Mr. Mulenga Mutila
Mr. Mundashi Musonda Micheal

Mulungushi Chambers
Stand No. 8, Permanent House
PO Box 36639
LUSAKA
Tel: 221980
Fax: 235897
Mr. Phiri Chivwara Kopeka
Mr. Simbao Mwamba Kenslick

Mungomba Associates
The Lawyers' Inn
42 Kudu Road, Kabulonga
PO Box 35476
LUSAKA
Tel: 260055/58
Fax: 262110
Mr. Mungómba Dísreali Willa

Mumba S. Kapumpa Advocates
Plot 2957 Benangombe Road, Woodlands
PO Box 33066
LUSAKA
Tel: 264229
Fax: 260664
Cell: (096) 762035
Email: mkapumpa@zamtel.zm
Mr. Kapumpa S Mumba

Munsaka Chambers
1st Floor Nsefu House
Room 5, 1st Floor Nsefu House
PO Box 50987
Lusaka
Tel/Fax: 227413
Mrs Virginia Agness Sondashi

Munyinda & Co
7th Floor Findeco House
Cairo Road
PO Box RW 50891
LUSAKA
Tel: 222277
Mr. Munyinda Mututwa Andrew

Muponda Chashi & Partners
6th Floor Woodgate House
PO Box 30284
LUSAKA
Tel: 224230
Cell: 097 771789/096 434534
Mr. Chashi Justin

Musa Dudhia & Co
Comesa
PO Box 31198
LUSAKA
Tel: 228426/30
Fax: 222603/227188
Email:
Dudhia Abdulla Ebrahim
Dudhia Ashard Abdulla
Dudhia Musa Isap Mahomed
Patel Gulam Farid

Mushipe & Associates
8th Floor Zimco House
PO Box 33813
LUSAKA
Tel: 231188
Fax: 262713
Ms. Mushipe Martha
Ms Rhoda Phiri

Mushota & Associates
1B 2nd Floor, West Suite
ZSIC House Chiparamba Road
P/Bag W 411
LUSAKA
Tel/Fax: 225014 / 097 773687
Mrs. Mushota Jabani Lillian

Mutemwa Chambers
Plot 685,4th Floor Lotti House
PO Box 30993
LUSAKA
Tel: 226136/237924
Fax: 221901
Mr. Mutemwa Mutemwa

Mvunga Associates
Anchor House
Sapele Road
PO Box 37988
LUSAKA
Tel: 226881
Fax: 234077
Prof. Mvunga Mphanza Patrick
Ms Sambo Towela

For additional analytical, business and investment opportunities information, please contact Global Investment & Business Center, USA at (202) 546-2103. Fax: (202) 546-3275. E-mail: rusric@erols.com

Mwiimbu & Co
3rd Floor Tazara House
PO Box 31645
LUSAKA
Tel: 237905 / 096 769625
Mr. Jack Jacob Mwiimbu

N

Nakonde Chambers
1st Floor Cha Cha Cha House
Cha Cha Cha Road
PO Box 31226
LUSAKA
Tel: 222427
Mr. Malewa Victor Kaona

Namukamba Chambers
1st Floor Permanent House
PO Box 34682
LUSAKA
Tel: 235454
Mr. Michelo Hichuumba Clement

NKM & Associates
PO Box 35822
LUSAKA
Tel: 229610
Mr. Mutuna Kalonde Nigel
Mr. Simuchoba Sibanze 095 705391

Nkwazi Chambers
PO Box 36870
LUSAKA
Tel: 254968
Mr. Munyama Bruce África
Mr. Nambeye Nancy

Nosiku Kawanambulu & Co
Stand No. 10524 Lumumba Road
MK Sports
PO Box 36857
LUSAKA
Tel: 261912
Mr. Sipalo Ngenda

Nyangulu & Co
Plot 2361, Design House
Sapele Road
PO Box 32049
LUSAKA
Tel: 221008

For additional analytical, business and investment opportunities information, please contact Global Investment & Business Center, USA at (202) 546-2103. Fax: (202) 546-3275. E-mail: rusric@erols.com

Mr. Mhango Ganjo Huck Norman
Mr. Kabwe Hobday
Judge Nyangulu Anthony John

Nyankhata Chambers
9 Ngwezi Road
Roma Township
PO Box 32049
LUSAKA
Tel: 290231
Mrs. Ngámbi Nkhata Daisy

O - P

Okware & Associates
Kulima House, 1st Floor
Cnr. Cha Cha Cha/Katunjila Roads
First Floor, Office No 106-108
PO Box 39569
LUSAKA
Tel: 236677 / 229035
Cell: 096 758222 / 095 703602
Mr. Okware Nicholas
Mr. Nicholas Chanda

P.M. Mwikisa & Co
3rd Floor Tazara House
Independence Avenue
P/Bag RW 403
LUSAKA
Tel: 222790
Mr. Mwikisa Wasamunu

Paul Palan & George
3rd Floor Premium House
Independence Avenue
Premium House
PO Box 34020
LUSAKA
Tel: 097 802566
Mr. Mulonda Palan

Patrick Zulu & Partners
5th Floor Society House Suite 509
PO Box 35516
LUSAKA
Tel: 220938
Mr. Munsanje Hodges Mark
Mr. Noyoo Noyoo

Paul Pandala Banda & Co
2nd Floor Southern Wing
Plot No. 163 Impala House

Cha Cha Cha
PO Box 50437
LUSAKA
Tel: 227638 / 231278
Cell: 097 779807 / 784461
Mr. Banda Pandala Paul
Mr. Kasonso Gozen Allan
Mr. Mubembe Joseph

Permanent Chambers
Sapele Road Memaco House
PO Box 35702
LUSAKA
Tel: 225884
Fax: 225049
Mr. Mubanga Willie Aubbie Crispin
Mr. Mandona Richard Nsofu

PH Yangailo
PO Box 35972
LUSAKA
Tel: 238195
Fax 238195
Mr. Yangailo Pengani Handerson
Mr. Ngulube Richard

Phoenix Partners
9th Floor Premium House
Independence Avenue
PO Box 34302
LUSAKA
Tel: 234621
Fax: 234620
Mr. Malila Mumba
Mr. Chanda Charles
Dr. F K M Sumaili

Pikiti & Co
No. 52 Church Road
Ndelefina Premises
PO Box 35716
LUSAKA
Tel: 226665
Fax: 237506
Mr. Pikiti Mweshi Mathew Joseph

R - S

RH Nketani & Co
Plot 104A Grosvenor Court
Room 3, Cairo Road
PO Box 36806
LUSAKA

Tel: 228931
Nketani Hisambi Reuben
RMA Chongwe & Co
Panganani Road
PO Box 31190
LUSAKA
Tel: 234440
Email: rma-co@zamnet.zm <mailto:rma-co@zamnet.zm>
Alternative Email: nkanga@iinet.com.au <mailto:nkanga@iinet.com.au>
Chongwe A M Rodger, Dr.

Sambo Kayukwa & Co
Stand 628, 1st Floor CUSA House
PO Box 36855
LUSAKA
Tel: 097 799141
Kayukwa Robert Godfrey

Shamwana & Co
Plot 9308 Independence Avenue
PO Box 32369
LUSAKA
Tel: 254839 / 253756
Fax: 251265
Email: shamwana@zamnet.zm <mailto:shamwana@zamnet.zm>
Mr. Shonga James Abyudi
Mr. Hachitapika Ruth Chimuka
Sharpe & Howard
1st & 2nd Floor Nalupembe House,
Stand 11723, Kabelenga Road,
PO Box 32587,
Tel: 222810/2/4, 232952; 232505
Fax: 224179
Email: s&h@zamnet.zm <mailto:s&h@zamnet.zm>
Mrs. Sharpe-Phiri Nicola Ann
Mr. Howard Guy Andrew
Ms.Theotis Ann Amanda
Mr. Kasonde Anthony
Ms. Katie Skippings
Ms. Veronica Scott
Ms Chipman Nelly

Shepande & Co
4th Floor Design House
PO Box 36939
LUSAKA
Tel: 237566/236046/221868
Fax: 238047
Mr. Shepande Mpolobe Kennedy

Silweya & Co
24c, 1st Floor
Technologist Building

PO Box 34426
LUSAKA
Tel: 221390
Mr. Silweya Henry

Simeza Sangwa & Associates
3rd Floor Woodgate House
PO Box 36824
LUSAKA
Tel: 227574
Fax: 220568
Mr. Banda James
Mr.Chipanzhya Mambwe
Mr. Sangwa Peter John
Mr. Simeza Mbonani Robert

Sinkamba & Associates
Indeco House
Cairo Road
PO Box 35352
LUSAKA
Tel: 097-780403
Mr. Sinkamba Owen

Solly Patel Hamir & Lawrence
4th Floor Woodgate House
PO Box 30605
LUSAKA
Tel: 229366/7
Fax: 225158
Mr. Patel Suliman

Sondashi & Co
Plot No. 1B
Chiparamba Road
Old UNDP Building
PO Box 50987
LUSAKA
Tel: 223373
Fax: 223373
Dr.Sondashi S Ludwig,

SS Phiri & Co
1st Floor Cha Cha Cha House
Cha Cha Cha Road
PO Box 36289
LUSAKA
Tel: 222543
Mr. Phiri Saulos Saidi

T - V

TS Chilembo Chambers
3rd Floor Tazara House
Dedan Kimathi Road
PO Box 37723
LUSAKA
Tel: 235983
Mr. Chilembo Todd Stewart

Veritas Chambers
Rooms 46-48
Carousel Shopping Centre
Stand No. 11052 Lumumba/Kafue Rds,
PO Box 30653
LUSAKA
Tel/Fax: 223922
Cell: 097 798763 / 805730
Mr. Sabi Mwape Samuel
Mr. Sikatana Mundia Fred

Verity and May Chambers
Ground Floor, Stand 7940/41
Kambendekela House
Dedan Kimathi Road
PO Box 31645
LUSAKA
Tel: 231185/222964
Fax: 222963
Email: izmbewe@zamnet.zm
Ms Kamanga Mwenya Priscilla
Ms Zeko Inonge Ireen Mbewe

W - Z

W Sithole Mwenda & Co
9th Floor Premium House
PO Box 37339
LUSAKA
Tel: 231890 / 238448
Fax: 238449
Mrs Mwenda Sithole Winnie

WM Kabimba & Co
3rd Floor Godfrey House
Longolongo/Kabelenga Road
PO Box 36571
LUSAKA
Tel: 238615/6
Fax: 238615
Mr. Kabimba Mwanacaambwa Wynter

WM Mumbuna & Co
4th Floor Bata House
PO Box 35472

For additional analytical, business and investment opportunities information, please contact Global Investment & Business Center, USA at (202) 546-2103. Fax: (202) 546-3275. E-mail: rusric@erols.com

LUSAKA
Tel: 235428/9
Cell: 096-430046
Mr. Mumbuna Wamui Mwenda

Zambezi Chambers
Ulendo Building
PO Box 32749
LUSAKA
Tel: 235689
Mr. Musanya Mukuka Alex
Zikonda & Associates
11th Floor Zimco House, Cairo Road
PO Box 34974
LUSAKA
Tel: 238504
Fax:238545
Mr. Zikonda Ray Anderson

Zulu & Co
3rd Floor Room 3 & 3A
Society House
PO Box 30917
LUSAKA
Tel: 223527
Mr. Zulu Saizi Sebastian

LEADING ATTORNEYS

LUSAKA

A

1. **Adams Aziz H.D., SC**, LL.B (UNZA July 1974), Advocate (June 1977), Solicitor (England and Wales Aug 84), A.D. Adams & Co., 1st Floor, Farmers House, Cairo Road, P.O. Box 33143. Tel: 228660, Fax: 228661 Specialisation: Banking, Commercial Law, Conveyancing, Civil Litigation, Constitutional Law, Company Law and Taxation.
2. **Akalutu Shepard**, LL.B, Advocate (Dec. 1988), Food Reserve Agency, Plot No. 7419, Manda Road, Food Reserve House, P.O. Box 34054, Tel: 286126 Fax: 286096/286097

B

3. **Banda Anessie Michael Bobo**, LL.B, Advocate (July 1988), Patents and Companies Registration Office, Part of Stand 8477 Longacres, Haile Selassie Avenue, Mwayi House, Tel: 255151 Fax: 255426 Email: pcro@zamnet.zm
4. **Banda Chifumu Kingdom**, SC, LL.B (1975), Advocate (July 1976), Chifumu Banda & Associates, Longolongo Road, Godfrey House, P.O. Box 31025. Tel: 233395/233059, Fax: 232203 Email: chifumu@zamtel.zm. Specialisation: Litigation, Criminal, Corporate, Conveyancing, Divorce, Arbitration, Legal Drafting, Commercial Transaction, Immigration, Wills and Probate.

For additional analytical, business and investment opportunities information, please contact Global Investment & Business Center, USA at (202) 546-2103. Fax: (202) 546-3275. E-mail: rusric@erols.com

5. **Banda James**, LL.B, Advocate (12 November 1999), Simeza Sangwa & Associates, 3rd Floor, Cairo Road, P.O. Box 36824, Woodgate House. Tel: 227574 Fax: 220568
6. **Banda Michael Chauba**, LL.B (UNZA Dec 1984), Advocate (Dec. 1985), Banda Watae Advocates, Plot 1716, Jacaranda Road, MSB Complex, P.O. Box 33939, Tel/Fax: 254678, Email: bwa@zamnet.zm Specialisation: Corporate Law
7. **Banda Nixon Mabvuto,** LL.B.(), Advocate (Z. Dec.1982), Standard Chartered Bank, Standard House, Cairo Road, PO Box 32238. Tel: 229242 Fax: 222092
8. **Banda Overs Masozi Mufwakawiri**, LL.B( ), Advocate(Dec 1986), Chifumu Banda & Associates, Godfrey House, Longolongo Roads, PO Box 31025, Tel: 233395/233059, Fax: 232203, Email: chifumu@zamnet.zm.
9. **Banda Paul Pandala,** LL.B (1991), Advocate (Dec 1993) Paul Pandala Banda & Co., 2nd Floor, Southern Wing, Plot No. 163 Impala House, Cha Cha Cha Road, , P.O. Box RW 50437. Tel: 779807/784461
10. **Bukali Domingo,** LL.B (Z. 1986), Advocate (Dec 1987), M. Musonda & Co., 3rd Floor, Permanent House, Cairo Road, Tel: 221382 Fax: 221383, Specialisation: Company Law, Insolvency Specialist, Legal Drafting, Conveyancing. Email: mmusonda@zamnet.zm
11. **Bwalya Barnabas,** LL.B, Advocate (June 2001), Judiciary, PO Box 50067, Tel: 251330.
12. **Bwalya Kelvin Fube**, LL.B (Dec. 1985), Advocate (Nov. 1986), KBF & Partners, 1st Floor, E.W. Tarry Building, Cairo Road, Box 34444. Tel: 236449 Tel/Fax: 236450 Specialisation: Investment, Commercial, Immigration, Criminal & Constitution Law.
13. **Bwembya Mutale Joseph R.,** LL.B, Advocate (October 1997), National Assembly, Parliament Building, Parliament Road, P.O. Box 31299, Tel: 292425/7 Fax: 292252

C

14. **Cave Paul Dodge Anthony**, LL.B (Hon. Society, Middle Temple UK – Feb. 1965), Cavmont Merchant Bank Ltd, Mukuba Pension House, Mukuba Pension House, P.O. Box 38474, Tel: 224286/7 Fax: 224304/224316
15. **Chaane George,** Barrister and Solicitor (June 1967), Advocate (1968), A.D. Adams & Co., Farmers House, Cairo Road, P.O. Box 33143, Tel: 228660 Fax: 226881. Specialisation: Litigation and Conveyancing
16. **Chaiwila Maurice Mwango**, LL.B (UNZA 1990), Advocate (May 1992), Chaiwila & Chaiwila Associates, 2nd Floor Permanent House "T Wing", No. 253 Cairo Road, P.O. Box 34750. Tel: 096 795621/431479 Specialisation: Property Consultant
17. **Chalwe Kunda Margaret**, LL.B, Advocate (1997), Zambia National Commercial Bank Ltd, Plot 2119, Head Office, P.O. Box 33611. Tel: 221358/223077 Fax: 223082
18. **Chanda Charles,** LL.B (UNZA 1996), Advocate (Z. 1996), C.C Chambers Cusa House.
19. **Chanda Henry Chilufya,** LL.B (UNZA July 1975), Advocate (Dec 1976), Henry Chanda & Co., Nkwazi House, Nkwazi/Chachacha Roads, PO Box 35364, Tel: 25315/229882
20. **Chanda Lubasi Joan**, LL.B, Advocate (1997), Mahtani Group of Companies, Cairo Road, Professional Insurance House, 5th Floor, PO Box 34376. Tel: 224124/224276/224256
21. **Chanda Mumbi Nicholas**, LL.B (UNZA 1996), Advocate (Z. November 1996),Nicholas Chanda & Associates, Suite No. 10, 1st Floor, Chester House, PO Box 39569, Tel: 229035, Fax: 229035, Cell:96 758222, Email: nichanda@zamtel.zm

For additional analytical, business and investment opportunities information, please contact Global Investment & Business Center, USA at (202) 546-2103. Fax: (202) 546-3275. E-mail: rusric@erols.com

22. **Chanda Mwamba**, LL.B, Advocate (Dec.2000), Judiciary, Plot 438, Independence Avenue, Supreme Court, PO Box 50067. Telephone: 251330 Ext. 110.

23. **Chanda Priscilla C.**, LL.B, Advocate (Apr. 2001), Ministry of Legal Affairs, Cell: 703476 Specialisation: General Practitioner.

24. **Chashi Justin,** LL.B (UNZA October 1984), Advocate (Dec 1985), Muponda Chashi & Partners, 6th Floor, Woodgate House, P.O. Box 30284. Tel/Fax: 224230/771789/96 434534.

25. **Chewe Annie Kangwa**, National Legal Clinic for Women, Musonda Ngosa Road, 110A/150, Villa Elizabetha, P/B E578, P.O. Box 30851. Tel: 220595 Fax: 234747

26. **Chibangula Gary Davies**, LL.B( ), Advocate (Dec 2001), Permanent Chambers, Pensions House, PO Box 35702, Tel: 225884 Fax: 225049 Cell: 096 754482 Email: permcham@zamnet.zm

27. **Chibesakunda Chibesa,** LL.B**,** Advocate (Dec 1992), Public Service Pensions Fund Board, Memaco House, P.O. Box 50588. Tel: 232035 Fax: 232319

28. **Chibesakunda Mwelwa,** LL.B**,** Advocate (February 1991), Corpus Globe, Plot No. 2386, Growell Building, Longolongo Road, P.O. Box 32115, Tel: 235480/1 Fax: 238657 Email: corpus@zamnet.zm Specialisation: Corporate and Commercial Law

29. **Chibesakunda Mwelwa Ng'ona,** Advocate (Dec 1967), National Assembly, Plot 5030, Parliament Building, Parliament Road, P.O. Box 31299. Tel: 292425/7 Fax: 292252

30. **Chibiya Muyoya,** LL.B (1990),Advocate (Dec.1991)Pensions and Insurance Authority, Cnr. Nationalist/John Mbita Rds, Former NCDP Building, P/B RW 30X, Tel: 250394, Email: pia@zamnet.zm

31. **Chibula Terence**, LL.B, Advocate (Dec. 1995), National Assembly, Parliament Building, P.O. Box 31299, Tel: 292425/7 Fax: 292252

32. **Chibundi Kafusha Philip,** LL.B**,** Advocate (Nov. 1999), Mulenga Mundashi & Co, Katondo St., Stand 29a/13, PO Box PO Box 34942, Tel: 235846/225886.

33. **Chibwe Chikwa Stephen**, LL.B, Advocate (1996), Ysakar Legal Practitioners, Suite No. 24. Kambendekela House, Dedan Kimathi Road, PO Box 33519, Tel: 236872/096 759771

34. **Chifuti Costain**, LL.B, Advocate (Dec. 2000), Judiciary Dept, Plot 438, PO Box 50067, Tel: 251330

35. **Chikampa George Hangoonta**, LL.B, Advocate (June 2001), (Address Unknown).

36. **Chikuni Priscilla**, LL.B, Advocate, Group3 Security Ltd, Plot 4974, Kabelenga Road, Lewis House, PO Box 31868. Telephone: 235322 Email: group3security@coppernet.zm

37. **Chilembo Oliver Bangala**, LL.B, Advocate (Dec. 1982), Chilembo & Co, Plot 2796, Chempro Building, PO Box 30584, Tel: 238465/6 Fax: 238234.

38. **Chilembo Todd Stewart,** LL.B (1984), Advocate (December 1985), T.S. Chilembo Chambers, 3rd Floor, Tazara House, Dedan Kimathi Road, P.O. Box 37723, Tel/Fax: 235983. Specialisation: Conveyancing and debt collection

39. **Chileshe Gilbert Chewe (Brig Gen)**, LL.B, Advocate, Chilupe and Co, 1st Floor Superannuation House, Ben Bella Road, PO Box 33204. Tel: 227878 Fax: 222768/9 Also: Embassy of Zambia, Washington Email: mubemba@aol.com

40. **Chilundu Watson**, LL.B (1996), Advocate (April 1997), Public Service Pensions Fund, Memaco Building, P.O. Box 50588. Tel: 232705-8

For additional analytical, business and investment opportunities information, please contact Global Investment & Business Center, USA at (202) 546-2103. Fax: (202) 546-3275. E-mail: rusric@erols.com

41. **Chilupe George Kabwe**, Advocate (8th Dec. 1978), Chilupe and Co., 1st Floor Superannuation House, Ben Bella Road, P.O. Box 33204, Tel: 227879.

42. **Chimembe Mwila Joseph**, Advocate (Dec. 1987), JMC & Associates, 2nd Floor, Cusa House, Stand 628, P.O. Box 34855, Tel: 238496. Specialisation: Conveyancing, Immigration, Citizenships and Criminal Law.

43. **Chimuka Constantine Haangala**, Solicitor (February 1975), Advocate (Ellis and Co., 1st and 2nd Floors, Farmers House, P.O. Box 31902, Tel: 227921/3, Fax: 227924 Telex: 45021. Specialisation: Conveyancing, Company and Commercial Law.

44. **Chimungu Tarsisius Chewe**, LL.B (UNZA 1982), Advocate (May 1985), Chimungu and Company, Ground Floor, Wing C, Permanent House, Cairo Road, P.O. Box 33693, Tel: 96-759145

45. **Chimwala P,M. H**., LL.B (December 1988), Zesco Limited, Great East Road, P.O. Box 33304, Tel: 225466 Fax: 222753

46. **Chintu Mulenga Hubert**, LL.B, Advocate (May 1991), Chintu & Company, Plot 685, Lotti House, Cairo Road, P.O. Box 30446, Tel: 237576/237548/223448.

47. **Chiyenge Chishala Eness,** LL.B ( ), Advocate (April 1983), Saleah Associates, No. 2, Mezzanine , Society House, PO Box 39012, Tel: 095 704436/096 756694

48. **Chinyanta Judith Mukaya Tembo**, LL.B (April 1988), Advocate (December 1988), Communications Authority, Legal Department, Plot 3141, Cnr Lumumba and Buyantanshi Road, Heavy Industrial Area, P.O. Box 36871, Tel: 246702/241236.

49. **Chipanzhya Mambwe**, LL.B, Advocate (March 1999), Messrs Simeza Sangwa & Associates, 3rd Floor, Woodgate House, Cairo Road, P.O. Box 36824. Tel: 227574, Fax: 220568

50. **Chipimo Elias Chileshe**, LL.B (UNZA), BCL (Oxon), Advocate (November 1989), Corpus Globe, Stand No. 2386, Growell Building, Longolongo Road, P.O. Box 32115, Tel: 235480/1, Fax: 238657, Email: corpus@zamnet.zm Specialisation: Corporate and Financial Services.

51. **Chipman Nelly**, LL.B (UNZA), Advocate (Dec 1998), Sharpe & Howard, 1st and 2nd Floors, Nalupembe House, Kabelenga Road, P.O. Box 32587, Tel: 222810/2/4, 232952, 232505 Fax: 224179 Email: s&h@zamnet.zm

52. **Chisanga Bikoko Aswell**, LL.B (UNZA 1989), Advocate (December 1990), National Pension Scheme Authority (NAPSA) Provident House, P.O. Box 51275RW, Tel: 228046-53, Fax: 228060, 293487 (Res).

53. **Chisanga Kangwa George**, Advocate (July 1993), Stanbic Bank (Z) Ltd, P.O. Box 31955, Tel: 229071, Fax: 225380/221152. Email: stanbic@zamnet.zm Specialisation: Business and Commercial, Corporate Advisory Services, International Joint Venture Agreements, Securities and Taxation.

54. **Chishimba Fraser**, LL.B (Dec. 1990), Advocate (Dec. 1991), Fraser & Associates, 1st Floor, Fintex House, Plot 1378, Dar-es-Salaam Place, Sapele Road, P.O. Box 35641. Tel: 227563/229387, Fax: 236893, Cell: 750772. Specialisation: Civil Litigation, Commercial Transactions, Probate, Corporate Law, Taxation and Conveyancing.

55. **Chisi Prince**, LL.B (UNZA 1993), Advocate (1994), Chifumu Banda & Associates, Godfrey House, Longolongo Road, P.O. Box 31025, Tel: 233395/233059. Specialisation: General

56. **Chisulo Samson Lee, SC,** LL.B, Advocate (1977), Sam Chisulo & Co., House No.1 Nyerere Road Prospect Hill, PO Box 50124, Tel: 253553/097 821430

For additional analytical, business and investment opportunities information, please contact Global Investment & Business Center, USA at (202) 546-2103. Fax: (202) 546-3275. E-mail: rusric@erols.com

57. **Chisunka Matthew Kasonde**, Advocate (Dec. 1983), Bank of Zambia, Bank Square, Cairo Road, P.O. Box 30080, and Tel: 228888, Fax: 221764.

58. **Chiti Lannette Kambole**, LL.B (Dec 1983), L.C & Company, Vintage Building, Plot No 5997, Great East Road, P.O. Box 37219, Tel: 290195/295151, Fax: 295176.

59. **Chiti Stanley Bwalya Kasonde**, Advocate (Dec. 1978), L.C & Company, Vintage Building, Plot No 5997, Great East Road, P.O. Box 37219, Tel: 290195/295151, Fax: 295176.

60. **Chitoshi Chishala Jnr**., LL.B, Advocate (April 1996), Zambia National Commercial Bank, Head Office, Plot 2119, P.O. Box 33611, Tel: 221358 Fax: 223082.

61. **Chiwale McRobby Vincent**, LL.B, Advocate (Dec. 1998), I.C. N'gonga & Co., Muyuni House, Plot 8116, 1st Floor, Room 3, Bombay Street, Kamwala, Tel: 220254/56.

62. **Chola Gertrude Shapi C.** , LL.B (1995), Advocate (April 1996), Zambia Revenue Authority, Revenue House, P.O. Box 35710, Tel: 227460, Fax: 221075.

63. **Chona Mainza Mathias**, SC, Barrister at Law (1958 Grays Inn, London), Advocate (October, 1963), State Counsel (July 1975), Mahachi Chambers, 6th Floor, Findeco House, P.O. Box 51093, Fax: 225063.

64. **Chongwe Ignatius Mumba,** LL.B, Advocate (2001), Legal Resources Chambers, 4th Floor, Woodgate House, PO Box 35162. Tel: 227484 Fax: 220658 Email: lrf@zamnet.zm

65. **Chongo Irene Musonda**, LL.B, Advocate(Dec.1993), Lloyd Siame and Company, 2nd Floor, CUSA House, P.O. Box 37418, Tel: 237241 Fax: 237242 Also at Ndola.

66. **Chongwe Rodger M.A**., Dr., RMA Chongwe and Company, Plot No. 1653 Panganani Road, P.O. Box 31190, Tel: 234440/ 97 776024/96 767598.Email: rma-co@zamnet.zm Alternative email: nkanga@iinet.com.au

67. **Chonta Chileshe Charles**, LL.B, Advocate (Dec 1995), Ellis and Co., Phillip Ellis House, 8 Tito Road, Off Church Road, P.O. Box 31902, Tel: 252709/738/809 Fax: 250802 Also at Ndola and Kitwe

68. **Chuula Chikosola Patrick**, LL.B Hons (1990), Advocate (1994), Jitesh Naik Advocate, Sitwe Plaza, Plot No. 742, Cha Cha Cha Road, P.O. Box 31176, Tel: 227216/7 Fax: 226928. Specialisation: General

69. **Chulu Jacob Elliot Laen**, LL.B, Advocate (Nov. 1979), Central Board of Health, Ndeke House, PO Box 35588, Tel: 253588/253179

70. **Chuulu Miyoba Matrine**, LL.B (April 1992), Advocate (December 1993), National Legal Aid Clinic for Women, stand No. 1109/150, Musonda Ngosa Road, P/B E578. Tel: 220595, Fax: 234747 or Women & Law in Southern Africa (WLSA), PO Box Tel: 255209/097 774617.

71. **Cornhill Gregory**, LL.B (June 1993), Advocate (1996), Fidelity Chambers, 9th Floor, Premium House, Independence Avenue, P.O. Box 38906, Tel/Fax: 231823 Email: gscom@zamnet.zm

D

74. **Dindi Noah Kaponda**, Dindi and Company, Plot 1B, Room 115, 1st Floor, Western Wing, Above Cairo Chemist, Chiparamba Road, P.O. Box 34972, Tel/Fax: 229875

75. **Dudhia Arshad Abdulla**, LL.B (E. August 1991), Advocate (Dec. 1992), Musa Dudhia & Co., Permanent House, Cairo Road, P.O. Box 31198, Tel: 228426-30, Fax: 222603. Specialisation: Commercial Litigation, Conveyancing and Matrimonial.

76. **Dudhia Abdul Ebrahim**, Barrister (February, 1961), Advocate (November 1965), Notary Public (June, 1979 Musa Dudhia & Co., Permanent House, Cairo Road, P.O. Box 31198, Tel: 228426-30, Fax: 222603. Specialisation: Conveyancing and Commercial Legal Work.

77. **Dudhia Musa Isap Mohamed**, Solicitor (E. February 1959), Advocate (Jan. 1960), Notary (March, 1965), Musa Dudhia & Co., Permanent House, Cairo Road, P.O. Box 31198, Tel: 228426-30, Fax: 222603. Email: musadud@zamnet.zm Specialisation: General Practitioner.

G

78. **Gani Ebrahim Adam**, Advocate (April, 1970), A.D. Adams & Co., Farmers House, Cairo Road, P.O. Box 33143, Tel: 228660 Fax: 228661

79. **Gondwe Buta**, LL.B (1984), Advocate (Dec. 1985), Development Bank of Zambia, Legal Department, Development House, Stand No. 29, Katondo Street, P.O. Box 33955, Tel: 228576-94, Fax: 222426, Telex: ZA 45040 (ADD "DEVE B"), Specialisation: General.

80. **Gondwe Lameck**, LL.B (April 28, 1999) Andrea Masiye and Company, Plot 974, Addis Ababa Drive, P.O. Box 30757. Tel: 254842.

H

78. **Hachitapika Chimuka Ruth**, LL.B, Advocate (12 May 2000), Shamwana & Co., Plot No. 9308 Independence Avenue, P.O. Box 32369, Tel: 254839/253756 Fax: 251265 Email: shamwana@zamnet.zm

79. **Haimbe Dilys Nama Njolomba**, LL.B (Z. 1985), Advocate (May, 1989), Lisulo & Company, Opp. UNZA Gate, Plot 5839 Nanshila Road, Kalundu. Tel: 294970 Cell: 97 794969

80. **Haimbe H. Mulambo**, LL.B, Advocate (June 2001), Makala & Co., Nairobi Place, 5th Floor, Woodgate House, PO Box 33431, Tel: 223895/226312

81. **Haimbe Mwangala Lubinda**, LL.B, Advocate (April 1995), Lusaka City Council, Civic Centre, Independence Avenue, P.O. Box 30077. Tel: 253114

82. **Hakasenke Claydon,** LL.B (1988), Advocate (August 1990), LL.M (Cantab. 1990) FCCS (1990), Hakasenke and Co., 1st Floor Insurance House, P.O. Box 35858, Tel: 238810/11, Direct Line: 238813, Fax: 238814.

83. **Hamakando Maambo Hamuzwe Fred,** LL.B (Z. 1976), Advocate (Z. Dec. 1978), Batoka Chambers, 5th Floor, Zimco House, Cairo Road, P.O. Box 33856. Tel: 234650 Fax: 228227.

84. **Hamanyanga Hamala George,** LL.B (UNN 1965), Advocate (April 19, 1971) Hamanyanga & Co., Grosvenor Court, Plot 104A, Cairo Road, P.O. Box 34417, Tel: 225642

85. **Hamanyanga Namwandi,** LL.B (UNZA 1991), Advocate (Z. Dec. 1992), Dip. WL (UNZA 1995), Zambia Revenue Authority, Revenue House, Kabwe Roundabout, P.O. Box 35710, Tel: 229744. email: hamanyan@zra.org.zm

86. **Hamir M Ali.., SC,** LL.B (UNZA 1970), Advocate (April 1971), Ali M.Hamir & Co, Westavia House, Plot No.9214, Off Los Angeles Road, P.O Box 36475, Tel: 88578/9, Fax: 288009. Email: amhamir@zamnet.zm

87. **Hamir Osman Mohammed.**, LL.B (UNZA 1993), Advocate (Dec.1993), LL.M (Cambridge),Ali M.Hamir & Co., Plot No.9214, Off Lumumba Road, Westavia House, P.O Box 36475Tel: 288578/9, Fax: 288009. Email: omhamir@zamnet.zm

For additional analytical, business and investment opportunities information, please contact Global Investment & Business Center, USA at (202) 546-2103. Fax: (202) 546-3275. E-mail: rusric@erols.com

88. **Hamir Farhana Quadri, LL.**B.(UNZA), Advocate(May 2002), Christopher Russell Cook & Company, 4th Floor, Woodgates House, Cairo Road, PO Box 34091, Tel: 229366 Email: sphl@zamnet.zm

89. **Han'gandu Nemba Kelvin,** LL.B (UNZA,1996), Advocate(Z.1996), Central Chambers, Lex House, Addis Ababa Road Round About, P.O Box 50468,Tel/Fax: 253610, Specialisation: Civil Litigation, Corporate, Litigation Law, Media , Libel.

90. **Howard Andrew Guy**, Advocate (Dec.), Sharpe & Howard, Stand No. 2374 Bata Boulevard, Lusaka Showgrounds, P/B RW 175X, Ridgeway. Tel:250677/255156 Fax: 252909 Cell: 096 753201/702389/750898 Email: howard@zamnet.zm

K

78. **Kabimba Wynter M**., LL.B (UNZA 1981), Advocate (1984), W.M Kabimba & Co., Godfrey House, 3rd Floor, Kabelenga/Longolongo Roads, P.O Box 36571, Tel: 238615/6, Fax: 238615. Specialisation: Corporate & Taxation Law, Civil. Email: wmk@zamnet.zm

79. **Kabonga Valentine A.L,** LL.B, Advocate (20 April 1979), Zambia Institute of Advanced Legal Education (ZIALE), Plot No. 9& 11, Andrew Mwenya Road, PO Box 30090. Tel: 254557/254581 Fax: 254620

80. **Kabwe Hobday**, LL.B (1994), Advocate (1996), Nyangulu & Co, Plot 2361, Design House, Sapele Road, P.O. Box 32049 Tel: 221008 Specialisation: Litigation, Corporate, Taxation, Conveyancing, Criminal and Commercial.

81. **Kachapulula Kandala Charles**, LL.B (1975), Advocate (Dec.1978) Union Bank (Z) Ltd. (In Liquidation), Zimco House, Cairo Road, PO Box 34940, Tel: 223314, Fax: 221866, Telex: 40112/45150. Specialisation: Commercial Transactions, Conveyancing, International Trade/Investment Agreements.

82. **Kaite John Kakungu**, LL.B, Advocate (December 1987) ZCCM Investments Holdings plc, Mukuba Pension House, Plot 5309, Dedan Kimathi Road, PO Box 30048, Tel: 229115/232388 Fax: 228561 Email: postp@zccm.zm

83. **Kajimanga Charles**, LL.B (Z.1983), LL.M (USA, Cornell May,1993), Advocate (Dec.1984), Kajimanga & Company, 5th Floor, 2nd Floor Godfrey House, Longolongo Road, P.O Box 50794, Tel: 234451 Fax: 234436 Cell: 700595 ckajima@zamnet.zm Specialisation: General.

84. **Kalikiti Alex**, LL.B (Sept.1993), Advocate (Sept 1994), Lusaka Water and Sewerage Company Ltd, Head Office, Plot 871 Katemo Road, Los-Angeles Road, P.O Box 50198, Tel: 250666/250776.

85. **Kalima Meebelo** (Nov 1998), Kalima Chambers, Plot/Stand No. 1, Addis Ababa Road, Kalima House, P.O. Box RW 50209, Tel: 255216/700927.

86. **Kalinde Nkole Leonard**, LL.B, Advocate (November 1996), Commerce Bank (In Liquidation), PO Box , Tel: 223781 Cell: 95 703604 Email: lkalinde@law.unza.zm

87. **Kalokoni Gideon James,** LL.B (UNZA 1996), Advocate (Z.1996), Zesco Limited, P.O. Box 33304, Head Office, Great East Road, Tel: 228084-94 Fax: 222753

88. **Kamanga Priscilla Mwenya** , LL.B (1987), Advocate (Feb.1990) Verity & May, Ground Floor, Kambendekela House, Suite No. 1, Cairo Road, PO Box 30123, Tel: 231185/222964, Fax: 222963 Email: izmbewe@zamnet.zm Specialisation: Conveyancing, Legal Drafting.

89. **Kamfwa Kasongo Obote**, LL.B (UNZA 1992), Advocate (Dec.1993), Zambia State Insurance Corporation Ltd., Premium House, Independence Avenue, P.O Box 30894, Tel: 225861, Fax: 224361, Telex:42521, Specialisation: General.

90. **Kamuwanga Beatrice Mwangala,** (DR), LL.B (1976), LLM (1979), PHD (Dec. 19988), Advocate (1989), Cert. in conflict Resolution (1989), Kamuwanga & Co.(formerly Transna Chambers), 5th Floor, ZIMCO House, P.O Box 33713, Tel: 221502, Fax: 223534 Specialisation: International Trade, Investment Law, Women Law and Development, International Tax law. Also: Zambia Law Development Commission, Tel: 250071

91. **Kamwendo Isaac,** Times Printpak (Z) Ltd, Legal Dept, Times House, Freedom Way, PO Box 30394, Tel: 229076

92. **Kamwi Eric Mutaba,** Advocate (November 1999), Electoral Commission of Zambia, PO Box 50274 Tel: 253155-7 Fax: 253884/250081

93. **Kanja Mpundu George**, LL.B, Advocate (2001), Palan & George, 3rd Floor, Premium House, Independence Avenue, Premium House, PO Box 34020. Tel: 097 802566

94. **Kaona Victor Malewa**, LL.B (UNZA 1993), Advocate (Oct. 1994), Nakonde Chambers, Cha Cha Cha House, 1st Floor, Cha Cha Cha Road, P.O. Box 31226, Tel: 222427

95. **Kapatamoyo Chama Maudy**, Advocate (Dec.1995), CKM & Associates, Chester House, Cairo Road, PO Box 38288 Cell: 097 792172 Specialisation: General Practitioner

96. **Kapilikisha Francis Chowa**, Advocate (April, 1996), Echo Temple & Chambers, Indeco House, Cairo Road, RW 51258. Tel: 220264/228561 Email: echo@zamnet.zm.

97. **Kapinga Peter**, ,LL.B (UNZA 1986), Advocate (July,88), Zambezi River Authority, Kariba House, Stand 32, Cha Cha Cha Road, P.O Box30233, Tel: 227970/1, Fax: 227498, 228401/2 Telex:ZA 42421 ZRA. Email: zaraho@zamnet.zm

98. **Kapita Astridah Kangwa**, Advocate (October 1997), Mainza & Company, 4th Floor, Chester House, Cairo Road, PO box 38143, Tel/Fax: 223126.

99. **Kapumpa S. Mumba**, LL.B, Advocate (October 1972), Mumba S Kapumba Advocates, Plot 2957 Benangombe Road, Woodlands, PO Box 33066. Tel: 264229 Fax: 260664 Email: mkapumpa@zamtel.zm

100. **Kasonde Andrew Mutale**, LL.B, Advocate (Z. 26 Nov. 1963) Barrister Solicitor, Grays Inn, London, Kasonde & Co, P.O Box 37548, Specialisation: General Practitioner.

101. **Kasonde Anthony**, LL.B, Advocate (2001), Sharpe & Howard, 1st & 2nd Floor Nalupembe House, Stand 11723, Kabelenga Road, PO Box 32587, Tel: 222810/2/4, 232952; 232505 fax: 224179 Email: s&h@zamnet.zm

102. **Kasonde Pixie Linda Mwila Yangailo**., LL.B (1993), Advocate (1993), PriceWaterhouseCoopers, Stand No. 2108, National Savings and Credit Bank Building, 7th Floor, Tel: 228809-10/220768 Fax: 220778 email: pixie.yangailo@zm.pwcglobal.com Specialisation: General Practitioner.

103. **Kasonde Patrick**. LL.B (, Advocate (April 1997), Zambia Telecommunications Co. Ltd, Indeco House, Cairo Road, PO Box 30099, Tel: 235613 Fax: 235611.

104. **Kasonso Gozen Allan**, Advocate (April,1996), Paul Pandala Banda & Co., 2nd Floor, Southern Wing, Plot No. 163 Impala House, Cha Cha Cha Road, , P.O. Box RW 50437. Tel: 779807/784461

105. **Kasote Donald Kirk,** Advocate (1990 May), Levy Mwanawasa & Company, Plot 6798 Chiwalamabwe Road, Olympia Ext., P.O. Box 31283, Tel/Fax: 292880 Email: mwaka@coppernet.zm

106. **Katayi Kabwe,** LL.B (Hons. 1992), Advocate (Dec.1993), Katayi & Co., First Alliance Premises, Cha Cha Cha Road, PO Box 50022 Tel: 096 759551

107. **Katongo Damson Chindeni,** LL.B (Hons.March 1967), Barrister & Solicitor (Aug.1968), Jaques & Partners, 4th Floor, Anchor House, Cairo Road, P.O Box 30275, Tel: 228080/1, Telex: ZA 42790, Fax: 226173 Email: jaques@zamnet.zm Specialisation: Commercial & Business.

108. **Katuta Bruno C.K,** LL.B, Advocate (April 1981), Lai-Loi Chambers, 3rd Floor Kulima House, Plot 317, Cha Cha Cha Road, PO Box 35981, Tel: 236674

109. **Kaulung'ombe Germand Mutale**, LL.B, Advocate (Dec. 1986), Marshall Chambers, Suite 406/7 Anchor House, Plot 1369-71,Cairo Road, PO Box 51230. Cell: 097 780256

110. **Kayukwa Godfrey R.,** LL.B (1982) Advocate (Dec.1983), Sambo Kayukwa & Co, CUSA House, Stand 628, 1st Floor, P.O. Box 36855 Cell: 97-799141

111. **Kayuma Mary Natchihulu Chitebe**, Advocate (Dec.1986), Stand No.25, Development Bank of Zambia, Development House, Katondo Street, P.O Box 33955, Tel: 24072. Fax: 222426 Also: M.C. Kayuma Associates, 5th Floor Anchor House, PO Box 33955, Tel: 231849. Also Ndola at PO Box 240098 Ndola.

112. **Kearns Thomas J Andrew**, LL.B, Advocate (Dec. 1998), Jacob & Partners, 8th Floor Zimco House, PO Box 36181 , Tel: 223917 Fax: 223916

113. **Kongwa Francis Situmbwa,** LL.B (), Advocate Kongwa and Company, Plot No.260, Lusaka High School Building, PO Box 36710. Tel: 226390

114. **Kunda Christina**, Advocate (Nov.1989), Corpus Globe, The Globe Building, Stand No.2386, Longolongo Road, P.O Box 32115, Tel: 235480/1, Fax: 238657. Specialisation: Corporate Advisory Litigation, Acquisitions, Privatisation. Email: tinakunda@mail.com

115. **Kunda George**, LL.B (Z.1980), Advocate (Z.28 April 1982), Solicitor (Supreme Court of England and Wales, June 1990), George Kunda and Co, Plot 6798 Chiwalamabwe Road, Olympia Ext., P.O. Box 31283, Tel/Fax: 292880 E-mail: geokunda@zamnet.zm, Specialisation: Civil and Criminal Litigation, Commercial Corporate, Land Litigation, Conveyancing, Business Transactions and Investment Law. Also Lu

116. **Kunda Irene Mwezi,** LL.B (Z.1981), Advocate (Z. Dec. 23,1983), Solicitor of the Supreme Court (England and Wales, June 1990), George Kunda & Co, Plot 6798 Chiwalamabwe Road, Olympia Ext., P.O. Box 31283, Tel/Fax: 292880 E-mail: geokunda@zamnet.zm.

117. **Kunkuta Musesha Chitundu Joseph, C.,** LL.B, Advocate (December,1978), Patents and Companies Registration,, Off Part of Stand 8471, Haile Selassie Road, Mwayi House, P.O. Box 32020. Tel: 255151/255025 Fax: 255426 Email: pcro@zamnet.zm

118. **Kwenda Inonge,** LL.B, Advocate (2001), Lukona Chambers, Lex House, Tito Road, P.O. Box 31160, Tel: 254748 Fax: 253166 Email: lukona@zamnet.zm Specialisation: Conveyancing, Litigation, Debt Collection, Commercial Transactions, Trade Marks and Patents.

L

119. **Lengesela Magoba Felix**, Advocate (Dec.1995), Lusaka City Council, Civic Centre, P.O Box 30077, Tel: 253114, Fax: 252141 - (DECEASED).

For additional analytical, business and investment opportunities information, please contact Global Investment & Business Center, USA at (202) 546-2103. Fax: (202) 546-3275. E-mail: rusric@erols.com

120. **Lipimile George**, LL.B, CIPA, ATA, Advocate (Sept.1988), MSc. (Intellectual Property), , Zambia Competition Commission, Cairo Road, Main Post Office, PO Box 32826. Tel: 222775 Fax: 222789 Specialisation: Intellectual Property

121. **Lisimba Mutakela,** LL.B (1995), Advocate (Nov.1996), Zambia National Commercial Bank Ltd, Cairo Road, PO Box 33611, Tel: 238878, Fax: 224056.

122. **Lisimba Vernon Munalula**, LL.B (1973), Advocate (Feb.1975) LLM (1981), Lisimba & Co., 4th Floor, ZIMCO House, Cairo Road, P.O Box 35929, Tel: 231771, Specialisation: Business Law.

123. **Liswaniso Theresa Mubutu Kampata**, LL.B, Advocate (November 1996), Development Bank of Zambia, Stand 29, Katondo Street, Development House, PO Box 33955. Tel: 228576-94, Fax: 222426

124. **Liweleya Munalula Michael**, LL.B (Dec.1984), Advocate (Z. Dec, 1986), Stock Broker (1994), Legal Counsel, Securities and Exchange Commission, 8th Floor, National Savings & Credit Bank Blg, Cairo Road North-End, P.O. Box 35165, Tel: 227012/225988, Fax: 225443, Cell: 096-757016 Email: liweleya@zamnet.zm Specialization: Securities Law.

125. **Locha Godfrey**, LL.B, Advocate (Nov. 1997), D.H.Kemp & Co., Plot 6941, Suez Road, Off Church Road Tel: 252381/255081 Fax: 255225.

126. **Lukonde Emmanuel Mukuka Orlando**, Advocate (Dec. 1991), Zambia Police Service, Head Quarters, Independence Avenue, P.O. Box 50103, Tel: 253545/252872.

127. **Lukwanda Gilbert X.**, LL.B, Advocate (1981), Small Enterprises Development Board (SEDB), Graphic Design House, Plot 629 Cairo Road, PO Box 35373. Tell: 222176 Email: sedb@zamnet.zm

128. **Lungu Grace Bubile**, LL.B, Advocate (26 Nov. 96), Simeza Sangwa & Associates, 3rd Floor, Woodgate House, PO Box 36824, Tel: 227574 Fax: 220568.

129. **Lungu Edgar C.**, LL.B, (Z.1981), Advocate (May, 1983), Andrea Masiye & Co., Lex House, Addis Ababa Round About, P.O Box 30757, Tel/Fax: 254842, Specialisation: Board Secretarial Practice and procedures.

130. **Lungu Helen,** LL.B, Advocate (2001), Libertas Legal Practitioners, Los Angeles Boulevard, PO Box 50843, Tel/Fax: 251784 email: nkonde@zamnet.zm

131. **Lungu Stephen**, LL.B (May 1992), Advocate (Dec. 1992), BP Zambia Ltd Mukuba Pension House, Dedan Kimathi Road, P.O Box 31999, Tel: 228684 Tel/Fax : 221512, Email: lungusm@arl.bp.com Specialisation :General Practitioner.

132. **Lwatula Mwenya**, H.E., DIP.S.W (Z.1967), Advocate (June 1975), Ellis and Company, P.O. Box 31902, Phillip Ellis House, No. 8 Tito Road. Also President Avenue, Berverly House, PO Box 71536, Ndola Also: Obote Avenue, PO Box 21300 Kitwe Email: elisanco@zamnet.zm or Embassy of China, 5 Dong si Jie, San Li Tun, Beijing, China Tel: 6532 1554/1526/1585(R)/1891 (F) email: zamem@pulbic.bta.net.cn

M

119. **Mabula Mulundu Elsie S.,** LL.B, Advocate (April 1986), Zambia National Tender Board, Katunjila Road, Kulima Tower, 11th Floor Room 7, PO Box 31009, Tel: 222855/220577 Fax: 220577. Email: tenders@zamnet.zm

120. **Mabula Tukiya Kankasa Dr,** LL.B (1980), LLM (Harvard 1982), Ph.D (London 1991), Stockbroker (1998), Advocate (15 Nov. 1996), Bank of Zambia, Bank Square, Cairo Road, P.O. Box 30080, Tel: 228888/222375, Specialisation: Commercial Law, Securities Law, Human Rights Law.

For additional analytical, business and investment opportunities information, please contact Global Investment & Business Center, USA at (202) 546-2103. Fax: (202) 546-3275. E-mail: rusric@erols.com

121. **Mabutwe Clement**, LL.B (UNZA 1975), Advocate (July 1976), Mabutwe and Associates, Plot No. 37, Ngumbo Road, Prospect Hill, P.O. Box 37991, Tel: 255767, Specialisation: Commercial and Banking Law.

122. **Machila Bradford,** LL.B (Hons), University of London (1990), Advocate (1991), Corpus Globe, The Globe Building, Stand No. 2386, Longolongo Road, PO Box 32115, Tel: 235480/1 Fax: 238657 Email: corpus@zamnet.zm; bradford@zamnet.zm Specialisation: Corporate Law, Commercial Law, Company Secretarial, Conveyancing, Banking and Insolvency.

123. **Mainza Remmy,** LL.B, Advocate (Oct.1994) Mainza & Company, 4th Floor, Chester House, Cairo Road, PO Box 38143, Tel/Fax: 223126.

124. **Majula Betty Mwaka**, LL.B, Advocate (Jan. 1992), Zambia Civic Education Association, Plot 2/1836, Azikiwe Close, Lucy Sichone Memorial House, P/B 239X, Tel: 229641 Email: mmajula@coppernet.zm

125. **Makala Kenny H.,** LL.B (UNZA 1984), Advocate (Dec. 1995), Makala & Co., Plot 2103, Nairobi Place, 5th Floor, Woodgate House, PO Box 33431, Tel: 233895 Email: khmakala@zamnet.zm. Specialisation: Banking, Conveyancing and Commercial Law.

126. **Makasa Robinson M**., BA (ED.1980), LL.B (Z. 1989), Advocate (Dec. 1992), M. Makasa & Company, 21st Floor, Findeco House, P.O. Box 310263. Tel: 237563 Fax: 282321 Specialisation: Litigation, Criminal, Civil, Conveyancing, Divorce, Wills and Probate, Commercial Transactions, Industrial Relations Law.

127. **Malambo Vincent Blackskin,** LL.B (UNZA Nov. 1983), Advocate (Dec. 1984), Advocate & Notary Public (Jan. 1995), Malambo & Silwamba Advocates & Notaries, 6th Floor, Kwacha House, Cairo Road, Private Bag E342, Tel: 225362, Fax: 225362/238601

128. **Malata Mwenya Flavia**, LL.B, Advocate (April 1995), Fraser Associates, 1st Floor, Fintex House, Dar-es-Salaam Place, Sapele Road, PO Box 35641, Tel: 229387/227563 Fax: 236893

129. **Malila Mumba**, LL.B (Z. 1987), LLM (Cantab. 1989), Advocate (1989), Phoenix Partners, 9th Floor, Premium House, Plot 7431 Independence Avenue, PO Box 34302. Tel: 234621, Fax: 234620. Specialisation: Corporate Law/Commercial Transactions.

130. **Mambwe Silas**, LL.B (UNZA 1992), Advocate (Dec. 1993), Zambia National Commercial Bank, Head Office, Cairo Road, PO Box 35036, Tel: 221355, Dir: 229640 Fax: 223085, Specialisation: General.

131. **Manda Mandy Munsaka**, LL.B, Advocate, Echo Temple & Chambers, Indeco House, Cairo Road, RW 51258. Tel: 228561 Email: echo@zamnet.zm.

132. **Mandhu Fatima,** LL.B, Advocate (Nov. 1990), ZCAS, Dedan Kimathi Road,Plot 5309, PO Box 35243. Tel:237737/232183/223095 Fax: 222542

133. **Mandona Richard Nsofu**, Advocate (April 1978), Permanent Chambers, Permanent Chambers, Sapele Road, MEMACO House, PO Box 35702, Tel: 225884/220372, Fax: 225049 Email: permcham@zamnet.zmAlso:3rd Floor, Provident House, 2nd Floor, P.O. Box 23215, Matuka Avenue. Tel: 220602 Fax: 228051. Also at Kitwe

134. **Mapara Rita,** LL.B, Advocate (12 May 2000), Central Chambers, Lex House, Addis Ababa Road Roundabout, Plot 874, PO Box 50468, Tel/Fax: 254815/253610, Email: cclaw@zamnet.zm.

135. **Masiye Andrea Sylvester**, Matriculation (1948), Army School of Education, Kenya, Army Instructors' Middle East Command, Egypt; LL.B (UNZA 1975); Advocate (Z.

For additional analytical, business and investment opportunities information, please contact Global Investment & Business Center, USA at (202) 546-2103. Fax: (202) 546-3275. E-mail: rusric@erols.com

20th April 1979), Member IBA (1984), Andrea Masiye & Co., Plot 974, Lex House, Addis Ababa Round About, P.O. Box 30757, Tel/Fax: 254842, 250941 Specialisation: Conveyancing, Corporate, Civil, Criminal Law and Commercial Transactions.

136. **Matembo Dorothy Matongo**, LL.B, Advocate (Nov. 1996), Zesco Limited, Head Office, Plot 6949 Great East Road, PO Box 33304, Tel: 228094

137. **Matibini Patrick**, LL.B (Dec. 1982), LL.M (Nov. 1989), Advocate (20th Dec. 1984), MNB Legal Practitioners, Stand 6131, 5th Floor Godfrey House, Longolongo Road, PO Box 34207, Tel: 236920/236134, Fax: 236134 Email: mnb@zamnet.zm

138. **Mathotho Stanley E.A.,** LL.B, Advocate (May 1983), Electoral Commission of Zambia, PO Box 50274 Tel: 253155-7 Fax: 253884/250081

139. **Mayowe Christopher**, LL.B, Advocate (Dec. 1992), Mayowe and Company, PO Box 31916, Plot No. 2516, Cha Cha Cha Road N/E, Tel: 235292

140. **Mbalashi Chilufya,** LL.B (UNZA 1981), Advocate (1982), LLM (Harvard Law School, USA 1988), Specialisation: Banking and Finance.

141. **Mbambara Anock**, LL.B, Advocate (Nov. 1997), Zambia State Insurance Corporation Ltd., Premium House, Independence Avenue, P.O Box 30894, Tel: 225861, Fax: 224361, Telex:42521, Specialisation: General.

142. **Mbewe Bonaventure Chikwakwa**, LL.B (Nov. 1998), Advocate (May 1990), Bank of Zambia, Bank Square, Cairo Road, P.O. Box 30080,Tel: 228888/222375, Specialisation: Insurance, Aviation, Corporate and Employment.

143. **Mbewe Cecilia Nseduluka**, LL.B, Advocate (Dec. 1996), National Assembly, Parliament Building, Parliament Road, Stand No. 5030, PO Box 31299. Tel: 292425

144. **Mensah Frank Joe**, B.A (1969), P.G.C.E (1972), LL.B (1986), Advocate (Dec. 1988), Achimota Chambers, Cha Cha Cha House, 1st Floor, Rooms 9-10, Tel: 223485, Fax: 223495, Specialisation: Civil, Criminal and Conveyancing.

145. **Mhango Ganje Norman Huck**, LL.B (Z. October 1977), Advocate (Z. Dec. 1978), Nyangulu and Co, Chuundu House, Heroes Place, P.O. Box 32409, Tel/Fax: 221008.

146. **Miaze Bornfree S**., LL.B (1991), Advocate (1992), Equity Chambers, 4th Floor, Kulima House, Katunjila Road, P.O. Box RW 51052, Tel: 224045/097-775022

147. **Mitcheley Anthony O.R.**, LL.B (Inner Tempe, London 1951),Advocate (July 1955), A.D. Adams & Co., Farmers House, Cairo Road, P.O. Box 33143, Tel: 228660 Fax: 228661

148. **Mittal Rajesh Chandra**, LL.B (Meerut University India), Advocate (1999), Cave Malik and Company, Mambilima House, Kabelenga Road, P O Box 34204. Tel: 096 766321/235486/231964. *Also* Caravelle House, Buteko Avenue, P.O. Box 70924. Tel: 610393/610394/614227 Ndola

149. **Miyanda Samuel S. Hon**, LL.B (1982), Advocate (1984), Miyanda and Associates, 3rd Floor, Cusa House, Cairo Road, PO Box 34949. Tel/Fax: 221441

150. **Mkandawire F. Maria**, LL.B, Advocate (Dec. 92), Bank of Zambia, Bank Secretariat, Cairo Road, P.O. Box 30080, Tel: 228888

151. **M'kandawire Mabeleka Susan**, LL.B (1995), Advocate (Dec. 95), Communications Authority, Plot No. 3141 Buyantanshi Road, P.O. Box 36871, Tel: 246702, Fax: 246701

For additional analytical, business and investment opportunities information, please contact Global Investment & Business Center, USA at (202) 546-2103. Fax: (202) 546-3275. E-mail: rusric@erols.com

152. **Mofya Nigel Letford**, LL.B (Z. 1985), Advocate (Z.Dec. 1988), Stand 20, 21,22, Mofya Chambers, Central Arcade Annex behind Society House, PO Box 31593, Tel: 235723

153. **Mondoloka Mwape**, LL.B (Z. November 1989), Advocate (Dec. 1990), Dip. Woman's Law (August 1995), Energy Regulations Board, PO Box 37631, Tel: 236002 Fax: 236003. Email: erb@zamnet.zm; mmondoloka@erb.org.zm Specialisation: Business and Corporate Law.

154. **Mooya Flora Kantu**, LL.B (Z. November 1983), Advocate (May 1985), Local Authorities Superannuation Fund, Superanuation Fund, Superannuation House, Stand No. 8363, Ben Bella Road, PO Box 34646, Tel: 222198/229643/7, Fax: 225863, Specialisation: General

155. **Mosha Billingtone**, LL.B, Advocate (Nov. 1999), AN Chambers, Makishi Road, PO Box 30851, Tel: 231767/224548/ 97 797855

156. **Mosho Lewis**, LL.B (UNZA 1994), Advocate (1995), Lusaka Stock Exchange, Lusaka Stock Exchange Building, Stand 2A, Society House, Cairo Road, P.O. Box 34523, Tel: 228391, Fax: 228608, Specialisation: Taxation, Civil, Criminal and Conveyancing.

157. **Moyo Milimo**, LL.B, Advocate (2001), Bank of Zambia, Bank Square, P.O. Box 30080, Tel: 222375, Fax: 222375,

158. **Mtamira Chesya Bwanausi**, LL.B (Dec. 1985), Advocate (), National Legal Clinic for Women, 110A/150 Musonda Ngosa Road, Villa Ellizabetha, P/B E578. Tel/Fax: Tel: 255209

159. **Mtonga Leya**, LL.B, Advocate (Nov. 97) Aero Zambia, Dedan Kimathi Road, ZNIB Building, P/B E717. Cell: 095 703076

160. **Mubanga D.K.**, LL.B, Advocate, Zambia Police Service, Headquarters, Independence Avenue, P.O. Box 50103, Tel: 253545/252872

161. **Mubanga Willie Aubie C.**, LL.B (Z.1975), Advocate (July 1977), Permanent Chambers, Sapele Road, MEMACO House, PO Box 35702, Tel: 225884/220732 Fax: 225049, Email: permcham@zamnet.zm Specialisation: General.

162. **Mubashi Hugo Chomba**, LL.B (July 1972), Advocate (Z. Jan. 1976), HC Mubashi & Co., Plot 5430 Kasangula Road, Kalundu, PO Box 35891, Tel: 290188, Cell: 702346. Specialisation: Corporate, Conveyancing.

163. **Mubembe Joseph**, LL.B (November 1980), Advocate (20 Dec. 1995), Army Headquarters, Arakan Barracks, 'A' Branch, Independence Avenue, P.O. Box 31931, Tel: (Dir) 263664, Fax: 254275, Specialisation: General. Also: Paul Pandala Banda & Co., 2nd Floor, Southern Wing, Plot No. 163 Impala House, Cha Cha Cha Road, P.O. Box RW 50437. Tel: 779807/784461.

164. **Mubonda Newton K.,** Advocate (Dec. 1986), D.H. Kemp & Co., Suez Road, Plot No. 6941, Off Church Road, P.O. Box 31000, Tel: 252381 Fax: 255081/255225.

165. **Mudenda Clement M.**, Advocate (Dec. 1995), National Legal Clinic for Women, 110A/150 Musonda Ngosa Road, Villa Ellizabetha, P/B E578. Tel/Fax: 220595 / 234747 Cell: 783284

166. **Mudenda Frederick Syamulandabala**, LL.B (UNZA),LLM (AU) Advocate (Dec. 1995), Lewis Nathan Advocates, Plot 3/110a, Musonda Ngosa Road, PO Box 37268, Tel: 233174/5, Fax: 229860.Email: LNA@Zamnet.zm

For additional analytical, business and investment opportunities information, please contact Global Investment & Business Center, USA at (202) 546-2103. Fax: (202) 546-3275. E-mail: rusric@erols.com

167. **Mufuzi Lass**, LL.B (Z. 1983), Advocate (.Dec 1984), Permanent Human Rights Commission, Independence Avenue, Mulungushi House, PO Box 33812, Tel: 251327/57

168. **Muhyila Austin Hinyungwe**, LL.B (Z. 1987), Advocate (Z. 1988), Global Partners, 5th Floor, Zimco House, Chainda Place, Cairo Road, P.O. Box 320186, Tel: 227974.

169. **Mukande Louis Mwikisa**, Advocate (Dec. 1982), Mukande & company, Salvation Army House, Stand 685, P.O. Box 30134. Tel: 239756, Fax: 220489.

170. **Mukata Keith Akakelwa**, LL.B, Advocate, Jacob & Partners, 8th Floor Zimco House, Cairo Road, PO Box 50570, Lusaka. Tel: 223917 Fax: 223916 Cell: 096 766131

171. **Mulamfu Beatrice Mukumbwa**, LL.B, Advocate (Oct. 1977), Beta Legal Consult Chambers, 6 Nyati Close, PO Box 50742. Tel: 250312 Fax: 250293 096-751370 Email: beta@zamnet.zm Specialisation: General

172. **Mulele Moses M.**, LL.B (Nov. 1986), Advocate (May 1993), National Assembly, Stand No. 5030, Parliament Road, Parliament Building, P.O. Box 31299, Tel: 292425/7 Fax: 292252

173. **Mulenga Charles**, LL.B, Advocate (Dec. 95), Zambia National Building Society, Century House, Stand 6915, Ground Floor, P.O. Box 30420. Tel: 229197, Fax: 225510.

174. **Mulenga Geoffrey Chilufya**, LL.B, Advocate (Nov. 1996), Legal Resources Chambers, 2nd Floor, Woodgate House, PO Box 35162. Tel: 227484 Fax: 220568 Email: lrf@zamnet.zm

175. **Mulenga Mutila**, LL.B, Advocate (May 1983), Mundashi Mulenga & Co., 3rd Floor, Development House, Katondo Street, P.O. Box 34972, Tel: 235846/225886 Fax: 235847

176. **Mulikita Njunga Mulikita**, LL.B Advocate (April 1995), Zambia Privatisation Agency, Privatisation Building, Nasser Road, P.O. Box 30819, Tel: 221467/223859.

177. **Mulonda Palan**, LL.B, Advocate (Dec. 1995), Palan & George**,** 3rd Floor, Premium House, Independence Avenue, PO Box 34020. Tel: 097-802566

178. **Mulonda Valerie Mutinta Mululuma**, LL.B (Oct. 1993), Advocate (October 1994), NAPSA, Lusaka House, Cnr. Lumumba/Ben Bella Roads, Plot 4459/7048, Cairo Road, P.O. Box RW 51275, Tel: 222705, Fax: 221195 Email: napsa@zamnet.zm Specialisation: General

179. **Mulwila John M, (Dr.),** LL.B (1974), LL.M (1977), PH.D (1980), Advocate (April 1987), Ituna Partners, 7th Floor, Zimco House, P.O. Box 32214, Tel: 223796/237882

180. **Mumba Andrew Dean Mwansa**, LL.B, Advocate (Oct. 1994), Sharpe & Howard, 1st & 2nd Floor Nalupembe House, Stand 11723, Kabelenga Road, PO Box 32587, Tel: 222810/2/4, 232952; 232505 fax: 224179 Email: s&h@zamnet.zm or Permanent Human Rights Commission Independence Avenue, Mulungushi Office Complex, P.O. Box 33812, Tel: 255387

181. **Mumba Alex John**, LL.B (Z. 1978), Advocate (Z.1979), LL.M (London, 1980), Advocate (Dec. 1980), AJM Associates, Carousel Shopping Centre, Cnr Lumumba/Kafue Roads, Rooms 28-30-32, 2nd Floor, P.O. Box 50540, Tel: 237725 Fax: 237743 Specialisation: Company and Commercial Law.

182. **Mumbuna Wamui Mwenda,** LL.B, Advocate (Nov. 1988), W.M. Mumbuna & Co, Bata house, 4th Floor, P.O. Box 35472 Tel: 235428/9 Cell: 096-430046 Fax: 235431

For additional analytical, business and investment opportunities information, please contact Global Investment & Business Center, USA at (202) 546-2103. Fax: (202) 546-3275. E-mail: rusric@erols.com

183. **Munakopa Lloyd**, LL.B, Advocate (Nov. 1996), Jitesh Naik Advocate, Sitwe Plaza, Cha Cha Cha Road, P.O. Box 31176, Tel: 227216-7, Fax: 226928, Email: jnaikadv@zamnet.zm

184. **Munalisa Lawrence**, LL.B, Advocate (May 1992) Ministry of Home Affairs, Old Cabinet Building, Independence Avenue, P.O. Box 50997. Tel: 254261.

185. **Munansangu Milimo Moono**, LL.B (UNZA), Advocate (March 1999), Lusaka City Council, P.O. Box 30077, Tel: 252996, Fax: 252141

186. **Mundashi Musonda Michael**, LL.B (Z.Dec. 1984), Advocate (Dec. 1985), Mundashi Mulenga & Co., 3rd Floor, Development House, Katondo Street, P.O. Box 34972, Tel: 235846 Fax: 235847. Specialisation: Insurance related work, Commercial Practice, Taxation laws, Custom and Excise.

187. **Mundia Christopher Lubasi**, LL.B (Z.Nov. 1979), Advocate (23 Nov. 1981), Dip. In Arb (June 2000 AFSA), CL Mundia and Company, 1st Floor, Bible House, Freedom Way, P.O. Box 35492, Tel: 220272/67/88 Fax: 294093 (Home) Specialisation: General, Arbitration and Mediation.

188. **Muneku Charles Nathaniel**, LL.B (UNZA 1983), Advocate (Dec. 1984), Charles and Charles Associates, 3rd Floor, Development House, P.O. Box 37619, Tel: 238801, Fax: 235789 Specialisation: General

189. **Muneku Noriana Mseteka**, LL.B, Advocate (Dec. 1998), Zambia National Building Society, 3rd Floor Century House, PO Box 30420. Tel: 231541/225510

190. **Mun'gomba Willa Disraeli**, BA, LL.B (1965), Barrister at Law (1968), Advocate (Nov. 1970), Mun'gomba Associates, The Lawyers' Inn, 42 Kudu Road, Kabulonga P.O. Box 35476, Tel: 260055/58 Telefax: 262110 Email: ncapcha@zamnet.zm Specialisation: Commercial Law, Banking, Investment & General Commercial transactions, International Law.

191. **Munsanje Hodges Mark**, LL.B (UNZA), Advocate (Dec. 1991), Patrick Zulu & Partners, 5th Floor, Suite 509, Society House, PO Box 35516, Tel: 220938 Specialisation General.

192. **Munyama Bruce Africa**, Barrister (July 1963), Advocate (June 1967), Nkwazi Chambers, Plot 6392 Duduza Chisizda Crescent, Opp. Ndeke Hotel P.O. Box 36870, Tel: 254968 Specialisation: Corporate and Tax Law.

193. **Munyinda Andrew Mututwa**, LL.B (UNZA Dec. 1971), Advocate (July 1976), Munyinda and Company, 7th Floor, Findeco House, Cairo Road, P.O. Box 50891, Also at 5th Floor, Zambia National Provident Fund, Mongu. Tel: 222277. Specialisation: Commerce, Stock Exchange, Financial Agreements, Construction Contracts.

194. **Musaba Keith K.**, LL.B (UNZA June 1993), Advocate (Dec. 1993), Law Bank, Attorneys at Law, Permanent House, P/B 442X, Ridgeway. Tel: 231490 Fax: 231096 Email: lawbank@zamtel.zm Specialisation: Corporate Law, Commercial and Business Law, Civil Litigation, Conveyancing, Legal Drafting & Banking.

195. **Musaluke Martin**, LL.B (Z. Aug. 1994), Advocate (Oct. 1994), Zambia Privatisation Agency, Nasser Road, PO Box 30819. Tel: 221467/223859 Also: Musaluke & Co.,

196. **Musanya Alex Mukuka**, LL.B (1975), Advocate (Dec. 1976), Zambezi Chambers, Ulendo Building, P.O. Box 32749.

197. **Musenga M Bob**, LL.B (UNZA 1996), Advocate (Z. Nov. 1996), Zambia Daily Mail, Longolongo Road, PO Box 31421, Tel/Fax: 225881

For additional analytical, business and investment opportunities information, please contact Global Investment & Business Center, USA at (202) 546-2103. Fax: (202) 546-3275. E-mail: rusric@erols.com

198. **Mushipe Martha**, LL.B (UNZA), Cert. H.R. (France/Switzerland), DWL (Zimbabwe), ASCZ, AHCZ, Advocate (Nov. 1988), Mushipe and Associates, 8th Floor, Zimco House, Cairo Road, PO Box 33813, Tel: 231188, Fax: 236303262713.

199. **Mushota Lilian Jabani**, LL.B, Advocate (.May 1985), Mushota and Associates, 1B, 2nd Floor, West Suite, ZSIC House, Chiparamba Road, P/B W411, Tel/Fax: 225014 Cell: 097 - 773687

200. **Musonda Edward**, LL.B, Advocate (12 May 2000), Lisulo & Company, Opp. UNZA Gate, Plot 5839 Nanshila Road, Kalundu. Tel: 294970 Cell: 97 794969

201. **Musonda Michael**, LL.B (Z. Nov. 1986), Advocate (Nov. 1987), LL.M (London, 1989), M. PHILL (Oxon 1991), M Musonda and Company, 3rd Floor Permanent House, P.O. Box 36470, Tel: 221382 Fax: 221383, Email: mmusonda@zamnet.zm Specialisation: International Business, Commercial and Corporate Law.

202. **Musyani Gertrude Mukata**, LL.B, Advocate (Nov. 1997), Corpus Globe, Growel Building, Longolongo Road, P.O. Box 32115, Tel: 235480/1 Fax: 238657 Specialiastion: Corporate, commercial, conveyancing and litigation

203. **Mutale Bonaventure C**., SC, LL.B, Advocate (Dec. 1976), Ellis and Company, Ellis and Co., Phillip Ellis House, 8 Tito Road, Off Church Road, P.O. Box 31902, Tel: 252709/738/809 Fax: 250802 email: elisanco@zamnet.zm **Also** at Ndola and Kitwe Specialisation: Litigation and International Intellectual Property.

204. **Mutemwa Mutemwa**, LL.B (Z. 1984), Advocate (Z. 1985), Mutemwa Chambers, Lotti House, Plot 685, 4th Floor, P.O. Box 30993, Cairo Road, Tel/Fax: 221901

205. **Mutti Kashumba Nellie Butete**, LL.B (1979), Advocate (Dec.1980), Lukona Chambers, Lex House, Tito Road, P.O. Box 31160, Tel: 254748 Fax: 253166 email: lukona@zamnet.zm Specialisation: Conveyancing, Litigation, Debt Collection, Commercial Transactions, Trade Marks and Patents.

206. **Mutuna Nigel Kalonde**, LL.B (UNZA 1985), Advocate (Nov. 1985), NKM & Associates, 8th Floor, Room 809, Anchor House, Lusaka Square, Cairo Road, P.O. Box 35822, Tel/Fax: 229610 Email: partner@nkmandassociates.com.zm

207. **Muuka Nawa Lishomwa**, Advocate (Dec. 1988), Zambia Revenue Authority, Revenue House, Kabwe Roundabout, Luanshya Road, P.O. Box 35710, Tel: 227460 Fax: 221075

208. **Muvwende Avin**, LL.B, Advocate (Dec. 1992), Zambia Revenue Authority, Revenue House, Kabwe Roundabout, Luanshya Road, P.O. Box 35710, Tel: 222828 Fax: 221075 Email: muvwende@zra.org.zm

209. **Muwamba Sekelebaka**, LL.B, Advocate (2001), Legal Resources Chambers, 2nd Floor, Woodgate House, PO Box 35162. Tel: 227484 Fax: 220568 Email: lrf@zamnet.zm

210. **Muyawala Moses Patrick**, LL.B (UNZA June 1993), Advocate (April 1996), Dzekedzeke & Co, Findeco House, 14th Floor, Cnr. Independence/Cairo Roads, P.O. Box 30685, Tel: 225582

211. **Mvunga Mphanza Patrick** (Prof), LL.B (Z.1970), LL.M (Harvard 1971), Advocate (Sept. 1973), PH.D (London 1978), Mvunga & Associates, Anchor House, Sapele Road, Box 37988, Tel: 226881 Fax: 234077

212. **Mwamba Emmah**, LL.B (1996), Advocate (1997), Ituna Partners, 7th Floor, Zimco House, Cairo Road, P.O. Box 32314, Tel: 223796 Fax: 222977

For additional analytical, business and investment opportunities information, please contact Global Investment & Business Center, USA at (202) 546-2103. Fax: (202) 546-3275. E-mail: rusric@erols.com

213. **Mwanakatwe Chipampe Paul**, Advocate (Dec. 1990), JMM Consultants, 6th Floor, Findeco House, P.O. Box 30481, Tel: 222201 Fax: 220126

214. **Mwanakatwe John Mupanga**, Barrister (England 1964), Advocate (Z.Jan. 1966), JMM Consultants, 6th Floor, Findeco House, P.O. Box 30481, Tel: 222201 Fax:220126 Specialisation: Legal Finance, Development Consultant.

215. **Mwananshiku Kampamba Pam**, LL.B, Advocate (2000), Ministry of Legal Affairs, Attorney General's Chambers, Fairley Road, PO Box RW 50106, Telephone 253686/252786

216. **Mwananshiku Slyvester Chibangu**, LL.B, Advocate ((Apr. 1994), Law Bank, Attorneys at Law, Permanent House, P/B 442X, Ridgeway. Tel: 231490 Fax: 231096 Specialisation: General

217. **Mwanawasa Kakubo Maureen**, LL.B, Advocate (Nov. 1996), Levy Mwanawasa & Company, Plot 6798 Chiwalamabwe Road, Olympia Ext., P.O. Box 31283, Tel/Fax: 292880 Email: mwaka@coppernet.zm

218. **Mwanawasa Levy Patrick**, SC, LL.B (1973), Advocate (June 1975), State Counsel (1992), Levy Mwanawasa & Company, Plot 6798 Chiwalamabwe Road, Olympia Ext., P.O. Box 31283, Tel/Fax: 292880 Email: mwaka@coppernet.zm

219. **Mwanda Florence,** LL.B. Advocate **()**Zambia Telecommunications Ltd**,** Legal Department, Lamya House, PO Box 30099 Tel: 235613

220. **Mwandenga Mudford Zachariah**, LL.B (October 1981), Advocate (Z. Dec. 1982), Zambia Privatisation Agency, Privatisation Building, Nasser Road, P.O. Box 30819, Tel: 221467 Fax: 221467 Fax: 225270 Specialisation: General

221. **Mwansa Achiume Charity Chola**, LL.B (Z.1981), Advocate (24 May 1988), Solicitor of England and Wales (1992), CC Mwansa & Co., 6th Floor, Kwacha House, Room 17, P.O. Box 50235. Tel:

222. **Mwansa Egipso**, LL.B, Advocate (2000), Judiciary, Supreme Court Building, PO Box 50067, Tel: 251330

223. **Mwansa E.B.M,** LL.B (Z.1981), Advocate (May 1983), EBM Chambers, Former Sheriff's Yard, Jacaranda Road, P.O. Box 32081, Tel/Fax: 252185 Cell: 703476 Specialisation: General Practitioner.

224. **Mwansa Ernest Chitumwa**, LL.B, Advocate (Dec. 1987), Ernest C. Mwansa & Partners, 163 Lumumba Road, P.O. Box 35868, Tel: 222229 Telefax: 225661

225. **Mwansa Kasumpa**, LL.B, Advocate (Nov. 1996), Zesco Limited, Plot 6949 Great East Road, PO Box 33304, Tel: 228094

226. **Mwanza Yona R**., LL.B, Advocate (April 1998), Permanent Chambers, PO Box 35702, Tel: 238195, Fax: 225049. Also: Kitwe at Provident House, Matuka Avenue, PO Box 23215 Email: permcham@zamnet.zm

227. **Mwape Darlington**, LL.B, Advocate (Dec. 1993), Lincoln Chambers, 1st Floor Salvation Army House, Cairo Road, PO Box 37489. Tel: 220476/220749

228. **Mweemba William Smith**, LL.B (Z. Nov. 1980), Advocate (Z. Dec. 1981), Barclays Bank of Zambia Ltd, Kafue House, Stand Nos. 2646, 2328-2330 7th Floor, P.O. Box 31396, Tel: 226076 (Dir), Fax: 226185 Specialisation: General.

229. **Mweemba Wilson**, LL.B, Advocate (8/4/98), Lowe Management Services Ltd, PO Box 31916, Stand 13969, Chandwe Musonda Road. Tel: 221562 or 220542

For additional analytical, business and investment opportunities information, please contact Global Investment & Business Center, USA at (202) 546-2103. Fax: (202) 546-3275. E-mail: rusric@erols.com

230. **Mwenda Leonard Jameson** (Bishop), LL.B, Advocate (May 1985), Anglican Diocese of Lusaka Church Road, Cathedral of the Holy Cross, PO Box 30183, Tel: (O)254789 (H) 264516 Email: angdiolu@zamnet.zm

231. **Mwenda Marjorie Grace,** B.A (1975), LL.B (1978), Advocate (1980), LL.M (1989), MG Johnson-Mwenda & Co, 1st floor, CUSA House, Cairo Road, Plot 628, P.O. Box 33645, Tel: 260-1-223261, Fax: 260-1-224692 Cell: 096-755579, Email: mgjm@coppernet.zm. Specialisation: Conveyancing, Intellectual Property, Commercial and Business Law and Mediation and Arbitration.

232. **Mwenda Winnie Sithole**, LL.B (1980), Advocate (Dec. 1981), LL.M (1990), W.Sithole-Mwenda & Co, 9th Floor, Premium House, P.O. Box 37339, Tel: 238448 Dir (236453) Dir: 231890 Fax: 238449, Specialisation: Corporate Law, Conveyancing and Commercial Law.

233. **Mwenya Anne Chibiliti,** Advocate (1992), Zambia Investment Centre, Los Angeles Boulevard, Plot 6457, P.O. Box 34580 Tel: 252130 Specialisation: Corporate and Investment Law Email: invest@zamnet.zm

234. **Mwenya Chibeka**, LL.B, Advocate (May 1989), Barclays Bank of Zambia Ltd, Kafue House, Stand Nos 2646, 2328-2330 7th Floor, P.O. Box 31396, Telefax: 228858 ext 666

235. **Mwenye Musa Juma**, LL.B, Advocate (Nov. 1999), Sharpe & Howard, 1st & 2nd Floor Nalupembe House, Stand 11723, Kabelenga Road, PO Box 32587, Tel: 222810/2/4, 232952; 232505 fax: 224179 Email: s&h@zamnet.zm Specialisation: General.

236. **Mwenzi Alice Mibenge**, LL.B (Univ. of Lon), Advocate (1998), Agriflora Ltd, Off Simon Mwansa Kapwepwe Road, P/B CH43, Tel: 283686 Fax: 220186 email: mwenzi@zamnet.zm

237. **Mwewa Gideon Katebe**, LL.B (UNZA 1992), Advocate (Dec. 1993), Gideon & Partners, 2nd Floor, Impala House, Cha Cha Cha Road, PO Box RW 50347 , Tel: 231278 Cell: 096 – 766413 Specialisation: General.

238. **Mwiche Kafula**, LL.B, Advocate (2001), Malambo & Silwamba, 6th Floor, Cairo Road, Kwacha House, PO Box E342, Tel/Fax: 238601

239. **Mwiimbu Jacob Jack**, LL.B (1984), Advocate (Dec. 1986), Mwiimbu & Co, Tazara house, 3rd Floor, PO Box 31645 Tel: 237905/096 769625

240. **Mwikisa Paul Wasamunu**, LL.B, Advocate (7th Dec. 1979), P.M. Mwikisa & Co, 3rd Floor, Tazara House, Independence Avenue, P.O. Box P/B 403X, Tel: 222790

N

240. **Naik Jitesh**, LL.B (1983), Advocate (Dec. 1984), Jitesh Naik Advocate, Sitwe Plaza, Cha Cha Cha Road, PO Box 31176, Tel: 227216-7, Fax: 226928 Email: jnaikadv@zamnet.zm Specialisation: Banking and commercial law, conveyancing, litigation, debt collection

241. **air Celine**, LL.B, Advocate (Nov. 1999), Ernst & Young, Katondo Street, Development House, PO Box 32385. Tel: 236120/227022

242. **Namachila S. C. Bernard** LL.B, Advocate, Local Government and Housing, Church Road, Ministry of Local Government and Housing, P.O. Box 50027, Tel: 254119/253195 Cell: 703141

243. **Nambeye Nancy**, LL.B, Advocate (12 May 2000), Nkwazi Chambers, Plot 6392 Duduza Chisizda Crescent, Opp. Ndeke Hotel P.O. Box 36870, Tel: 235310

For additional analytical, business and investment opportunities information, please contact Global Investment & Business Center, USA at (202) 546-2103. Fax: (202) 546-3275. E-mail: rusric@erols.com

244. **Nchito Mutembo**, LL.B, Advocate(Dec. 1992), MNB Legal Practitioners, 3rd and 4th Floors, Godfrey House, Stand No. 6131, Longolongo Road, PO Box 50349, Tel: 236920/236134, fax: 236134 email: nchima@zamnet.zm

245. **Nchito Nchima Manley**, LL.B (Z.Nov. 1986), Advocate (Dec. 1987), MNB Legal Practitioners, 3rd and 4th Floors, Godfrey House, Stand No. 6131, Longolongo Road, PO Box 50349, Tel: 236920/236134, fax: 236134 email: nchima@zamnet.zm

246. **Ndhlovu Hope Mukatimui**, LL.B, Advocate (2000), Afronet, Plot 7539, Lukasu Road, PO Box 31145, Tel: 251813/4.

247. **Ndhlovu Humphrey Hlazo**, (H.C), Advocate (June 1975), HH Ndhlovu & Co., Woodgate House, 3rd Floor, Room 307, Cairo Road, PO Box 35789 Tel: 220541

248. **Ndhlovu Masauso Nelson**, BA (1972), LL.B (1983), Advocate (May 1985), Chifumu Banda & Associates, Longolongo Road, Godfrey House, P.O. Box 31025. Tel: 233395/233059, Fax: 232203 Email: chifumu@zamtel.zm

249. **Ndhlovu Matiya**, LL.B, Advocate (Nov. 27, 1997), Central Chambers, Plot 874 Tito Road, Lex House, PO Box 50465, Tel: 254610 Fax: 254815 Email: cclaw@zamnet.zm

250. **Ndhlovu Telephone Kay**, LL.B (1992), Advocate (1993), National Airports Corporation Ltd, St/Plot No. 947/M, Airport Road, Lusaka International Airport, PO Box 30175, Tel/Fax: 271044 Specialisation: Aviation

251. **Neves Drastrass Maria Sanana**, LL.B, Advocate (Nov. 1986), Zambia Privatisation Agency, Privatisation Building, Nasser Road, P.O. Box 30819, Tel: 221467 Fax: 221467 Fax: 225270 Specialisation: General

252. **Ng'ambi Nkhata Daisy**, LL.B (1975), LL.M (University of London, 1978), Advocate (April 1983), Nyankhata Chambers, Alick Nkhata Avenue, Lukundo House Tel: 263637 / 227174

253. **Ng'anjo Nathan**, LL.B (UNZA 1994), Advocate (1995), Finance Bank Zambia Ltd, Legal Department, Chanik house, Cairo Road, PO Box 37102 Tel: 221614 Specialisation: General.

254. **Ng'onga Isiah Chifumbe**, Advocate (Dec. 1984), IC N'gonga & Co, Plot 186 Bombay Street, Muyuni Complex Building, 1st Floor, Room 3, PO Box 36309, Tel: 220254/56 Fax: 220254.

255. **Ng'onomo Beatrice Feleni Makomo**, LL.B, Advocate (Jan 1972), Hamanyanga and Co., Grosvenor Court, Plot 104A, PO Box 34417, Tel: 225642

256. **Ngenda Akalemwa**, LL.B, Advocate (Nov. 1997), Makala & Co, 5th Floor, Woodgate House, PO Box 33431, Tel: 223895/237461 Fax: 226312 email: khmakala@zamnet.zm

257. **Ngenda Benjamin Lubinda**, LL.B (Z.1977), LL.M (Temple Univ. Philadelphia 1992), Advocate (1978), Notary Public (March 1985), Solicitor (England and Wales, March 1990), Attorney (New York Oct. 1977), Ben Ngenda Advocates, Westavia House, Stand No. 16875 Nangwenya Road, Le Ciel Plaza, PO Box 34844. , Cell: 097-771854 Email: BNgenda@excite.com Specialisation: Corporate Finance and International Transactions.

258. **Ngenda Chrispin Mbindawina**, LL.B (1982), Advocate (Dec. 1984), Christopher Russell Cook & Co, Woodgate House, 4th Floor, Cairo Road, PO Box 34091, Tel: 229366-70 Fax: 225713/225158, Telex: ZA 43130 (DECEASED)

For additional analytical, business and investment opportunities information, please contact Global Investment & Business Center, USA at (202) 546-2103. Fax: (202) 546-3275. E-mail: rusric@erols.com

259. **Ngenda Sipalo**, Advocate (Dec. 1980), Ngenda Chambers, Stand No. 10524, Lumumba Road, Opp. Govt Stores, PO Box 36852. Tel: 231581/ 96 759598/261912

260. **Ngoma Agnes Mkalimo,** Advocate (April 1982), AN Chambers, Makishi Road, PO Box 30851, Tel: 231767/224548/ 97 778196

261. **Ngoma Mwaka Samudengu**, Advocate (Dec. 1992), Zambia National Oil Company, Indeco House, Cairo Road, PO Box 34595. Tel: 222134 Fax: 220144 Email: znoc@zamnet.zm

262. **Ngulube Anderson**, LL.B (1996), Advocate (April 1997), JB Sakala & Co., Permanent House, Cairo Road, Wing "A", Ground Floor, PO Box 34279. Tel: 226885 Fax: 224443

263. **Ngulube Richard,** LL.B, Advocate (2001), PH Yangailo & Co, Woodgate House, 4th Floor, P.O. Box 35972, Tel: 238195, Specialisation: Conveyancing, Civil Litigation, Patents & Trade Marks.

264. **Ngwira William,** LL.B, Advocate (Nov. 1996), Libertas Legal Practitioners, Los Angeles Boulevard, Plot 4833, PO Box 50843, Tel: 251784 Cell: 096 435033 Cell: 772145 Email: nkonde@zamnet.zm

265. **Njobvu Corinth A.J**, Pub. Admin (1976), LL.B (1987), Advocate (1994), Christopher Russell Cook & Co, 4th Floor, Woodgate House, Cairo Road, PO Box 34091, Tel: 229366 Fax: 225713/225158

266. **Nketani Reuben H.**, BA (UNZA 1971), LL.B (UNZA 1981), Advocate (April 1982), RH Nketani & Co, Plot 104A Grosvenor Court, Cairo Road, Room 3, PO Box 36806. Tel: 228931

267. **Nkhata Masauso**, LL.B, Advocate (Nov. 1999), Lusaka City Council, Independence Avenue, Civic Centre, PO Box 30077, Tel: 250877/252141.

268. **Nkonde Sunday Bwalya**, LL.B, Advocate (Nov. 1989), Libertas Legal Practitioners, Plot 4833 Los Angeles Boulevard, PO Box 50843, Tel: 251784 Cell: 772145

269. **Noyoo Noyoo**, LL.B (Z.Dec. 1990), Advocate (Z.May 1992), Patrick Zulu & Partners, 5th Floor, Suite 509, Society House, PO Box 35516, Tel: 220938 Cell: 097 775378 Specialisation: General Practitioner.

270. **Nsemukila Katuta Kosta**, Advocate (May 1991), Katuta & Company, 4th Floor, CUSA House, PO Box FW110, Tel: 235134 Fax: 235843

271. **Nyangulu Anthony John**, Comm., LL.B (UNZA 1970), Advocate (Jan. 1972), Nyangulu & Co, S/N 1377 Sapele Road, Design House, PO Box 32049, Tel: 221008 Fax: 225677.

272. **Nyembele Lagos**, LL.B (Z), Advocate (April 1978), Phillip Ellis House, 8 Tito Road, Off Church Road, P.O. Box 31902, Tel: 252709/738/809 Fax: 250802 Also at Ndola and Kitwe Specialisation: Litigation and International Intellectual Property.

273. **Nyirenda Malaro**, LL.B (Aug. 1995), Advocate (Dec. 1995), Union Bank (Z) Ltd. (In Liquidation), Zimco House, Cairo Road, PO Box 34940, Tel: 223314, Fax: 221866, Telex: 40112/45150.

274. **Nyirongo Gavu,** Advocate (Nov. 1996), NAPSA, Lumumba Road, Lusaka House, PO Box 33790, Tel: 225226

O

For additional analytical, business and investment opportunities information, please contact Global Investment & Business Center, USA at (202) 546-2103. Fax: (202) 546-3275. E-mail: rusric@erols.com

240. **Okware Nicholas**, Advocate (Nov. 1996), Okware and Associates, Office No. 106-108 Kulima House, First Floor, Cnr. Cha Cha Cha/Katunjila Roads, PO Box 39569, Tel: 236677 , 229035 Cell: 097 772455, Email: okware@zamnet.zm

P

240. **Patel Gulam Farid**, LL.B (Jan. 1960), Advocate (May 1974), Musa Dudhia & Co, Permanent House, PO Box 31198, Tel: 228426-30 Fax: 222603, Specialisation: Conveyancing, Commercial Legal Work, General Practitioner.

241. **Patel Kanti** K., LL.B (Z. 1972), Advocate (Z.April 1973), Solicitor of the Supreme Court of England and Wales (1989), Christopher Russell Cook & Co., Woodgate House, Cairo Road, PO Box 34091, Tel: 229366-70, Fax: 225713//225158. Email: crc@zamnet.zm Specialisation: Banking and Finance, Commercial, Conveyancing, Company, Trade Marks & Patents.

242. **Patel Suliman** M., Barrister at Law (Lincolns Inn, London), Advocate (Z. August 1964), Solly Patel Hamir & Lawrence, 4th Floor Woodgate House, PO Box 30605, Specialisation: Conveyancing and Commercial Law. Tel: 229366-70 Fax: 225158/225713

243. **Patel Younus Asmal**, LL.B (Z. 1979), Advocate (Z.Dec. 1981), Asmal & Co, Plot 9249, Delhi Street, Fidelity Building, 2nd Class Trading Area, PO Box 36626, Tel: 244025/226210 Fax: 236538, Specialisation: Conveyancing, Consultation of all multi legal aspects of human life.

244. **Penza Chibulu Jane**, LL.B (Z.1982), Advocate (Z.April 1984), BA (Z.1977), RDS Investments Ltd, Plot No. 4171 Nangwenya Road, Cnr. Kabelenga/Longolongo Roads, PO Box 35703, Tel: 223877/222498 Fax: 223876.

245. **Phiri Chivwara Kopeka**, LL.B (1977), Advocate (Dec. 1978), Mulungushi Chambers, 1st Floor, Permanent House, Stand No. 8, Cairo road, PO Box 36639, Tel: 221980 Fax: 235987/235896

246. **Phiri Elita Mwikisa**, LL.B, Advocate (Z. Dec. 1988), Zambia Investment Centre, PO Box 34580. Tel: 255241 Fax: 252150 Email: invest@zamnet.zm

247. **Phiri Jack**, LL.B (June 1993), Advocate (Oct. 1993), Advocate (Oct. 1994), Lloyd Siame and Company, 2nd Floor, CUSA House, P.O. Box 37418, Tel: 237241 Fax: 237242 Also at Ndola.

248. **Phiri Moses**, LL.B (Z.1985), Advocate (Z.1986), M. Phiri & Partners, Plot No. 4749, Lubwa/Beit Road, Rhodespark, PO Box 38582. Tel: 250017 Fax: 250027.

249. **Phiri Ngaitila Zifela**, LL.B (UNZA 1992), Advocate (Dec. 1998), Afronet, Plot 7539, Lukasu Road, PO Box 31145, Tel: 251813/4 Email: ngaitila@afronet.org.zm

250. **Phiri Rhoda,** LL.B, Advocate (2001), Mushipe and Associates, 8th Floor, Zimco House, Cairo Road, PO Box 33813, Tel: 231188, Fax: 236303262713.

251. **Phiri Saidi Saulos**, LL.B (1973), Advocate (Nov. 1978), SS Phiri & Co., 1st Floor, Cha Cha Cha Road, Cha Cha Cha House, PO Box 36289. Tel: 222543.

252. **Pikiti Matthew Joseph Mweshi**, BA (1978), LL.B (1982 UNZA), Advocate (April, 1984), Pikiti & Co., 52 Church Road, Ndelefina Premises, PO Box 35716, Tel: 226665 Fax: 237506, Specialisation: General Practitioner.

253. **Punza Leonard Simbwalanga**, LL.B, Advocate (March 1999), Zambia Police, Police Headquarters, P.O. Box 50103, Tel/Fax 253545 Cell: 096 766252 Email: lpunza@yahoo.com

For additional analytical, business and investment opportunities information, please contact Global Investment & Business Center, USA at (202) 546-2103. Fax: (202) 546-3275. E-mail: rusric@erols.com

254. **Roberts Alfred**, LL.B (UNZA 1989), Advocate (Dec.1990), LL.M (Cantab. 1992), Solicitor (1992), Finance Bank, 5th Floor, Finance House, PO Box 37102, Tel: 224276/223586/229735, Specialisation: Banking, Corporate, International and General Transaction.

S

255. **Sabi Samuel Mwape**, LL.B, Advocate (Nov. 1999), Corpus Globe, The Globe Building, Stand No. 2386, Longolongo Road, PO Box 32115, Tel: 235480/1 Fax: 238657 Email: corpus@zamnet.zm

256. **Sakala Chimbeka Kamilon**, LL.B, Advocate (April 1994), Jaques Partners, PO Box 30275, Anchor House, Cairo Rd, Tel: 228081 Fax: 226173

257. **Sakala David O**., LL.B (1995), Advocate (April 1996), Mabutwe & Co, 37 Ngumbo Road, Prospect Hill, PO Box 37991 Tel: 255767

258. **Sakala Kondwa Emily Chibiya**, LL.B, Advocate, J.B. Sakala & Co., Permanent House, Wing "A", Ground Floor, Cairo Road, PO Box 34279. Tel: 226885 Fax: 224443 Email: chiyak@yahoo.com

259. **Sambo Nsunka R.K**., LL.B (UNZA 1981), Advocate (Dec. 1983), University of Zambia, Legal Counsel, PO Box 32379, Tel: 253952/294540.

260. **Sambo Towela Pamela**, LL.B, Advocate (12 May 2000), Mvunga Associates, Mvunga & Associates, Anchor House, Sapele Road, Box 37988, Tel: 226881 Fax: 231636.

261. **Sameta Lydia**, LL.B (UNZA), LL.M (Kings College London), Advocate (Dec. 1992), PriceWaterhouseCoopers, 7th Floor, National Savings and Credit Bank Building, Cairo Road, PO Box 30942, Tel: 228808/10, Fax: 220768, lydia.sameta@zm.pwcglobal.com Specialisation: Corporate Insolvency Law, Employment and International Economic Law.

262. **Sampa Anne Mwanza,** LL.B, Advocate (July 1988), Zambia National Commercial Bank, Cairo Road, ZANACO Headquarters, P.O. Box 33611, Tel: 221358 Fax: 223082

263. **Sampa Christopher M,** LL.B (Z. UNZA 1990), Advocate (1991), CM Sampa & Co., Esco Building, Kabelenga Avenue, PO Box 38209, Tel: 233052 Specialisation: General Practitioner.

264. **Sampa Norman**, LL.B, Advocate (Nov. 1999), MNB Legal Practitioners, Stand 6131, 5th Floor Godfrey House, Longolongo Road, PO Box 34207, Tel: 236920/236134, Fax: 236134 Email: mnb@zamnet.zm

265. **Samulela Maureen**, LL.B, Advocate (Nov.1999), Miyanda & Associates, 3rd Floor CUSA House, Cairo Road, PO Box 34949. Tel: 238474/ 96766417.

266. **Sangwa John Peter**, LL.B (UNZA 1989), Advocate (7th Dec. 1990), LL.M (UNZA 1996), Simeza Sangwa & Associates, 3rd Floor, Woodgate House, PO Box 36824, Tel: 227574 Fax: 220568. Specialisation: Corporate and Commercial Law.

267. **Scott Veronica**, LL.B, Advocate (2001), Sharpe & Howard, 1st & 2nd Floor Nalupembe House, Stand 11723, Kabelenga Road, PO Box 32587, Tel: 222810/2/4, 232952; 232505 fax: 224179 Email: s&h@zamnet.zm

268. **Shapi Chola CG**, LL.B (1995), Advocate (April 1996), Zambia Revenue Authority, Revenue House, Plot 9401, PO Box 35710, Tel: 227460 Fax: 221075 Ext.119 Emapil shapic@zra.org.zm

For additional analytical, business and investment opportunities information, please contact Global Investment & Business Center, USA at (202) 546-2103. Fax: (202) 546-3275. E-mail: rusric@erols.com

269. **Sharpe-Phiri Nicola Ann**, LL.B (1991), Advocate (Dec. 1992), Sharpe & Howard, 1st & 2nd Floor Nalupembe House, Stand 11723, Kabelenga Road, PO Box 32587, Tel: 222810/2/4, 232952; 232505 Fax: 224179 Cell: 096 750272 Email: s&h@zamnet.zm Specialisation: Conveyancing, Corporate, Commercial transactions, civil litigation, Domestic.

270. **Shepande Kennedy Mpolobe**, LL.B (1991), Advocate (1993), BA (1995), Shepande & Co., 4th Floor, Design House, PO Box 36939, Tel: 237566/236046/221868, Fax: 238047.

271. **Shezongo Namuyoba Joyce**, LL.B (UNZA 1991), Advocate (Nov. 1992), National Legal Aid Clinic for Women, Plot 110/150 Villa Elizabetha, P O Box 34777, Tel: 253975

272. **Shonga James Abyudi**, Advocate, Shamwana & Co., Plot No. 9308 Independence Avenue, P.O. Box 32369, Tel: 254839 / 253756 Fax: 251265, email: shamwana@zamnet.zm , Specialisation: Corporate and Commercial Law.

273. **Siakalima Zunga**, LL.B (Z.Nov. 1985), Advocate (Z.Dec. 1986), Bango Associates, Plot 9686 Chudleigh, PO Box 50072. Tel: 294013.

274. **Siame Natasha Tumelo**, LL.B, Advocate (12 May 2000), Duly Motors Ltd, Cnr. Ben Bella/Freedom Way, PO Box 31956. Tel: 237553, 237607 Fax: 237551

275. **Siampwili Patrick**, LL.B, Advocate (Nov. 1999), MNB Legal Practitioners, Kabelenga/Longolongo Roads, Godfrey House, PO Box 34207, Tel: 236921 Fax: 234019. email: mnb@zamnet.zm

276. **Siamutwa Charles**, LL.B (1995), Advocate (Nov. 1996), Zesco Limited, Head Office, PO Box 33304, Tel: 228084-94 Fax: 222753 Email: zesco@zesco.co.zm

277. **Siamuzyulu Maimbo Febby**, National Legal Clinic for Women, Plot 110A/150, Musonda Ngosa Road, Villa Elizabetha, P/B E578. Tel: 220595

278. **Sibanda Pamela**, LL.B, Advocate (Nov. 1997), National Legal Clinic for Women, Plot 110A/150, Musonda Ngosa Road, Villa Elizabetha, P/B E578. Tel: 220595 Fax: 234747

279. **Sichombo Daniel Miyoba**, LL.B (1987), Advocate (1989), Lusaka Water and Sewerage Company Ltd, Katemo Road, PO Box 50819, Tel: 252578. Email: dsichombo@hotmail.com Specialisation: Business and Corporate Law.

280. **Sichone Frightone,** LL.B, Advocate (2001), Ministry of Lands, Mulungushi House, PO Box 50694. Tel: 252288/252323/252320

281. **Sikatana Mundia Fred**, LL.B (1973), Advocate, Veritas Chambers, Rooms 46-48, St. 11052 Carousel Shopping Centre, Lumumba/Kafue Roads, PO Box 30653, Tel/Fax: 223922 Cell: 097 798763/805730. Specialisation: Human Rights, Law and Development.

282. **Sikatele Cecilia,** LL.B, Advocate (2001), Ministry of Lands, Mulungushi House, PO Box 50694. Tel: 252288/252323/252320

283. **Sikota Sakwiba**, BSc.Law & Politics (Keele University UK – 1980), Advocate (Dec. 1981), Post Grad Dip, Inter. Law (UNZA 1982), Central Chambers, Lex House, Addis Ababa Road Roundabout, Plot 874, PO Box 50468, Tel: 253610 Fax: 254815, Email:cclaw@zamnet.zm, Specialisation: Civil Litigation, Corporate, Litigation Law, Media, Libel.

284. **Silwamba Eric Suwilanji**, LL.B, Advocate (Dec. 1984), Malambo & Silwamba Advocates and Notaries, 6th Floor, Kwacha House, Cairo Road, P/B E342, Tel: 238601 Fax: 225362.

285. **Silweya Henry**, LL.B (UNZA 1970), Advocate (24 Jan. 1972), Post Graduate (June 1976), Cambridge University (UK), Silweya & Co., 24c 1st Floor Technologist Building, PO Box 34426. Tel: 221390, Specialisation: Land Administration. *Also:* 2nd Floor Liso House, Musi-o-Tunya Road, PO Box 61153, Livingstone.

286. **Silweya Towa**, LL.B, Advocate (May 1993), Legal Assistant Project (UNHCR), Office of the Commissioner for Refugees (MHA), Chipowa Road, Rhodespark. Tel: 255474/097 849869.

287. **Simbao Mwamba Kenslick**, LL.B (UNZA 1977), Advocate (Dec. 1978), Mulungushi Chambers, Stand No. 8, Permanent House, Cairo Road, PO Box 36639, Tel: 221980/221911, Fax: 235897 Specialisation: General Practitioner.

288. **Simeza Robert Mbonani**, LL.B (1989), Advocate (Z. Dec. 1990), Simeza Sangwa & Associates, 2nd Floor, Woodgate House, PO Box 36824. Tel: 227474 Fax: 220568.

289. **Simuchoba Sibanje**, LL.B, Advocate (Dec. 1985), NKM & Associates, 8th Floor, Anchor House, Cairo Road, PO Box 35822, Tel/fax: 229610 Cell: 705391 Email: sibanze@zamtel.zm

290. **Simukoko Geoffrey Wamusula**, LL.B (Z. 1973), Advocate, (May 1974), MBA (Leeds 1983), G.W. Simukoko and Company, Plot 11994 Off Lake Road, Woodlands. Tel: 264403/255733 PO Box 38247.

291. **Simumba-Kawama Goma**, LL.B, Advocate (Nov. 1996), Anglo-American Corporation, PO Box 31986, 74 Independence Avenue Tel: 251633/096 766158 Email: kmgoma@hotmail.com

292. **Sinkamba Owen**, LL.B (UNZA 1994), Advocate (Dec. 1995), Sinkamba & Associates, Indeco House, Cairo Road, PO Box 35352, Tel: 097-780403

293. **Sitali Butler Asimbuyu, Capt. (rtd)**, LL.B, (Z.1985), Advocate (Z.Aug.1987), Cavmont Merchant Bank Ltd, Dedan Kimathi road, Mukuba Pension House, PO Box 38474. Tel: 224286 Fax: 224280/6

294. **Situmbeko Chocho**, LL.B, Advocate (2001), Legal Resources Chambers, 2nd Floor, Woodgate House, PO Box 35162. Tel: 227484 Fax: 220568 Email: lrf@zamnet.zm

295. **Sitwala Sachika**, LL.B (UNZA 1988), Advocate (Dec. 1993), B.Sc. ED (UNZA 1978), Lighthouse Chambers, Stand No. 110A/150 Villa Elizabetha, Musonda Ngosa Road, PO Box 37072, Tel: 242527 Cell: 096 758002/763140 Fax: 292958 (Home). *Also:* Independence Avenue, Plot 153 Findeco House, PO Box 910153 Tel: 07-221324/221579/221605, *Mongu*. Email: lhselaw@zamtel.zm

296. **Siwale Mungeni**, LL.B, Advocate (Dec. 1995), National Water Supply & Sanitation Council, Plot 164 Mulombwa Close, Fairview Tel: 226941/2 Fax: 226904 Cell: 096 435167 Email: mungenism@zamnet.zm; nwasco@zamnet.zm

297. **Siwila Amos**, LL.B (Z.Nov. 1986), Advocate (Z.July 1988), Zambia National Commercial Bank Ltd, Cairo Road, PO Box 33611, Tel: 2238878, Fax: 224056.

298. **Skippings Katie A**, LL.B, Advocate (2001), Sharpe & Howard, 1st & 2nd Floor Nalupembe House, Stand 11723, Kabelenga Road, PO Box 32587, Tel: 222810/2/4, 232952; 232505 Fax: 224179 Cell: 096 750272 Email: s&h@zamnet.zm

For additional analytical, business and investment opportunities information, please contact Global Investment & Business Center, USA at (202) 546-2103. Fax: (202) 546-3275. E-mail: rusric@erols.com

299. **Sondashi Ludwig S. Dr**., (FILGA, 1972), LL.B (1978), Advocate (Nov. 1978), LL.M (1985), Ph.D (1990), Sondashi and Co., Plot No. 1B, Chiparamba Road, Old UNDP Building, PO Box 50987, Tel: 223373, Specialisation: Consultant in Constitution, Administrative and Local Government Laws.

300. **Sondashi Virginia Agness**, Certificate in Accounts (1980), LL.B (1993), Advocate (Oct. 1995), Munsaka Chambers, 1st Floor Nsefu House, Room 5, PO Box 50987, Tel/Fax: 227413, Specialisation: General Practitioner.

301. **Songolo Philimon,** LL.B, Advocate (2001), MNB Legal Practitioners, Stand 6131, 5th Floor Godfrey House, Longolongo Road, PO Box 34207, Tel: 236920/236134, Fax: 236134 Email: mnb@zamnet.zm

302. **Sumaili F.K.M**, Dr., LL.B, Advocate (12 May 2000), Phoenix Partners, 9th Floor, Premium House, Plot 7431 Independence Avenue, PO Box 34302. Tel: 234621 Fax: 234620.

T

303. **Tafeni Clement Francis**, LL.B, Advocate (June 29, 2001), Legal Resources Chambers, Woodgate house, PO Box 35162. Tel: 221263 Email: lrf@zamnet.zm

304. **Tembo Mtukuzi Tukuza**, LL.B, Advocate (Nov. 1998), Grant Thornton Associates Ltd, , Mukuba Pension House, PO Box 30885. Tel: 227722/28 Fax: 223774 Email: gthorntn@zamnet.zm

305. **Theotis Amanda D**., LL.B (1996), Advocate (1996), Sharpe & Howard, 1st & 2nd Floor Nalupembe House, Stand 11723, Kabelenga Road, PO Box 32587, Tel: 222810/2/4, 232952; 232505 Fax: 224179 Email: s&h@zamnet.zm

306. **Theu Jordan**, LL.B (Z.April 1988), Advocate (Z.Nov. 1989), Dip. Dev. Studies (Cantab, August, 1989), NAPSA, Lusaka House, Stand 6031 Lumumba/Ben Ben Roads, PO Box RW 51275, Tel: 224869

307. **Ticklay Abdul Aziz**, LL.B (1976), LL.M 1979), Advocate (Dec. 1980), Dip in Air and Space Law (1985), AA Ticklay & Co. Plot No. 12794, Last Shop House, Mumbwa Road, PO Box 32953, Tel: 271308 Specialisation: Company Law, Immigration Law, International Business Law.

308. **Torgbor Edward Nu Adja**, Judge, LL.B (Grays Inn London, Jan 1968), Advocate (Z.Feb. 1979), Mung'omba Associates, 42 Kudu Road, PO Box 35476. Tel: 260055 Fax: 262110

V

309. **Vundamina Kyansenga**, LL.B, Advocate (1996), National Airports Corporation Ltd, St/Plot No. 947/M, Airport Road, Lusaka International Airport, PO Box 30175, Tel/Fax: 271044 Specialisation: General

W

303. **Watae Sydney**, LL.B., Advocate (Dec. 1993), United States Agency for International Development, USAID Mission, PO Box 32481, Tel: 254303/6 Email: swatae@us.gov.za Also: Banda Watae & Co.

304. **Willombe Bevin Chansa**, LL.B, Advocate (Jan 1972), MMW & Co, Electra House, PO Box 31619. Tel: 097 786737

305. **Wina Muwindwa Mbile**, LLB (1996), Advocate (1997), Zambia Electricity Supply Corporation Ltd, Great East Road, P.O. Box 33304, Tel: 228086/8. Email: zesco@zesco.co.zm

For additional analytical, business and investment opportunities information, please contact Global Investment & Business Center, USA at (202) 546-2103. Fax: (202) 546-3275. E-mail: rusric@erols.com

306. **Wood Albert Mark**, LL.B (Z. 1983), Advocate (Z. Dec. 1984), AM Wood & Co, Advocates and Notaries, 3rd Floor, Godfrey House, PO Box 30028. Tel: 237957, Fax: 237963, Email: markwood@zamnet.zm Specialisation: Conveyancing, Civil Litigation, Patents & Trade Marks.

307. **Wright Jonathan Henry A.**, LL.B, Advocate (Dec. 1995), Malambo & Silwamba, 6th Floor, Cairo Road, Kwacha House, PO Box E342, Tel/Fax: 238601

Y

303. **Yangailo Pengani Handerson**, LL.B (Z. 1990), Advocate (Z. Dec. 1991), PH Yangailo & Co, Woodgate House, 3rd Floor, P.O. Box 35972, Tel: 238195/96, Specialisation: Conveyancing, Civil Litigation, Patents & Trade Marks.

304. **Young Pio Amilha**, LL.B, Advocate (2001), Corpus Globe, The Globe Building, Stand No. 2386, Longolongo Road, PO Box 32115, Tel: 235480/1 Fax: 238657 Email: corpus@zamnet.zm

305. **Yousuf Musa Ahmed Adam**, LL.B, Advocate (April 1964), A.D. Adam & Co, No. 6941 Suez Road, PO Box 33143. Tel: 228660 Fax: 228661

Z

303. **Zaheeda Essa**, LL.B Hons, Advocate (1998), DH Kemp & Co, Plot No. 6941, Suez Road, PO Box 31000, Tel: 252381/ 255081, Fax: 255225

304. **Zaloumis Mwangala Frances**, LL.B, Advocate (Dec. 1990), Dove Chambers, PO Box 39538, Cell: 097 789579

305. **Zaloumis Sarandos Martin Joseph,** LL.B, Advocate (3/4/96), Dove Chambers, Plot 106/7 E.W. Tarry's Building, Cairo Road, PO Box 39538. Tel: 221030/97 789579

306. **Zeko Irene Inonge Mbewe**, LL.B (1986), Advocate (Dec. 1987), LLM (1992) Verity & May, Ground Floor, Kambendekela House, Suite No. 1, Cairo Road, PO Box 30123, Tel: 231185/222964, Fax: 222963 Email: izmbewe@zamnet.zm Specialisation: Legislative Drafting.

307. **Zikonda Anderson Ray**, LL.B (Z.1977), MCL (George Washington University, USA, Dec. 1980), Advocate (Dec. 1983), Solicitor of Supreme Court, England and Wales (1993), Legal Practitioner, Kingdom of Tonga, South Pacific (1994), Zikonda & Associates, 11th Floor, Zimco House, Cairo Road, PO Box 34974. Tel: 260-1-238504, Tel/Fax: 260-1-238545, Specialisation: Corporate Law and Intellectual Property

308. **Zulu Douglas**, LL.B, Advocate (Z. Dec. 2000), Judiciary, Plot 438, Independence Avenue, Supreme Court, PO Box 50067. Tel: 251330

309. **Zulu George**, LL.B (Nov. 1986), Advocate (Z.Dec 1987), Zambia Electricity Supply Corporation Ltd, Great East Road, P.O. Box 33304, Tel: 228084/9 Fax: 222753, Email: zesco@zesco.co.zm Specialisation: Courtroom – Civil, Industrial and Criminal Litigation and Conveyancing.

310. **Zulu Ian,** LL.B (1992), Advocate (April 1995), I. M. Zulu & Associates, 2nd Floor Eagle House, Former Chuundu House, PO Box 31190, Tel: 234440 Cell: 097 776024 / 096 767598 Email: ianmz@coppernet.zm

311. **Zulu Lekiwe Angela,** LL.B (Z), Advocate (May 1992), Atlas Partners, Plot 2374 Reedbuck Building, PO Box 34630, Tel: 251243 Fax: 251245.

312. **Zulu Leslie Chembe**, LL.B, Advocate (April 1994), LC Zulu and Company, AMI Head Office Building, 3535 Lumumba/Malambo Roads, PO Box 30131. Tel: 246191/6 Fax: 246192 Cell: 762110

For additional analytical, business and investment opportunities information, please contact Global Investment & Business Center, USA at (202) 546-2103. Fax: (202) 546-3275. E-mail: rusric@erols.com

313. **Zulu Lucas Mangani**, LL.B, Advocate (10 May 1991), Luangeni Chambers, Stand 12500 Kafue/Lumumba Road Junction, Caroussel Building, PO Box 37493, Tel/Fax: 234650 Cell: 96 762043.

314. **Zulu Sebastian Saizi**, Advocate (Dec. 1967), Zulu & Co., 3rd Floor Room 3 & 3A, Society House, PO Box 30917. Tel: 223527.

CHAMBESHI | CHILILABOMBWE | CHINGOLA | CHIPATA | CHOMA | DAR-ES-SALAAM | KABWE | KASAMA | KALULUSHI

Lombe Chongo W., LL.B, Advocate (May 1998), NFB Africa Mines plc, PO Box 22592, Kitwe. Tel: 721666/721601-8

Mumba Rodney Musonda, LL.B, Advocate (May 1983), Chililabombwe Municipal Council, P.O. Box 210023, Tel: 382234, Fax: 382945

Banda Wilson, LL.B (1992), Advocate (1993) Fidelity Chambers, Bwafwano House, 2nd Floor and Rooms 201 and 202, P.O. Box 10661 Tel: 312898 Fax: 313773. Also Fidelity Chambers, 11 Ghandi Street, Tel: 312583/096 902978. Also: Premium House, Independence Avenue, P.O. Box 38906, Lusaka

Mataa Nawa, LL.B, Advocate (1995), Zambia Consolidated Copper Mines Ltd, Fern Avenue, General Offices, P.O. Box 10063, Tel: 344079 Fax: 312498 Email: nawa@hotmail.com Specialisation: Corporate Law.

Ndulo Matyola, LL.B (UNZA), BSc. (Norway), Advocate, Zambia Consolidated Copper Mines Ltd, Fern Avenue, General Offices, P.O. Box 10063, Tel: 344079 Fax: 312498

Sumbwe Roy Mambwe, LL.B (Z), Advocate (Z. May 1989), Mhango & Co, Bwafwano House, Kwacha Street, P.O. Box 11123 Tel/Fax: 311078, Telex: ZA 54029 Specialisation: General

Banda Chikakula T.A., B.A (Makerere 1967), LL.B (UNZA 1976), Advocate (Dec 1, 1978) Katete Chambers, Findeco House, Parirenyantwa Road, P.O. Box 511071, Tel: 21330

Tembo Samuel Jeremiah Bezaliel, LL.B, Advocate (1976), SJB Chambers, Findeco House, Parirenyatwa Road, PO Box 511102. Telefax: 21311 / 21584

Ngandu Artwell Munyongwe, LL.B (UNZA), Advocate, Messrs A.M Ngandu & Co., Livingstone Road, Total Service Station Building, P.O. Box 630255. Tel: 20136.

Phiri Chilombo M. Bridget, LL.B, Advocate (2001), Judiciary, Magistrates Court, PO Box 630335. Tel: 21275/211

Chanda M.S.M, LL.B (Hons Dec. 1976), Advocate (Dec. 1978), Tazara, Stand No. 50 Nyerere Road, Tazara Headquarters, P.O. Box 2834. Tel (Res) 72402.

Chishimba Bornwell Kasumpa, LL.B, Advocate (8th Dec. 1978), Chishimba and Co., Plot 214B, Independence Way, Justinian Chambers Building, P.O. Box 80971 Tel: 224283/222514.

For additional analytical, business and investment opportunities information, please contact Global Investment & Business Center, USA at (202) 546-2103. Fax: (202) 546-3275. E-mail: rusric@erols.com

Kabesha D. Mulilo, LL.B, Advocate (Dec. 1986), Kabesha & Co, 3rd Floor, Mukuni House, Eastern Wing, Stand No. 210 Independence Way, Mukuni House P.O. Box 81484, Tel: 222596 097 780511 Fax: 222713/222288.

Mukuka Edward Mulenga, LL.B, Advocate (Dec 1982), E.M. Mukuka & Co., 1st Floor, Plot 71 Davy House, Freedom Way, P.O. Box 80471. Tel: 225052/097 822245.

Musonda Patrick Chileshe, LL.B (Z. 1987), Advocate (Dec. 1988), Zambia Railways Ltd, Plot/Stand No. 110, Head Office, Cnr Ghana/Buntungwa Street, P.O. Box 80935. Tel: 05-223893 / 097 793133

Mwansa Abraham, LL.B, Advocate (April 1998) Legal Resources Chambers, Butungwa Street, Chitanda House, PO Box 81183, Tel: 05-221581 Email: lrfkb@zamnet.zm

Nsefu Millo Abel Alick, Advocate (April 1982), Zambia Railways, Head Office, Plot/Stand No. 110, Cnr Ghana/Buntungwa, P.O. Box 80935. Tel: 222201 Fax: 224411.

Singini Brian Mataya, LL.B (1987), Advocate (1988), Zambia Railways, Head Office, Cnr Ghana/Buntungwa, P.O. Box 80935. Tel: 222201/096 785540 Fax: 224411.

Sinkende Jeremiah, LL.B, Advocate (Dec.1993), Zambia/China Mulungushi Textiles, Head Office Plot 2419 Kabwe-Ndola Road, PO Box 81091. Tel: 222311/2 Fax: 224916

Ndhlovu Elack Davison, LL.B, Advocate (Dec. 1978), Luso Chambers, D E House, Plot No. 265, President Avenue, P.O. Box 260365. Tel: 731504

KITWE

1. **Akabondo Imonda**, LL.B, Advocate (Dec. 1993), Mopani Copper Mines plc, Central Street, Nkana West, P.O. Box 22000 Tel: 247555.
2. **Banda Elijah Chola,** LL.B (Z), Advocate (Z.Dec. 1986), MNB Legal Practitioners, Mukuba Pension House, President Avenue, , P.O. Box 20817. Tel: 231863 Fax: 231862 Email: mnbkitwe@zamnet.zm
3. **Besa Christopher Mutale,** LL.B, Advocate (2001), MNB Legal Practitioners, Mukuba Pension House, President Avenue, P.O. Box 20817. Tel: 231863 Fax: 231862 Email: mnbkitwe@zamnet.zm
4. **Chaila Julia C. Z.,** LL.B, Advocate (Dec.1984), Copperbelt Energy Corporation plc, 23rd Avenue, Nkana East, P.O. Box 20819, Nkana East, Tel: 223466/245555 Fax: 223445/244040.
5. **Chamutangi Peter Musengu,** LL.B (UNZA 1974), Diploma (Cambridge University 1982) Certificate Training for Trainers (Ireland 1986), Advocate (Oct. 1976), ZCCM Holdings plc, Kantanta Street, P.O. Box 20172, Tel: 245142 Fax: 223445, Specialisation: General
6. **Chileshe Dennis Bendix**, LL.B (UNZA Nov. 1998), Advocate (Nov 1989), LL.M (London), Copperbelt University, Jambo Drive, P.O. Box 21692. Tel: 222066/225155, Fax: 222469 / 096 903170
7. **Chisanga Mwenya Fulgency**, LL.B (UNZA), Advocate (Dec. 1993), Ellis & Company, Afcom House, Obote Avenue, P.O. Box 21500, Kitwe. Tel: 226966/226518 Fax: 226639
8. **Chisuse Kuminyanga C.**, K.C. Chisuse & Associates, 3rd Floor, Ex Legal and General Building, 3rd Floor, P.O. Box 22055. Tel: 229545, Fax: 229546. Specialisation: General (DECEASED).
9. **Chizu Honest Amon**, LL.B (UNZA), Advocate (1999), Kitwe Chambers, Plot 495/6, City Square, Permanent House, P.O. Box 21745. Tel: 222990, Fax: 225682.

For additional analytical, business and investment opportunities information, please contact Global Investment & Business Center, USA at (202) 546-2103. Fax: (202) 546-3275. E-mail: rusric@erols.com

10. **Chugan Mohan**, LL.B (1974), Advocate (1975), Chugan & Co. 3rd Floor, Legal and General Building, City Square, P.O. Box 20891, Tel: 228997 Fax: 222124
11. **Forrest William Myles**, M.A. (GEOG, 1956), Dip.(Management Tech). 1956, Law Society of England, Qualifying Exam (1969), Advocate (Dec. 1976), Forrest Price & Co, Marble House, P.O. Box 21966, Tel: 224866/224580, Fax: 221096. Specialisation: Family/Matrimonial, Company/Commercial Law.
12. **Kamanga Patricia N.S**., LL.B, Advocate (1988), P.S. Kamanga & Co., Katilungu House, Plot 27, 3rd Floor, Room 1, Obote Avenue, P.O. Box 20445. Tel: 229316 Fax: 229317
13. **Kauseni Adam Jack**, LL.B, Advocate (May 1990), Holstens Trucking, Plot No. 1259, Freetown House, Freetown Road, PO Box 23101. Tel: 231855
14. **Kaweche Baldwin B**, LL.B, Advocate (April 1978), Kaweche & Co, Room 209, 2nd Floor Marbel House, Plot 2498, City Square, Room 209, P.O. Box 20441. Tel: 225490/230784 Fax: 225490 (DECEASED)
15. **Lubamba Laban**., LL.B (Hons) (UEA) 1967, Advocate, (August 1968), Jaques & Partners, Insurance House, City Square, P.O. Box 21766, Tel: 222933/222540/229171, Fax: 229177, Telex: ZA 52690
16. **Lwambano Frank M.**, LL.B, Advocate (Dec.1988), Ellis and Company, Afcom House, Plot 384, Obote Avenue, P.O. Box 21500. Tel: 226966/226518 Fax: 226639/222933/229171
17. **Malama Steven Caution Mwaba**, LL.B (Hons) (UEA) 1967, Advocate (August 1968), Jaques & Partners, Insurance House, City Square, Plot 101P.O.Box 21766, Tel: 222933/222540/229171, Fax: 229177, Telex: ZA 52690 Cell: 096 787859
18. **Masengu Michael G.,** LL.B (UNZA October 1977), Advocate (Dec. 1979), Michael Masengu & Co., Leanor House, Top of the Post Office, Parklands Shopping Centre, P.O. Box 20909, Tel/Fax: 229903.
19. **Mazumba Douglas**, LL.B (UNZA 1996), Advocate (Z. November 1996), Douglas & Partners, 4th Floor Bowmaker House, PO Box 21699. Tel:
20. **Mbewe Jacob**, LL.B (1996), Advocate (28 Nov.1997), Mbewe & Co., Room 143, 1st Floor Nchanga House, P.O. Box 20264, Tel/Fax: 245366 Specialisation: Civil Litigation, Commercial Transactions, Probate, Corporate Law, Taxation and Conveyancing.
21. **Mbindo Kafunya**,LL.B, Advocate (4 Dec. 1987) Jaques & Partners, Insurance House, City Square, P.O.Box 21766, Tel: 222933/222540/229171, Fax: 229177, Telex: ZA 52690
22. **Michelo Victor Namobe**, LL.B, Advocate (Oct.1994), Kitwe City Council, Nsansa Lane, Civic Centre, PO Box 20070, Tel: 228796 Fax: 224698.
23. **Mkokweza Charles C.L**., LL.B (UNZA), Advocate (1998), Corpus Globe, PO Box 21225, Mukuba Pension House. Tel: 222739/224530, Fax: 222852 Email: corpuscb@zamnet.zm. Specialisation: Corporate Law, Commercial Law, Taxation, Employment Law and Competition Law.
24. **Moono Lacane**, LL.B, Adv. (April 1996), Messrs Hangala and Company, 2nd Floor, Afcom House, Obote Avenue, Room 90, P.O. Box 23511. Tel: 231207.
25. **Mukumbi Jonas**, LL.B, Advocate (July 1976), Mukumbi & Co., Provident House, Matuka Avenue, P.O. Box 22940. Tel: 221644/221475 Fax: 221475
26. **Mulongo Jasper**, LL.B, Advocate (Dec. 20, 1995), Zamtel Ltd, Dury Lane/Kantanta Street, Regional Headquarters, PO Box 21410, Tel: 220199 Fax: 220299
27. **Mumba Batholomew Sampa**, Sampa Mumba & Co, 6th Floor, Bowmaker House, Stand No. 1093, City Square, P.O. Box 22854. Tel/Fax: 228314 (DECEASED)
28. **Mwaba Lamba Mwila**, LL.B, Advocate, Ellis & Co, Afcom House, Obote Avenue, P.O. Box 21500. Tel: 226966/226518 Fax: 226639
29. **Mwanza Robert Yona**, LL.B, Advocate (April 1998), Permanent Chambers, Provident House, 2nd Floor, P.O. Box 23215, Matuka Avenue. Tel: 220602 Fax: 228051
30. **Nachula Rita Noah Nsokolo**., LL.B (UNZA 1982), Advocate (Z.April 1984), Kitwe Chambers, Permanent House, Plot 495/6, City Square, P.O. Box 21745, Tel: 222990/225682.

31. **Nalwamba Judith Mwaka**, LL.B (UNZA 1988), Advocate (1999), Copperbelt University, P.O. Box 21962. Tel: 227946 Fax: 229354.
32. **Nyirenda William Boli**, LL.B, Advocate (Z. 1981), Solicitor (England and Wales 1991), Ezhuga Musonda and Co., Obote Avenue, Angoni House, P.O. Box 22144, Tel: 228414/228955/227557, Fax: 220539. Specialisation: Finance Law, Securitinisation, Conveyancing and Litigation.
33. **Nyirongo Gavu**, LL.B, Advocate (Z. Nov. 1996), Ezhuga Musonda and Co., Obote Avenue, Angoni House, P.O. Box 22144, Tel: 228414/228955/227557, Fax: 220539.
34. **Pendwe Philemon J.C**., LL.B, Adv, Simwanza Pendwe & Co, 1st Floor, Mukuba House, President Avenue, P.O. Box 21593. Tel: 221770 Fax: 221388.
35. **Simwinga Derrick Ali**, Kitwe City Council, Civic Centre, Nsansa Lane, P.O. Box 20070. Tel: 228796 Fax: 224698.
36. **Twumasi Samuel Gyamera Atta**, LL.B, Advocate (5 Dec.1986), Kitwe Chambers, Plot 495/6, Permanent House, City Square, P.O. Box 21745. Tel: 225682.
37. **Zaloumis Irene T.M**., (Dec. 1979), Kitwe City Council, Nsansa Lane, P.O. Box 20070. Tel: 228796 Fax: 224698

For additional analytical, business and investment opportunities information, please contact Global Investment & Business Center, USA at (202) 546-2103. Fax: (202) 546-3275. E-mail: rusric@erols.com

BUSINESS TRAVEL

US STATE DEPARTMENT SUGGESTIONS

COUNTRY DESCRIPTION: Zambia is a developing southern African country. Tourist facilities outside of well-known game parks are not fully developed. The capital is Lusaka.

ENTRY/EXIT REQUIREMENTS: A passport and visa are required. A visa should be obtained in advance. American citizens arriving for tourism or business at Lusaka International Airport or major land borders, can obtain a one-entry visa for 25 dollars (US) or a multiple entry visa for 80 dollars (US). Long-term visitors or persons coming for employment may also obtain a visa at the border. All Americans who are not residents of Zambia must pay an airport departure tax of 20 dollars (US).

In an effort to prevent international child abduction, many governments have initiated procedures at entry/exit points. These often include requiring documentary evidence of relationship and permission for the child's travel from the parent(s) or legal guardian not present. Having such documentation on hand, even if not required, may facilitate entry/departure.

SAFETY AND SECURITY: U.S. citizens are advised to avoid all travel in Zambia's Northern Luapula Province, including the entire Lake Mweru lakefront, and in directly adjacent areas in the northern province near the border with the Democratic Republic of Congo (DRC) due to instability in the area. In December 2000, military action near the DRC town of Pweto caused armed combatants and refugees to flood into northeastern Zambia. Armed gunman occasionally attack vehicles near the DRC-Zambian border.

U.S. Government personnel are restricted from traveling to the northeast Zambian border region, and from using the Pedicle Road, which traverses the southeast portion of DRC between Mufulira in Copperbelt Province and Mansa in Luapula Province unless they have received prior permission to travel to those areas.

Large numbers of travelers visit tourist destinations, including South Luangwa National Park and Victoria Falls, without incident. However, in 1998, armed gunmen attacked cars traveling on the Lusaka-Mongu Road in the immediate vicinity of the Kafue National Park. American citizens are advised defer any unnecessary travel to the region along the western border with Angola, where conditions remain unsettled as a result of periodic cross-border military activity. Armed gunman occasionally attack traffic near the western border with Angola, and, in the past, bombs have fallen into Zambian territory.

Land mines in the Gwembe Valley near Sinazongwe (along the southwest end of Lake Kariba on the Livingstone to Siavonga Road) make travel to that area potentially hazardous. U.S. citizens are advised not to travel on this road and not to drive off established roads in this area.

U.S. citizens should avoid political rallies and street demonstrations and maintain security awareness at all times.

CRIME: Crime in Zambia is widespread. Armed carjackings, muggings and petty theft are commonplace in Lusaka and other major cities, especially in downtown commercial districts and housing compounds. Carjackers target four-wheel drive vehicles, but anyone who does not practice sound security procedures may be targeted. Thieves steal possessions from automobiles and public transport vehicles stopped in traffic. Lock car doors and roll up windows at all times. Travel at night is particularly risky, both in Lusaka and on roads outside of the city.

The loss or theft abroad of a U.S. passport should be reported immediately to local police and to the nearest U.S. Embassy or Consulate. The pamphlets *A Safe Trip Abroad* and *Tips for Travelers to Sub-Saharan Africa* provide useful information on protecting personal security while traveling abroad and on travel in the region in general. Both are available from the Superintendent of Documents, U.S. Government Printing Office, Washington, D.C. 20402, via the Internet at http://www.access.gpo.gov/su_docs, or via the Bureau of Consular Affairs home page at http://travel.state.gov/.

MEDICAL FACILITIES: Government hospitals and clinics are often understaffed and lack supplies. Private medical clinics in major cities can provide reasonable care in many cases, but major medical emergencies usually require medical evacuation to South Africa or the U.S. Basic medical care outside of major cities is extremely limited. Doctors and hospitals often expect immediate cash payment for health services.

MEDICAL INSURANCE: The Department of State strongly urges Americans to consult with their medical insurance company prior to traveling abroad to confirm whether their policy applies overseas and whether it will cover emergency expenses such as medical evacuation. U.S. medical insurance plans seldom cover health costs incurred outside the United States unless supplemental coverage is purchased. Further, U.S. Medicare and Medicaid programs do not provide payment for medical services outside the United States. However, many travel agents and private companies offer insurance plans that will cover health care expenses incurred overseas including emergency services such as medical evacuations.

When making a decision regarding health insurance, Americans should consider that many foreign doctors and hospitals require payment in cash prior to providing service and that a medical evacuation to the U.S. may cost well in excess of 50,000 dollars (US). Uninsured travelers who require medical care overseas often face extreme difficulties, whereas travelers who have purchased overseas medical insurance have, when a medical emergency occurs, found it life-saving. When consulting with your insurer prior to your trip, ascertain whether payment will be made to the overseas healthcare provider or whether you will be reimbursed later for expenses you incur. Some insurance policies also include coverage for psychiatric treatment and for disposition of remains in the event of death.

Useful information on medical emergencies abroad, including overseas insurance programs, is provided in the Department of State's Bureau of Consular Affairs brochure *Medical Information for Americans Traveling Abroad*, available via the Bureau of Consular Affairs home page or autofax: (202) 647-3000.

OTHER HEALTH INFORMATION: Information on vaccinations and other health precautions may be obtained from the Centers for Disease Control and Prevention's hotline for international travelers at 1-877-FYI-TRIP (1-877-394-8747); fax 1-888-CDC-FAXX (1-888-232-3299), or via the CDC's Internet site at http://www.cdc.gov/.

TRAFFIC SAFETY AND ROAD CONDITIONS: While in a foreign country, U.S. citizens may encounter road conditions that differ significantly from those in the United States. The information below concerning Zambia is provided for general reference only, and may not be totally accurate in a particular location or circumstance.

Safety of Public Transportation: Poor
Urban Road Conditions/Maintenance: Fair
Rural Road Conditions/Maintenance: Poor
Availability of Roadside Assistance: Poor

Driving on Zambian roads can be hazardous. Since most roads do not have shoulders or sidewalks, pedestrians and livestock use the roadways both day and night. While the main roads in Lusaka are maintained, many secondary roads are in poor repair. Driving at night can be hazardous and is discouraged. Mini-buses and cars break down often. When breakdowns occur, local drivers place a few branches behind the car to indicate trouble, but this is hardly visible at night. Many drivers use their high beams at night to detect stopped vehicles and pedestrians.

There are no emergency services for stranded drivers. It is advisable to have a cell phone when undertaking a trip outside of town, although many parts of the country do not yet have cell phone service. During the rainy season (end of October to mid-March), travelers who do not have a four-wheel drive vehicle will encounter problems driving on rural roads. The stretch between Lusaka and Livingstone is more difficult during that time of year, as well as the Great East Road and roads in the eastern and northern parts of the country. The road from Lusaka to the Copperbelt cities of Ndola and Kitwe is generally in good shape year-round. It is not unusual to see elephants and antelopes on or near the road while driving to Victoria Falls or in the vicinity of the Kafue National Park.

Mini-buses serve as the primary means of inter-city travel in Zambia. They are often overcrowded and seldom punctual. City traffic is comprised mostly of cars and mini-buses; motorcycles are rare. Over 1,000 car accidents, many alcohol-related, were reported in 2000. No American citizens have been involved in serious car accidents. Carjackings occur in Lusaka during the daytime. For security reasons, the Embassy discourages travelers from driving on rural roads, especially near the borders with DRC and Angola. American citizens who must drive there are encouraged to drive in convoy and to carry cellular phones and two-way radios.

Seat belts are mandatory, as are helmets for motorcyclists. A child's seat is not mandatory. Traffic circulates on the left side of the road. There is no is no left turn on red, however, many motorists do turn. The speed limit is 50 km/30 mph in Lusaka and 100 km/60 mph outside of city limits. However, speed limits are rarely respected and most cars drive 80 km/50 mph in the city and 120 km/75 mph outside town. It is not unusual to see four-wheel drive vehicles, trucks and buses driving at even higher speeds on the stretch between Lusaka and Livingstone. Drivers under the influence of alcohol who are involved in accidents are tested at Lusaka's University Teaching Hospital (UTH) and then taken to court. The penalty for drivers involved in an accident resulting in injury is 6,000 Kwacha (approximately 2 US dollars).

For additional general information about road safety, including links to foreign government sites, see the Department of State, Bureau of Consular Affairs home page at http://travel.state.gov/road_safety.html. For specific information concerning Zambian driving permits, vehicle inspection, road tax and mandatory insurance, contact the Zambia National Tourist Board at www.zntb@zamnet.zm. The Road Safety Commission is responsible for road safety in Zambia, telephone 260-1-25-24-38 or 25-19-77.

AVIATION SAFETY OVERSIGHT: As there is no direct commercial air service by local carriers at present, or economic authority to operate such service, between the U.S. and Zambia, the U.S. Federal Aviation Administration (FAA) has not assessed Zambia's Civil Aviation Authority for compliance with international aviation safety standards.

For further information, travelers may contact the Department of Transportation within the U.S. at 1-800-322-7873, or visit the FAA Internet home page at http://www.faa.gov/avr/iasa/. The U.S. Department of Defense (DOD) separately assesses some foreign air carriers for suitability as official providers of air services. For information regarding the DOD policy on specific carriers, travelers may contact DOD at (618) 229-4801.

CRIMINAL PENALTIES: While in a foreign country, a U.S. citizen is subject to that country's laws and regulations, which sometimes differ significantly from those in the United States and may not afford the protections available to the individual under U.S. law. Penalties for breaking the law can be more severe than in the United States for similar offenses. Persons violating Zambian

For additional analytical, business and investment opportunities information, please contact Global Investment & Business Center, USA at (202) 546-2103. Fax: (202) 546-3275. E-mail: rusric@erols.com

laws, even unknowingly, may be expelled, arrested or imprisoned. Penalties for possession, use, or trafficking in illegal drugs in Zambia are strict and convicted offenders can expect jail sentences and heavy fines.

U.S. citizens importing prescription drugs into Zambia without a physician's prescription may be arrested and incarcerated. Travelers should carry their prescription drugs and medications in original labeled containers, as well as the written prescription from their physician. Persons overstaying their visa or attempting to work while on a tourist visa risk imprisonment and deportation.

Zambian police do not always provide the U.S. Embassy with timely notification of the arrest of American citizens. If you are detained, insist on your right to contact a U.S. Consular Officer.

CURRENCY ISSUES: American Express and Visa cards are accepted in major supermarkets, restaurants, stores and hotels in Lusaka and Victoria Falls. American travelers cannot withdraw money from ATMs unless they have an account with a bank in Zambia. U.S. travelers checks are easy to cash provided travelers have identification. There are no currency restrictions in Zambia.

PHOTOGRAPHY RESTRICTIONS: Travel to military areas and photographing military facilities are prohibited. Authorities may also challenge photography of areas other than tourist attractions.

DANGERS POSED BY WILD ANIMALS: Travelers are advised that, even in the most serene settings, the animals are wild and can pose a threat to life and safety. Travelers are cautioned to observe all local or park regulations and heed all instructions given by tour guides.

CHILDREN'S ISSUES: For information on international adoption of children and international parental child abduction please refer to our Internet site at http://travel.state.gov/children's_issues.html or telephone (202) 736-7000.

REGISTRATION/EMBASSY LOCATION: U.S. citizens living in or visiting Zambia are encouraged to register with the Consular Section of the U.S. Embassy in Lusaka at the corner of Independence and United Nations Avenues, and to obtain updated information on travel and security in Zambia. U.S. citizens may contact the American Embassy during regular work hours, Monday through Thursday from 8:00 a.m. to 5:00 p.m., and on Friday from 8:00 a.m. to 12:30 p.m. The telephone number is (260-1) 250-955. After hours, the Embassy duty officer can be reached at (260-1) 252-234. The mailing address is P.O. Box 31617, Lusaka, Zambia. The telephone number is (260-1) 250-955 or 250-230; the fax number is (260-1) 252-225.

IMPORTANT INFORMATION

BUSINESS CUSTOMS

Zambia inherited the British legal system at independence in 1964. Business law is based mostly on British law, and business customs are similar to those in the U.S. and Europe.

TRAVEL ADVISORY AND VISAS:

Visas are required for U.S. passport holders, and it is highly recommended that travelers obtain visas in advance of arrival. Multiple entry visas may be obtained from the Embassy of the Republic of Zambia, 2419 Massachusetts Avenue, NW, Washington DC 20008, telephone (202) 265-9717. A multiple entry visa costs forty U.S. dollars, and a single entry visa costs twenty-five dollars. Zambian Embassy officials generally require a letter of invitation from the individual or entity in Zambia with whom one intends to do business. Tourist visas may be obtained at the border pr at the airport upon arrival. These visas are usually single entry visas valid for 3 months and cost twenty dollars.

Crime is a problem in Zambia. Mugging is relatively rare, but car thefts and house and car break-ins are not uncommon. The Copperbelt towns along the border with the Democratic Republic of Congo (Zaire) have seen periodic surges in crime due to problems across the border. There are no internal travel restrictions in Zambia, although areas around military bases may have restricted access. Police/traffic checkpoints do occur, fining vehicles deemed not to meet safety regulations. Many observers see this as corruption problem.

Medical facilities are generally limited. Doctors and hospitals often require immediate cash payment for health care services. Medical insurance covering air ambulance evacuation is highly advisable. For the most recent travel information on Zambia, call (202) 647-5225. For fax information, call (202) 647-3000, or check "travel.state.gov" on the Internet.

HOLIDAYS:

Anticipated Zambian Holidays in the year 2002 are:

January 1 New Years Day
March 12 Youth Day
March 29 Good Friday
March 30 Holy Saturday
March 31 Easter Sunday
April 1 Easter Monday
May 1 Labor Day
May 25 African Freedom Day
July 2 Heroes Day
July 3 Unity Day
August 7 Farmers Day
October 24 Independence Day
December 25 Christmas Day

BUSINESS INFRASTRUCTURE

English is the official language and the language of government and business in Zambia.

There are weekly or more frequent airline connections to Lusaka from London, Dar es Salaam, Harare, Johannesburg, Lilongwe, Nairobi and among other cities. Domestic flights are available between Lusaka, Ndola or Kitwe (Copperbelt Province), Mfuwe and Chipata (Eastern Province), Livingstone (Southern Province), and Kasama (Northern Province). There are also five flights per week from Johannesburg to Ndola and four per week from Johannesburg to Livingstone.

The railway system is rundown and undergoing restructuring. Passenger train travel is unreliable and can be uncomfortable. There are numerous private city bus lines, but they are overcrowded and often unsafe. There are well-maintained and affordable luxury coach services on inter-city runs, including Lusaka-Harare, Lusaka-Johannesburg, and Livingstone -Lusaka- Copperbelt routes.

Road transportation is the preferred means of transport for many goods. The road network is uneven: quite good on some stretches and abysmal on others.

Zambia is landlocked and goods come in and out via air freight, or four ports: Dar es Salaam, Tanzania; Beira, Mozambique; Durban, South Africa; and Walvis Bay, Namibia.

Telecommunications are generally adequate but can be unreliable, especially during the rainy season. Cellular service is currently offered in Lusaka, Copperbelt towns, and some towns along the line of rail. International telephone calls are expensive, about 8 U.S. dollars per 3 minute call to the U.S., including tax. AT&T's USA Direct service is available, as well as similar services to Britain, Sweden and some other European countries. A number of callback service companies are operating, although their legality and blocks their operations are disputed by the parastatal telephone company, ZAMTEL. Fax machines are widely used in Zambia. The Internet is also becoming a popular communications tool.

Good quality housing is available but generally in short supply, particularly for rental housing.

Malaria is endemic in Zambia; cases occur in Lusaka, as well. Prophylaxis is strongly recommended if traveling outside the city. HIV prevalence is very high in Zambia, with estimated rates of 30-40% of the adult population in urban areas. The water in major city hotels is safe. When traveling outside the major cities, water should be filtered and boiled if possible.

Fresh meat, dairy products, fruits and vegetables are readily available and of high quality. Most processed food is imported from South Africa and is available in urban supermarkets, although it may be expensive. Lusaka has a number of good restaurants.

Guide For Business Representatives: This guide is available for sale by the Superintendent of Documents, U.S. Government Printing Office, Washington DC 20402, Tel: (202) 512-1800; Fax: (202) 512-2250. Business travelers to Zambia are encouraged to seek appointments with U.S. Embassy Lusaka officials. Such visitors should contact the Commercial Section in advance. The Commercial Section can be reached at Tel: (260-1) 250-955 or Fax: (260-1) 252-225.

MAJOR CITIES

LUCAKA

Lusaka is a city whose bustling chaos has a certain charm that is just Zambia.

The tourist passing through the capital may not see any reason to stay, but Lusaka is the product of a country battling to find its way in a new world, caught between colonial beginnings, years of socialist independence and now democracy. It typifies the problems many African countries face as they find their "independent" footing in world that's surging ahead.

The fascinating thing about Lusaka is its energy. Not perhaps of the same ilk as the Big Apple, but an African energy, propelled by that need to survive.

Lusaka is as much a part of "the real Africa" as the rich national parks and stunning scenery. Well over 60% of its 2 million inhabitants are unemployed, but there are surprisingly few beggars. Although petty theft occurs, most people try to make an honest living, selling their wares or services and smiling to boot.

The markets are a hive of activity, the thousands of stalls are filled and cleared every day. A myriad of motor spares dealers, restaurants, hairdressers, fishmongers, fruitsellers and rows and rows of "salaula" - discarded clothing from the West sold to Africa by the bale.

Venture out to a nightclub or roadside shebeen and "get in the groove", so to speak, of the local people. Dance the night away to the sounds of rhumba, kwela, techno or good old rock 'n roll.

But Lusaka is also a city undergoing a facelift. A walk around the city will reveal new shops- including a new market and a multi-million dollar shopping mall under construction; smart fast food outlets; freshly mended roads old buildings being refurbished and the transformation of the city's parks.

For many, this is the perfect example of what economic liberalisation has done for the country. And viewed from the villages, Lusaka is the glittering capital which still persuades rural Zambians to take the bus there in search of jobs and dreams.

The capital covers an area of over 70km sqare and is one of the fastest-growing cities in central Africa. It's population almost trebled in the immediate post-independence era and continues to grow daily. There has been no influx control and the city is bursting at the seams. Grossly inadequate municipal facilities are hard-pressed to cope with the ever-increasing demand.

It is a sprawling, unplanned metropolis with many multi-storey buildings, high-walled suburbs and busy shanty towns. Fast-growing industrial development has brought together people of many nationalities, making it a bustling centre for economic, political and cultural activities.

The city lies at the junction of the main highways to the north, east, south and west at an altitude of 1 300m above sea level. There are air links to most of the major tourist destinations in Zambia from Lusaka International Airport.

The shops are mainly grouped along the broad double carriageway of Cairo Rd, but the government buildings are about 6km away along Independence Ave.

For maps of the city, try the **Zambian National Tourist Board**, the craft shop at the Pamodzi Hotel or the Map Centre, Mulungushi House, opposite the US embassy.

There is a local magazine called the **Lusaka Lowdown** which is a mine of information on what's happening in town and full of useful adverts for local services and products. Check out the online version.

CLIMATE

The most appealing factor to many who have made Lusaka their home is the superb climate. Warm sunny summers, interspersed with cooling thunderstorms and mild winters with loads of sunshine.

It can get very hot between October and March if there's no rain. The average rainfall, between November and April, is about 950mm. Summer temperatures range from 20 degrees to 32 degrees C. Winter temperatures from 10 degrees to about 26 degrees. Humidity is usually below 40%.

For additional analytical, business and investment opportunities information, please contact Global Investment & Business Center, USA at (202) 546-2103. Fax: (202) 546-3275. E-mail: rusric@erols.com

GETTING THERE

Lusaka is close to the centre of Zambia between the eastern and western bulges. **All major routes to the east, west, north and south flow through the city**.

The Great North Road comes down from Tanzania via Kapiri Mposhi, and is about 1 100km from the Tanzanian border.

The Great East Rd from Chipata to Lusaka is 570km.

The road from Livingstone in the south meets up with the "Kafue Road" and is 470km long. From the Chirundu border with Zimbabwe, the route is well paved and 136km long.

The Mongu road coming in from the west via the **Kafue National Park** is 591km long.

The domestic railway goes to Livingstone, Kapiri Mposhi and the Copperbelt. The Tanzania Zambia Railway - Tazara - comes down as far as Kapiri Mposhi, where the Zambia Railways train links it to Lusaka. Buses arrive from Harare, Lilongwe, Johannesburg, Livingstone and the Copperbelt.

Lusaka International Airport, which is 14km from the city centre, receives most international flights.

Zambian Airways will flies to and from Johannesburg and currently has scheduled flights to Mfuwe, Chipata, the Copperbelt and Livingstone.

Zambia Skyways has scheduled domestic flights to Lusaka from: Ndola, Kasama, Kasaba Bay, Mongu, Livingstone, Mfuwe and Chipata.

InterAir Flies into Ndola from Johannesburg and Entebbe from where a connecting flight to Lusaka can be taken.

Getting around -

No scheduled bus services - taxis range from 12 seater minibuses to dilapidated cars to good dial up cabs to chauffeur driven vehicles.

WHERE TO STAY

Accommodation in Lusaka is plentiful and there are choices to suit all tastes and budgets. From Five star hotels, Well known hotel chains, Game lodges on private game reserves, to motels and quiet guesthouses in the suburbs.

A few kilometres from the CBD are the three top hotels, the **Holiday Inn,** the **Inter-Continental Hotel** and the **Pamodzi.**

For cheaper accommodation try the **Fairview Hotel, Chrismar, Hillview, Kafue Rd Garden, Garden House** or **Ndeke Hotels.** The oldest hotel in the City is the **Lusaka Hotel** just off Cairo Rd.

Comfortable Guesthouses in the suburbs include the **Wayside Bed & Breakfast** just 4km South of the City Centre, and **Juls Guesthouse** just off the Great East Rd. Lusaka's newest Lodge **Villa Lodge Gardens** and another one with very convenient shopping access **Chita Lodge.**

There are various motels in and around town which offer basic but reasonably priced accommodation.

RESTAURANTS AND NIGHTLIFE

See Supplement

SHOPPING

Most of the banks and many bureaux de change can be found along Cairo Road.

For groceries and general **supplies**, the newly opened Manda Hill shopping centre is where it's all at. This is Lusaka's first shopping mall and it's becoming a big hit with an excellent range of shops and boutiques. There's also a big supermarket in Cairo Rd. There are several suburban shopping centres, not of the mall type, but with a variety of shops that usually supply anything you need, mostly imported from Zimbabwe or South Africa and a little pricey. These are called Kabulonga, Northmead and Woodlands.

If not for shopping, but just for the experience of how the local masses shop, a visit to one of Lusaka's **markets** is a must. It's an interesting experience and well worth a visit, if just for the colourful and lively atmosphere. The Soweto Market is two roads west of Cairo Road, and the other opposite the Tazara building in Independence Ave. A new, smarter, roofed market has just been built along Freedom Way.

Curios and crafts can be found at Zambili in Luanshya Rd. The Book House shop, in the Manda Hills Shopping Center. Zintu Handicrafts are at the Holiday Inn. Moore Pottery on Kabalenga Road has an excellent range of ceramics, and Zintu Za Nyimba at the bottom end of Panganani Road sells a wide range of locally made wooden furniture, batiks, candle holders, lamps shades, hand-dyed cloths and carvings. Definitely worth a visit. Hope House in Luanshya Road is a charitable organisation providing support to Aids victims and sell a range of home-made crafts.

For **Gemstones** and fine **jewellery**, try **Jagoda** at the Holiday Inn or the Intercontinental Hotel.

You can buy **film** and get photographs processed at Phoenix Photographics halfway down Cairo Road. Books can be found at Tower Books at the Castle in Makeni, the Book House SHop at Manda Hills and Mary's Bookshop on the Leopards Hill Rd.

A word of warning - Lusaka is famous for car thieves, pick-pockets and bag snatchers, but if you have someone who can mind your vehicle and keep a good grip on your bags, it's quite safe.

SIGHTSEEING

A good place for locally hand-crafted curios is the **Kabwata Cultural Village**, which is in the suburb of Kabwata along Burma Road. The residents are carving all day and a wide variety of items are for sale at reasonable prices. Test your bargaining skills.

Lusaka National Museum on Independence Avenue is undoubtedly one of the most attractive public buildings in the city.This cultural history museum tells the story of Zambia in four main sections; ethnography, witchcraft, history and contemporary art. The ground floor presents the works of artists from Zambia's independence (1964) to date: contemporary paintings, sculpture and ceramics. With no national art gallery, this provides the visitors with a rare opportunity to sample Zambian Art. The upper floor houses historical and cultural artifacts. Particularly fascinating is the witchcraft exhibit which will give the visitor the opportunity to learn about a part of Zambian life that is rarely discussed, but is deeply imbedded in every sphere of daily life. Facilities: The museum has a small library, a small conference room and a snack shop. Opening hours: 9am-4. 30pm daily; closed public holidays. Admission: US$2 adults, US$1 children. Guided tours possible. Parking available.

Bente Lorens Ceramic Studio in Longacres has a fine collection of bowls, plates and ornaments which are also for sale. **The Henry Tayali Visual Arts Centre** at the showgrounds has a fine selection of works by Zambian artists. Single-exhibitor and group shows are held every month. Open daily from 10h00. (See listings for Galleries)

Kalimba Reptile Park has an impressive collection of snakes, all found in the surrounding area, crocodiles, tortoises and some of the most unusual chameleons found in Africa. The park is set in a lush garden with a kids playground, putt putt course and a verandah where refreshments are served. Head out of town on the Great East Road towards the airport and turn left at the last Caltex garage before the airport turnoff. Follow the signs for about 11km. The park, which is part of a fish farm, also sells fresh frozen fish and crocodile tails, as well as a range of crocodile bags, purses, belts, etc.
Mundawanga Park has been renovated and is back operating.

The Aylermer May Cemetery in Lagos Rd, Rhodes Park. This was Lusaka's first Cemetery and is currently undergoing extensive renovations.

There are several car-hire companies in Lusaka to help you get around: see **car hire** listings for contact numbers.

DAY TRIPS

Lilayi Game Ranch, 20 minutes outside of town, is set on a 700 hectare farm, a part of which has been uncultivated and left in its pristine bush state. There are 19 different antelope species but no predators,so they're a lot less skitttish than in the national parks. Over 200 birds species have been recorded here, which can be spotted on walking trails, game drives or horseback trails. Bookings are essential .

Chaminuka Private Game Reserve just 45 minutes north of Lusaka offers a superb wildlife Safari and lunch in beautiful surroundings. One can also take a horseback trail through the Reserve, go fishing, enjoy a swim, play tennis and relax in their outdoor jacuzzi and sauna. The Reserve has more species of animals than any other game park in Zambia, including, lion cheetah, giraffe, elephant, ostrich and even the elusive sitatunga. It does offer day package special which can be found at the rates section of their web site.

Another reason to visit Chaminuka is their extensive **Art Gallery** . Historically the Sardanis family have been serious promoters of Zambian Art. Chaminuka, has a collection of more than 1000 pieces of art, ranging from traditional artefacts collected in over 35 countries in Africa, to contemporary sculpture and painting collections.

Zambili Crafts and Cafe D'Afrique near the centre of town is a great place to stop over for lunch. Traditional foods and cultural performances, situated in Kalundu.

JLazyJ Farm is a 1 500 hectare bird sanctuary also 20 minutes from town. The owner will take you horseback riding through the pristine miombo woodland or one can simply do walks and birdwatching on one's own.

Trotover Equestrian Centre offers horseback hacks through indigenous forest with natural obstacles, or birdwatching walks. This is a great spot for a family picnic - with a pool and a few streams.

Foxdale Ostrich Farm

Lechwe Game and Fish Farm is within an hour of Lusaka on the banks of the Kafue River. The river's proximity attracts many waterbirds. Sixteen different antelope species can be seen in the

For additional analytical, business and investment opportunities information, please contact Global Investment & Business Center, USA at (202) 546-2103. Fax: (202) 546-3275. E-mail: rusric@erols.com

woodlands and floodplains of the area. On offer are horse trails and boat rides down the river. Booking essential.

At the **Kafue Marina**, also within an hour's drive from town, one can hire a boat or canoe and there are picnic facilities with barbecues and rondavels. Take the Kafue Road out of town and turn left just before the Kafue Bridge, followed by another left and a right. (See listings for Daytrips)

LIVINGSTON

Named after the famous Victorian missionary explorer, Dr. David Livingstone, the Town was established in 1905. As a major European settlement, the town was made the capital of Northern Rhodesia in 1911. As the capital, it enjoyed excellent facilities far superior to anything in the country, as can be seen from the surviving Edwardian colonial buildings that line the city's main road, and even had the distinction of having the country's first newspaper.

The capital was moved to Lusaka in 1935 and the bustling city has become a quiet town, a little neglected but still retaining a special charm. The proximity to the Zambezi River and the spectacular Victoria Falls has led it to become a base for travelers from all over the world wanting to explore this Seventh wonder of the World.
Stop in at the Adventure Centre for a wide range of adventure activities, services and shops. There are several Adventure Companies offering Riverboarding, White water rafting, Canoeing, Horse riding trails, Abseiling, local tours to the Victoria Falls and around Livingstone. There are Safari operators, a Restaurant, an Internet Cafe, a Backpackers Lodge and an excellent Arts and Crafts Gallery. You'll find them in Mosi-o-Tunya road heading towards the Falls (corner of Nakatindi rd out to Kazungula) Don't miss it! You can also book all these adventures from the Pocket Guide Office at the Victoria falls Border post on the Zambian side. Two great new books on Dr. Livingstone just released - order here

GETTING THERE

- **Zambian Airways** has scheduled planes to Livingstone from Lusaka and will soon be flying from Livingstone to Johannesburg.

- **Zambia Skyways** has scheduled flights to Livingstone from Lusaka.

By Road, Livingstone can be approached from three directions. If you're coming **from Zimbabwe,** cross the border at the town of Victoria Falls over the famous Victoria Falls Bridge, carry straight on this road for about 11 kilometres. **From Botswana**, cross the border at Kazungula by ferry, and continue east for about 60kms. **From Lusaka**, Livingstone is 470 kms. Take the southbound Kafue Road out of Lusaka and just after the Kafue River Bridge, turn right towards Mazabuka. This road leads straight to Livingstone.

WHERE TO STAY

In Livingstone Town itself there are 3 hotels, and several backpackers establishments

- **Wasawange Lodge** in Libala Drive which is also the road to the airport, has very comfortable ethnically decorated chalets with all the conveniences of a modern hotel.

For additional analytical, business and investment opportunities information, please contact Global Investment & Business Center, USA at (202) 546-2103. Fax: (202) 546-3275. E-mail: rusric@erols.com

- The **New Fairmount** Hotel in Mosi o Tunya Rd and the Northwestern Hotel have standard air-conditioned rooms and a Casino and night club.

- **Ngolide Lodge** in Mosi-o-Tunya Rd, Livingstone offers comfortable, affordable accommodation in a convenient location, just 8 kms from the falls.

- **Fawlty Towers** is right in the middle of Livingstone on the Mosi-o-Tunya Road in the Adventure Centre and has great inexpensive accommodation with a pool.

There are several hotels and lodges in the Victoria Falls area and along the Zambezi, providing a wide range of accommodation.

- **Stanley Safari Lodge** is the newest lodge in the area opening June 2002. It has a direct view over the spray of the Victoria Falls and the National Park. They are offering excellent opening specials at the moment.

- **Tongabezi** is a very stylish lodge built from stone and set into the surrounding cliffs. It has comfortable safari tented accommodation on the rivers edge as well as three stone, wood and thatch chalets on the cliff edge overlooking the river. They also have island camps in the Zambezi River.

- **Taita Falcon Lodge** is perched on the edge of the cliffs and has superb views of the spectacular Batoka gorge.

- **Zambezi Royal Chundu Fishing and Safari Lodge** is further upstream of the Zambezi.

- **Mukolo Island Tented Camp** run by the stylish Chilongozi Safari Company who also conduct canoeing safaris on the upper Zambezi.

- **Chundukwa Tree Lodge** Camp has wood and thatch chalets on stilts over the River and offers horse trails and canoeing.

- **Thorntree** is another bush camp up river with spacious tented accommodation on the rivers edge.

- The newest additions are the **River Club** on the banks of the Zambezi and the **Waterfront**. Sun International is planning a luxurious complex to open in 2001.

- **Kubu Cabins** is a quaint bush lodge about 25kms up river with an excellent riverside site, renowned for superb food and a quiet homely atmosphere. This lodge is currently being refurbished.

- **Mawala Lodge** is 30 kms upstream of Victoria Falls with an upstairs bar and dining area offering great views of the Zambezi and wildlife coming down to the rivers edge to drink.

- A new **Sun International Resort** just opened very close to the Falls. There are two hotels, **The Zambezi Sun** (3 star hotel) as well as **The Royal Livingstone** (5 star hotel). Each of the hotels has its own design, specific character and identity. The needs of the widest possible range of clients are provided for, including families and corporate and conference groups, as well as top end individual travellers.

RESTAURANTS

Several new restaurants have opened in Livingstone recently:
Utsav is the first Indian Restaurant to appear in Livingstone - found in the main Mosi-o-tunya rd.

They also have a take-away section called Exciting Biting !
The Laughing Dragon is a new Chinese establishment just off the main rd near the **Hungry Lion.**
Hippo's pub behind Fawlty Towers serves great meals and has a pool table and darts.
ZigZag also doubles as a booking office for various adventures as well as a small shop but serves lunches and cakes on the pavement.
The **Pigs Head**, Kabompo Road is one of the local pubs, also serving food.
Eatrite Fast Foods, in the main road
For excellent light lunches with good wholesome food try **Pilgrims** just on the outskirts of Town on the way to the Falls. They also have a curio shop there.
Chanters is a good new restaurant in Lukulu Rd with accommodation as well.
Flying Pizza on the main rd near the Adventure Centre serves great pizzas, shwarmas, burrittos, soft drinks.
The **Waterfront** always has meals available on their great terrace on the river's edge
Both **Sun International Hotels** have several good restaurants although they're quite pricey.

CURIO SHOPS

African Visions is a great new addition to Livingstone with a wide selection of Zambian and other African works of art and craftwork. Find them at the **Adventure Centre** in Mosi-o-Tunya Rd.
Kubu Crafts sells fine wood crafted furniture among other curios and souvenirs.

GETTING AROUND

Imperial Car Hire offers a full range of vehicles to tour around Livngstone, and the Falls. AJ Car Hire and Tours offers chauffeur driven cars or self drive hire and takes tours around the area as well as airport transfers.
Makoro Quest, Bundu Adventures and **Bushtracks Africa** also do day trips and transfers

SUPPLEMENTS

GOVERNMENT OFFICES

MINISTRY	TELEPHONE
Agriculture, Food and Fisheries	Tel: 251537
Auditor General	Tel: 25241
Commerce, Trade and Industry	Tel: 228301
Communications and Transport	Tel: 251444
Community Development and Social Services	Tel:227840
Defence	Tel: 251211
Education	Tel: 227636
Energy and Water Development	Tel: 263870
Environment and Natural Resources	Tel: 229410/229419
Finance	Tel: 250544
Foreign Affairs	Tel: 252666
Health	Tel: 253040/45
Home Affairs	Tel: 254261
Information and Broadcasting	Tel: 227840
Labour and Social Security	Tel: 227840
Lands	Tel: 252288
Legal Affairs	Tel: 251588
Local Government and Housing	Tel: 253077
Mines and Minerals development	Tel: 252990
Office of the President	Tel: 260312
Science, Technology and Vocational Training	Tel: 229673
Sports, Youth and child Development	Tel: 227158
Tourism	Tel: 227645
Works and Supply	Tel: 353244

US AND COUNTRY CONTACTS

U.S. Embassy Lusaka

Ambassador David B. Dunn

Deputy Chief of Mission Robert Whitehead
Economic/Commercial Chief Troy Fitrell
Commercial Officer Daniel Ebert
Commercial Specialist Vedruna Santana

U.S. mailing address: 2310 Lusaka Pl., Washington DC 20521-2310.

International mailing address: United States Embassy, PO Box 31617, Lusaka, Zambia.

Street address: Corner of United Nations and Independence Avenues, Lusaka, Zambia.

Telephone: 260 1 250-955
Fax: 260 1 252-225

ZAMBIAN GOVERNMENT AND INDUSTRY

Ministry of Commerce, Trade and Industry, Permanent Secretary Dr. Moses Banda, PO Box 31968, Lusaka, Zambia. Tel: 260 1 223-617.

Ministry of Finance, Permanent Secretaries Mrs. Stella M. Chibanda and Mr. BoniFace Nonde, PO Box RW 50062, Lusaka, Zambia. Tel: 260 1 250-657 and 260 1 251-843.

Zambia Privatization Agency (ZPA), Chief Executive Stuart Cruickshank, PO Box 30819, Lusaka, Zambia. Tel: 260 1 223-859.

Zambia Investment Center (ZIC), Director Dr. Mbikusita Lewanika, PO Box 34580, Lusaka, Zambia. Tel: 260 1 255-240.

Zambia Association of Chambers of Commerce and Industry (ZACCI), Chairman George Chabwera, PO Box 30844, Lusaka, Zambia.
Tel: 260 1 252-369

COUNTRY MARKET RESEARCH

Price Waterhouse, Senior Partner Jack Ward, PO Box 30942, Lusaka, Zambia. Tel: 260 1 228-809

COMMERCIAL BANKS

1. S. Sridhar
   Managing Director
   Citibank Zambia Limited
   Citibank House, Chachacha Road
   P.O. Box 30037
   Tel: 260-1-229025
   Fax: 260-1-226258

   2. Margaret Mwanakatwe
   Managing Director
   Barclays Bank of Zambia Limited
   Kafue House, Cairo Road
   P.O. Box 31936

Lusaka, Zambia
Tel: 260-1-228858-66
Fax: 260-1-222519
Telex: ZA 41570

3. John Janes
Managing Director
Standard Chartered Bank Limited
Cairo Road
P.O. Box 32238
Lusaka, Zambia
Tel: 260-1-229242
Fax: 260-1-222092
Telex: 260-41660 or 45420

4. Archibald Macleod
Managing Director
Stanbic Bank Zambia Limited
Corporate House, Cairo Road
P.O. Box 32111
Lusaka, Zambia
Tel: 260-1-282441
Fax: 260-1-221152

5. Jia Zaisen
Managing Director
Bank of China (Zambia) Limited
Amandra House, Ben Bella Road
P.O. Box 34550
Lusaka, Zambia
Tel: 260-1-238711
Fax: 260-1-235350

6. Keith Stewart
Managing Director
Cavmont Mercahnt Bank Limited
Mukuba Pension House, Dedan Kimathi Road
P.O. Box 32222
Lusaka, Zambia
Tel: 260-1-224280
Fax: 260-1-224304

7. M. Wadood
Managing Director
Finance Bank Zambia Limited
Chanik House, Cairo Road
P.O. Box 36762
Lusaka, Zambia
Tel: 260-1-223587
Fax: 260-1-227290
Telex; ZA 40338

8. S. Gupta
Managing Director

For additional analytical, business and investment opportunities information, please contact Global Investment & Business Center, USA at (202) 546-2103. Fax: (202) 546-3275. E-mail: rusric@erols.com

First Alliance Bank Limited
Chachacah Road
P.O. Box 36326
Lusaka, Zambia
Tel: 260-1-229303
Fax: 260-1-228441
Telex: ZA 40794

9. A.K. Misra
Managing Director
Indo-Zambia Bank Limited
Cairo Road,
P.O. Box 35411,
Lusaka, Zambia
Tel: 260-1-224653
Fax: 260-1-225090
Telex: ZA 40631

10. Friday C. Ndhlovu
Managing Director
Investrust Merchant Bank Limited
AFE House, Freedom Way
P.O. Box 32344,
Lusaka, Zambia
Tel: 260-1-238733
Fax: 260-1-237060

11. Godfrey Msiska,
General Manager
New Capital Bank Limited
Anchor House, Cairo Road
P.O. Box 36452
Lusaka, Zambia
Tel: 260-1-229508
Fax: 260-1-224055
Telex: ZA 43830

12.. Samuel B. Musonda
Managing Director
Zambia National Commercial Bank
Plot 33454, Cairo Road
P.O. Box 33611
Lusaka, Zambia
Tel: 260-1-228979
Fax: 260-1-223106
Telex: ZA 42360

WASHINGTON-BASED U.S. GOVERNMENT CONTACTS

Karl Albrecht, Zambia Desk Officer (AF/S), Department of State, Washington DC, 20520. Tel: 202 647-9858.

Office of the Coordinator for Business Affairs, Department of State, tel.: 202 746-1625.

Deborah Henke Rogers, Zambia Desk Officer (ANESA/OA), Department of Commerce, Washington DC, 20230. Tel: 202 482-4227.

TPCC Trade Information Center Number: 1 800 USA-TRADE.

Trade Assistance and Promotion Office, Foreign Agricultural Service, Department of Agriculture, tel.: 202 720-7420.

FOREIGN DIPLOMATIC MISSIONS

IN LUSAKA - DIALING CODE 260+1+ NUMBER

COUNTRY	**ADDRESS**	**POST**	**TELEPHONE**	**FAX**	**TLX/EMAIL**
ANGOLA	Plot No. 6660, Mumana Rd. Olympia Park Ext	Box: 31595	Tel: 291142, 290346	292595	ZA 41940
BOTSWANA	Diplomatic Triangle	Box: 31910	Tel: 250555 / 250019 /	Fax: 253895	ZA 41710
CANADA	5119 United Nations Ave	Box: 31313	Tel: 250833	Fax: 254176	ZA 42480 isaka@paris03.x400.gc.ca
CHINA.	7430 Haile Selassie Ave	Box 31975.	Tel: 252410/253770	Fax: 251157	Tlx:41360
CUBA.	5574 Magoye Road.Kalundu	Box 33132	Tel:291308	91586	Tlx:40349 ssikulem@zamnet.zm
DENMARK	Dunduza Chisidza Crescent	Box 50299	Tel:254182 / 253750	Fax: 254618	ZA 43580
EGYPT	5206 United Nations Avenue	Box: 32428	Tel: 254149	Fax: 252213	Tlx: 40021
EUROPEAN UNION	Plot 4899 Los Angeles Boulevard, Lusaka		250711, 251140, 255586,255585	250906, 252336	info@zam.eudel.com
FINLAND.	74 Independence Avenue,	Box 50819	Tel: 251988 /252026	Fax: 254981	Tlx:43460 finemb@zamnet.zm
FRANCE	74 Independence Avenue	Box 30062	Tel:251332/251340	Fax: 254475	Tlx:41430 frcooparobase@zamnet.zm

GERMANY.	5209 United Nations Avenue,	Box 50120	Tel: 250644/251259 251262	Fax: 254014	Tlx:41410
GREECE	54 Joseph Mwila Rd, Rhodes Park	Box: 31587	Tel: 231020/231064	Fax: 231061	.
INDIA,	Pandit Nehru Rd	Box: 32111	Tel:253006/253158 /9/60	Fax: 254118	Tlx:41420
IRELAND.	6663 Katima Mulilo road, Olympia Park Extension,	Box 34923	Tel:290482/291124 292288	Fax: 290482	Tlx:43110
ITALY	Diplomatic Triangle, Independence Ave	Box 31046	Tel 250775/250783 250781	Fax: 254929	Tlx 43380 italyzam@zamnet.zm
JAPAN.	3218 Haile Selassie Avenue.	Box 34190	Tel: 251555/252036 252039	Fax: 253488	Tlx:41470 jez@zamnet.zm
KENYA	United Nations Ave.	Box: 50298	Tel: 250772/250742	Fax: 253829	ZA 40270 kenhigh@zamnet.zm
KOREA	92 Mutandwa Rd, Roma	Box 30584	Tel:292380	Fax: 225368	.
MALAWI HIGH COMMISSION	Bishops Rd, Kabulonga	Box 50425	Tel: 265764/9	Fax: 265765	ZA 41840
MOZAMBIQUE	Plot 9592 Kacha Rd, Northmead	Box 34877	Tel: 220333/239135	Fax: 220345	Tlx:45900
NAMIBIA	6968 Kabanga Rd, Rhodes Park	Box: 30577	Tel: 252250/250968	Fax: 252497	.
NETHERLANDS	5208 United Nations Ave	Box 31905	Tel:253819/253590 253994	Fax: 253733 250200	Tlx:40211 nlgovlus@zamnet.zm
NIGERIA	5203 United Nations Ave	Box: 32598	Tel: 253177 / 253268/253265	Fax: 253560	ZA 41280
NORWAY.	Plot No.245/65 Birdcage Walk Haile	Box 34570	Tel:252188/252625.	Fax: 253915	ZA 40100

	Selassie Avenue,				
PORTUGAL	23 Yotem Muleya Rd Woodlands	Box 33871	Tel: 253720/260296	Fax: 253896	Tlx:40010.
ROMANIA	2 Leopards Hill Road, Kabulonga,	Box 31944	Tel:262182/262239	.	ZA 40668
RUSSIA	Plot No. 6407, Diplomatic Triangle,	Box 32355	Tel:252183/252128 /252120	Fax: 253582	Tlx:40341
SAUDI ARABIA	4896 Los Angeles Blvd	Box: 34411	Tel: 253266 /253325	Fax: 253449	Tlx:45550.
SOMALI	Plot No.G3/377A Kabulonga	Box 34051	Tel:262119/263944.	Fax: 253582	Tlx:40270
SOUTH AFRICA	D26 Cheetah Rd, Kabulonga	Private Bag W369	Tel: 260999	Fax: 263001	sahc@zamnet.zm
SWEDEN.	Alick Nkatha Ave, Longacares	Box 30788	Tel: 251711	Fax: 254049	ZA 41820 swedem@zamnet.zm
TANZANIA	Ujaama House, United Nations Ave,	Box: 31219	Tel: 253320/253222 253323/4	Fax: 254861	ZA 40118 tzrplsk@zamnet.zm
UNITED KINGDOM	Independence Ave,	Box: 50050	Tel: 251133	Fax: 253798	ZA 41150 brtn@zamnet.zm
UNITED STATES	United Nations Ave,	Box: 31617	Tel: 250955	Fax: 252225	ZA 41970 usembass@zamnet.zm
ZAIRE	1124 Parirenytwa Rd Rd. Box 71234,	Box: 31287	Tel; 213343 / 229044 /5	.	.
ZIMBABWE	Haille Selassie Rd	Box: 33491	Tel: 254006/12/18	Fax: 253582	Tlx:45800

ZAMBIAN MISSIONS ABROAD

COUNTRY	**ADDRESS**	**PHONE**	**FAX**	**TELEX/EMAIL**

ANGOLA	106/108, Run Rei Katyavala Maculusso PO Box 1496 Luanda	Tel: 244-2-331145/ 331241	Fax: 244-2-331241	Telex:998-3439
BELGIUM	1060 Brussels 469 Avenue Moliere	Tel: 32-2-343-5649	Fax: 32-2-347-4333	Telex: 846-63102 ZAMNREP B
BOTSWANA	P.O. Box 362 1118 Queen's Road, Zambia House, The Mall, Gaberone	Tel: 267-351-951 267-351-952	Fax: 267-353-952	Telex: 991-2416
CHINA	Beijing (Peking) 5 Dongsijie San-Li-Tun	Tel: 8610-5321778 /5321554 8610-8610-5321891	Fax: 8610-532-1891	Telex: 085 -22388 zamem@public.bta.net.cn
DEMOCRATIC REPUBLIC OF CONGO	54-58, Avenue de L'Ecole, Gombe. B.P. 1144, Kinshasa	Cell: 48456	Fax: 2431-2123151	
	Corner Rues/Lufira, Zone Lubumbashi. B.P.596, Lubumbashi	Tel: 222309		
EGYPT	25 Abdel Monein Riad Sreet, Mohandesein. POBox 253 Dokki. Cairo 12311	TEL: 202-3610281/2/3	Fax: 20-2-361-0833	Telex: 927-2262
ETHIOPIA	Addis Ababa, Old Airport Area Higher 23 Kebele 12, Addis Ababa. P.O. Box 1909	Tel: 251-1-711-302	FAX: 2511-711566	Telex: 976-21065 zam.emb@telecom.net.et
GERMANY	5300 Bonn 2, Bad Godesberg, Mittelstrasse 39	Tel: 49-228-376-811/2/3 49-228-376-813	Fax: 49-228-379-536	Telex: 841-88551 Bosa d zambianbonn@t-online.de
INDIA	New Delhi 110057 F-8/22 Vasant Vihar	Tel: 91~1l~6847681/ 6846848/ 6845862	Fax: 91-11-6147928	zambiand@nde.vsnl.net.in
JAPAN	10-2, Ebarn 1-Chome, Shinagwa-Ku Tokyo 142,	Tel: 813-34910121	Fax: 813-34910123	zamet@crisscross.com

KENYA	Nyerere Road City Hall Annex, Box 48741, Nairobi	Tel: 254-2-724-850 254-2-724-796 254-2-724-799	Fax: 254-2-718-494	zambiacom@swiftkenya.com
MALAWI	Box 30138, Plot 40/2 Capital Hill, Lilongwe 3	Tel: 265-731-911	Fax: 784349	Telex: 988-4181
MOZAMBIQUE	Avenida Kenneth Kaunda, 1286 PO BOX 4655, Maputo.	Tel: 258-1-492-452 491307	Fax: 2581-491893	Telex: 946-6415
NAMIBIA	22 Sam Nujoma Drive CnrMandume Nddemufayo Road. POBox 22882, Windhoek	Tel: 264 61-237610/1 264-61-237611	Fax: 264-61-228-162	Telex: 964-0485
NIGERIA	18 Festival Road, Victoria Island. POBox 6119, Lagos	Tel: 2341-2690426/7	Fax: 2341-2690426	
RUSSIA	Prospect Mira 52 Moscow	Tel: 7-095-288-5001 2885092	Fax: 7-095-975-2056	zambia@online.ru
SOUTH AFRICA	P.O. Box 12234, Pretoria, 1159 Ziervogel St. Arcadia. Off Hamilton St.P.O.BOX 12234 Hartifield 0028	Tel: 27-12-3262223	Fax: 27-012-3262140	
SWEDEN	Stockholm, Engelbrektsgatan 7 Box 26013	Tel: 468-799040	Fax: 468-796850	zamembas@algonet.se
SWITZERLAND	The United Nations Office -Geneva 17-19 Chemin Du Champ-D'anier, Geneva, 1209 Le Petit Saconnex	Tel: 41-22-788-5330 41-22-788-5331 41-22-788-5330/1	Fax: 41-022-788-5340	Telex: 415200
TANZANIA	5 & 8 Ohio/Sokoine Drive P.O. Box 2525 Dar-es-Salaam	Tel:255-27-2621	Fax: 255-112977	zhcd@rah.com
UNITED KINGDOM	2 Palace Gate, Kensington, London W8 5NG	Tel: 44-171-589-6655	Fax: 44-171-581-1353	Telex: 851-263544

UNITED NATIONS	9th Floor, 800 Second Avenue. New York, NY 10017. USA	Tel: 1-212-7581110	Fax: 1-212-7581319	zmbun@undp.org
USA	Washington, D.C. 20008 2419 Massachusetts Avenue N.W.	Tel: 202-265-9717 202-265-9718 202-265-9719	Fax: 202-332-0826	zambia@purple.tmn.com
ZIMBABWE	Box 4698, Zambia House, 48 Union rd, Harare.	Tel: 263 4-773782	Fax: 263 4-776782	Telex: 987-24698

ADVETISING COMPANIES

ADVENTURE	**COMPANY**	**BASE**	**TEL**	**FAX**	**EMAIL**
ABSEILING	Abseil Zambia	Livingstone	Tel: 3-323454	3-324440	theswing@zamnet.zm
BUNJI JUMPING	African Extreme	Livingstone	Tel: 03 324156	Fax: 03 324157	extreme@zamnet.zm
FISHING	Barotseland Fishing Tours	Lusaka	Telefax: 01 222571	Fax: 01 225491	.
	Mutemwa Camp	Lusaka	Tel: 03 3213220	Fax: 03 321320	remote.africa@satmail.bt.com
	Maziba Bay River Safaris.	Sioma, Zambezi River	Mobile: +27 82-3380896 / +27 (0)82-6809876	Tel/Fax: +27(0)15-7810205	zambezia@mweb.co.za
	Maziba Bay River Safaris.	Sioma	00 264 61225762	00 264 61225762	kessler@iafrica.com.na
	Sakazima Island	W. Province	Tel: 2711 4651534	.	.
	Ndole Bay	Lake Tanganyika	Tel: + 27 (0)12 347 2499	Fax: + 27 (0)12 347 4628	sundown@iafrica.com
	Nkamba Bay	Lusaka	Tel: 01 287291	Fax: 01 287677	nkamba@zamnet.zm
MICROLIGHTING HELICOPTERS FIXED WING	Batoka Sky	Livingstone	Tel: 03 320058 cell: +263 11 407573	Fax: 03 323095	reservations@batokasky.co.zm

	Remote Africa Safaris	South Luangwa	Tel: 01 252163	Fax:062 45059	remote.africa @satmail.bt.com
	Maziba Bay River Safaris.	Sioma, Zambezi River	Mobile: +27 82-3380896 / +27 (0)82-6809876	Tel/Fax: +27(0)15-7810205	zambezia@mweb.co.za
HORSE TRAILS	Chundukwa Adventure Trails	Livingstone	Tel: 03 324006	Fax: 03 324452	chunduka@zamnet.zm
	Chaminuka Private Game Reserve	45 mins north of Lusaka	Tel: +260 1 222694 / 225432	Fax: +260 1 222815	chaminuk@aol.com
	Lilayi Game Ranch	Tel: 01 228682	Fax: 01 222906	lilayi@zamsaf.co.zm	
LAKE CAMPING	Cipembere	Siavonga	Tel: 511358	Fax: 511249	.
HOUSEBOATING	Gwembe Safaris	Lake Kariba	Tel: 032 20021	Fax: 032 20054	gwemsaf@zamnet.zm
	Hooligan	Siavonga	Lusaka,262281 /260989	250342 / 44 code 007	.
	Matusadona	Siavonga	Tel: 01 252518 Tel: 01 511358	Fax: 01 252859 Fax: 01 511249	.
CANOEING	African Experience	Lunga River, Kafue NP	Tel: 27 11 888 8015	Fax: 27 11 888 5435	safariafrica@experience.co.za lafex@icon.co.za
	Bundu Adventures	Livingstone, Zambezi	Tel:03 324407	Fax: 03 324406	zambezi@zamnet.zm
	Changa Changa Adventures	Luangwa River	Tel: 290146 Cell: 751302	Fax:295546	rshenton@zamnet.zm
	Chundukwa Adventure Trails:	Livingstone, Zambezi R	Tel: 03 23235	Fax: 03 323224/324006	chunduka@zamnet.zm
	Karibu Safaris	Lower Zambezi River	Tel: +2711 -31-839774	Fax +2711 -31-831957	karibusa@iafrica.com
	Makora Quest	Livingstone, Zambezi	Tel: 03 321679	Fax: 03 320732	quest@zamnet.zm

	Safari Par Excellenc e	Livingstone, Zambezi	Tel: 03 321320	Fax: 03 321320	zambezi@africaonline.co.zw
	Sobek Canoe Adventure s	Zambezi Gorge and Lower Zambezi	Tel: 01 511168	Fax: 01 511168	eagles@zamnet.zm
	Tongabezi	Livingstone, Lower Zambezi	Tel: 03 323235	Fax: 03 323234	tonga@zamnet.zm
	Tafika	Luangwa River	Tel: 03 321320	Fax: 062 45059	remote.africa@satmail.bt.com
RAFTING	Bundu Adventure s	Livingstone	Tel:03 324407	Fax:03 324406	zambezi@zamnet.za
	Maziba Bay River Safaris.	Sioma, Zambezi River	Mobile: +27 82-3380896 / +27 (0)82-6809876	Tel/Fax: +27(0)15-7810205	zambezia@mweb.co.za
	Raft Extreme	Livingstone	Tel: 03 322370	.	.
	Safari Par Excellenc e	Livingstone	Tel: 01 2236741	Fax:01 224915	atd@zamnet.zm
WALKING SAFARIS	Remote Africa Safaris	Mfuwe	Tel/Fax: 260-62-45059	.	remote.africa@satmail.bt.com
	Shiwa Safaris	Lusaka	Tel: 01 228682	Fax 222906	safcom@zamnet.zm
	Chundukwa Adventure Trails:	Livingstone	Tel: 323235	Fax: 323224/324006	chunduka@zamnet.zm
	Robin Pope Safaris	South Luangwa	Tel: 062 45090	Fax: 062 45051	rps@super-hub.com
	Star of Africa	South Luangwa	Tel: (263-9) 41715, 41837	Fax: (263-9) 229909	star_of_africa@telconet.co.zw
SCUBA DIVING	Tanganyika Lodge	Lake Tanganyika	Tel: 224616	Fax:224915	atd@zamnet.zm
	Kalambo Lodge	Lake Tanganyika	Tel:224616	Fax: 224915	atd@zamnet.zm
RIVER BOARDING	Serious Fun	Livingstone	Tel: 260 3 323912	Fax: 321850	.

ZAMBEZI BOAT CRUISES	Bwaato Adventures	Livingstone	Tel: 03 324106	324227	.
	Victoria Falls River Safaris	Livingstone	Tel: +260 3 324115 Cell: +263 11 230655	Fax: +260 3 322083	riversafaris@zamnet.zm
HIKING TRAILS	Changa Changa	Luangwa RIver	Tel:03 324407	Fax: 03 324406	zambezi@zamnet.zm
	Taita Falcon Lodge	Batoka Gorge Victoria Falls	Tel / Fax: 260 3 321850 (office)	Cell: 263 11 208387 (lodge)	taita.falcon@outpost.co.zm
SAFARI EXPEDITIONS	African Horizons	Zambia/Botswana	Tel: 260 3 323432		ahorizon@zamnet.zm
	Africa Original Expeditions	Lusaka	Tel (2601) 265362	Fax: (2601) 261472	anzac@zamnet.zm
	Royal Barotse Safaris	Western Zambia	Tel: +264 (0)61-225949 Cell: +264 81-1241162	Fax: +264 61-225949	barotse@iafrica.com.na
	Zambia Outdoors	All Zambia	Telefax: (0)1179 606494		info@zambiaoutdoors.co.uk

HOTELS

Lusaka and Surrounds

LUSAKA	ADDRESS	TEL / FAX	E- MAIL
CHAINAMA HOTEL	Great East Rd	Tel: 292451/6 Fax: 290809	.
CHAMINUKA	45mins north of Lusaka	Tel: 01 233303/4 Fax: 01 233305	chaminuk@aol.com
PROTEA SAFARI LODGE	Chisamba	Tel: 226589 Fax: 221175	chisamba@zamnet.zm
FRINGILLA GUESTHOUSE	50kms north Lusaka	Tel: 611199	fringill@zamnet.zm
FAIRVIEW HOTEL	Church Rd	Tel: 212954	fairview@zamnet.zm
GARDEN HOUSE HOTEL	Mongu Rd	Tel: 233004/3 Fax: 251734	.

CHRISMAR HOTEL	Los Angeles Boulevard	Tel: 253036 Fax: 253036	chrismar@zamnet.zm.
HILLVIEW HOTEL	Kafue Rd Lusaka	Tel:233250 Fax: 252779	.
HOLIDAY INN	Church Rd	Tel: 251666 Fax: 253529	holinn@zamnet.zm
INTER-CONTINENTAL HOTEL	Haille Selassie Ave.	Tel: 250000/250600 Fax:251880	lusaka@interconti.com
KAFUE ROAD GARDEN HOTEL	.	Tel: 274646 Fax:252779	
LECHWE LODGE	Box 31522	Tel: 222083/84/73, Fax: 222684	kflechwe@zamnet.zm
LILAYI LODGE	Box 30093	Tel: 228682/3, Fax: 222906	lilayi@zamnet.zm
LUSAKA HOTEL	Cairo Rd	Tel: 229049, Fax: 225726	
MUMANA PLEASURE RESORT	10446 Great East Road Box 35530	Tel: 260 1 291860/3 Fax: 260 1 291863	mumana@zamnet.zm
NDEKE HOTEL	Off Los Angeles Blvd. Box 30815.	Tel:251734 Fax: 252779	
NEW LONDE HOTEL		Tel:212061/227966 Fax: 254005.	
PAMODZI HOTEL	Church RdBox 35450	Tel: 254455 Fax: 250995	pamodzi@zamnet.zm
VILLA LODGE GARDENS	Ibex Hill	Tel:260870 Fax: 260870	villa@coppernet.zm
CHISAMBA	ADDRESS	TEL / FAX	E- MAIL/website
IBIS GARDENS		Tel: 01-233766, 05 - 221950, Tel/Fax 01 - 233764.	Ibis@zamnet.zm
PLOUGHMANS ARMS HOTEL	Main Rd.	Tel 10430	

KABWE	ADDRESS	TEL / FAX	E- MAIL
TUSKERS HOTEL		Tel: 222077 222498 Fax: 222076	tuskers@zamnet.zm
Western Zambia			
SOLWEZI	ADDRESS	TEL / FAX	E- MAIL
SAKATANGO HOTEL	Box 110071, Solwezi	Tel: 821224	
MONGU	ADDRESS	TEL / FAX	E- MAIL
LYAMBAYI HOTEL	Box 910193, Mongu	Tel: 221138 Fax: 221138	
NGULU HOTEL	Box: 910308.	Tel: 221028/221258 Fax: 221286	
SIR MWANAWINA MOTEL	Box 53, Mongu	Tel: 22148 Fax: 221856	

NORTHERN ZAMBIA

KASAMA	ADDRESS	TEL / FAX	E- MAIL
KASAMA HOTEL	Main Rd	Tel: 221188	
KWACHA RELAX HOTEL	Box : 410053, Kasama	Tel:221124	
MBALA	ADDRESS	TEL / FAX	E- MAIL
ARMS HOTEL	Box 420161, Mbala	Tel: 450585	
NEW GRASSHOPPER INN	Box 420093, Mbala	Tel: 450589	
MKUSHI	ADDRESS	TEL / FAX	E- MAIL
FOREST INN	Box 810064, Mkushi	Tel/Fax: 362188	r.shenton@zamnet.zm
MPIKA	ADDRESS	TEL / FAX	E- MAIL
CRESTED CRANE HOTEL	Box 450125, Mpika	Tel: 370694	

MPULUNGU	ADDRESS	TEL / FAX	E- MAIL
KALAMBO LODGE	Box 34065 Lusaka	Tel: 235382 Lusaka, Fax: 235381	atd@zamnet.zm
NKUPI LODGE	PB 8, Port Mpulungu	Tel: 455166	
TANGANYIKA LODGE	PB 59 Mpulungu	Tel: 224248, Fax: 224265	atd@zamnet.zm
MISHEMBE	Lake Tanganyika	Tel: 04 221615.	
SHIWA NGANDU	ADDRESS	TEL / FAX	E- MAIL
KAPISHYA HOT SPRINGS SHIWA NG'ANDU	Shiwa Ng'andu Estate	Tel: 01 228682 Fax: 222906	safcom@zamnet.zm
CHIRUNDU	ADDRESS	TEL / FAX	E- MAIL
NAMBADWE MOTEL			
GWABI LODGE	Box 30813	Tel: 250772	gwabi@zamnet.zm
KANYEMBA LODGE	Box 30815, Lusaka	Tel: 252779	

SOUTHERN ZAMBIA

CHOMA	ADDRESS	TEL / FAX	E- MAIL
CHOMA HOTEL	Box 630805, Choma	Tel: 20189	
MAMBUSHI CHALETS	Gwembe Safaris Box 630162, Choma	Tel:20021 Fax: 20054	gwemsaf@zamnet.zm
KALOMO	ADDRESS	TEL / FAX	E- MAIL
KALOMO HOTEL	Box 620110	Tel: 65188	
MAZABUKA	ADDRESS	TEL / FAX	E- MAIL
MAZABUKA GARDEN HOTEL	Box 30815	Tel: 251734	

LIVINGSTONEand VICTORIA FALLS	ADDRESS	TEL / FAX	E- MAIL
KUBU CABINS	PO Box 60748, Livingstone	Tel: 324093, Fax: 324091	
LIVINGSTONE ISLAND TENTED CAMP	PB 286x, Ridgeway, Lusaka	Tel: 2601 265814 Fax: 2601 262291	tim@chilongozi.com
MUKOLO ISLAND TENTED CAMP	PB 286x, Ridgeway, Lusaka	Tel: 2601 265814 Fax: 2601 262291	tim@chilongozi.com
NGOLIDE LODGE	P.O. Box 60186 Livingstone	Tel: 3 321091/2 Fax: 3 321113 Cell: 00 263 11 406712	ngolide@zamnet.zm
MAWALA LODGE	P.O.Box 60273, Lvingstone	Fax: 260-3-324455, Tel: 260-3-321935 Cell 263-11-213720 / 263-11-724711	mawala@zamnet.zm
TAITA FALCON LODGE	Livingstone	Tel:03321850	taita-falcon@zamnet.zm
THE ROYAL LIVINGSTONE	Sun International S.A.	Tel: 2711 780-7878 Fax: 2711 780-7061	fitres@sunint.co.za
TONGABEZI LODGE	P Bag 31Livingstone	Tel: 323235, Fax: 3232242	tonga@zamnet.zm
WASAWANGE LODGE	Box 60278 Livingstone	Tel: 260-332-4066, Fax: 260-332-4067	lisbwa@zamnet.zm
ZAMBEZI RIVER TREE LODGE	Chundukwa Adventure Trails	Tel: 324452 Fax: 324006	chunduka@zamnet.zm
ZAMBEZI ROYAL CHUNDU LODGE	Box: 60889	Tel: 321772 Johannesburg: (2711)Tel: 9533224	chundu@icon.co.za

ZAMBEZI SUN	Sun International S.A.	Tel: 2711 780-7878 Fax: 2711 780-7061	fitres@sunint.co.za
MUTEMWA CAMP Upper Zambezi	50 km from the border at Katima Mulilo	Tel: +27 (0)11 888 2431 Fax: +27 (0)11 888 5798	mutemwa.lodge@mweb.co.za
MONZE	ADDRESS	TEL / FAX	E- MAIL
MONZE HOTEL	Box 660267, Monze	Tel: 50089	
SIAVONGA	ADDRESS	TEL / FAX	E- MAIL
EAGLES REST CHALETS	Box 1, Siavonga	Tel/fax: 01 511168	eagles@zamnet.zm
LAKE KARIBA INN	Box 117, Siavonga Box 33565 Lusaka	Tel: 511269/249 Fax: 511188	Tel: 01 253768 Fax: 01 252518
LEISURE BAY LODGE	Box 68 Siavonga	Tel: 01 511135/6 or Lusaka: 01 252779	
MANCHINCHI BAY LODGE	Box 115, Siavonga	Tel: 511299/399	
LAKE SAFARI LODGE	Box 30, Siavonga	Tel: 511148 / 511200 Fax: 511103	
LAKE KARIBA			
CHETE ISLAND LODGE	UTC:	Tel: 260-32-324413, 321122,321210	westisl@id.co.zw
CHIKANKA ISLAND CAMPS	Gwembe Safaris Box 630162, Choma	Tel:20021 Fax: 20054	gwemsaf@zamnet.zm

RESTAURANTS

Hotel Restaurants

Holiday Inn	Garden Grill	Famous for great breakfasts and buffet feasts.
	Golden Spur	Best salad bar in town, varied menu for the whole family
	McGinty's	Pub meals and atmosphere in Irish tradition
Inter-Continental	Savannah Grill	Best international and Zambian Cuisine (open March 2001)
	Olive Grove	Mediterranean Restaurant (open March 2001)
	Safari Bar	Cosy meeting place for drinks and cocktails (open March 2001)
	Makumbi	Great view, stylish a la carte menu and resident band. Speciality nights Monday - Italian, Friday - African Drums.
Pamodzi	Jacaranda	
	Rendezvous	
Lilayi Lodge	Lodge Restaurant	The most beautiful setting, adventurous buffet selection

Chinese Restaurants	
The Continental	
The Giant Dragon	
Memories of China	
Sichuan	Family run restaurant with a great selection of authentic dishes to feast on
Indian Restaurants	
Arabian Nights	The menu, decor and costumed staff are a pleasant escape from the norm
Danny's	An extensive menu of Indian dishes, as well as good steaks.
Dil	Buffet or a la carte meals prepared by the resident Indian chef
Shenai	A very popular venue for great indian food, a la carte
European Cuisine	
Cosmo Club	
Fra Gigi	Italian home cooking prepared by imported italian chef.
Hibiscus	A very professional staff serving beautifully prepared and presented food

Marco Polo	Attention to detail and presentation of fine food make this a must do venue
Miscellaneous	
Chantal's	
Chit Chat	Currently one of Lusaka's most popular lunch time hang out's Great menu, good food, great outdoor setting.
Club	
Golden Bull	Seafood and steaks
Jaylin	Creole menu and the best pepper steak in the world
Le Coulis D'Or	
Mr Pete's	Famous for their spare ribs and nightclub.
Pizza Island	Halaal pizza's, schwarma's and grilled chicken to sit down or take away
Spitfire Grill	Outdoor grill, bar, music, casino and chinese restaurant to choose from
Pubs	
Browns	Colourful spacious pub with music, and live bands on occasion
Chasers	Great pub meals and cocktails with a friendly efficient staff
Eureka	Popular meeting place, poole table, dart board and a legionary barman
Safari Bar Inter-Continental Hotel	Cosy meeting place for drinks and cocktails (open March 2001)
Soul Provider	One of Lusaka's best kept secrets, very relaxed venue with music
Night Clubs / Music Venues	
8000 RPM	Techno night club, gets going after 11pm
Black Velvet	Night club
Browns	Pub
Cafe D'Afrique	Delcious food and excellent cultural entertainment Every night from 8-20 September. Otherwise Thurs-Fri - Saturdays.
Chantals	
Chez n' Temba	Rumba club

Cosmopolitan	Night club
Jungle	Night club
Mike's Car Wash	Rumba club
Mr Pete's	Night club
Polo Grill	Live music weekends
Coffee Shops	
Cafe' d'Afrique	Coffee and cake, great lunches and cultural evenings with traditional food
Chit Chat	Coffee, teas and cake, great lunches, playground for kids
El Toro	Great lunches and gateaux prepared daily by Rosita, stay or take away
La Patisserie	Cupaccino, espresso, fresh cakes, bread and savouries and sandwichesl
Rhythms Cafe Inter-Continental Hotel	Wide range of speciality coffees and cocktails
Tit Bits	
Twembe	Italian pizza and pasta, pies and coffees served at outside tables or to go
Take Aways	
CHEF'S HOUSE	
EL TORO	Order in advance from full meals to burgers and samoosa's.
FOOD FAYRE	Regular fastfoods
LAFASTFOODS	Chinese, ice-cream, burgers
MERRYLAND	All sorts of stuff
TONTOS	Chicken menu's
LA PATISSERIE	Baked on the premises, bread, cakes, croissants, plus a variety of lunches
PIZZA PIZZA PIZZA	Pizza's, chinese food, and grilled chicken to take home
NANDO'S	Chicken the Portuguese way, chicken burgers, pitta breads, salads et al
TWEMBE	Pizza and pasta, rolls, pies, beer and more

STRATEGIC STATISTICS

Monthly Inflation (%)	4.2
Year to date inflation (%)	16
Exchange Rates: K/US\$ K/GBP K/SAR	 1,313.29 2,193.94 288.58
Interest Rates (%)	45
Treasury Bill Rates: 28 days 91 days 182 days	 19.6 26.3 25.8
Gross Domestic Product (USD)	1,345,000
GDP Per Capita (USD)	245.00
Total population	9,00,000
Population growth rate(%)	3.5
GDP Growth rate(%) (1997)	2.8

THE CROSS-BORDER INITIATIVE IN EASTERN AND SOUTHERN AFRICA

EXECUTIVE SUMMARY

The Cross-Border Initiative (CBI) comprises a common policy framework developed by fourteen participating countries in Eastern and Southern Africa and the Indian Ocean, with the support of four co-sponsors; the International Monetary Fund, the World Bank, the European Union, and the African Development Bank. The participants are Burundi, Comoros, Kenya, Madagascar, Malawi, Mauritius, Namibia, Rwanda, Seychelles, Swaziland, Tanzania, Uganda, Zambia, and Zimbabwe; Mozambique has also indicated its intention to join. The policy framework aims to facilitate cross-border economic activity by eliminating barriers to the flow of goods, services, labor, and capital, and to help integrate markets by coordinating reform programs in several key structural areas, supported by appropriate macroeconomic policies. The initiative places the responsibility for determining how to implement the agreed policy measures at the national level.

The **four key elements of the Initiative** are:

- liberalizing foreign exchange systems by eliminating restrictions on current account transactions and certain capital transactions, and establishing unified interbank spot foreign exchange markets;
- dismantling nontariff barriers on imports and exports, eliminating tariffs on trade between CBI participants, and lowering tariffs on a nonpreferential (MFN) basis to agreed or lower levels;

- strengthening domestic financial markets by, inter alia, improving prudential and supervisory capacity of central banks; and
- simplifying and liberalizing investment procedures.

The purpose of this paper is to take stock of the achievements under the CBI in each of the four areas mentioned above. The paper takes into account recent developments through end-December 1998. Regarding the **liberalization of foreign exchange systems**, most countries had removed restrictions on current account transactions by end-1998. In addition, a handful of countries liberalized substantially capital account transactions while the remaining countries took partial steps to ease such controls, including those affecting equity investments among the participating countries. On the **exchange rate regime**, most countries met the CBI objective of introducing a flexible exchange rate system within the context of a unified inter-bank foreign exchange market.

On **trade liberalization and facilitation**, significant but uneven progress was achieved. Many of the participating countries made substantial progress toward meeting the CBI targets on tariffs. Although, none of the countries fully eliminated intraregional tariffs, virtually all countries implemented preference margins for other CBI participants ranging between 60—80 percent. Progress on MFN liberalization was mixed; (i) three countries met the target of lowering the maximum tariff rate to 20—25 percent; (ii) six countries met the target of reducing the number of nonzero tariff bands to no more than three; and (iii) three countries where data are available, met the target of reducing their weighted average tariff rates to no more than 15 percent. Nevertheless, tariff exemptions remained widespread, including for imports by governments, parastatals, nongovernmental organizations, and for goods related to foreign-financed projects and those under the various investment codes. The pace of trade reform reflected, in part, concerns on the potential adverse impact on fiscal revenue.

Notable progress was achieved in reducing **nontariff barriers** to imports. Most countries eliminated import quotas and bans, as well as import licensing requirements. Moreover, the monopoly power previously exercised by state marketing boards or state controlled enterprises in regard to exporting, importing, and price setting was significantly reduced in most of the countries. Although export duties and export marketing monopolies remained in place in about half the countries, only a few countries continued to maintain export restrictions. Finally, substantial progress was also achieved in some key areas of **trade facilitation**, including implementing the harmonization of road transit charges, and the introduction of the Road Customs Transit Document and of a single goods customs declaration form.

Good progress was made in reforming the **domestic financial sectors to** improve their efficiency. Most countries moved to the use of indirect monetary instruments to control monetary aggregates, and administered interest rates were phased out and replaced with market-based mechanisms. Increased attention was devoted to strengthening the powers of central banks to enforce prudential regulations and to provide autonomy in conducting monetary policy. All CBI countries had either adopted or were in the process of adopting Basle capital adequacy standards, and several countries required that the capital ratio be above the minimum 8 percent of risk-weighted assets. In addition, most of the countries had prudential limits on connected/single borrower transactions, as well as on single/aggregate foreign exchange exposures. There was a substantial increase in the number of banks in some countries, including a significant presence of foreign owned banks, but in other countries, the degree of competition in financial markets was still limited to a few operators.

Progress was made in the area of **investment deregulation**. There was substantial simplification of approval procedures (particularly through the establishment of a one-stop investment approval authority). The publication of investment codes was completed by ten participants, and substantive progress made in the remaining countries. However, with the exception of a few countries, most of the investment codes included some form of tariff exemptions. There was slow

For additional analytical, business and investment opportunities information, please contact Global Investment & Business Center, USA at (202) 546-2103. Fax: (202) 546-3275. E-mail: rusric@erols.com

progress in concluding double taxation agreements, in the cross-listing of stocks, and in **facilitating labor mobility** (visa protocol, residence/work permits, and short-term entry permits).

I. INTRODUCTION

1. As described in earlier papers[1], the Cross-Border Initiative (CBI) comprises a common policy framework developed by fourteen participating countries in Eastern and Southern Africa and the Indian Ocean[2], with the support of four co-sponsors—the Fund, the World Bank, the European Union (EU), and the African Development Bank. The policy framework aims to facilitate cross-border activity by eliminating barriers to cross-border flows of goods, services, labor, and capital, as well as to integrate markets through a coordination of reform programs in the areas of trade, exchange systems, domestic banking and payment systems, and investment regulations, supported by appropriate macroeconomic policies. The CBI has avoided the creation of new institutions, placing responsibility at the national level for the design and implementation of measures to support the agreed policy framework.

2. To this end, a set of "core" measures were articulated in a Concept Paper[3], which was adopted at the First CBI Ministerial Meeting in Uganda in August 1993 (Box 1). A Second Ministerial Meeting, held in Mauritius in March 1995, endorsed a "Road Map" for further trade liberalization that included the elimination of tariffs on intraregional trade and the convergence of external tariffs to a trade-weighted average of 15 percent, both by October 1998. At the Third Ministerial Meeting, held in Zimbabwe in February 1998, the participating countries decided to continue and broaden the CBI, and agreed that the future focus should emphasize investment facilitation issues, and the harmonization of national and regional policies toward a conducive environment for efficient investment and trade flows. [4]

3. Under the CBI, each participating country was expected to: (i) create a Technical Working Group (TWG) comprised of representatives of the public and private sectors that would identify and report on the main impediments to the cross-border activities outlined in the Box, and would suggest a common program of action to be implemented at the national level; (ii) establish a Policy Implementation Committee (PIC), comprised of officials with the authority to design and implement a specific program of policy measures[5]; and (iii) complete a Letter of CBI Policy (LCBIP) specifying the steps that the country would take to implement the various measures, including regulatory changes and a timetable which would be endorsed by the co-sponsors. [6]

4. As one of the co-sponsors, the Fund's role was to ensure that each LCBIP was consistent with progress toward a stable macroeconomic framework. The CBI objectives and the schedule of implementation of the various measures have been featured in staff discussions in the context of Article IV consultations and use of Fund resources, and have been taken into account in considering technical assistance requests. For countries undertaking structural adjustment in the context of Fund-supported programs, actions included in the LCBIPs have been built in, and coordinated with, the adjustment program. The CBI has also been featured in staff discussions with nonparticipating countries to apprise them of emerging policy trends with wider implications.

5. The purpose of this paper is to take stock of the achievements of the CBI since its inception in 1993. It is, of course, important to mention that measures in areas such as improving financial intermediation were underway before the CBI began and were undertaken for domestic reasons rather than considerations regarding regional cooperation and harmonization. Section II describes progress in implementing the measures specified in the four areas of the CBI policy framework as of December 1998—foreign exchange systems, trade regimes, domestic banking and payments systems, and investment regulations. Finally, Section III discusses the remaining agenda and the issues to be addressed.

Box. Key Elements of the CBI Framework

For additional analytical, business and investment opportunities information,
please contact Global Investment & Business Center, USA
at (202) 546-2103. Fax: (202) 546-3275. E-mail: rusric@erols.com

Exchange Systems

- Complete elimination of restrictions on current account transactions, and relaxation of restrictions for some capital transactions to liberalize direct investment and investment in regional equity markets.
- Establish unified interbank spot-foreign exchange markets by 1996.

Trade Liberalization and Facilitation

- Dismantle nontariff import barriers on a most-favored-nation (MFN) basis. Short negative lists for reasons of health and security could be retained. Where immediate elimination is not feasible, participants should agree with the Fund on a schedule for their removal, normally within one year.
- Eliminate all quantitative restrictions on exports to all countries, except for a short negative list.
- Eliminate tariffs on intraregional trade by October 1998 for products originating in the CBI area.
- Aim at a harmonized external tariff with no more than three nonzero bands, a maximum rate of 20—25 percent, and a weighted average rate of 15 percent by October 1998.
- Implement harmonized transit charges and introduce: a road customs transit document, a single goods declaration document, and a bond guarantee scheme.

Domestic Banking and Payments Systems

- Strengthen regulatory and prudential functions of central banks and domestic financial markets.
- Eliminate impediments to entry by regional and extraregional financial institutions, and enable specialized financial institutions—including offshore banking facilities—to participate in providing equity and export credit facilities.

Investment Regulations

- Simplify and liberalize investment approval procedures; consolidate investment codes and all regulations into a single published document.
- Establish one-stop investment centers to process investment applications within 45—60 days, with automatic approval in the absence of valid objections.
- Process residence and employment permits within four weeks; relax or eliminate visas on a reciprocal basis; allow freer movement in border areas.
- Authorize stock exchanges to list and trade equities from other stock

For additional analytical, business and investment opportunities information, please contact Global Investment & Business Center, USA at (202) 546-2103. Fax: (202) 546-3275. E-mail: rusric@erols.com

exchanges in the region.

II. POLICY IMPLEMENTATION AND ISSUES

A. Liberalization of Foreign Exchange Systems

Developments

6. Under the CBI framework, participants are expected to eliminate exchange restrictions on current account transactions in a nondiscriminatory manner and to relax certain types of capital transactions. The liberalization of the capital account referred principally to transactions associated with long-term, non-debt-creating, foreign direct investments (FDI) rather than to short-term capital. The main focus of the reform was to improve the regulatory environment for investments, both domestic and foreign; progressively harmonize investment incentives; and encourage investment in regional equity markets (see Section D below). In light of the fragility of the domestic financial system (elements of which were to be addressed within the Initiative; see Section C), the liberalization of short-term capital inflows was not perceived to be a priority. In regard to foreign exchange markets, the objective was to establish unified, interbank spot-exchange *markets* no later than 1996. Such markets would, in turn, set the stage for more diversified operations, including forward cover, and liberalization of foreign currency accounts.

7. With regard to the removal of exchange restrictions on current account transactions, 12 of the 14 CBI countries have accepted the obligations under Article VIII, sections 2, 3, and 4 as of December 1998 (compared with only two in 1993) (Table 1)[7]. Regarding the capital account, Kenya, Malawi, Mauritius, Uganda, and Zambia have substantially liberalized capital account transactions, while Comoros and Madagascar have taken steps to ease controls, including on the repatriation of portfolio outflows. Tanzania and Zimbabwe also took steps in the latter regard.

8. Exchange arrangements vary widely, with 9 participating countries maintaining a floating exchange rate system in the context of unified interbank exchange markets (Tables 2 and 3)[8]. Controls on foreign currency accounts for residents and foreign entities have been lifted, with the exception of Burundi, Comoros, Namibia, Seychelles, Swaziland, and Zimbabwe. Finally, although some progress has been made over the last three years in easing foreign exchange repatriation and surrender requirements, most countries continue to impose such controls (Table 4). Competition in foreign exchange markets has also been enhanced with the licensing of nonbank foreign exchange bureaus in nine countries. Forward cover through commercial banks and other authorized dealers is available in nine countries. In addition, Kenya, Tanzania, and Uganda (the East African Cooperation (EAC) countries) have agreed that their respective currencies be fully accepted within the EAC countries, and that the currencies be quoted by banks and foreign exchange bureaus.

B. Trade Liberalization and Facilitation

Developments

9. The CBI framework called for a coordinated and time-bound reduction of trade barriers at the regional level, and with third countries on an MFN basis. The specifics of the trade reform agenda and the timetable for implementation included: (i) effective October 1995, increasing from 60 percent to 70 percent the intraregional tariff preference for countries that had not yet done so; (ii) elimination of tariffs on intraregional trade by October 1998, with an increase in the preference rate to 80 percent by October 1996 and to 90 percent by 1997; and (iii) a harmonized external tariff to be adopted by October 1998 consisting of no more than three nonzero bands, a trade weighted average tariff rate of no more than 15 percent, and a maximum rate of 20—25 percent[9]. With regard to nontariff barriers (NTBs), countries were expected to dismantle import licensing

For additional analytical, business and investment opportunities information,
please contact Global Investment & Business Center, USA
at (202) 546-2103. Fax: (202) 546-3275. E-mail: rusric@erols.com

requirements and similar NTBs on an MFN basis, except for a short "negative list" for noneconomic reasons such as security, health, and environment. Quantitative restrictions on exports to all countries were to be eliminated, except for a small negative list for the same noneconomic reasons.

10. By end-December 1998, many of the participating CBI countries had either met or made substantial progress toward meeting CBI targets for trade liberalization (Tables 5 and 6). Significant progress on tariff reduction on intraregional trade was achieved. Although, none of the countries met the target for eliminating intraregional tariffs by end-December 1998, Kenya, Madagascar, Tanzania, Uganda, and Zimbabwe, had implemented an 80 percent preference margin, while Burundi, Comoros, Malawi, Mauritius, Rwanda, and Zambia had increased the preference margin to 60—70 percent. Moreover, Kenya, Tanzania, and Uganda have indicated a desire to accelerate tariff reductions on trade between them, in the context of the EAC Agreement. Namibia and Swaziland could not change their preference margins because they are members of the Southern African Customs Union (SACU). Seychelles has not made any progress on increasing the preference margin.

11. Regarding the reduction of the maximum tariff rate, Kenya, Uganda, and Zambia met the CBI target of 20—25 percent by end-December 1998 [10]. In addition, Madagascar, Malawi, and Tanzania reduced their maximum rates to 30 percent, while Comoros and Rwanda lowered theirs to 40 percent. Although some reductions have taken place in the remaining six countries, the maximum rates remain high in Mauritius, Namibia, and Swaziland (in the range of 70—80 percent); and substantially higher in Burundi and Zimbabwe (100 percent), and Seychelles (200 percent).

12. Comoros, Kenya, Madagascar, Rwanda, Uganda, and Zambia met the target of reducing the number of nonzero bands to no more than three, by end-December 1998—Uganda's two tariff bands went beyond the target. Burundi, Malawi, and Tanzania had 4—5 tariff bands, and the least amount of progress was recorded in the cases of Mauritius, Seychelles, and Zimbabwe with 8, 9, and 17 bands, respectively, and the SACU countries which continued to have multiple tariff bands.

13. Information on the weighted average tariff rate is not available for all countries. Among the countries with such information, the CBI target of an average tariff rate of no more than 15 percent was met with substantial margins in Kenya, Uganda, and Zambia. Using the more widely available unweighted average tariff rate, six countries (Malawi, Namibia, Rwanda, Swaziland, Uganda, and Zambia) have averages that are either around or below 15 percent. Kenya and Madagascar had unweighted average rates of about 18 percent, and the rest of the countries had unweighted average rates ranging from 21.8 percent (Tanzania) to 35 percent (Burundi). Limited progress was made in reducing other duties and charges (ODCs) and in amalgamating them into the basic tariff structure, mainly because of revenue concerns. Malawi, Seychelles, Tanzania, and Zambia met the CBI objective, while Burundi, Comoros, Namibia, Rwanda, Uganda, and Zimbabwe had ODCs below 15 percent, and Madagascar and Mauritius had ODCs of up to 40 percent and 400 percent, respectively.

14. Although notable progress was achieved in reducing import NTBs, particularly those related to bans, quotas, and licensing requirements, the record on dismantling state monopolies and eliminating discriminatory taxes and reducing tariff exemptions has been mixed (Table 7 and 8). The CBI countries have eliminated all import quotas and bans, with the exception of Namibia (which has quotas for imports of used cars and clothing, and seasonal bans on some agricultural products), Uganda (which has a ban on cigarettes that is expected to be eliminated by July 1999), Seychelles (which has semiannual quotas on all imports) and Swaziland (which maintains seasonal bans on some agricultural products). Import licensing requirements have been eliminated in most CBI countries, with the exception of Namibia, Seychelles, and Zimbabwe. The monopoly power previously exercised by state marketing boards or state controlled enterprises

For additional analytical, business and investment opportunities information, please contact Global Investment & Business Center, USA at (202) 546-2103. Fax: (202) 546-3275. E-mail: rusric@erols.com

with regard to exporting, importing, and price setting was significantly reduced in all countries with the exception of Comoros, Mauritius, Namibia, Seychelles, Swaziland, and Tanzania. Similarly, progress was mixed in eliminating discriminatory higher rates of excise duty and/or value-added tax on certain imports which remain in half of the CBI countries (Burundi, Kenya, Mauritius, Seychelles, Tanzania, Uganda, and Zambia). Tariff exemptions remain widespread, including for imports by governments, parastatals, nongovernmental organizations, and for goods related to foreign-financed projects and those under the various investment codes.

15. Substantial progress was achieved in reducing impediments to exports (Table 9). By end-December 1998, only Zambia and Zimbabwe maintained export bans and quotas, respectively, while export licenses were required in only three countries (Kenya, Namibia, and Zimbabwe). Export duties remained in place in Burundi, Comoros, Rwanda, Swaziland, Tanzania, and Zimbabwe, while Burundi, Namibia, Seychelles, Swaziland, and Zimbabwe still maintained marketing monopolies.

16. Substantial progress was achieved in some key areas of trade facilitation. With the exception of the SACU countries (Namibia and Swaziland) and the island economies, the rest of the CBI countries implemented the harmonization of road transit charges, and introduced the Road Customs Transit Document (Table 10)[11]. In addition, a single goods customs declaration form was introduced by most countries, except in Burundi, Malawi, and Rwanda, where information is not available. In contrast, however, no country had yet introduced a bond guarantee scheme by the end of the CBI period.

Assessment of progress

17. The extent of trade liberalization achieved in the CBI countries can be assessed using an index of aggregate trade policy restrictiveness.[12] Under the CBI, considerable progress has been made in trade reforms, mainly in the context of adjustment programs supported by the Fund and the World Bank. Five countries moved to open trade regimes, compared to zero at the inception of the initiative; another three countries had moderately restrictive trade regimes, the same number as at the beginning of the initiative; and the remaining six countries continued to have relatively restrictive trade regimes (Figure 1 and Table 11).

18. Based on the index, the most ambitious reformers were Kenya, Madagascar, Malawi, Rwanda, Uganda, and Zambia, as they reduced their restrictiveness ratings by 4—5 points and achieved open trade regimes (except Kenya which moved from the restrictive to the moderate category). In contrast, Burundi, Comoros, Seychelles, and Zimbabwe made no progress in trade liberalization; moreover, Seychelles and Zimbabwe continued to have a rating of "10" on the index.

19. As a group, the CBI countries reduced their rating on the index by an average of 2.4 points compared to 1.7 for a select group of non-CBI African countries.[13] As a result, although the CBI countries had more restrictive trade regimes at the beginning of the Initiative, by end-1998 their trade regimes were, on average, less restrictive (5.9) than those of the select group of non-CBI countries (6.2). However, the CBI countries still remain, on average, markedly more restrictive than countries in other regions. While 43 percent of the CBI countries would be classified as having highly restrictive trade regimes, only 17 percent of the economies of the rest of world (excluding non-CBI African countries) would be classified as highly restrictive (Figure 2). Similarly, only 36 percent of the CBI countries would be classified as open compared with 52 percent for the rest of the world. Of course, the rating for the rest of world masks a wide dispersion among the various regions of the world, with industrialized countries as a group having the lowest rating of 4 and the Middle Eastern countries having the highest rating of 5.5, compared with 5.9 for CBI countries.[14] It is important to note that good practice countries (Chile, Colombia, New Zealand, and Singapore) have a rating of 1.5, and that Uganda and Zambia, with ratings of 2, are very near this level.

For additional analytical, business and investment opportunities information, please contact Global Investment & Business Center, USA at (202) 546-2103. Fax: (202) 546-3275. E-mail: rusric@erols.com

Factors influencing achievement of CBI trade reform objectives

20. Several reasons have been cited for the delay in implementing trade policy reforms. These included: civil unrest (Burundi, Comoros and Rwanda); the concern about potential adverse impact of trade reform on government revenues (Comoros, Tanzania and Zimbabwe) and hence on macroeconomic stability; and membership in other regional trading arrangements (RTAs). The fiscal impact of trade reform depends on the nature of the reforms introduced and the specific circumstances of the country.[15] In order to offset any possible adverse effect on revenues, the reduction in tariffs should be accompanied by a tariffication of NTBs on imports and exports, and the elimination of tariff exemptions. However, even in those circumstances where trade liberalization might lead to a short-term loss in revenues, the appropriate response should be to adopt offsetting measures—if on the revenue side preferably by less-distorting and more broad-based taxes that are applied equally to both imports and domestic production.

21. The excessive number of RTAs which the CBI countries are members may indeed have interfered with the pace of trade liberalization. As shown in Figure 3 and Table 12, the CBI countries are members of five different RTAs: the Common Market for Eastern and Southern Africa (COMESA), EAC, IOC, SACU, and the Southern Africa Development Community (SADC). These countries are faced with conflicting obligations, different and uncoordinated strategies, inconsistent external liberalization goals, and different and conflicting rules and administrative procedures. For example, under the COMESA Treaty, 80 percent preferences were to have been provided by the member states to each other by 1998 and 100 percent by 2000. In contrast, under the more accelerated CBI framework, the complete elimination of intra-CBI tariffs was envisaged to take place by end-October 1998. As for the SADC, intraregional preferences are also envisaged, but over eight years beginning in 2000.

C. Reform of the Domestic Financial Sector

Developments

22. The development of a sound financial sector and efficient payment systems are viewed as essential for increasing cross-border flows and market access. To ensure the soundness of financial institutions, the CBI framework called for intensified efforts to improve prudential and supervisory capacity of central banks so as to encourage development of the commercial banking sector and other financial institutions, and to strengthen the domestic payments system. Additional measures included developing foreign trade financing instruments and establishing correspondent banking relationships within the region.

23. At the commencement of the Initiative, virtually all CBI countries relied on bank-by-bank credit ceilings and administered interest rates as key instruments of monetary policy. Government interference was prevalent, through directed credit allocations, heavy borrowing from central banks to finance large fiscal deficits, and maintenance of negative real interest rates. With respect to the institutional structure, a proper legal framework for the independence of central banks was largely absent, entry by domestic and foreign commercial banks was restricted and led to concentrated ownership structures, and regulation and supervision were inadequate to ensure the soundness of financial institutions.

24. Despite the variety of problems, there has been good progress in improving the efficiency of the financial system. In the banking system, direct monetary instruments in the form of individual bank credit ceilings and selective credit controls have been phased out in all countries except Comoros; most countries now use indirect monetary instruments such as open market operations, changes in liquidity requirements, and standing discount facilities (Table 13).[16] Administered interest rates have been phased out and replaced with market-based mechanisms in almost all countries except Comoros and Seychelles.[17]

For additional analytical, business and investment opportunities information, please contact Global Investment & Business Center, USA at (202) 546-2103. Fax: (202) 546-3275. E-mail: rusric@erols.com

25. Financial market developments can also be gauged by the presence of active primary and secondary markets for public debt instruments, an interbank money market, and a stock exchange. Most CBI countries, with the exception of Comoros, Rwanda, and possibly Burundi have fairly active primary markets for government and central bank securities with weekly auctions, and/or tap sales between auctions. The existence of secondary markets is more limited, with active markets being present only in Kenya, Malawi, Zambia, and Zimbabwe. Secondary markets have been slow to develop, owing in part to the existence of high liquidity requirements, the lack of infrastructure and capacity, as well as lingering doubts about the soundness of some banks. The latter factor has confined active interbank markets to Kenya, Malawi, Mauritius, Namibia, Zambia, and Zimbabwe. Stock exchanges exist in several countries, but it could be argued that only the stock exchanges in Kenya, Namibia, Zambia, and Zimbabwe are relatively active.

26. Attention has also been devoted to central banks' powers to enforce prudential regulations. To this end, legislation was enacted or revised during 1993—98 in Madagascar, Namibia, Seychelles, Swaziland, Uganda, and Zambia (Table 14). In Comoros and Zimbabwe, the supervisory and regulatory role continues to be shared by the government and the central bank. In principle, central banks have full autonomy in most countries, except in Comoros, Kenya, Tanzania, and Zambia, where autonomy is partial.[18]

27. Roughly half the CBI countries have either fully or substantially implemented financial sector reform programs. An evaluation of the development of foreign trade instruments and the removal of impediments to entry indicate that considerable progress has also been achieved in the majority of countries. The increased focus on financial sector reform issues has also coincided with an expansion of financial markets in most of the countries. Thus, the number of commercial banks has increased to more than 50 in Kenya; 21 in Zambia; 20 in Uganda and 18 in Tanzania. At the same time, all countries with the exception of Comoros and Malawi have foreign banks operating in their countries; and Kenya, Malawi, Tanzania, and Uganda have taken measures to reduce government ownership or privatize state-owned banks and to review existing licensing procedures before licensing additional new banks. The payment system appears to be satisfactory in ten of the participating countries although efficiency is high in only a few (Mauritius, Namibia, and Swaziland).

Assessment of progress

28. Despite recent progress in several areas, the degree of competition in financial markets in a number of countries remains limited to a few operators, and there is only a thin supply of financial instruments. The market for treasury and central bank bills remains narrow in most of the participating countries, to the extent that the frequent reason attributed to the lack of secondary markets in public debt is the absence of a sufficient amount of outstanding public paper. In this context, changes in reserve and liquidity ratios have been extensively used as the preferred monetary instrument. Such uses (together with the high level of nonperforming loans) are often cited as contributing to the wide spreads between deposit and lending rates.

29. Supervisory practices have improved significantly in most of the CBI countries. All CBI countries have either adopted or are in the process of adopting the Basle standard for capital adequacy requirement of 8 percent; and in several countries the capital ratio is above the minimum requirement. Most of the countries have prudential limits on connected/single borrower transactions, as well as on single/aggregate foreign exchange exposures.

D. Reform of Investment Regulations

30. Another major objective of the CBI involved reforming the regulatory environment for direct investments, and the progressive harmonization of the structure of investment incentives. In regard to the regulatory environment, participating countries agreed to simplify and codify all

For additional analytical, business and investment opportunities information, please contact Global Investment & Business Center, USA at (202) 546-2103. Fax: (202) 546-3275. E-mail: rusric@erols.com

investment-related regulatory provisions into a single published document that would be widely available; establish one-stop investment centers that would process all applications between 45 days and 60 days; and grant automatic approval in the absence of objections at the end of that period. Other specific measures called for participants to conclude avoidance of double taxation agreements on a bilateral basis; authorize the cross-listing of stocks from other exchanges in the region; and expedite the processing of residence and work permits, and relax visa requirements for investors. In addition, participating countries were expected to become members of the Multilateral Investment Guarantee Agency, and where necessary, of bilateral investment guarantee agencies such as Overseas Private Investment Corporation. The ratification of a suitable amended form of the Multilateral Industrial Enterprise Charter was also encouraged.[19]

31. Overall progress in the area of investment deregulation has been mixed. There has been almost full liberalization of approval procedures (in particular establishing a one-stop investment approval authority), and the publication of investment codes has been completed by 10 participants, and the remaining countries have made substantive progress (Table 15). However, with the exception of a few countries, most of the investment codes include tariff exemptions. With regard to the statute of limitation, only 6 participants have fully implemented it. There has also been slow progress with regard to double taxation agreements and cross-listing of stocks.

32. Overall progress in regard to the facilitation of labor market issues (visa protocol, residence/work permits, and short-term entry permits) has also been mixed. Most of the non-island economies have taken action on short-term entry permits for border residents, while the EAC countries—Kenya, Tanzania, and Uganda—no longer require visas for their citizens to travel between their countries. There has been little progress in the processing of residence and work permits except for Kenya, Namibia, Tanzania, Uganda, and Zambia.

III. THE REMAINING AGENDA

33. In the context of a gradual return to macroeconomic stability, good progress has been achieved in most of the CBI countries in the liberalization of exchange systems over the last few years. This is reflected in the widespread elimination of restrictions on external current transactions, the shift towards market-based exchange rates, and the move (mainly in respect of inflows) towards liberalizing external capital transactions related largely to FDI. The movement towards liberalization, moreover, has reduced reliance on direct controls, and correspondingly increased the role of macroeconomic policies. In particular, macroeconomic policies have become the key instruments in promoting exchange rate stability and containing inflationary pressures. Some countries, however, still need to remove the remaining restrictions on current account transactions. To strengthen investor confidence and the export environment there is also the need to further liberalize capital account transactions on FDI and to liberalize foreign exchange repatriation and surrender requirements.

34. Although some of the CBI countries have made significant progress in trade liberalization going well beyond the CBI objectives to achieve open trade regimes, others continue to have either moderately or highly restrictive trade regimes. Ideally, the countries classified as having moderately to highly restrictive trade regimes need to move to open trade regimes, say, over the next three years. Moreover, countries should continue to persevere with trade reform by lowering their maximum tariff rates to no more than 15 percent (in line with the current maximum rate for Uganda), and reducing the number of nonzero tariff bands to 2 or 3 and their unweighted average tariff rates to no more than 10 percent over the medium term.

35. The continuing existence of other duties and charges outside the basic tariff structure needs to be eliminated. The amalgamation of these charges into the tariff structure would reduce its complexity and improve its transparency and efficiency. With regard to NTBs, much remains to be done, especially in the areas of state monopolies and discriminatory taxes. Given that NTBs are the most distortionary aspects of a trade regime, the future agenda should focus attention on

For additional analytical, business and investment opportunities information, please contact Global Investment & Business Center, USA at (202) 546-2103. Fax: (202) 546-3275. E-mail: rusric@erols.com

eliminating them as a priority. By making the trade regimes more transparent and less distorted, such an agenda would help make these economies more efficient and competitive. More determined efforts will be needed to eliminate or reduce sharply tariff exemptions. This would serve the purpose of strengthening the fiscal position and introducing more transparency into the trade regimes.

36. The difficulties caused by overlapping RTAs needs to be addressed. Ideally, while trade liberalization should be undertaken on an MFN basis, the extension of tariff preferences to other members of RTAs is likely to enhance trade creation and lessen trade diversion, if accompanied by liberalizing on an MFN basis. In this light, it would be important that the overlapping regional trade arrangements in Eastern and Southern Africa (see Annex I) harmonize the various goals and objectives of the different RTAs, coordinate them more efficiently, and make their objectives more internally consistent so as to (i) avoid negating some of the potential gains from regionalism and undermining the potential improvement in the investment climate that arise from a larger market and improved transparency; (ii) introduce common and simple (rather than conflicting) rules of origin into the trading process; (iii) prevent costly duplication of administrative effort; and (iv) reinforce the reform momentum by consolidating the political capital needed to pursue reforms. CBI participants should make every effort to achieve these goals and accelerate the ongoing efforts at trade facilitation.

37. As a practical matter, rationalizing the current multiple RTAs would be facilitated by accelerating reduction of external tariffs on an MFN basis and removing NTBs. Such an action by one country, or group of countries, could increase the pressure on others to follow suit to prevent intraregional trade and investment from being diverted away from them. In addition, more frequent contacts between all the countries in the region might provide a forum for discussion on adopting a common set of objectives, adopting common rules and regulations and reducing administrative complexity, and for resolving policy disagreements. For example, it would be useful to explore the possibility of inviting COMESA and SADC to join the CBI Steering Committee. Rationalization of the multiple RTAs would enlarge markets, improve transparency, and reduce administrative costs, thus providing a better climate for trade and investment.

38. Despite recent progress in several areas, much work also remains to be done to develop the financial systems to achieve the objectives of the CBI. The authorities need to work toward increasing competition in the financial system by accelerating the pace of privatization of banks, in a transparent manner, and by granting further autonomy to central banks—legally and in practice. Further, macroeconomic stability and the resulting lower inflation rate will ensure that real interest rates are positive and help raise financial savings, and thus the development of money and capital markets. There is also the need to strengthen regulation and supervision to help achieve financial system soundness, which is an important element for macroeconomic stability. The introduction of a transparent safety net, such as a well defined and limited deposit insurance scheme, rather than reliance on blanket government guarantees, would help increase market discipline. It should be pointed out that the prevalence of state-owned banks makes it hard to credibly refuse to bail out such banks in case of failure.

39. Increased investment (both domestic and foreign) in participating countries is crucial for real per capita economic growth and diversification. As mentioned earlier, the Third Ministerial Meeting held in Zimbabwe (February 1998) requested the co-sponsors to prepare a Road Map for Investment Facilitation to be discussed at the Fourth Ministerial Meeting to be held in 1999. The paper outlining this road map, which has now been finalized by the co-sponsors, indicates that while there has been an upturn in the average real per capita growth in recent years, growth in sub-Saharan Africa and the CBI countries needs to be raised and diversified to ensure a significant improvement in living standards in the near future. To this end, gross investment in the CBI countries needs to be increased to at least 25 percent of GDP, as suggested by the Global Coalition for Africa. Foreign direct investment, which had increased only marginally compared to other developing countries, should be allowed to play an important role in this process. The main

lessons of experience drawn by the Paper are that investor confidence is linked not only to the perception of the robustness of reforms, but also to their consistent implementation over time; that reform efforts (which usually take a long time) have not been consistent and sustained enough to regain investor confidence; and that a concerted effort is needed, over an extended period, to firmly establish improved general conditions for attracting investment and build a better image. The Paper identified eight essential conditions for attracting investment: political stability, good governance, macroeconomic reform and stability, trade liberalization, exchange system liberalization, market integration, investment deregulation, and consistency in policy application. Since it would not be feasible to tackle all aspects of investment facilitation at one and the same time, the Paper suggests immediate actions in selected priority areas. They consist of actions to accelerate implementation of the CBI trade reform agenda; investment promotion at the regional and national level; selective legal and judicial reforms; selective tax reforms; and steps to raise awareness and spur the private sector to deliver improvements in services and performance.

40. In implementing the remaining agenda, participation of the private sector through the TWGs will continue to be important. Experience under the CBI suggests that the TWGs have emerged as a crucial part of the CBI process by contributing to ownership and effective implementation of reforms.

REGIONAL ORGANIZATIONS IN EASTERN AND SOUTHERN AFRICA, AND THE INDIAN OCEAN

A. The Common Market for Eastern and Southern Africa (COMESA)

41. The COMESA was established in November 1993, superseding the Preferential Trading Agreement (PTA) for Eastern and Southern African states.[20] The aims and objectives of the COMESA Treaty and Protocols are to facilitate the removal of structural and institutional weaknesses of its members through the creation and maintenance of:

- a full free trade area guaranteeing the free movement of goods and services produced within the COMESA region, and the removal of all nontariff barriers;
- a customs union under which goods and services imported from non-COMESA countries will attract a single tariff rate;
- the free movement of capital and investment supported by the adoption of common investment practices;
- a gradual establishment of a payments union based on the COMESA Clearing House, and the eventual establishment of a common monetary union; and
- the adoption of common visa arrangements, leading eventually to the free movement of bona fide persons.

42. The fulfilment of the complete COMESA mandate is regarded as a long-term objective. To become more effective as an institution COMESA has defined its priorities over the next 3—5 years as being "The Promotion of Regional Integration Through Trade and Investment." Under the COMESA program, activities in respect of trade liberalization, trade facilitation, payments systems, institutional support, competition policy, investment road maps, strengthening the private sector, and immigration and free movement of persons will be undertaken.

43. The COMESA program includes the establishment of a Free Trade Area (FTA) by the year 2000, to be achieved by the annual reduction of intra-COMESA tariffs. As of end-December 1998, eight countries had achieved a reduction of 80 percent, and six other countries achieved reductions of 60—70 percent. All COMESA countries have reiterated their commitment to achieve

For additional analytical, business and investment opportunities information, please contact Global Investment & Business Center, USA at (202) 546-2103. Fax: (202) 546-3275. E-mail: rusric@erols.com

a FTA by October 2000, and over half are in a position to make such a transition without having to effect large additional preferences. Member countries have also agreed to adopt a formula on the rules of origin for preferential trade that require the local content to be not less than 35 percent of the ex-factory cost of the goods. COMESA member states have further agreed to establish a customs union with a common external tariff (of 0 percent, 5 percent, 15 percent, and 30 percent) by 2004. In the area of trade facilitation, the COMESA Secretariat is implementing a program to improve the transport and communications systems of the region. These include the adoption of Harmonized Road Transit Charges, a Yellow Card (vehicle insurance) Scheme, Customs Bond Guarantee Scheme, and an Advance Cargo Information System. To provide the required financial infrastructure and service support, COMESA has created specialized institutions in the form of a Trade and Development Bank, a Reinsurance company, and the COMESA Clearing House.[21] Institutional support in the form of a Court of Justice, formally created in June 1998, establishes COMESA as an institution with rules which can be enforced through a court of law. The Court will adjudicate and arbitrate on, inter alia, unfair trade practices, interpretation of the treaty, and ensuring that members comply with agreed decisions. In regard to immigration and the free movement of persons, four countries are already in full compliance, while others have committed themselves to fully implementing the protocol. The protocol on the free movement of persons will be implemented in several stages, with the first stage—the removal of visa requirements—to be completed by the year 2000.

B. The Southern African Development Community (SADC)[22]

44. In August 1992, a formal treaty providing for the establishment of SADC was adopted, superseding the Southern African Development Coordination Conference (SADCC).[23] This treaty called for the broadening of cooperation among member states in 20 sectors, including transport, health, tourism, mining, and water.

45. The SADC Trade and Development Protocol, signed in August 1996, seeks to establish a SADC Free Trade Area eight years after ratification and the gradual elimination of tariffs and NTBs to trade in the interim. The Protocol has been ratified by only five member states. Others are in agreement on a tariff liberalization program, currently being negotiated by the 11 original signatories of the Trade Protocol. This program is less ambitious than the one agreed by its own member countries under the CBI and under the COMESA. Current proposals call for the removal of all intraregional tariffs within eight years, but do not cover the liberalization of trade with non-SADC countries. Also, unlike agreements under the CBI, proposals regarding trade liberalization among SADC countries allow for special treatment of so-called "sensitive products" (in agriculture, agro-industry, and manufacturing), involving a slower phase-in for import tariff reductions. Moreover, some of the proposals being considered leave open the possibility of excluding some goods/sectors altogether from the trade liberalization exercise.

46. South Africa, on behalf of its partners in the South African Customs Union (SACU),[24] has offered to reduce its tariffs at a faster pace than non-SACU SADC countries, although a number of "sensitive" goods—dairy products, wheat, sugar, cotton, fabrics, leather footwear, and vehicles—will be subject to a slower liberalization process. Negotiations within SADC are being held each month under a Trade Negotiating Forum framework. The aim is to reach agreement on a full schedule of tariff reductions before the SADC Summit in August 1999.

C. Southern African Customs Union (SACU)

47. The Southern African Customs Union (SACU) was established in 1910 between the newly established Union of South Africa and the separate protectorates of Botswana, Lesotho, and Swaziland. The agreement was renegotiated in 1969 to reflect increases in the partner country shares of regional imports. Namibia became a member of SACU in 1990. The aims of the SACU

For additional analytical, business and investment opportunities information, please contact Global Investment & Business Center, USA at (202) 546-2103. Fax: (202) 546-3275. E-mail: rusric@erols.com

are to encourage economic development and diversification, in particular in the less-advanced member countries, and afford all parties equitable benefits arising from intra-Union and international trade. The Customs Union Commission, comprising representatives of all the contracting parties, is the supreme consultative body of SACU and meets annually.

48. Under the SACU agreement, members apply the customs, excise, sales, antidumping, countervailing and safeguard duties, as well as related laws, set by South Africa, to goods imported to the common customs area from third countries outside the Union. A SACU member may enter separately into, or amend, trade agreements with a country outside the common customs area, provided the terms of such agreements or amendments do not conflict in any way with the provisions of the SACU agreements. Members may not impose duties or quantitative restrictions on goods grown, produced or manufactured in the SACU area and they may not impose any duties on importation, from any other member, of goods which were imported from outside the common customs area. Each member has its own legislation on quantitative restrictions on goods imported from outside the SACU area. Members, other than South Africa, may, following consultations, apply additional duties or increase duties for protection of infant industries. Rebates, refunds, and drawbacks granted by member countries must be identical, except in specified circumstances. Exceptional trade restrictions by a member may also be justified. There are marketing arrangements under which agricultural imports from other SACU countries may be restricted.

49. All customs, excise, sales and additional duties collected by SACU members are pooled and distributed to members. The shares of BLNS countries are determined on the basis of a revenue-sharing formula and the residual is allocated to South Africa. The original 1910 revenue sharing formula was based on the respective contribution of the BLNS countries to total imports into, and consumption of excisable goods produced within, the SACU area. The 1969 formula provided for an enhancement factor of 42 percent of the shares of the BLNS countries; this factor was introduced to compensate the BLNS countries for negative effects resulting from their participation in SACU. These effects were: (i) the price-increasing effect of the customs union for the BLNS countries and the implicit protection for South African industry; (ii) the industrial polarization resulting from the tendency of industries to locate within the customs union to choose sites in South Africa; and (iii) the loss of fiscal discretion experienced by the BLNS partners because South Africa retained tariff-setting power for the region. Nontariff barriers applied by South Africa also had a negative effect on the size of the revenue pool. Subsequently, the revenue sharing formula was renegotiated in 1975 and a "stabilization factor" was added in 1978, operating retrospectively to 1974/75, to reduce fluctuation in the revenue shares accruing to the BLNS countries. The stabilization factor was centered on a mean of 20 percent of the tax base, with a lower bound of 17 percent and an upper bound of 23 percent. The tax base refers to the sum of duty-inclusive imports, c.i.f., and excise tax-inclusive value of goods produced in the Union and consumed in a particular BLNS country.

D. Commission for East African Cooperation (EAC)

50. The EAC between Kenya, Uganda, and Tanzania was established in November 1993, and is the most recent in a long line of regional integration arrangements between these three countries.[25] Through regional cooperation, the EAC seeks, inter alia, to:

- strengthen and consolidate cooperation in agreed fields with a view to bringing about equitable development among member states;
- establish a single market and investment area in the region; and
- promote sustainable utilization of the region's natural resources and effective protection of the environment.[26]

For additional analytical, business and investment opportunities information, please contact Global Investment & Business Center, USA at (202) 546-2103. Fax: (202) 546-3275. E-mail: rusric@erols.com

51. The main policy organs of the EAC are: the Summit of the Heads of State, the Permanent Tripartite Commission, the Coordination Commission, and the Secretariat. Since the launching of the EAC, the Tripartite Commission has concentrated on the identification and elimination of physical and policy related constraints, which could slow progress in the establishment of a single market and investment area. Accordingly, much of the work has focussed on formulation of programs to ease the movement of people, goods, services and capital; provide adequate and reliable basic infrastructure; harmonize standards, specifications, trade documentation and investment policies; harmonize macroeconomic and sectoral policies; provide trade financing and other facilities ancillary to the growth of exports; and achieve convertibility of the three East African currencies.

52. As a result of these activities, the EAC has achieved (i) full convertibility of the three East African currencies within the region; (ii) full liberalization of the external current account, and progress towards liberalization of the capital account; (iii) holding of pre- and post-budget consultations in order to harmonize monetary and fiscal policies; (iv) synchronization of the budget day of the three member countries; (v) development of a macroeconomic framework for the region to guide countries towards economic convergence; (vi) launching of the EAC Development Strategy, 1997—2000, which provides for guidelines for economic and social development; (vii) formation of an East African Securities Regulatory Authority to facilitate the establishment of an East African Stock Exchange and cross-listing of stocks; (viii) formation of East African Business Council, comprising private sector organizations to promote cross-border trade and investments; and (ix) the execution of tripartite agreements for the avoidance of double taxation, road transport, and inland waterways. In addition, efforts are underway to eliminate internal tariffs by July 1, 2000, for the launching of an East African passport, and the identification of a EAC designated transport network.

E. The Indian Ocean Commission (IOC)

53. The IOC was established in December 1982 by Madagascar, Mauritius, and Seychelles, with the objective of promoting cooperation in trade, agriculture, fishing and ecosystem conservation, as well as cooperation in the cultural, scientific, technical and educational areas. While the IOC has developed a wide variety of regional programs, cooperation in the economic sector has been a priority, as reflected in the implementation of an Integrated Regional Program for Development of Trade (PRIDE)[27].

54. The overall objective of PRIDE is to strengthen regional trade integration, specifically by lifting the technical and financial constraints on the private sector of its members. PRIDE is expected to increase business competitiveness, enhance the quality of traded goods, and improve the availability and reliability of trade data. PRIDE has two main components: a macroeconomic component consisting of a general framework of actions to liberalize trade in goods and services, investment, capital movements, and the movement of people;[28] and a microeconomic component aimed at facilitating business contacts and partnerships such as participating in trade exhibitions and organizing trade missions.

55. As the IOC member states are also members of COMESA, they subscribe to the trade integration strategy of COMESA. The IOC has also been actively involved in all the preparatory meetings of the CBI, and expects to be involved in its implementation, particularly in those areas that fall within its purview.

For additional analytical, business and investment opportunities information, please contact Global Investment & Business Center, USA at (202) 546-2103. Fax: (202) 546-3275. E-mail: rusric@erols.com

www.ingramcontent.com/pod-product-compliance
Lightning Source LLC
LaVergne TN
LVHW080030210926
848481LV00011B/3147